PRACTICAL OBJECT-ORIENTED DESIGN WITH UML

Second Edition

PRACTICAL OBJECT-ORIENTED DESIGN WITH UML

Second Edition

Mark Priestley

The **McGraw·Hill** Companies

London   Boston   Burr Ridge, IL   Madison, WI   New York   San Francisco
St. Louis   Bangkok   Bogotá   Caracas   Kuala Lumpur   Lisbon   Madrid
Mexico City   Milan   Montreal   New Delhi   Santiago   Sao Paulo   Seoul
Singapore   Sydney   Tokyo   Toronto

Practical Object-Oriented Design with UML, Second Edition
Mark Priestley
ISBN 0077103939

 **Education**

Published by McGraw-Hill Education
Shoppenhangers Road
Maidenhead
Berkshire
SL6 2QL
Telephone: 44 (0) 1628 502 500
Fax: 44 (0) 1628 770 224
Website: www.mcgraw-hill.co.uk

British Library Cataloguing in Publication Data
A catalogue record for this book is available from the British Library

Library of Congress Cataloguing in Publication Data
The Library of Congress data for this book has been applied for from the Library of Congress

Senior Development Editor: Caroline Howell
Marketing Manager: Alice Duijser
Senior Production Editor: Eleanor Hayes

Cover design by Fielding Design Ltd
Printed and bound in the UK by Bell and Bain Ltd, Glasgow

The McGraw-Hill Companies

CONTENTS

PREFACE

> Mr Palomar's rule had gradually altered: now he needed a great variety of models, perhaps interchangeable, in a combining process, in order to find the one that would best fit a reality that, for its own part, was always made of many different realities, in time and in space.

> *Italo Calvino*

This book aims to provide a practical and accessible introduction to object-oriented design. It assumes that readers have prior knowledge of an object-oriented programming language, ideally Java, and explains both the principles and application of UML. It is aimed principally at students in the later years of an undergraduate or Masters course in Computer Science or Software Engineering, although I hope that other audiences will find the book useful.

The overall strategy of the book is to emphasize the connections between design notations and code. There are many excellent books available which discuss systems analysis and design with UML, but fewer that pay detailed attention to the final product, the code of the system being developed. UML is at bottom a language for expressing the designs of object-oriented programs, however, and it seems natural to consider the notation and meaning of the language from this perspective. I have also, over the years, found this to be a good way of imparting to students a concrete sense of what the design notations actually mean.

The book has two main objectives related to this overall philosophy. The first is to provide a complete example of an object-oriented development using UML, starting with a statement of requirements and finishing with complete executable code which can be run, modified and extended.

This objective of course places limits on the size of the example that can be considered. To get round this, the book takes as its paradigm system architecture a typical stand-alone desktop application, supporting a graphical user interface and interfacing to a relational database. Within this framework, the text examines the development of some core functionality, and leaves extensions of the system to be worked out as exercises.

The second objective is to provide a tutorial introduction to those aspects of UML that are important in developing this kind of application. Much emphasis is placed on clearly explaining the constructs and notation of the design language, and demonstrating the close relationship between the design and the implementation of object-oriented programs. These issues are treated rather superficially in many books. If they are not clearly understood, however, it is difficult to make correct use of UML.

UML is a large and complex language, and when one is learning it there is a danger of being overwhelmed by details of the notation. In order to avoid this, the book uses a subset of UML that is sufficient to develop desktop applications. The most significant omissions are any coverage of concurrency, activity diagrams and anything other than a brief mention of deployment diagrams. These aspects of the language are obviously important for 'industrial-strength' applications of UML, but these lie somewhat outside the experience of the intended audience of this book.

STRUCTURE OF THE BOOK

Following an introductory chapter, Chapter 2 introduces the basic concepts of object modelling in the context of a simple programming example. Chapters 3 to 7 contain a more extended case study of the use of UML, while Chapters 8 to 12 present the most important UML notations systematically. These two sections are independent of each other, allowing different reading strategies as shown in Figure P.1. Chapter 13 discusses strategies for implementing UML designs and Chapter 14 provides a general discussion of some of the underlying principles of object-oriented design.

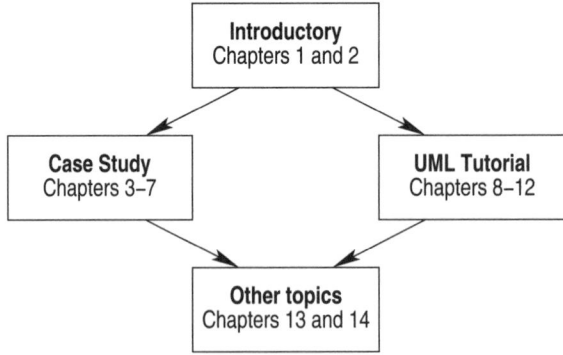

Figure P.1 Chapter dependencies

CHANGES IN THE SECOND EDITION

The most significant change in the second edition is that the diagram editor example has been replaced by a new case study based on a simple booking system for a restaurant. This provides an application with more 'real-world' context than the diagram editor, and is one which many students find easier to relate to. It also allows concepts of different architectural layers to be introduced more naturally than before, and these topics are now covered explicitly in Chapters 4 to 7.

Although the focus of the book is on language rather than process, it is impossible to divorce the two entirely in any practical approach. In the new Chapter 3, the book now includes an explicit discussion of some issues in the development of software processes and provides an outline sketch of the Unified Process.

The remaining chapters are very much the same as in the previous edition, though minor changes have been made throughout the book, both in content and presentation. To make room for the new chapter and case study, some material has had to be omitted from this edition, most noticeably the second case study. All the material that has been omitted, including the diagram editor example, will be made available from book's website.

FURTHER RESOURCES

A web page for the book provides access to the source code for the examples used in the book, solutions to all exercises and material from the first edition. It can be found at the following URL:

```
http://www.mcgraw-hill.co.uk/textbooks/priestley
```

An instructor's manual, including slides, the diagrams used in the book and additional exercises, is available to *bona fide* academics who have adopted the book for classroom use. Information on how to obtain the manual can be found on the publisher's website.

ACKNOWLEDGEMENTS

In the preparation of this new edition, my most significant debt is to my students who have made use of the earlier editions, and also sat through earlier presentations of the restaurant booking system. I am indebted to Michael Richards for the initial idea for this case study.

INTRODUCTION TO UML

According to its designers, UML, the Unified Modeling Language, is 'a general-purpose visual modeling language that is used to specify, visualize, construct and document the architecture of a software system'. This chapter explains how models are used in the software development process, and the role of a language such as UML. The high-level structure of UML is described, together with an informal account of its semantics and the relationship between design notations and code.

1.1 MODELS AND MODELLING

The use of models in the development of software is extremely widespread. This section explains two characteristic uses of models, to describe real-world applications and also the software systems that implement them, and then discusses the relationships between these two types of model.

Models of software

Software is often developed in the following manner. Once it has been determined that a new system is to be built, an informal description is written stating what the software should do. This description, sometimes known as a *requirements specification*, is often prepared in consultation with the future users of the system, and can serve as the basis for a formal contract between the user and the supplier of the software.

The completed requirements specification is then passed to the programmer or project team responsible for writing the software; they go away and in relative isolation produce a program based on the specification. With luck, the resulting program will be produced on time, within budget, and will satisfy the needs of the people for whom the original proposal was produced, but in many cases, sadly, this does not happen.

The failure of many software projects has led people to study the way in which software is developed, in an attempt to understand why projects fail. As a result, many suggestions have been made about how to improve the software development process. These often take the form of *process models* describing a number of activities involved in development and the order in which they should be carried out.

Process models can be depicted graphically. For example, Figure 1.1 shows a very simple process, where code is written directly from the system requirements with no intervening steps. As well as showing the processes involved, as rectangles with rounded corners, this diagram shows the artefacts produced at each stage in the process. When two stages in a process are carried out in sequence, the output of one stage is often used as the input to the next, as indicated by the dashed arrows.

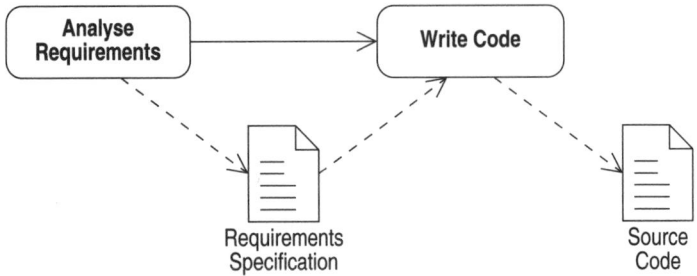

Figure 1.1 A primitive model of software development

The requirements specification produced at the start of a development can take many forms. A written specification may be either a very informal outline of the required system or a highly detailed and structured functional description. In small developments the initial system description may not even be written down, but only exist as the programmer's informal understanding of what is required. In yet other cases a prototype system may have been developed in conjunction with the future users, and this could then form the basis of subsequent development work. In the discussion above all these possibilities are included in the general term 'requirements specification', but this should not be taken to imply that only a written document can serve as a starting point for subsequent development.

It should also be noted that Figure 1.1 does not depict the whole of the software life cycle. In this book, the term 'software development' is used in rather a narrow sense, to cover only the design and implementation of a software system, and many other important components of the life cycle are ignored. A complete project plan would also cater for crucial activities such as project management, requirements analysis, quality assurance and maintenance.

When a small and simple program is being written by a single programmer, there is little need to structure the development process any more than in Figure 1.1. Experienced programmers can keep the data and subroutine structures of such a program clear in their minds while writing it, and if the behaviour of the program is not what is expected they can make any necessary changes directly to the code. In certain situations this is an entirely appropriate way of working.

With larger programs, however, and particularly if more than one person is involved in the development, it is usually necessary to introduce more structure into the process. Software development is no longer treated as a single unstructured activity, but is instead broken up into a number of subtasks, each of which usually involves the production of some intermediate piece of documentation.

Figure 1.2 illustrates a software development process which is slightly more complex than the one shown in Figure 1.1. In this case, the programmer is no longer writing code based on the requirements specification alone, but first of all produces a structure chart showing how the overall functionality of the program is split into a number of modules, or subroutines, and illustrating the calling relationship between these subroutines.

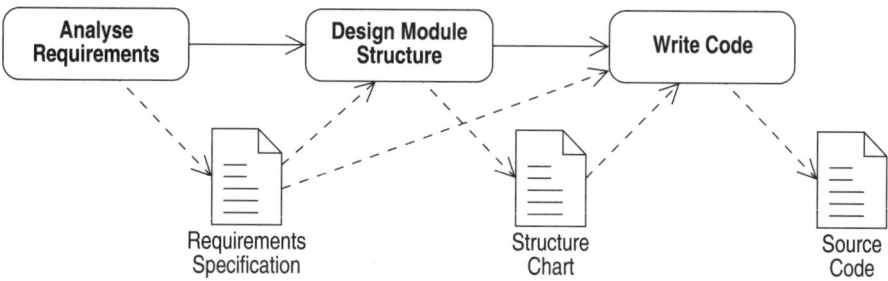

Figure 1.2 A more complex software development process

This process model shows that the structure chart is based on the information contained in the requirements specification, and that both the specification and the structure chart are used when writing the final code. The programmer might use the structure chart to clarify the overall architecture of the program, and refer to the specification when coding individual subroutines to check up on specific details of the required functionality.

The intermediate descriptions or documents that are produced in the course of developing a piece of software are known as *models*. The structure chart mentioned in Figure 1.2 is an example of a model in this sense. A model gives an abstract view of a system, highlighting certain important aspects of its design, such as the subroutines and their relationships, and ignoring large amounts of low-level detail, such as the coding of each routine. As a result, models are much easier to understand than the complete code of the system and are often used to illustrate aspects of a system's overall structure or architecture. An example of the kind of structure that is meant is provided by the relationships between subroutines documented in the structure chart above.

As larger and more complex systems are developed and as the number of people involved in the development team increases, more formality needs to be introduced into the process. One aspect of this increased complexity is that a wider range of models is used in the course of a development. Indeed, software design has sometimes been defined as the construction of a series of models describing important aspects of the system in more and more detail, until sufficient understanding of the requirements is gained to enable coding to begin.

The use of models is therefore central to software design, and provides two important benefits, which help to deal with the complexity involved in developing almost any significant piece of software. First, models provide succinct descriptions of important aspects of a system that may be too complex to be grasped as a whole. Second, models provide a valuable means of communication, both between different members of the development team and also between the team and outsiders such as the client. This book describes the models that are used in object-oriented design and gives examples of their use.

Models of applications

Models are also used in software development to help understand the application area being addressed by a system, before the stages of system design and coding are reached. Such models are sometimes referred to as *analysis models* as opposed to *design models* such as the structure chart discussed above. The two types of model can be distinguished by the fact that, unlike design models, analysis models do not make any reference to the properties of the proposed software system, but aim instead to capture certain aspects and properties of the 'real world' business.

In general terms, analysis and design models fulfil the same needs and provide the same sorts of benefit. Both software systems and the real-world systems that they are supporting or interacting with tend to be highly complex and very detailed. In order to manage this complexity, descriptions of systems need to emphasize structure rather than detail, and to provide an abstract view of the system. The exact nature of this abstract view will depend on the purposes for which it is produced, and in general several such views, or models, will be needed to give an adequate overall view of a system.

Characteristically, analysis models describe the data handled in an application and the various processes by which it is manipulated. In traditional analysis methods, these models are expressed using diagrams such as logical data models and data flow diagrams. It is worth noticing that the use of analysis models to describe business processes predates, and is independent of, the computerization of such processes. For example, organization charts and diagrams illustrating particular production processes have been used for a long time in commerce and industry.

Relationship between analysis and design models

It is likely that both analysis and design models, as defined above, will be produced in the course of the development of any significant software system. This raises the question of what kind of relationship exists between them.

The process of system development has traditionally been divided into a number of phases. An analysis phase, culminating in the production of a set of analysis models, is followed by a design phase, which leads to the production of a set of design models. In this scenario, the analysis models are intended to form the input to the design phase, which has the task of creating structures that will support the properties and requirements stated in the analysis models.

One problem with this division of labour is that in many cases the languages and notations used for the production of analysis and design models have been very different. This leads to a process of translation in moving from one phase to the next. Information contained in the analysis models must be reformulated in the notation required for the design models.

Clearly, there is a danger that this process will be both error-prone and wasteful. Why, it has been asked, go to the trouble of creating analysis models if they are going to be replaced by design models for the remainder of the development process? Also, given that notational differences exist between the two types of model, it can be difficult to be certain that all the information contained in an analysis model has been accurately extracted and represented in the design notation.

One promise of object-oriented technology has been to remove these problems by using the same kinds of model and modelling concepts for both analysis and design. In principle, the idea is that this will remove any sharp distinction between analysis and design models. Clearly, design models will contain low-level details that are not present in analysis models, but the hope is that the basic structure of the analysis model will be preserved and be directly recognizable in the design model. Apart from anything else, this might be expected to remove the problems associated with the transfer between analysis and design notations.

A consequence of using the same modelling concepts for analysis and design is to blur the distinction between these two phases. The original motivation behind this move was the hope that software development could be treated as a 'seamless' process: analysis would identify relevant objects in the real-world system, and these would be directly represented in software. In this view, design is basically a question of adding specific implementation details to the underlying analysis model, which would be preserved unchanged throughout the development process. The plausibility of this view will be considered in more detail in Section 2.10 once the main concepts of object-orientation have been discussed in more detail.

The purpose of this book is to explain the modelling concepts used by object-oriented methods, and to show how models can be expressed in the notation defined by UML. The focus of the book is on design and the use of design models in the development of software, but the same modelling concepts apply equally well to the production of analysis models. Analysis is a skill distinct from design, and there is much to learn about the techniques for carrying it out effectively, but the resulting analysis models can perfectly well be expressed using the notation presented in this book.

1.2 METHODOLOGIES

Software development, then, is not simply a case of sitting down at a terminal and typing in the program code. In most cases the complexity of the problem to be solved requires that intermediate development steps are taken, and that a number of abstract models of the program structure are produced. These points apply equally well to developments involving only one programmer and to conventional team developments.

Over the years, many different strategies for developing software have been tried out, and those that have been found particularly successful or widely applicable have been formalized and published as *methodologies*. In software engineering circles, the term 'methodology' is often used (or misused) simply to mean a suggested strategy or method for developing software systems. Process models such as Figures 1.1 and 1.2, which show a number of development activities and the artefacts produced at each stage, illustrate some of the essential aspects of a methodology. A description of an 'industrial-strength' methodology, however, would be a great deal more complicated than either of those diagrams.

Methodologies offer guidance on at least two important aspects of software development. First, a methodology defines a number of models that can be used to help develop a system. As explained in the previous section, a model describes a particular aspect of a system at an abstract level, and therefore enables discussions about the system to proceed at a suitably high level without becoming involved too soon in low-level details. A methodology will also define a set of formal notations in which the recommended models can be written down and documented. Often these formal notations are graphical, thus giving rise to the wide use of diagrams in software development. The models together with the notation in which the models are documented are sometimes referred to as the *language* defined by the methodology.

As well as defining a language, a methodology defines various activities involved in software development, and specifies the order in which these activities ought to be carried out. Together, these define a model of the development *process*, and a process model can be illustrated in diagrams such as Figures 1.1 and 1.2. The process defined by a methodology is often defined much less formally than the language, and usually a large amount of flexibility is envisaged, allowing the methodology to be used in a wide variety of situations, for applications with differing requirements and even with programmers who may be disinclined to design a program before writing it.

The process defined by a methodology can be thought of as defining an outline schedule or plan for a project. Each stage in such a process defines particular 'deliverable work products', as shown in Figures 1.1 and 1.2, and the forms of these deliverables are usually specified by the language of the methodology. As well as helping in the technical aspects of software development, this suggests that the use of a methodology can be of great assistance in project management.

Classification of methodologies

Great similarities exist between many of the methodologies that have been published, and based on these it is possible to group methodologies into a number of broad classes. The similarities arise from the fact that different methodologies can be based on a common understanding of how to describe the underlying structure of software systems. As a result, related methodologies will often recommend the use of very similar models in development. Sometimes, of course, the relationship between two models can be obscured by the fact that different notation is used for them. These surface differences can hide, but do not remove, the underlying structural similarities.

A well-known class of methodologies is the so-called *structured methods*, including structured analysis, structured design and their many variants. The characteristic model used by these methodologies is the data flow diagram, which illustrates how data is passed between the different processes in a system. Structured methods picture a software system as being made up of a collection of data that can be processed by a number of functions external to the data. These methodologies are particularly appropriate for the design of data-rich systems, and are often used in the development of systems destined for implementation on relational databases.

A different class of methodologies consists of those described as *object-oriented*. Although there are similarities between the notation used in some object-oriented and structured methodologies, the object-oriented methods are based on a completely different understanding of the basic structure of software systems. This understanding is embodied in the *object model* described in Chapter 2.

Although notational details differ widely, there has been a high level of agreement among different object-oriented methodologies about the kinds of model that can usefully be applied when carrying out an object-oriented development. Because of this, it is quite possible to talk about object-oriented design in a generic manner, without being constrained by the definitions of one methodology. It is important to use a consistent and clearly defined notation, however, and in this book that of the Unified Modeling Language will be used.

1.3 THE UNIFIED MODELING LANGUAGE

The Unified Modeling Language (UML) is, as its name suggests, a unification of a number of earlier object-oriented modelling languages. The three principal designers of UML had each previously published their own methods, and UML was intended to integrate the insights of these three methods, and to encourage the spread of object-oriented techniques by making available a single widely recognized notation. This integration was aided by the common framework shared by the original methods, and also by the fact that the three individuals concerned joined the same company.

Because of its impressive pedigree, and assisted by its adoption as a standard by the Object Management Group, UML generated a lot of interest in the software industry even before its publication in a definitive form, and it can be expected to continue as the dominant object-oriented modelling notation for the foreseeable future.

UML made a significant departure from earlier methodologies in clearly and explicitly differentiating the language used to document a software design from the process used to produce it. As its name states, UML defines a language only, and as such provides no description or recommendations relating to the process of development. This eminently sensible approach recognizes that there is very little consensus in the software industry about process, and a growing recognition that the choice of process is crucially affected by the nature of the product and the environment in which the development will take place. UML is intended to be a well-defined language which can be productively used with a wide range of different processes.

The remainder of this section discusses some of the basic high-level concepts of UML and describes the ways in which UML classifies models and presents them to software developers.

Views

UML is informed by a vision of the structure of software systems known as the *4+1 view model*. The UML version of this model is shown in Figure 1.3. As this figure clearly indicates, the model gets its name from the fact that a system's structure is described in five views, one of which, the use case view, has a special role to play in integrating the contents of the other four views.

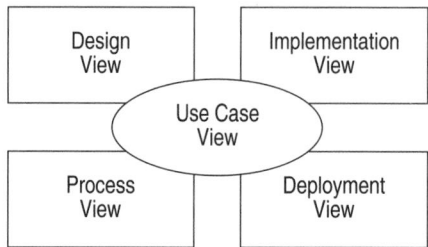

Figure 1.3 The 4+1 view model

The five views shown in Figure 1.3 do not correspond to particular formal constructs or diagrams that can be described in UML. Rather, each view corresponds to a particular perspective from which a system can be examined. Different views highlight different aspects of the system that are of interest to particular groups of stakeholders. A complete description of the system can be formed by merging the information found in all five views, but for particular purposes it may be sufficient to consider only the information contained in a subset of the views.

The *use case view* defines the system's external behaviour and is of interest to end users, analysts and testers. This view defines the requirements of the system, and therefore constrains all the other views, which describe certain aspects of the system's design or construction. This is why the use case view has a central role and is often said to drive the development process.

The *design view* describes the logical structures that support the functional requirements expressed in the use case view. It consists of definitions of program components, principally classes, together with specifications of the data they hold, and their behaviour and interactions. The information contained in this view is of particular interest to programmers, as the details of how the system's functionality will be implemented are described in this view.

The *implementation view* describes the physical components out of which the system is to be constructed. These are distinct from the logical components described in the design view and include such things as executable files, libraries of code and databases. The information contained in this view is relevant to activities such as configuration management and system integration.

The *process view* deals with issues of concurrency within the system, and the *deployment view* describes how physical components are distributed across the physical environment, such as a network of computers, that the system runs in. These two views address non-functional requirements of the system such as fault-tolerance and performance issues. The process and deployment views are relatively undeveloped in UML, compared in particular with the design view, which contains much of the notation that would informally be thought of as design-related.

Models

Different views, then, correspond to different perspectives from which a system can be examined. The information relevant to each view is recorded in the various types of model defined by UML. For example, a use case model presents the information in the use case view in such a way that it is accessible to the intended audience of that view.

Models may also be produced at different levels of abstraction, or at different stages of the development process. For example, as explained in Section 1.1, it is common to define analysis and design models of a system at different stages of the development process. It then becomes important to define the relationship between these models and to ensure their mutual consistency.

Model elements

The word 'model' is used rather loosely in writing about UML. Sometimes it refers to the totality of information stored about the system being developed, encompassing all the five views, sometimes described as the *system model*. More often, it refers to the subset of that information contained in a single view.

The defining property of a model that is shared by all these usages is that a model consists of a collection of *model elements*. These are the 'atoms' of modelling, and UML defines a wide range of different types of model element, including such familiar concepts as classes, operations and function calls. A model is a structure built up of a number of interrelated model elements.

If a CASE tool is being used to support development, it will maintain a database storing all the information that has been declared about the model elements known to the system. The sum total of this information makes up the system model.

Diagrams

A model is normally presented to a designer as a set of *diagrams*. Diagrams are graphical representations of collections of model elements. Different types of diagram present different information, typically about either the structure or the behaviour of the model elements they depict. Each diagram type has rules stating what kinds of model elements can appear in diagrams of that type, and how they are to be shown.

UML defines nine distinct diagram types, which are listed in Table 1.1 together with an indication of the views with which each is characteristically associated.

Table 1.1 UML's diagram types

	Diagram	View
1	Use case diagram	Use case view
2	Object diagram	Use case and design views
3	Sequence diagram	Use case and design views
4	Collaboration diagram	Use case and design views
5	Class diagram	Design view
6	Statechart diagram	Design and process views
7	Activity diagram	Design and process views
8	Component diagram	Implementation view
9	Deployment diagram	Deployment view

Confusingly, diagrams are sometimes referred to as models, as both contain information about a set of model elements. The basic distinction between the two concepts is that a model describes the logical structure of the information, whereas a diagram is a particular physical presentation of it. If a CASE tool is being used, the model would correspond to the information that the tool might store in a database, and diagrams to particular graphical representations of all or part of this information.

UML diagrams are largely graphical in form, because most people find such representations easier to work with than purely textual representations of complex structures. Graphical notations are rather limited in terms of what they can easily express, however, so it is common to supplement UML with a textual specification language such as the Object Constraint Language, described in Chapter 12.

Understanding UML

Learning UML, then, involves coming to understand two related things. First, it is necessary to understand the various types of model element and how they can be used in UML models. Second, the details of the various different types of diagram need to be learnt, along with the relationship between the graphical form of the diagrams and the model elements they represent.

The structure of models is formally defined in the UML specification by means of a *metamodel*, a term which means 'model of a model'. The metamodel is rather like the definition of a programming language: it defines the different types of model element, their properties and the ways in which they can be related.

It is possible to describe the metamodel explicitly, but it is more common when one is initially learning UML to focus on the *syntax*, or legal structure, of the different types of diagram. In this book, the symbols used to represent different model elements will be introduced informally as the various types of diagram are discussed.

As well as learning the syntax of UML's diagrams, it is important to understand their *semantics*, or what they mean. Design languages are best understood in terms of the properties of the artefacts being designed. In the case of UML, these artefacts are usually object-oriented programs, and in this book the connection between design models and code will be emphasized as a means of coming to understand UML.

1.4 DESIGN MODELS AND CODE

The relationship between design and code is more subtle than it at first appears, and this section explains in more detail exactly what the relationship is. The importance of the relationship is that the meaning of much of the UML notation can be understood in terms of the run-time properties of object-oriented programs.

The models used in the design of a system present an abstract view of it, and an implementation adds enough detail to make these models executable. If the design documentation is consistent with the source code, this means that the models present an abstract view of the structure and properties of the code. This relationship is shown on the left-hand side of Figure 1.4.

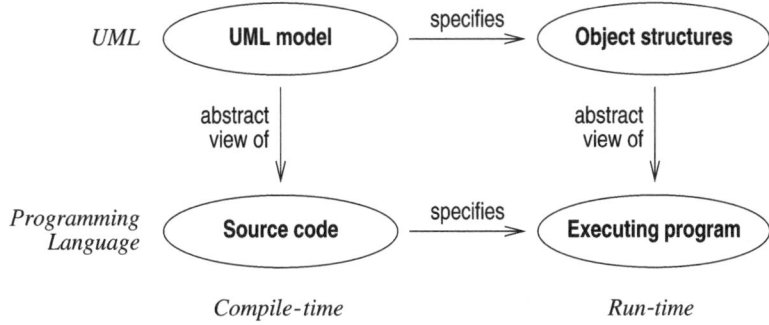

Figure 1.4 Relationships between models and code

Both design documentation and source code can be described as *compile-time* artefacts. Source programs, written in languages such as Java or C++, are documents which define the behaviour that we want a program to exhibit, and must be compiled and executed before they have any effect. UML design diagrams are also documents which specify the general structure and behaviour of a system, even though it may not be possible to directly translate them into executable code.

Once it is compiled and executed, a program has a variety of *run-time* properties, as shown at the lower right of Figure 1.4. At the lowest level, these can be described as the effect the program has on a computer's processor and memory when the program is running. When writing a program, programmers often try to visualize the behaviour and effects of the code, but it is unusual for them to think in terms of the raw addresses and binary data that is being manipulated by the machine. Instead, they tend to work with an abstract model of what is happening when a program runs.

In particular, programmers in object-oriented languages tend to use abstract models of program execution which talk in terms of objects being created and destroyed as a program runs, and objects knowing about other objects and being able to communicate with them. These abstract models are called *object structures* in Figure 1.4. The arrow on the right-hand side of the diagram indicates that object structures are abstractions of what really happens when a program runs, in the same sort of way as a design diagram is an abstraction of the information contained in a source program.

The significance of all this is that object structures, the abstract models that we use to understand programs, can also be used to explain what UML's design models mean, as indicated by the top arrow in Figure 1.4. This means that object-oriented models and programs are describing essentially the same thing, and explains how design models can be translated into code while preserving the properties specified in the design. It also means that UML can largely be understood in terms of concepts that are familiar from programming.

Two conclusions can be drawn from this discussion. First, the diagrams defined in a language such as UML are not just pictures, but have a definite meaning in terms of what they specify about the run-time properties of systems. In this respect, diagrams are just like programs, but more abstract.

Second, the model that is used for explaining the meaning of UML notations is very similar to the models that object-oriented programmers use to help them visualize the behaviour of the programs they are writing. Thus UML and object-oriented languages have the same semantic foundations, which means that it is relatively easy to implement a design, or conversely to document an existing program, with some confidence that the two representations of the system are consistent.

Chapter 2 illustrates these points in detail. It describes the object model and the ways in which object structures can be defined in UML, and shows how diagrams can be used to document the structure and properties of programs.

1.5 THE SOFTWARE DEVELOPMENT PROCESS

UML is a modelling language, not a process, and a project using UML has also to decide what development process to use with it. There is much less agreement among software developers about what development processes are appropriate than there is about modelling notation. It has even been recommended that each project should begin by defining a suitable process, taking into account the nature of the system being developed, the size and experience of the development team and other factors.

A process model, the Unified Software Development Process, was developed in parallel with UML, by the same group of methodologists. The Unified Process incorporates much experience of managing software projects, while at the same time trying to preserve the flexibility in process that seems to be required.

Chapter 3 gives a brief account of the development of the principles underlying the Unified Process, and also describes how UML is typically used with a development based on the Unified Process.

1.6 SUMMARY

- Most non-trivial software developments use some *methodology*, even if only a very informal one. This often involves the production of *models* to help understand the structure and design of the system.

- Methodologies define both a *language* and a *process*. The language defines the models to be used and the notation for expressing them. The process defines how and when to produce the various models.

- A variety of methodologies, both *structured* and *object-oriented*, have been defined. UML is a *language* for expressing object-oriented design models, not a complete methodology.

- UML describes a system from a number of *views*, which represent properties of the system from various perspectives and relative to various purposes.

- Views are presented in *models*, which define a number of *model elements*, their properties and the relationships between them.

- The information contained in a model is communicated in graphical form, using various types of *diagram*.

- Design models and source code share a common semantic foundation, the *object model*. This ensures that it is possible to maintain a close relationship between the design and the code of a system.

1.7 EXERCISES

1.1 A fanciful description of a methodology for having a meal might include the following steps: plan the menu; do the shopping; cook the meal; eat the meal; wash the dishes. Define a suitable 'deliverable' for each step in the process. Does the deliverable produced by each stage serve as input, in some sense, to the next? If not, should it? Draw a diagram similar to Figures 1.1 and 1.2 to illustrate this process.

1.2 Try to illustrate the details of a software development methodology you are familiar with using diagrams similar to Figures 1.1 and 1.2.

1.3 Do you agree that it is desirable, or even possible, to separate the study of a design language from that of a process that uses the language? Does the same answer hold for programming languages?

1.4 Consider the relative merits of graphical and textual instructions and documentation for the following tasks:
   (*a*) programming a video recorder;
   (*b*) changing a wheel on a car;
   (*c*) getting to a friend's house that you have never visited before;
   (*d*) cooking a new and complex recipe;
   (*e*) describing the structure of the organization that you work within.
Can you identify any common features of the tasks you have identified as being most suitable for graphical support? Does the activity of software design share these features?

2

MODELLING WITH OBJECTS

Object-oriented programming and design languages share a common understanding of what software is and how programs work. The *object model* is the common computational model shared by UML and object-oriented programming languages. Programming and design languages express facts about programs at different levels of abstraction, but our understanding of both types of language is based on the abstract description of running programs that is provided by this model.

This chapter describes the essential features of the object model, introducing them in the context of a simple application. The notation provided by UML for illustrating these concepts is presented and the chapter also illustrates how they can be implemented, thus making clear the close connections between design and programming languages.

2.1 THE OBJECT MODEL

The object model is not a specific UML model, but a general way of thinking about the structure of programs. It consists of a framework of concepts that underlie object-oriented design and programming activity. As the name suggests, the fundamental property of the object model is that computation takes place in and between *objects*.

Individual objects are responsible for maintaining part of a system's data and for implementing aspects of its overall functionality. When a program is running, an object is typically represented by an area of memory containing, among other things, the data stored by that object. Objects also support methods, or functions, to access and update the data that they contain. Objects therefore combine two fundamental aspects of computer programs, namely data and processing, that are kept separate in other approaches to software design.

A program is more than a collection of isolated objects, however. Relationships between the data stored in individual objects must be recorded, and the global behaviour of the program only emerges from the interaction of many distinct objects. These requirements are supported by allowing objects to be linked together. This is typically achieved by enabling one object to hold a reference to another, or in more concrete terms, to know the location of the other object.

The object model therefore views a running program as a network, or graph, of objects. The objects form the nodes in the graph, and the arcs connecting the objects are known as *links*. Each object contains a small subset of the program's data, and the structure of the object network represents relationships between this data. Objects can be created and destroyed at run-time and the links between them can also be changed. The structure, or topology, of the object network is therefore highly dynamic, changing as a program runs.

The links between objects also serve as communication paths, which enable objects to interact by sending *messages* to each other. Messages are analogous to function calls: they are typically requests for the receiving object to perform one of its methods and can be accompanied by data parameterizing the message. Often, an object's response to a message will be to send messages to other objects and in this way computation can spread across the network, involving many objects in the response to an initial message.

It is possible to describe the structure of the object graph in a running program and to trace the effect of individual messages: a debugger would be a suitable tool for doing this. It is not normally feasible to write programs by defining individual objects, however. Instead, structural descriptions of *classes* of similar objects are given, defining the data that they can hold and the effect that execution of their methods has. The source code of an object-oriented program, therefore, does not directly describe the object graph, but rather the properties of the objects that make it up.

The role of the object model in design

In the context of design, the importance of the object model is that it provides a semantic foundation for UML's design notations. The meaning of many features in UML can be understood by interpreting them as statements about sets of connected, intercommunicating objects.

UML diagrams can be drawn to represent particular run-time configurations of objects. It is much more common, however, to draw diagrams that play the same role as source code, defining in a general structural way what can happen at run-time. These diagrams fall into two main categories. *Static* diagrams describe the kinds of connections that can exist between objects and the possible topologies that the resulting object network can have. *Dynamic* diagrams describe the messages that can be passed between objects and the effect on an object of receiving a message.

The dual role of the object model makes it very easy to relate UML design notations to actual programs, and this explains why UML is a suitable language for designing and documenting object-oriented programs. The remainder of this chapter illustrates this by using some basic UML notations to document a simple program.

A stock control example

In manufacturing environments, where complex products of some sort are being assembled out of component parts, a common requirement is to keep track of the stock of parts held and the way in which these parts are used. In this chapter we will illustrate the object model by developing a simple program that models different kinds of parts and their properties, and the ways in which these parts are used to construct complex assemblies.

The program will have to manage information describing the different parts known to the system. As well as maintaining information about the different types of part in use, we will assume that it is important for the system to keep track of individual physical parts, perhaps for the purposes of quality assurance and tracking.

For the purposes of this example, we will assume that we are interested in the following three pieces of information about each part.

1. Its catalogue reference number (an integer).
2. Its name (a string).
3. The cost of an individual part (a floating point value).

Parts can be assembled into more complex structures called *assemblies*. An assembly can contain any number of parts and can have a hierarchical structure. In other words, an assembly can be made up of a number of subassemblies, each of which in turn is composed of parts and possibly further subassemblies of its own.

A program which maintained information about parts, assemblies and their structure could be used for a number of purposes, such as maintaining catalogue and inventory information, recording the structure of manufactured assemblies and supporting various operations on assemblies, such as calculating the total cost of the parts in an assembly or printing a listing of all its parts. In this chapter we will consider one simple application, a query function that will find out the cost of the materials in an assembly by adding up the costs of all the parts it contains.

2.2 CLASSES AND OBJECTS

The data and functionality in an object-oriented system is distributed among the objects that exist while the system is running. Each individual object maintains part of the system's data and provides a set of methods that permit other objects in the system to perform certain operations on that data. One of the hard tasks of object-oriented design is deciding how to split up a system's data into a set of objects that will interact successfully to support the required overall functionality.

A frequently applied rule of thumb for the identification of objects is to represent real-world objects from the application domain by objects in the model. One of the major tasks of the stock control system is to keep track of all the physical parts held in stock by the manufacturer. A natural starting point, therefore, is to consider representing each of these parts as an object in the system.

In general there will be lots of part objects, each describing a different part and so storing different data, but each having the same structure. The common structure of a set of objects which represent the same kind of entity is described by a *class*, and each object of that kind is said to be an *instance* of the class. As a first step in the design of the stock management system, then, we might think of defining a 'part' class.

Once a candidate class has been identified, we can consider what data should be held by instances of that class. A natural suggestion in the case of parts is that each object should contain the information that the system must hold about that part: its name, number and cost. This suggestion is reflected in the following Java class.

```
public class Part
{
  private String name ;
  private long    number ;
  private double cost ;

  public Part(String nm, long num, double cst) {
    name   = nm ;
    number = num ;
    cost   = cst ;
  }

  public String getName()   { return name ; }
  public long    getNumber() { return number ; }
  public double getCost()   { return cost ; }
}
```

The UML notion of a class is very similar to that found in programming languages such as C++ and Java. A UML class defines a number of *features*: these are subdivided into *attributes*, which define the data stored by instances of the class, and *operations*, which define their behaviour. Generally speaking, attributes correspond to the fields of a Java class and operations to its methods.

In UML, classes are represented graphically by a rectangular icon divided into three compartments containing the name, attributes and operations of the class, respectively. The UML representation of the `Part` class above is shown in Figure 2.1.

The top section of the class icon contains the name of the class, the second section contains its attributes and the third section its operations. Programming language types can be used in operation signatures and a colon is used to separate the type from the name of an attribute, parameter or operation. UML also shows the access levels of the various features of the class, using a minus sign for 'private' and a plus sign for 'public'. Constructors are underlined to distinguish them from normal instance methods of the class.

Full details of the UML syntax are given in Chapter 8, but it is worth noting at this point that much of the detail shown in Figure 2.1 is optional. All that is required is the compartment containing the name of the class: other information can be omitted if it is not required in a particular diagram.

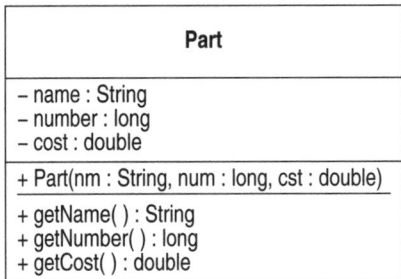

Figure 2.1 The `Part` class represented in UML

Object creation

Classes are defined at compile-time, but objects are created at run-time, as instances of classes. Execution of the following statement results in the creation of a new object. This involves two steps: an area of memory is first allocated for the object and then it is suitably initialized. Once the new object is created, a reference to it is stored in the variable `myScrew`.

```
Part myScrew = new Part("screw", 28834, 0.02) ;
```

Graphical notation for depicting individual objects and the data held in them is defined by UML. The object created by the line of code above could be depicted in UML as shown in Figure 2.2.

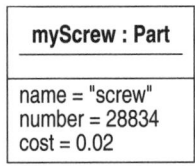

Figure 2.2 A part object

The object is represented by a rectangle divided into two compartments. The upper compartment contains the object's name followed by the name of its class, both underlined. Objects do not have to be named, but where a variable is associated with an object it is sometimes useful to use the variable name to name the object as well. An object's class is always shown when it is known. A common stylistic convention is to choose class names that start with an upper-case letter and object names that start with a lower-case letter.

Data is held in objects as the values of attributes. The lower compartment of an object icon contains the names and current values of the object's attributes. This compartment is optional, and can be omitted if it is not necessary to show the values of an object's attributes on a diagram.

2.3 OBJECT PROPERTIES

A common characterization of objects states that an object is something which has state, behaviour and identity. These notions are explained in more detail below, together with the related notion of encapsulation. The various terms are also related to those features of a class definition that implement them.

State

The first significant feature of objects is that they act as containers for data. In Figure 2.2, this property of objects is pictured by including the data inside the icon representing the object. In a pure object-oriented system all the data maintained by the system is stored in objects: there is no notion of global data or of a central data repository as there is in other models.

The data values contained in an object's attributes are often referred to as the object's *state*. For example, the three attribute values shown in Figure 2.2 comprise the state of the object 'myScrew'. As these data values will change as a system evolves, it follows that an object's state can change too. In object-oriented programming languages an object's state is specified by the fields defined in the object's class, and in UML by the attributes of the class. The three attribute values shown in Figure 2.2 therefore correspond to the three fields defined in the Part class defined in Section 2.2.

Behaviour

In addition to storing data, each object provides an *interface* consisting of a number of operations. Normally some of these operations will provide access and update functions for the data stored inside the object, but others will be more general and implement some aspect of the system's global functionality.

In programming languages, an object's operations are defined in its class, as a set of methods. The set of operations defined by an object defines that object's interface. For example, the interface of the part class defined in Section 2.2 consists of a constructor, and access functions to return the data stored in an object's fields.

Unlike attributes, operations are not shown on object icons in UML. The reason for this is that an object provides exactly the operations that are defined by its class. As a class can have many instances, each of which provides the same operations, it would be redundant to show the operations for each object. In this respect, an object's behaviour differs from its state as, in general, different instances of the same class will store different data, and hence have a different state.

Identity

A third aspect of the definition of objects is that every object is distinguishable from every other object. This is the case even if two objects contain exactly the same data and provide exactly the same set of operations in their interface. For example, the following lines of code create two objects that have the same state, but are nevertheless distinct.

```
Part screw1 = new Part("screw", 28834, 0.02) ;
Part screw2 = new Part("screw", 28834, 0.02) ;
```

The object model assumes that every object is provided with a unique *identity*, which serves as a kind of label to distinguish the object from all others. An object's identity is an intrinsic part of the object model and is distinct from any of the data items stored in the object.

Designers do not need to define a special data value to distinguish individual instances of a class. Sometimes, however, an application domain will contain real data items that are unique to individual objects, such as identification numbers of various kinds, and these data items will often be modelled as attributes. In cases where there is no such data item, however, it is not necessary to introduce one simply for the purpose of distinguishing objects.

In object-oriented programming languages, the identity of an object is usually represented by its address in memory. As it is impossible for two objects to be stored at the same location, all objects are guaranteed to have a unique address, and hence the identities of any two objects will be distinct.

Object names

UML allows objects to be given names, which are distinct from the name of the class the object is an instance of. These names are internal to the model and allow an object to be referred to elsewhere in a model. They do not correspond to any data item that is stored in the object; rather, a name should be thought of as providing a convenient alias for an object's identity.

An object's name is distinct from the name of a variable that happens to hold a reference to the object. When one is illustrating objects it is often convenient, as in Figure 2.2, to use as an object's name the name of a variable containing a reference to that object. However, more than one variable can hold references to the same object and a single variable can refer to different objects at different times, so it would be easy for this convention, if widely applied, to lead to confusion.

Encapsulation

Objects are normally understood to *encapsulate* their data. This means that data stored inside an object can only be manipulated by the operations belonging to that object, and consequently that an object's operations cannot directly access the data stored in a different object.

In many object-oriented languages, a form of encapsulation is provided by the access control mechanisms of the language. For example, the fact that the data members of the 'Part' class in Section 2.2 are declared to be private means that they can only be accessed by operations belonging to objects of the same class. Notice that this class-based form of encapsulation is weaker than the object-based form, which allows no object to have access to the data of any other object, not even that belonging to objects of the same class.

2.4 AVOIDING DATA REPLICATION

Although it is attractively straightforward and simple, it is unlikely that the approach to modelling parts adopted in Section 2.2 would be satisfactory in a real system. Its major disadvantage is that the data describing parts of a given type is *replicated*: it is held in part objects and, if there are two or more parts of the same type, the data will be repeated in each relevant object. There are at least three significant problems with this.

First, it involves a high degree of redundancy. There may be thousands of parts of a particular type recorded by the system, all sharing the same reference number, description and cost. If this data was stored for each individual part, a significant amount of storage would be used up unnecessarily.

Second, the replication of the cost data in particular can be expected to lead to maintenance problems. If the cost of a part changed, the cost attribute would need to be updated in every affected object. As well as being inefficient, it is difficult to ensure in such cases that every relevant object has been updated and that no objects representing parts of a different kind have been updated by mistake.

Third, the catalogue information about parts needs to be stored permanently. In some situations, however, no part objects of a particular type may exist. For example, this might be the case if none had yet been manufactured. In this case, there would be nowhere to store the catalogue information. It is unlikely to be acceptable, however, that catalogue information can only be stored when parts exist to associate it with.

A better approach to designing this application would be to store the shared information that describes parts of a given type in a separate object. These 'descriptor' objects do not represent individual parts. Rather, they represent the information associated with a *catalogue entry* that describes a type of part. Figure 2.3 illustrates the situation informally.

This new design requires that, for each distinct type of part known to the system, there should be a single catalogue entry object which holds the name, number and cost of parts of that type. Part objects no longer hold any data. To find out about a part it is necessary to refer to the catalogue entry object that describes it.

This approach solves the problems listed above. Data is stored in one place only, so there is no redundancy. It is straightforward to modify the data for a given type of part: if the cost of a type of part changed, only one attribute would have to be updated, namely the cost attribute in the corresponding catalogue entry object. Finally, there is no reason why a catalogue entry object cannot exist even if no part objects are associated with it, thus addressing the problem of how part information can be stored prior to the creation of any parts.

2.5 LINKS

The design of the stock control program now includes objects of two distinct classes. Catalogue entry objects hold the information that applies to all parts of a given type, whereas each part object represents a single physical part.

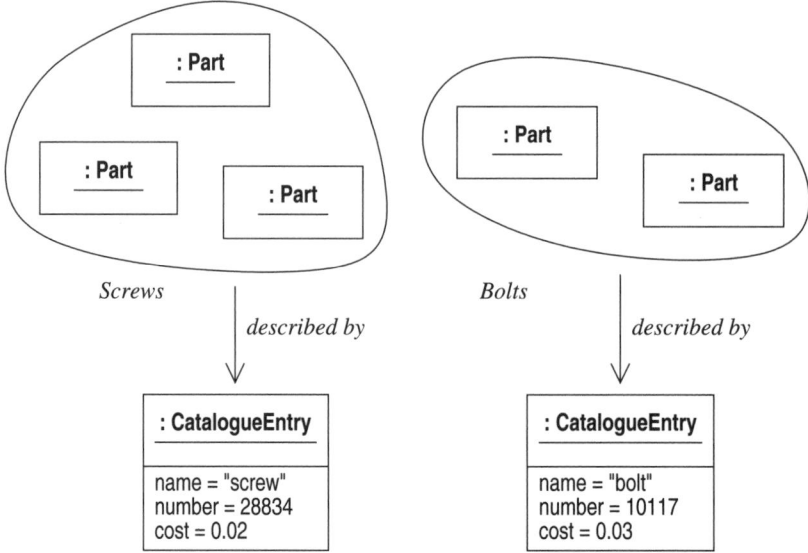

Figure 2.3 Parts described by catalogue entries

There is a significant relationship between these classes, however: in order to obtain a full description of a part, it is necessary to look not only at the part object but also at the related catalogue entry object that describes it.

In practical terms, this means that the system must record, for each part object, which catalogue entry object describes it. A common way of implementing such a relationship is for each part object to contain a reference to the relevant catalogue entry, as shown below. The catalogue entry class now contains the data describing parts, and parts are initialized with, and store a reference to, a catalogue entry.

```
public class CatalogueEntry
{
  private String name ;
  private long    number ;
  private double cost ;

  public CatalogueEntry(String nm, long num, double cst) {
    name   = nm ;
    number = num ;
    cost   = cst ;
  }

  public String getName()    { return name ; }
  public long   getNumber() { return number ; }
  public double getCost()    { return cost ; }
}
```

```
public class Part
{
  private CatalogueEntry entry ;

  public Part(CatalogueEntry e) {
    entry = e ;
  }
}
```

When a part is created, a reference to the appropriate catalogue entry object must be provided. The rationale for this is that it is meaningless to create a part of an unknown or unspecified type. The following lines of code show how part objects are created using these classes. First, a catalogue entry object must be created, but then it can be used to initialize as many part objects as required.

```
CatalogueEntry screw
   = new CatalogueEntry("screw", 28834, 0.02) ;
Part s1 = new Part(screw) ;
Part s2 = new Part(screw) ;
```

As explained in Section 2.2, the fields of a class are often modelled in UML as attributes of the class. However, if a field contains a reference to another object, such as the `entry` field in the `Part` class above, this approach is not appropriate. Attributes define data that is held inside objects, but catalogue entry objects are not held within parts. Rather, they are separate objects which can exist independently of any part objects, and can be referenced from many parts at the same time.

The fact that one object holds a reference to another is shown in UML by drawing a *link* between the two objects. A link is shown as an arrow pointing from the object holding the reference to the object it refers to and it can be labelled at the arrowhead with the name of the field that holds the reference. The objects created by the lines of code above can therefore be modelled in UML as shown in Figure 2.4.

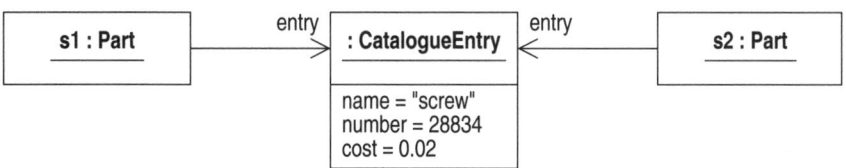

Figure 2.4 Links between objects

The arrowhead on the link indicates that it can only traversed, or *navigated*, in one direction. This means that a part object knows the location of the catalogue entry object it is linked to, and so has access to its public interface. This does not imply that the catalogue entry has any access to, or even any knowledge of, the part objects that reference it. Access in the other direction could only be provided by storing references to parts in catalogue entries, and thereby making the link navigable in both directions.

Object diagrams

An *object diagram* is a diagram that shows objects and links between them. Figure 2.4 is a very simple example of an object diagram. Object diagrams are a way of presenting in a visual form the structure of the object graph discussed in Section 2.1: they give a 'snapshot' of the structure of the data in a system at a given moment.

In a structure of linked objects, information is recorded in two distinct ways. Some data is held explicitly as attribute values in objects, but other information is held purely structurally, by means of links. For example, the fact that a part is of a given type is represented by the link between the part object and the appropriate catalogue entry: there is no data item in the system which explicitly records the type of a part.

2.6 ASSOCIATIONS

Just as the shared structure of a set of similar objects is defined by means of a class, the common properties of the links between those objects can be defined by means of a relationship between the corresponding classes. In UML, a data relationship between classes is called an *association*. Links are therefore instances of associations, in the same way that objects are instances of classes.

In the stock control example, then, the links in Figure 2.4 must be instances of an association between the part and catalogue entry classes. Associations are shown in UML by means of a line connecting the related classes; the association corresponding to the links above is shown in Figure 2.5. Notice that, for the sake of clarity, the diagram does not show all the information known about the catalogue entry class.

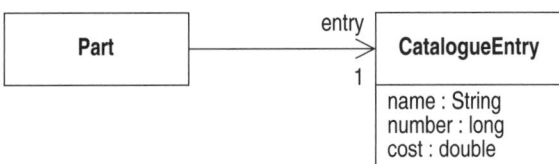

Figure 2.5 An association between two classes

This association models in UML the definition of the `entry` field in the `Part` class. As this field holds a reference, the association is shown as being navigable in only one direction. Like the corresponding links, it is labelled at one end with the name of the field. A label placed at the end of an association in this way is known as a *role name*: its positioning reflects the fact that the name 'entry' is used inside the part class to refer to the linked catalogue entry objects.

The association end is also labelled with a *multiplicity constraint*, in this case the figure '1'. A multiplicity constraint states how many instances a given object can be linked to at any one time. In this case, the constraint is that every part object must be linked to exactly one catalogue entry object. The diagram specifies nothing about how many parts can be linked to a catalogue entry object, however.

Multiplicity constraints give valuable information about a model, but it is important also to be aware of what they do not say. For example, a reasonable property to demand of the stock control system is that a part should always be linked to the same catalogue entry object, as the physical parts being modelled cannot change from one type to another. The multiplicity constraint shown does not enforce this, however: the constraint that there should only be one linked catalogue entry at any given time does not imply that it will be the same one at every time.

It is worth noticing that the Java `Part` class given above does not in fact implement the multiplicity shown in Figure 2.5. As the value `null` is a legal value for a reference field in Java, it would be possible for a part object not to be linked to any catalogue entry, if `null` was provided as an argument to the part constructor. This contradicts the multiplicity constraint that a part should always be linked to exactly one catalogue entry object. A more robust implementation of the `Part` class might check for this at run-time, and perhaps throw an exception if any attempt was made to initialize a part with a null reference.

Class diagrams

Just as object diagrams show collections of objects and links, *class diagrams* contain classes and associations. Figure 2.5 is therefore a simple example of a class diagram.

Whereas object diagrams show particular states of a system's object graph, class diagrams specify in a more general way the properties that any legal state of the system must satisfy. For example, Figure 2.5 states that at any given time the object graph of the stock control system can contain instances of the classes 'Part' and 'CatalogueEntry', and that each part object must be linked to exactly one catalogue entry. If the program gets into a state where a link connects two catalogue entries, say, or a part is not linked to a catalogue entry, an error has occurred and the program is in an illegal state. By a natural terminological extension, object diagrams are referred to as being instances of class diagrams if they satisfy the various constraints defined on the class diagram.

2.7 MESSAGE PASSING

The examples earlier in this chapter have illustrated how data in an object-oriented program is distributed across the objects in the system. Some data is held explicitly as the values of attributes, but the links between objects also carry information, depicting the relationships that hold between objects.

This distribution of information means that typically a number of objects need to interact in order to accomplish any significant functionality. Suppose, for example, that we want to add a method to the `Part` class enabling us to retrieve the cost of an individual part. The data value representing the cost of the part is not held in the part object, however, but in the catalogue entry object that it references. This means that the new method must call the `getCost` method in the catalogue entry class in order to retrieve the data, as shown in the following implementation.

```
public class Part
{
  public double cost() {
    return entry.getCost() ;
  }

  private CatalogueEntry entry ;
}
```

Now if a client holds a reference to a part and needs to find out its cost, it can simply call the `cost` method as follows.

```
Part s1 = new Part(screw) ;
double s1cost = s1.cost() ;
```

UML represents method calls as *messages* that are sent from one object to another. When one object calls another's method, this can be viewed as a request for the called object to perform some processing, and this request is modelled as a message. Figure 2.6 shows the message corresponding to the call `s1.cost()` in the code above.

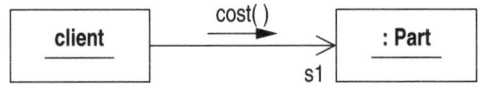

Figure 2.6 Sending a message

The client object in Figure 2.6 has an object name but no class name. The 'cost' message could be sent to a part by objects of many different classes, and the class of the sender of the message is irrelevant to understanding the message and the part object's response to it. It is therefore convenient to omit the class of the client from object diagrams like Figure 2.6, which illustrate particular interactions.

The client code holds a reference to the part object, in the variable `s1`, and this is shown in Figure 2.6 as a link, as before. The reference also enables the client to call the methods of the linked object, however, and this means that in UML links between objects also represent communication channels for messages. Messages are shown on object diagrams as labelled arrows adjacent to links. In Figure 2.6 a client object is shown sending a message to a part object asking it for its cost. Messages themselves are written using a familiar 'function call' notation.

When an object receives a message, it will normally respond in some way. In Figure 2.6 the expected response is that the part object will return its cost to the client object. However, in order to retrieve the cost, the part object must call the `getCost` method in the linked catalogue entry object. This can be represented by a second message, as shown in figure Figure 2.7.

Figure 2.7 also illustrates UML's notation for showing return values from messages. The value returned is written before the message name and separated from it by the assignment symbol ':='. As Figure 2.6 shows, this notation can simply be omitted when the return value is not being shown, or when no value is returned.

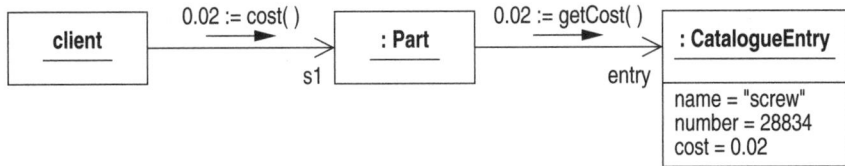

Figure 2.7 Finding the cost of a part

The semantics of the messages shown above are those of normal procedural function calls. When an object sends a message to another object, the flow of control in the program passes from the sender to the object receiving the message. The object that sent the message waits until control returns before continuing with its own processing.

2.8 POLYMORPHISM

As well as maintaining details of individual parts, the stock control program must be capable of recording how they are put together into assemblies. A simple assembly, containing a strut and two screws, is shown in Figure 2.8. Notice that irrelevant attributes of the catalogue entry class have been left out of this diagram.

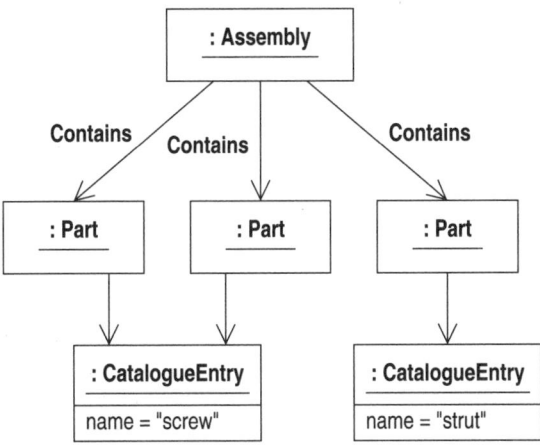

Figure 2.8 A simple assembly

In Figure 2.8 the information about which parts are contained in the assembly is represented by the links connecting the assembly object to the part objects. These links are labelled not with role names but with an *association name*. Association names describe the relationship that holds between the linked objects. The name is often chosen, as here, so that a sentence describing the relationship can be constructed out of the association name and the names of the linked classes. In this case, a suitable sentence might be that 'an assembly contains parts'.

An implementation of the assembly class must provide a way of holding references to an unspecified number of parts. A simple way of supporting this is for the class to contain a data structure that can hold references to all the parts in the assembly, as shown below.

```
public class Assembly
{
  private Vector parts = new Vector() ;

  public void add(Part p) {
    parts.addElement(p) ;
  }
}
```

The association that the links in Figure 2.8 are instances of is shown in Figure 2.9. Like the links, it is labelled with an association name, written in the middle of the association rather than at the end. The symbol '*' at the association end is a multiplicity annotation meaning 'zero or more'. On this diagram, it specifies that an assembly can be linked to, or can contain, zero or more parts.

The diagram in Figure 2.9 also documents the implementation of the association in the code above, by labelling the association end with the role name 'parts', corresponding to the field used to store references in the `Assembly` class. In general, associations and links can be labelled with any combination of name and role name required to make the meaning of the diagram clear.

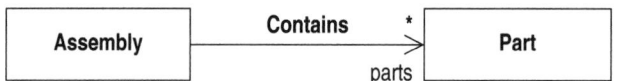

Figure 2.9 An association between assemblies and parts

It is not enough, however, for an assembly to be modelled simply as a collection of parts. Assemblies can have a hierarchical structure, where parts may be assembled into subassemblies, and subassemblies put together with other subassemblies and parts to make higher-level assemblies, to any required degree of complexity. A simple example of this is shown in Figure 2.10, which introduces a subassembly into the structure shown in Figure 2.8.

In order to achieve a hierarchical structure, an assembly must be able to contain both parts and other assemblies. This means that, unlike Figure 2.8, where the links labelled 'Contains' all connected an assembly object to a part object, in Figure 2.10 they can also connect an assembly object to another assembly.

Like many programming languages, UML is strongly typed. Links are instances of associations, and the objects connected by a link must be instances of the classes at the ends of the corresponding association. In Figure 2.8 this requirement is satisfied: every link labelled 'Contains' connects an instance of the assembly class to an instance of the part class, as specified in Figure 2.9.

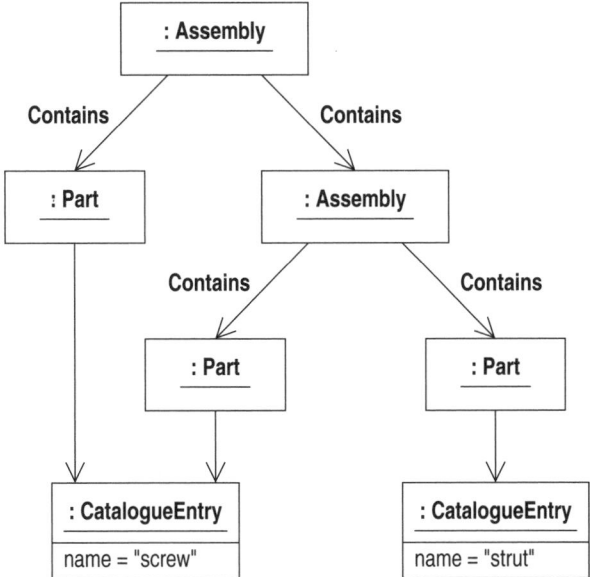

Figure 2.10 A hierarchical assembly

This requirement is violated in Figure 2.10, however, because a 'Contains' link connects the top-level assembly instance not to a part object, but to an instance of the assembly class. If we want to model hierarchical assemblies, the objects at the 'contained' end of these links must not be constrained to belong solely to the 'Part' class, as specified in Figure 2.9, but to either of the 'Part' or 'Assembly' classes. This is an example of *polymorphism*: this word means 'many forms' and suggests that in some situations objects of more than one class need to be connected by links of the same type.

Implementation of polymorphism

UML, being strongly typed, does not allow links to connect objects of arbitrary classes. For polymorphic links like those shown in Figure 2.10, it is necessary to specify the range of classes that can participate in the links. This is normally done by defining a more general class and stating that the specific classes that we wish to link are specializations of the general class.

In the stock control program, we are trying to model situations where assemblies can be made up of *components*, each of which could be either a subassembly or an individual part. We could therefore specify that the 'Contains' links connect assembly objects to component objects, which, by definition, are either part objects or other assembly objects, representing subassemblies.

In object-oriented languages the mechanism of *inheritance* is used to implement polymorphism. A component class could be defined, and the part and assembly classes defined to be subclasses of this class, as shown below.

```
public abstract class Component { ... }

public class Part extends Component { ... }

public class Assembly extends Component
{
  private Vector components = new Vector() ;

  public void add(Component c) {
    components.addElement(c) ;
  }
}
```

Unlike the earlier implementation of the `Assembly` class, which defined a method to add a part to an assembly, the corresponding method here adds a component to the assembly. At run-time, however, the actual objects that are created and added to an assembly will be instances of the part and assembly classes, not of the component class itself. The semantics of inheritance in Java means that references to subclasses can be used wherever a reference to a superclass is specified. In this case, this means that references to both parts and assemblies can be passed as parameters to the add function, as both of these classes are subclasses of the component class, which specifies the type of the function's parameter.

The implementation of the assembly class is potentially even more polymorphic than this, as it uses the Java library class `Vector`, which can hold references to objects of any kind, to store the component references. The restriction to components is enforced by the type of the parameter of the `add` method, which provides the only way that clients can add components to the assembly.

Polymorphism in UML

The implementation of polymorphism in this example arises from the interplay of two different mechanisms. First, the assembly class is defined so that it can hold references to a number of component objects and, second, inheritance is used to define subclasses representing the different type of components that exist. The programming language rules then mean that an assembly can store references to a mixture of the different types of component.

The `extends` relationship of Java is represented in UML by the relationship of *specialization* between classes: if class E is defined by extending class C, then E is said to be a specialization of C. This relationship is also referred to as *generalization* if it is being viewed as the relationship a superclass has to its subclasses: an equivalent description would be to say that C is a generalization of E. Generalization, or specialization, is depicted in UML class diagrams by means of an arrow linking the subclass in the relationship to the superclass. These relationships are distinguished visually from associations by the shape of the arrowhead. Figure 2.11 shows the specialization relationships between the classes in the stock control example.

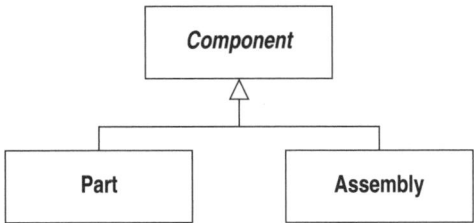

Figure 2.11 Generalization relationships between components

Unlike associations, generalizations do not have 'instances' that appear on object diagrams. Whereas associations describe the ways in which objects can be linked together, generalization describes the situations in which an object of one class can be *substituted* for an object of another. Because of this, the notion of multiplicity is not applicable to generalizations, and generalization relationships are usually not labelled.

Finally, we can redefine the association in Figure 2.9 to take into account the generalization in Figure 2.11. The resulting situation is shown in Figure 2.12. This diagram also documents the implementation of the Component, Part and Assembly classes given above.

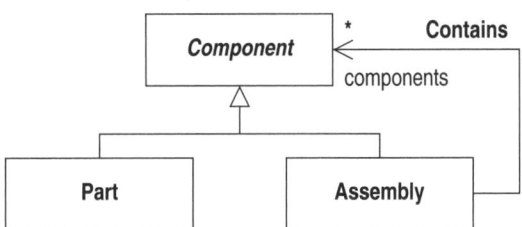

Figure 2.12 A model permitting hierarchical assemblies

Figure 2.12 states that assemblies can contain zero or more components (the association), each of which can be either a part or an assembly (the generalization). In the latter case, we have the situation where one assembly is contained inside another, and therefore this class diagram permits the construction of hierarchical object structures such as the one shown in Figure 2.10.

Abstract classes

Unlike the part and assembly classes, we never expect to create instances of the component class. Parts and assemblies correspond to real objects or constructions in the application domain. The component class, however, is a representation of a concept, namely the fact that parts and assemblies can be considered as specific examples of a more general notion of component. The reason for introducing the component class into the model was not to enable the creation of component objects, but rather to specify that parts and assemblies are in certain circumstances interchangeable.

Classes like 'Component', which are introduced primarily to specify relationships between other classes in the model, and not to support the creation of new types of objects, are known as *abstract classes*. As illustrated above, Java allows classes to be declared to be abstract and, in UML, this can be shown by writing the class name in a slanting font, as shown in Figures 2.11 and 2.12.

2.9 DYNAMIC BINDING

If an assembly object is passed a message asking for its cost, it can satisfy this request by asking its components for their cost and then returning the sum of the values it is returned. Components that are themselves assemblies will send similar 'cost' messages to their components. Components that are simple parts, however, will send a 'getCost' message to the linked catalogue entry object, as shown in Figure 2.7.

Figure 2.13 shows all the messages that would be generated if the assembly object at the top of the hierarchy in Figure 2.10 were sent a 'cost' message. Notice how in an object-oriented program a single request can easily give rise to a complex web of interactions between the objects in the system.

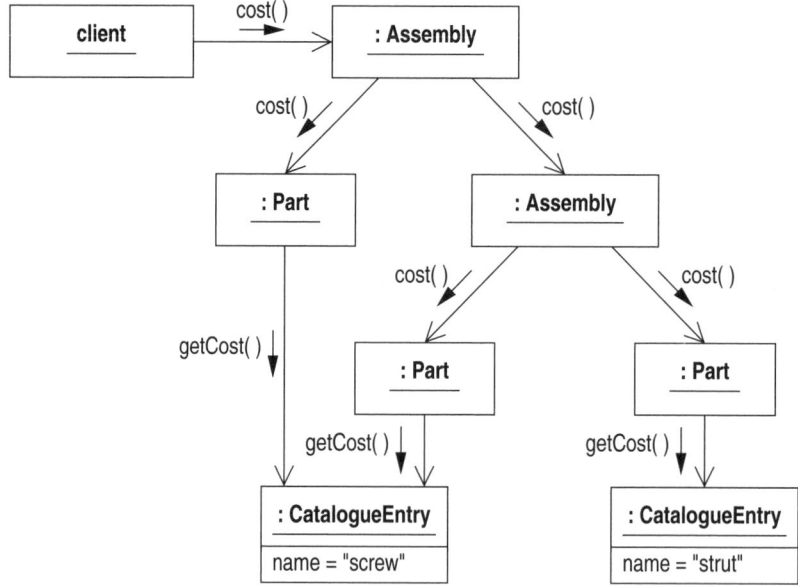

Figure 2.13 Message passing in the hierarchy

In this interaction, assembly objects work out their cost by sending the same message, namely 'cost', to all their components. The object sending the message does not know, and in fact need not know, whether a particular component is a part or an assembly. It simply sends the message and relies on the receiving object interpreting it in an appropriate manner.

The actual processing carried out when a 'cost' message is received will depend on whether it has been sent to an assembly or a part object. This behaviour is known as *dynamic*, or *late*, *binding*: essentially, it is the receiver, not the sender, of a message who decides what code is executed as a result of the message being sent. In polymorphic situations, the type of the receiver of a message may not be known until run-time, and hence the code to be executed in response to messages can only be selected at run-time.

In Java, this behaviour is obtained simply by declaring the cost function in the component class and then redefining it in the part and assembly classes to provide the required functionality for each of those classes, as shown in the following extracts from the relevant classes. Other languages have different ways of providing late binding: in C++, for example, the mechanism of virtual functions must be used.

```java
public abstract class Component
{
  public abstract double cost () ;
}

public class Part extends Component
{
  private CatalogueEntry entry ;

  public double cost() {
    return entry.getCost() ;
  }
}

public class Assembly extends Component
{
  private Vector components = new Vector() ;

  public double cost() {
    double total = 0.0 ;
    Enumeration enum = components.elements() ;
    while (enum.hasMoreElements()) {
      total += ((Component) enum.nextElement()).cost() ;
    }
    return total ;
  }
}
```

2.10 THE APPLICABILITY OF THE OBJECT MODEL

This chapter has discussed the basic features of the object model, and the close connection between the concepts of the object model and those of object-oriented programming languages has been emphasized. The object model is used at all stages of the software development life-cycle, however, from requirements analysis onwards, and it is important to examine its suitability for these activities.

It is often said that the object-oriented viewpoint is inspired by our everyday way of looking at the world. We do in fact perceive the world as consisting of objects that have various properties, interact with each other and behave in various characteristic ways, and the object model is said to be a reflection of this common sense view. It is sometimes further claimed that, as a result of this, modelling with objects is very easy, and that the objects required in a software system can be found simply by examining the real-world domain being modelled.

It is certainly the case that in some systems there is a fairly direct correspondence between some of the real-world objects being modelled and some of the software objects, but this analogy cannot be taken as a terribly helpful guide to building object-oriented systems. The overriding aims in designing software are to produce systems that meet the users' requirements, are easily maintainable, easy to modify and reuse, and that make efficient use of resources.

In general, however, there is little reason to expect that simply copying the objects perceived in the real world will result in software that has these desirable properties. For example, the straightforward representation of parts as part objects in Section 2.2 was shown in Section 2.4 to lead to significant problems of efficiency and maintainability, and there was even some doubt as to whether it could meet the functional requirements of the system. Another typical example of poor design arising from overemphasizing the properties of real-world objects is given in Section 14.5.

Furthermore, the message-passing mechanism used for communication between objects in the object model does not seem to represent accurately the way that many events happen in the real world. For example, consider a situation where two people, not looking where they are going, bump into each other. It is very counterintuitive to think of this as a situation where one of the people sends a 'bump' message to the other. Rather it seems that an event has taken place in which each person is an equal and unintentional participant. For this kind of reason, some object-oriented analysis methods recommend modelling the real world in terms of objects and events, and only introduce messages relatively late on in the design process.

Clearly there are cases where real-world objects, and in particular agents, can be thought of as sending messages to other objects. The most significant strengths of the object model arise not from its suitability as a technique for modelling the real world, however, but from the fact that programs and software systems that have an object-oriented structure are more likely to possess a number of desirable properties, such as being easy to understand and maintain.

Object-orientation is most helpfully understood as a particular approach to the problem of how to relate data and processing in software systems. All software systems have to handle a given set of data and provide the ability to manipulate and process that data. In traditional procedural systems the data and the functions that process the data are separated. The system's data is thought of as being stored in one place, and the functionality required by an application is provided by a number of operations, which have free access to any part of the data, while remaining essentially separate from it. Each operation has the responsibility of picking out the bits of data that it is interested in from the central repository.

An observation that can immediately be made about this kind of structure is that most operations will only use a small fraction of the total data of the system, and that most pieces of data will only be accessed by a small number of operations. What object-oriented approaches attempt to do is to split up the data repository and integrate pieces of data with the operations that directly manipulate them.

This approach can provide a number of significant technical advantages over more traditional structures. In terms of ease of understanding, however, the benefits of object-oriented design seem to arise not from the fact that the object model is particularly faithful to the structure of the real world, but rather from the fact that operations are localized together with the data that they affect, instead of being part of a large and complex global structure.

2.11 SUMMARY

- Object-oriented modelling languages are based on an abstract *object model*, which views a running system as being a dynamic network of interacting objects. This model also provides an abstract interpretation of the run-time properties of object-oriented programs.

- Objects contain data and a set of operations to manipulate that data. Every object is distinguishable from every other object, irrespective of the data held or operations provided. These properties of objects are known as the *state*, *behaviour* and *identity* of an object.

- A *class* describes a set of objects that share the same structure and properties. These objects are known as the *instances* of the class.

- Objects typically prevent external objects from having access to their data, which is then said to be *encapsulated*.

- *Object diagrams* show a set of objects, at run-time, together with the links between them. Objects can be named, and the values of their attributes can be shown.

- Objects co-operate by sending *messages* to other objects. When an object receives a message it executes one of its operations. Sending the same message to different objects can result in different operations being executed.

- Interactions between objects, in the form of messages, can be shown on object diagrams, together with parameters and return values.

- *Class diagrams* provide an abstract summary of the information shown on a set of object diagrams. They show the same kind of information as is typically found in a system's source code.

- A rule of thumb that is often used in object-oriented modelling is to base a design on the objects found in the real world. The suitability of designs arrived at in this way needs to be evaluated carefully, however.

2.12 EXERCISES

2.1 Draw a complete class diagram describing the final state of the stock control program described in this chapter, including any attributes and operations defined in the code extracts.

2.2 Assume that the following lines of code are executed.

```
CatalogueEntry frame
  = new CatalogueEntry("Frame", 10056, 49.95) ;
CatalogueEntry screw
  = new CatalogueEntry("Screw", 28834, 0.02) ;
CatalogueEntry spoke
  = new CatalogueEntry("Spoke", 47737, 0.95) ;

Part screw1 = new Part(screw) ;
Part screw2 = new Part(screw) ;

Part theSpoke = new Part(spoke) ;
```

(*a*) Draw a diagram showing the objects that have been created, their data members and the links between them.

(*b*) The following code creates an assembly object and adds to it some of the objects created earlier.

```
Assembly a = new Assembly() ;
a.add(screw1) ;
a.add(screw2) ;
a.add(theSpoke) ;
```

Draw a diagram showing the objects involved in the assembly a after these lines have executed, and the links between them.

(*c*) Execution of the following line of code can be shown as a cost() message being sent to the assembly a.

```
a.cost() ;
```

Add onto your diagram the messages that would be sent between objects during execution of this function.

2.3 The object diagrams in Figure Ex2.3 depict impossible states of the stock control program, according to the class diagrams in Figures 2.5 and 2.12. Explain why.

2.4 On a single diagram, illustrate the following using the UML notation for objects, links and messages.

(*a*) An object of class Window, with no attributes shown.

(*b*) An object of class Rectangle with attributes *length* and *width*. Assume that the rectangle class supports an operation to return the area of a rectangle object.

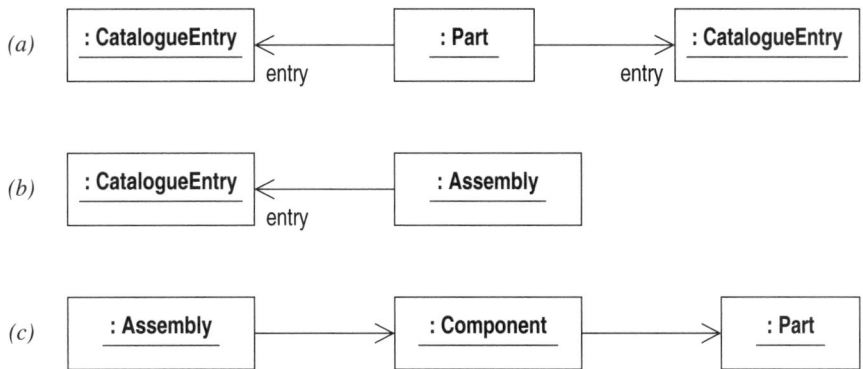

Figure Ex2.3 Illegal states of the stock control program

(*c*) A link between the window and rectangle objects, modelling the fact that the rectangle defines the screen co-ordinates of the window.

(*d*) The window object sending a message to the rectangle asking for its area.

Draw a class diagram showing `Window` and `Rectangle` classes with the properties mentioned in this question.

2.5 Suppose that an environmental monitoring station contains three sensors, namely a thermometer, a rain gauge and a humidity reader. In addition, there is an output device, known as a printer, on which the readings from these three sensors are shown. Readings are taken and transcribed onto the printer every five minutes. This process is known as 'taking a checkpoint'.

(*a*) Draw an object diagram showing a plausible configuration for these objects, and include on the diagram the messages that might be generated in the system every time a checkpoint is taken. Assume that a checkpoint is initiated by a message sent from a timer object to the monitoring station.

(*b*) Does your diagram clearly show the order in which messages are sent? If not, how might this be shown?

(*c*) Draw a class diagram summarizing the structure of the monitoring station.

2.6 A workstation currently has three users logged into it, with account names A, B and C. These users are running four processes, with process IDs 1001, 1002, 1003 and 1004. User A is running processes 1001 and 1002, B is running process 1003 and C is running process 1004.

(*a*) Draw an object diagram showing objects representing the workstation, the users and processes, and links to represent the relationships of a process running on a workstation and a user owning a process.

(*b*) Consider an operation which lists information about the processes that are currently running on a workstation. It can either report on all the current processes or, if invoked with a suitable argument, the processes for a single specified user. Discuss what messages would need to be passed between the objects shown in part (*a*) in order to implement this operation.

2.7 An alternative design for the program discussed in this chapter might do away with the part and catalogue entry classes and instead represent each different type of part by a distinct class. The model could, for example, contain 'screw', 'strut' and 'bolt' classes. The reference number, description and cost of each type of part would be stored as static data members in the relevant class, and individual parts would simply be instances of this class.

(*a*) What difference would this change make to the storage requirements of the program?

(*b*) Define an assembly class for this new design. What assumptions do you have to make to ensure that assemblies can contain parts of different types?

(*c*) Draw a class diagram documenting this new design.

(*d*) It is likely that new types of parts will have to be added to the system as it evolves. Explain how this can be done, first in the original design presented in this chapter and second in the alternative design being considered in this question.

(*e*) In the light of these considerations, which of the two design proposals do you think is preferable, and in which circumstances?

2.8 Suppose that a new requirement is defined for the stock control system, to maintain a count of the number of parts of each type that are in stock and not currently being used in assemblies. Decide where this data should be kept and draw messages on a suitable object diagram to show how the count is decremented every time a part is added to an assembly.

2.9 A 'parts explosion' for an assembly is a report that shows, in some suitable format, a complete list of all the parts in an assembly. Extend the stock management program to support the printing of a parts explosion for an assembly. Illustrate your design by including messages on an object diagram representing a typical assembly, such as the one shown in Figure 2.8.

2.10 In Section 2.5 it was stated that it would be an error to create a part object without linking it to a suitable catalogue entry object. However, the constructor of the part class that was presented in that section did not enforce this constraint, as it did not check whether the catalogue entry reference passed to it was not null. If it was null, a part object would be created that was not linked to any catalogue entry. Extend the constructor defined there to deal with this problem in a sensible way.

SOFTWARE DEVELOPMENT PROCESSES

As discussed in Chapter 1, two major components of every software development methodology are a description of a process for carrying out the activity of software development and a set of notations for documenting the results of that process. It was further noted that UML is a language, not a methodology, and was not specifically designed to support any specific process. The diagrams and notation defined by UML can be successfully used with a wide range of different processes.

This chapter describes the evolution of some ideas about the software development process, starting with the first widely known process models and finishing with a brief description of the Unified Process. While almost certainly not the final word in process modelling, it is interesting to consider the Unified Process in conjunction with UML because both were developed by the same group of researchers. The chapter concludes by discussing the logical relationships between different UML diagrams that are emphasized by the Unified Process.

3.1 THE WATERFALL MODEL

Early attempts to define a process for the development of software were largely based on ideas taken from other engineering disciplines and applied to the new area. A key idea was to identify a number of distinct activities involved in producing software, such as design, coding and testing, and to define the order in which they should be carried out. This led to process models such as the classic 'waterfall' model, shown in Figure 3.1.

The exact number and naming of the stages varies in different versions of the waterfall model, but in all versions the process moves systematically from high-level, declarative descriptions of what the system should do, through detailed descriptions, ultimately in code, of how it will do it, and finishes with a number of stages describing the activities involved in the deployment and subsequent operation of the system.

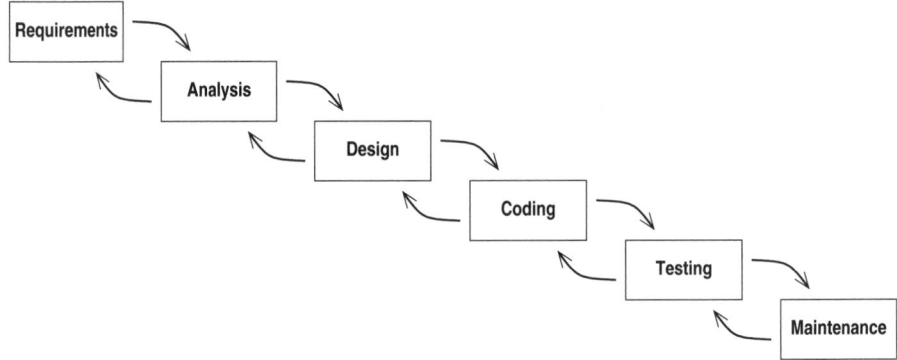

Figure 3.1 A waterfall model (Royce, 1970)

Most waterfall models, therefore, provide a model for the entire life-cycle of a software system, not just its development. The development of the system forms a very large part of the model, however, and is certainly the part that has received most attention in the literature of software engineering.

Each stage in the waterfall defines a separate activity. Successive stages in the waterfall are linked by arrows, and the downward arrows show the temporal ordering of the stages. The basic structure of the model therefore implies that the different stages are to be carried out consecutively. The process envisaged is not like building a house, where electricians, plumbers, roofers and so on might be working on the building simultaneously, but more like a production line, where the analysts, for example, complete their work and then hand the product over to the designers for the next stage. Implicit in this model is the expectation that at each stage the work done will be documented in some way, and that this documentation will be handed on and will form the basis for the work that is done at the next stage.

The waterfall model therefore presents an idealized picture of software development, in which a project would begin by documenting the requirements, move through the activities of analysis and design, and then code and test the system. After deployment the system would be maintained as long as it remained in service. This flow of work through the stages is what has given the name 'waterfall' to this type of model.

In practice, of course, projects are rarely developed in such an unproblematic manner. More typically, working on one stage will reveal problems, errors and omissions in the work that was done at the previous stage. Rather than proceeding on the basis of faulty work, it is obviously sensible to correct the problems before proceeding. The upward arrows in the diagram represent this feedback process whereby work done at one stage may cause revision and reworking of the previous stage.

It is not made explicit in Figure 3.1 whether this feedback can extend backwards over more than one stage. Some original versions of the model restricted feedback to the previous stage in the process only. Although attractive from a managerial point of view, this can seem like a rather arbitrary restriction. If, for example, coding uncovers significant problems in the design of the system, it is quite conceivable that these problems might themselves be serious enough to require changes to the work done at the analysis stage. The fact that the problems happened to be discovered at the coding stage rather than during a design review, say, does not seem a compelling reason to rule out making the required changes to the analysis.

In summary, then, the waterfall model represents the application of an intuitive, sensible and general-purpose engineering approach to software engineering. It emphasizes the importance of planning for an activity before carrying it out, and therefore provides a valuable counterweight to a prevalent tendency in software development to start coding without giving any thought to the overall architecture or structure of the program. Related to this, it recommends a top-down approach, whereby a system is described first at a high level of abstraction and more detail is added as the development continues. Finally, it provides, at least in theory, a strong management tool for controlling software projects: using this model, projects can be given a clear structure, with milestones at the end of each stage when the completed documentation for that stage is produced ready for the next stage.

In practice, however, application of the waterfall model did not live up to its promise to provide a way of structuring software projects so that they would be controllable, resulting in the delivery of correctly functioning systems on time and within budget. Two prominent reasons for this failure are the way the model manages the risks involved in a project and the treatment of the system's requirements in the model.

Risk management in the waterfall model

Contrary to what the waterfall model suggests, software development, particularly of new or complex systems, remains a highly unpredictable activity. There are numerous examples of software projects that have failed or been cancelled because they contain errors that would be too expensive to correct, or problems with performance that make the system unusable, or because they simply cannot be made to work reliably. One major goal of any development process is to find ways of minimizing the risk that a project will end in disaster.

Despite a great deal of work on techniques for developing provably correct software, testing remains a crucial part of any software development process. Although far from perfect, testing is the most effective method known of gaining any assurance that a program does what it is supposed to do in a reasonable time and does not have unexpected side effects.

In the absence of other techniques, then, it is only when a system is tested that developers get any information about the actual, as opposed to the planned, behaviour of the system. If there are major problems with the functionality or performance of a system, they will not be uncovered until the system is tested.

In the waterfall model, the testing activity is postponed until a late stage in a development. Some testing may be carried out earlier than the model suggests, for example if during the coding stage programmers test the modules they are working on, but the model proposes that the system is tested as a whole only when the earlier stages in the process are complete.

By its nature, then, the waterfall model proposes that much of the risk in a project is postponed to near the end of the development lifecycle. If testing is the most effective way known to uncover problems, and if testing is largely postponed until other activities have been completed, it follows that in a project managed according to waterfall principles there will always be a significant risk of major problems only being discovered at the end of the development.

Problems uncovered in testing are by no means caused only by coding errors. It is not uncommon for testing to reveal that the analysis stage was based on faulty assumptions, or made choices that have guided all the subsequent development but which have turned out to be unworkable.

Potentially, then, testing can reveal problems that go right back to the beginning of a project. In the worst case, this can mean that all subsequent work is flawed and has to be redone. In cost terms, this means that no practical bounds can be placed on the cost of fixing the problems uncovered in testing, which of course has serious consequences for the management and control of software projects.

System requirements in the waterfall model

The waterfall model assumes that requirements capture is a discrete step within the process, like testing, but this time one that occurs at the start of a project. It is assumed that a definitive statement of a system's requirements can be produced, on which subsequent development can be based. Experience has shown this to be an unrealistic assumption, and one that has led to many problems and failures in system development.

There appear to be a number of reasons why making a definitive statement of requirements at the start of a software project is harder than in other areas. First, the requirements for many software systems are extremely complex, and it is difficult to anticipate every circumstance that must be considered and to define suitable responses unambiguously. This means that it is often unrealistic to expect that even a consistent requirements statement can be achieved at the start of a project.

Second, many software projects are required to fit into dynamic and rapidly changing environments. Consider, for example, a complex trading system being written by a financial company. The requirements for such a system will be affected by a number of external factors, including the business practices of the company and the legal framework within which it trades. Over the period of system development, it is quite likely that both of these factors will change significantly, as part of normal business operation, but both types of change would typically mean that the system's requirements statement required significant alteration.

Finally, it has been observed that participation in the process of system development can change the users' perception of what is required from a system. Even when a system has been developed in accordance with the original specification, users frequently report that the result is not what they were expecting or required. A number of reasons have been suggested for this. There may, for example, be problems with the process by which the original requirements were obtained in consultation with users: assumptions made by the users may not have been explicitly brought out, or may have been misinterpreted by the people documenting the requirements, for example. In other cases, the experience of seeing a system take shape suggests to users alternative ways in which they could make use of it, so that by the time it is delivered the business requirements for the system have in fact changed.

3.2 ALTERNATIVES TO THE WATERFALL MODEL

Two major problems that have been identified with the waterfall model, then, are the management of risk within projects and the assumption that a definitive statement of requirements can be produced at the start of a project. Both of these problems come from the waterfall model's insistence, at least in theory, that development is largely a process of carrying out a fixed set of activities in a more or less determined order.

In response to these problems, a number of alternative accounts of the software development process were produced, two of which are described in this section. The innovations proposed by these new models have been adopted by current process models, including the Unified Process.

Evolutionary models

In response to what was perceived as the over-rigid structure of the waterfall model, a number of proposals were made suggesting that software should be developed in a more 'evolutionary' manner. Typically, this meant that development should start with the production of a prototype system implementing, or perhaps only simulating, a small part of the core functionality of the complete system.

This prototype could then be discussed with the users, who would also be able to gain first-hand experience of using the system. Feedback from the users would then guide subsequent development, and the prototype would evolve into a more complete system, with small increments of functionality being added at any given stage and repeated consultations with the users taking place.

By involving users in the development process, evolutionary methods hoped to avoid the problem of discovering at the end of a project that the system developed was not what the users needed, thus addressing one of the weaknesses of the waterfall model. Similarly, the emphasis on developing a series of working prototypes meant that the evolving system was being tested from an early stage in a project, making it possible to identify problems early in a project and spread risk across the life cycle.

The weaknesses of the evolutionary model are largely to do with the management and predictability of projects run on these lines. By the nature of the model, it is very difficult to see how project managers could sensibly plan a project, or allocations of work within it. Furthermore, the model gives no guarantee that the evolutionary process will in fact ever converge on a stable system, and no strategy for coping if this does not happen. Lastly, there is no guarantee with an evolutionary process that the overall architecture of the system that emerges will be such that maintenance activities, such as fixing errors and implementing changes to the system, can be effectively performed.

The spiral model

The spiral model was developed in an attempt to develop an explicit software process that addressed the weaknesses of the waterfall model, but preserved more of its traditional management-oriented virtues than the evolutionary model. Figure 3.2 illustrates the structure of the spiral model.

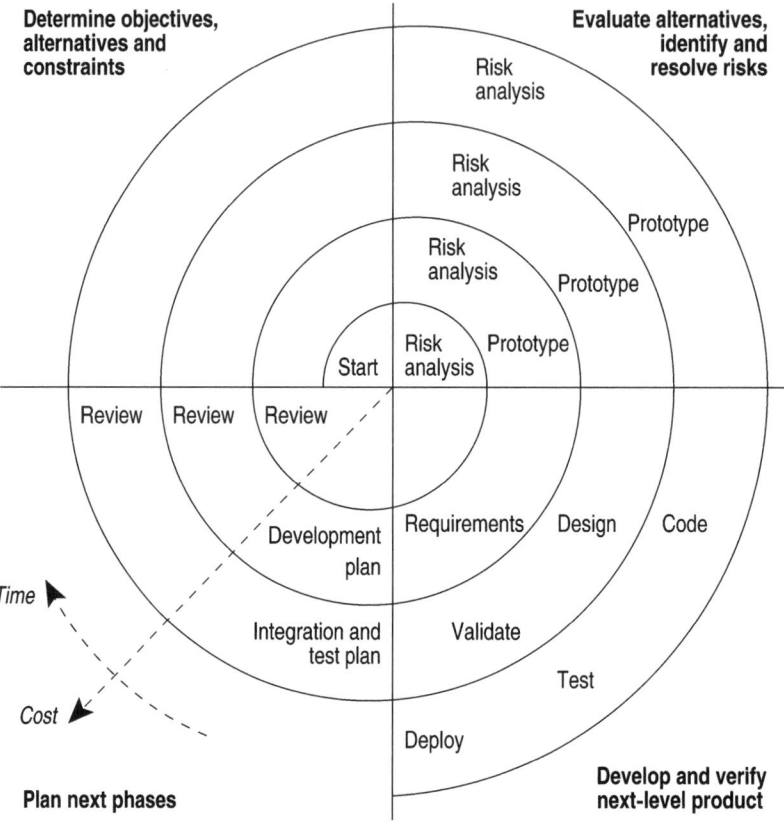

Figure 3.2 The spiral model (after Boehm, 1988)

As its name suggests, the spiral model breaks away from the linear structure presented by the waterfall model and instead pictures software development as progressing in a series of *iterations*, repeatedly revisiting the same stages and activities. Progress on the project is visualized as moving clockwise round the spiral in Figure 3.2, starting from the centre of the diagram and ending at a point on the periphery where the project is finished.

The model has two main dimensions, shown by the dashed arrows in Figure 3.2. The distance from the centre indicates the cost incurred on the project up to a certain point. Expository diagrams like Figure 3.2 show the cost increasing at a constant rate, but a spiral depicting a real project would be much less regularly structured.

The cumulative angular displacement from the starting point indicates the time that has past since the beginning of the project. Again, this is not a linear metric; rather, each complete rotation represents a single iteration of the project, but different iterations will involve different activities and will not all take the same elapsed time.

The four quadrants of the diagram represent the four main activities that the model proposes should be undertaken in each iteration. Each iteration begins in the top-left quadrant, by considering the objectives for the iteration, the various alternative solutions that should be considered and the constraints under which a solution must be developed. Once these have been determined, a risk analysis is carried out, as shown in the second quadrant. The aim of this is to ensure that each iteration focuses on the highest risks threatening the project. Following risk analysis, prototypes might be constructed to help evaluate possible approaches to resolving the risks, before committing to a detailed development.

Once the current risks have been identified and resolved, each iteration continues with a phase of product development and verification. Depending on the stage the project has reached, this phase could consist of different activities. Figure 3.2 shows subsequent iterations following a traditional trajectory from requirements through analysis to coding, but this ordering is not a necessary feature of the spiral model. Each development phase includes a validation step, such as testing the code that has been written in that phase.

Finally, each iteration finishes with a review of the work done in the iteration, and plans are made for the subsequent iteration.

The major innovation of the spiral model, then, is to propose that a development be structured as a formal series of *iterations*. Each iteration contains an explicit consideration of the risks to the project, and the work done in that iteration is intended to address the highest perceived risk. The risks can vary greatly, depending on the nature of the project, and they are not limited to potential technical problems: factors such as scheduling and budget control are prominent sources of risk.

It follows that the spiral model does not provide a single definitive process model in the simple way that the waterfall model does. Rather, it proposes that project planning should take place throughout the lifetime of a project, and that managers must be prepared to modify the plan in the light of progress made and the risks perceived at any given time.

Depending on the nature of the risks affecting a given project, the spiral model can in some circumstances come to resemble other process models. For example, if for a particular project the risks associated with requirements capture are low, but project management is perceived as a high risk, the spiral model applied to the project might well approximate the waterfall model very closely. If the highest risk attaches to developing a complex new user-interface, however, the spiral model may well end up resembling an evolutionary approach, because of the need to develop operational code that can be tested with users as soon as possible.

Finally, it is worth noticing another relationship between the waterfall and spiral models. As Figure 3.2 illustrates, individual iterations within the spiral can themselves follow a series of stages reminiscent of the waterfall model.

Iterative and incremental development

The evolutionary and spiral models therefore identified two important properties that an improved software development process should possess. First, software development should take place *incrementally*: rather than planning to complete the whole system in one concentrated burst of development effort, it is better to develop core functionality first, to the level of getting a working, if restricted, system, and then add the remaining functionality piecemeal, in a series of increments.

This approach has the benefit of producing working code early in the project life cycle. As well as reducing risks, by demonstrating the feasibility of the project, this approach also addresses the problem of requirements specification. Users are able to gain experience of a working system and then use this experience to feed back changes and suggestions into the subsequent development.

Second, the spiral model proposes that software projects be managed as a series of *iterations*, rather than as a single pass through the various activities identified in the waterfall model. Although explicitly proposed as a way of managing risk within a project, the original spiral model can also address the issue of managing requirements change: if this is identified as a significant risk, an iteration could consist of constructing a suitable prototype with a view to eliciting feedback from the users.

Current process models attempt to reconcile the advantages of incremental and iterative development with the traditional structuring of the process provided by the waterfall model. The most prominent such model currently is the Unified Software Development Process, which is discussed in the next section.

3.3 THE UNIFIED PROCESS

A software process that wants to draw upon what has been learned from the history of software development has to find a way to integrate two insights that at first appear rather contradictory. Despite the criticisms that have been made of the waterfall process, its identification of the different activities involved in software development and the characteristic artefacts that are produced by each is still very widely adopted. There seems to be some permanent value in activities such as requirements analysis and design, which are carried out before coding begins.

It is not clear, however, how these activities should be fitted into an iterative and incremental process. Insofar as these approaches emphasize the early production of code, they seem to leave little room for separate activities of analysis and design.

The Unified Process attempts to reconcile these two forces with the overall model of the development process shown in Figure 3.3. In this diagram, time flows from left to right, with the project progressing through a number of phases and iterations, and the vertical axis of the diagram shows a rather traditional list of development activities, or *workflows* in Unified Process terminology. The most prominent message of the diagram, indicated by the shaded areas corresponding to each workflow, is that each activity can occur in any iteration, but that the balance of activities within an iteration will alter as the project progresses from inception to completion.

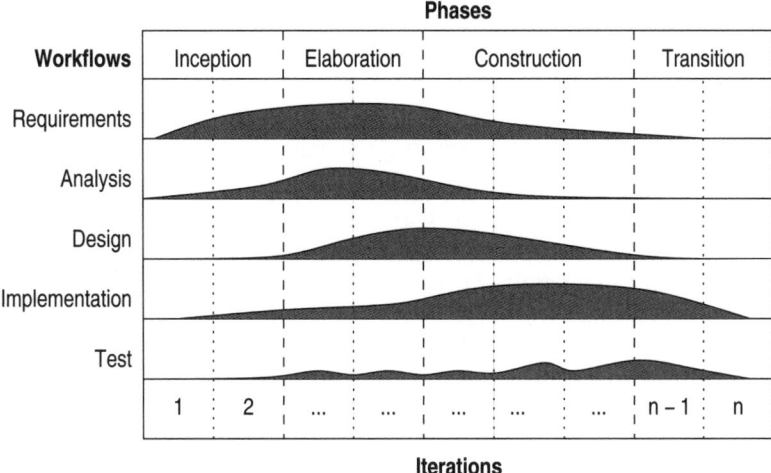

Figure 3.3 An overview of the Unified Process (after Jacobson *et al.*, 1999)

The four phases terminate with *milestones*, not shown on the diagram, which are intended to capture the points within the project lifecycle where significant management decisions and evaluation of progress can be made. The inception phase is primarily concerned with project planning and risk evaluation. The elaboration phase is concerned with defining the overall architecture of the system. In the construction phase, the system is built, ending with a release that can be delivered to the customers for beta testing. The transition phase covers the period of beta testing and terminates with the release of the completed system.

Within each phase there can be a variable number of iterations. As the diagram suggests, an iteration will typically be structured as a mini-waterfall process. An iteration should result in an incremental improvement to the product being constructed. Often, particularly towards the end of a project, each iteration will result in an increase in the functionality that has been fully implemented, but other outcomes are possible. For example, an iteration that resulted in a reworking of some aspect of the system's architecture could be very valuable if it meant that subsequent iterations were able to proceed more effectively.

3.4 THE ROLE OF MODELS IN DEVELOPMENT

The Unified Process assumes that the use of models plays an important role in any software development activity. Models are used to document the evolving system at the different levels of detail implied by the various workflows. The Unified Process was co-developed with UML, and includes very explicit recommendations about how and when the various UML diagrams can be used to support the activities involved in each workflow.

Section 3.5 describes the relationships that the Unified Process identifies between the various UML diagram types. Even if the full process is not being used, these relationships provide valuable insights into how best to use UML to document a development. Before considering this in detail, however, it is worth considering briefly other views on the use of models in software development.

The evolutionary processes discussed briefly in Section 3.2 made little use of, and in some cases were actively hostile to, models of software, but were focused much more on the development of the code of a system. This line of thought has recently been taken up again by the Extreme Programming (XP) movement. As with the older evolutionary models, XP views itself as being in opposition to processes that make extensive use of models and explicit processes in software development. These two aspects of XP are independent, however, and worth considering separately.

The traditional use of models is that they are produced in advance of writing code, and that the code is then written in accordance with the outlines contained in the models. Subsequent development, say in a later iteration, should start by updating the models and then proceed in an orderly way to update the code based on them. Clearly, this process will only work if the models and the code are kept consistent.

A typical scenario, however, is that when an iteration is coded, the design is adapted in more or less significant ways by programmers in the light of their experience in implementing it. It is uncommon in this situation for the design models to be kept in step with the code, with the result that, when the next iteration starts, the design models are inconsistent with the code, and there is no guarantee that changes to the design can efficiently be applied to the code.

This is a real problem for development teams. One response is to emphasize the notion of *round-trip engineering*, which proposes that tools be developed which will enable design and code to be kept consistent, and to evolve together as a project progresses. An alternative response, proposed by XP and related approaches, is to remove the problem by maintaining only one set of documentation. As the source code is the essential product of any development, XP recommends that all work be carried out on the code exclusively. Models can be used within an iteration, if the team finds their use helpful, but they are not preserved and do not form part of the permanent documentation of the system.

There is therefore a significant fault line between model-based accounts of software development and alternative accounts, which focus exclusively on code, and these two tendencies can be identified in writing on software development over many years.

In other respects, there are many similarities between the Unified Process and XP, which can be taken as the current representatives of these two traditions. For example, both emphasize the importance of basing development on a requirements statement structured round a description of the tasks that users perform with the system. These are known as *use cases* in UML and *stories* in XP. Both are explicitly iterative and incremental approaches, recommending that core functionality be implemented and tested as soon as possible, and both recognize that as further increments are added the design of the system may need to evolve quite dramatically, a process known as *refactoring* in XP.

XP is explicitly aimed at small to medium-sized developments. A team size of around ten is often mentioned, and the core of XP is a set of working practices such as pair programming, the development of automated test cases in advance of coding and very frequent product integration, which could be adopted in the context of a small and cohesive team. By contrast, the Unified Process is claimed to be applicable to projects of all sizes, and has much more to say about the overall top-down management of such projects.

3.5 THE USE OF UML IN THE UNIFIED PROCESS

The Unified Process envisages typical uses for the various UML diagrams within the context of a development project. A consequence of this is that there are certain relationships between the UML diagrams which are worth bearing in mind even if they are being used independently of a structured process. This section discusses and summarizes these relationships, and they will be applied in the development of the case study in the following chapters.

Requirements

The Unified Process places a great emphasis on the capture of system requirements using use cases. A sketch of the UML support for this process is given in Figure 3.4.

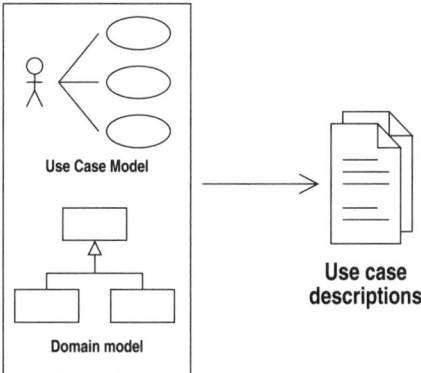

Figure 3.4 Requirements capture using UML

The use cases and actors in the system, and the relationships between them, are captured in a UML use case model. This is often supported by a *domain model*, a simple class diagram documenting the important business concepts and their relationships. The importance of the domain model is that it establishes the terminology that will be used for writing the descriptions of the use cases and offers some hope of removing ambiguity and lack of clarity in these descriptions. Often, it is helpful also to produce a *glossary* listing and defining the key terms in the system.

The most important part of the requirements documentation, however, is the textual description of the use cases. It is here that the important details of the system's functionality are considered and documented. UML does not, however, define a standard form for use case descriptions, so it is necessary for a project to define the template that will be used for writing these. Many different templates have been evolved, and the possible contents of use case descriptions are discussed in detail in Section 4.3.

A use case-driven process

The Unified Process is described as being 'use case-driven': this simply means that systematic use is made of the use cases at later stages in the process. The central use of use cases in analysis and design is shown in Figure 3.5.

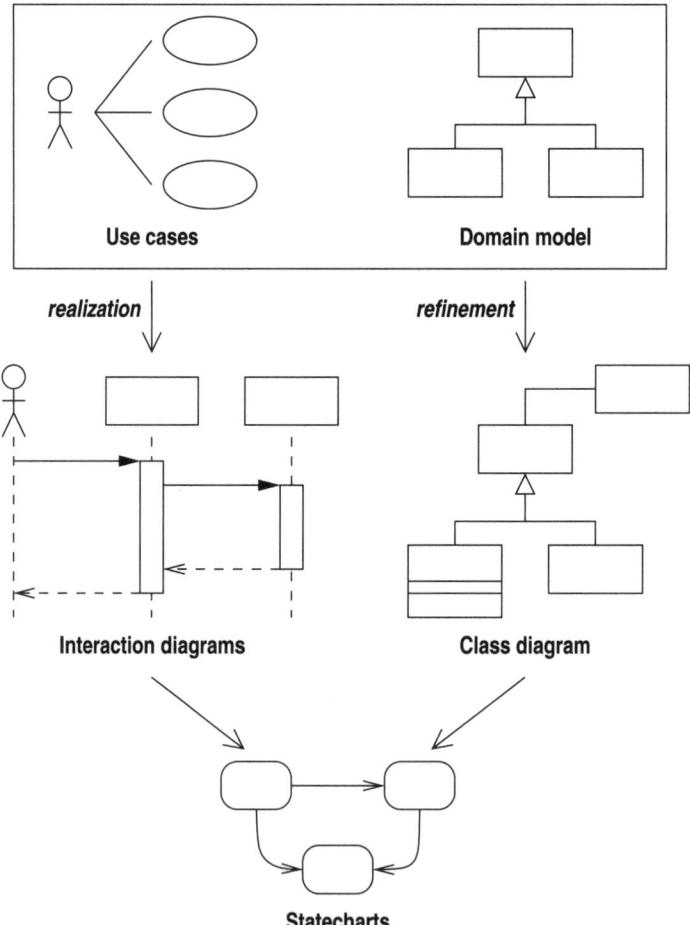

Figure 3.5 Realization and refinement with use cases

The most important activity here is that of *realization* of the use cases. A realization is a high-level implementation of a use case, expressed using a UML *interaction diagram*. It therefore shows how the functionality of the use case will be provided by the system, as a series of interactions between objects. The objects in the realizations are taken from the classes defined in the domain model.

Naturally, the domain model will not define everything that is needed to realize the use cases. Realization typically reveals the need for additional classes and redefined relationships between classes, as well as forcing the designer to specify in greater detail the attributes and operations that are required to support the interactions. This process of *refinement* evolves the initial domain model into a more comprehensive class diagram, which contains enough detail to form a basis for implementation.

The important point here is that development of the class model does not proceed in isolation. Rather, the changes that need to be made are all motivated by the process of realizing the use cases. This means that the class diagram evolves in such a way that designers can have some confidence that the classes specified will in fact support the required functionality. This is often not the case if a complex class diagram is produced separately from a consideration of object interactions.

Finally, based on the realizations and detailed class diagram, *statecharts* can be developed for those classes that require them, documenting the lifecycles of instances of those classes. Figure 3.5 therefore shows in outline how the production of the major UML models is directly informed by the contents of the use case model.

Once the models shown in Figure 3.5 have been produced, they can be directly used to guide the implementation of the system, a process examined in more detail in Chapters 7 and 13. The final significant influence of the use cases on the development process is in the production of test cases for the system. Tests can be systematically derived from use cases to provide acceptance tests for the system: that the use cases can be run successfully is a reasonable guarantee that the system performs some useful business function for the users.

3.6 SUMMARY

- The *waterfall model* envisaged the software development process as a highly structured sequence of distinct activities, or stages, starting with requirements analysis and ending with testing and deployment.

- By suggesting that testing be carried out late in the lifecycle, the waterfall model postpones an unacceptable amount of risk to the end of a project, when it is often too late to address it economically.

- The assumption that a definitive statement of requirements could be produced at the start of a project is another problem for projects based on the waterfall model.

- Alternative models, such as *evolutionary* models and the *spiral* model, attempted to address the problems of the waterfall model by recommending *incremental* and *iterative* approaches to software development.

- These ideas have been adopted by current methodologies, most prominently the *Unified Process*.

- The Unified Process makes extensive use of the models defined by UML, and this suggests a number of relationships that can be used to structure a system's documentation.

3.7 EXERCISES

3.1 Section 3.1 discussed the risk that late testing of a system poses in software development. Is this a problem unique to software engineering or do other branches of engineering face similar problems? Is there anything in the nature of the artefacts being engineered that causes this to be a problem? How have engineers in other areas got round the problem?

3.2 It was suggested in Section 3.1 that there is a problem if a software development process assumes that a definitive statement of requirements can be produced at the start of a project. Is this an equally significant problem for other areas of engineering? If so, is there anything in the nature of the artefacts being engineered that causes this to be a problem in specific areas? How have engineers in other areas got round the problem?

3.3 Why does the spiral model propose that each iteration includes the activity of producing the plans for the next iteration?

3.4 Can you find examples of processes that are incremental without being iterative, or iterative without being incremental?

3.5 Open source development has been widely discussed as a radical alternative to traditional development methods, and it can claim some notable successes, such as the Linux operating system. Discuss how open source development could be characterized using the process concepts presented in this chapter. Some suggestions for reading on open source development can be found in the references at the end of the book.

4

RESTAURANT SYSTEM: BUSINESS MODELLING

In the following four chapters, a simple case study will be considered and a complete development presented, from requirements capture to implementation. The goal is to illustrate the use of the UML notation in software development, and this will be done by considering a single iteration through four of the major workflows identified by the Unified Process, namely requirements, analysis, design and implementation.

As the case study is intended to emphasize the products of development rather than the process, the structure of these workflows as defined by the Unified Process will not be considered in detail. Instead, the activities involved in the development are introduced rather informally, with UML notations being introduced where there is a genuine need for them.

4.1 INFORMAL REQUIREMENTS

The system to be developed is intended to support the day-to-day operations of a restaurant by improving the processes of making reservations and allocating tables to customers. The restaurant currently operates a manual booking system using hand-written forms stored in a large folder.

An example of the current manual booking form is given in Figure 4.1. Each row on this form corresponds to a particular table in the restaurant. Bookings are entered for a particular table, and the number of 'covers', or diners expected, is recorded for each booking, so that a suitably sized table can be allocated. The restaurant runs three sittings in an evening, known as the 'pre-theatre', the 'dinner' and the 'supper' slots, but as the form illustrates, these slots are not strictly adhered to and bookings can be made for time periods that span more than one slot. Finally, a contact name and phone number are recorded for each booking.

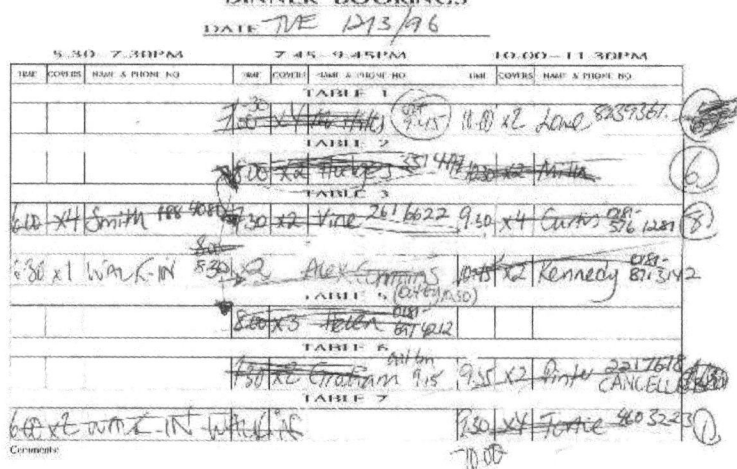

Figure 4.1 A manual booking sheet

Annotations are made to the booking sheet to record various events. When a party arrives and is seated at its table, the corresponding booking is crossed out. If the party is seated at a table other than the one booked, this is shown by drawing an arrow from the original booking to the new table. If a customer phones to cancel a booking, and it cannot be physically erased from the sheet, a note is made that the booking has been cancelled. Other pieces of information, such as the time by which a table must be vacated, can also be written on the sheet.

Diners can of course eat at the restaurant without making an advance booking, if a free table is available. This is known as a 'walk-in' and is shown on the sheet as a booking to record table occupancy, but no record of the customer's name or telephone number is made.

The need for a computerized system

The restaurant management has identified a number of problems with the manual system. The system is slow, and the booking forms quickly become difficult to read. This can lead to operational problems, such as customers being prevented from making a booking because it is not obvious from the form that there is in fact a table free. There is no backup system: if a sheet gets destroyed, the restaurant has no record of what bookings have been made for that evening. Finally, it is very time-consuming to get even simple management data, such as the rate of table occupancy, from the existing booking sheets.

For these reasons, among others, the restaurant would like to develop an automated version of the existing booking sheet. The new system should display the same information as the existing sheet, and in roughly the same format, to make it easy for restaurant staff to transfer to the new system. When new bookings are recorded, or changes made to existing bookings, the display should be immediately updated, so that restaurant staff are always working with the latest information available.

The system must make it easy to record significant events that take place when the restaurant is open, such as the arrival of a customer. Operation of the system will be as far as possible by direct manipulation of the data presented on the screen. For example, it should be possible to change the time of a booking, or the table it is allocated to, simply by dragging the booking to an appropriate place on the screen.

Defining an iteration

Iterative and incremental approaches suggest that the first iteration of a system should deliver just enough core functionality to enable the system to provide some positive business value. In the case of the restaurant booking system, the basic requirements are the ability to record bookings and to update booking sheet information when the restaurant is open. If this much functionality were available, it would be possible to use the system as a replacement for the existing booking sheets, and then to develop additional functionality in later iterations.

4.2 USE CASE MODELLING

Among the different possible views of a system, the *use case view* is considered to be central to UML. The use case view describes the externally visible behaviour of the system. Insofar as software development begins with a consideration of the requirements of the proposed system, therefore, the use case view establishes the forces that will drive and constrain subsequent development.

The use case view presents a structured view of a system's functionality. It does this by defining a number of *actors*, which model the roles that users can play when interacting with the system, and describing the *use cases* that those actors can participate in. A use case describes a specific task that a user can achieve with the system. The use case view contains a set of use cases, which should define the complete functionality of the system, or at least the functionality defined for the current iteration, in terms of the tasks that can be achieved with its help.

Ideally, the use case view should be comprehensible to clients, end users, domain experts, testers and anybody else whose involvement with the system does not require detailed knowledge of its structure and implementation. The use case view does not describe the organization or structure of a software system. Its role is to impose a constraint on designers, who must come up with a structure that will provide the functionality specified in the use case view.

Use cases

Use cases are the different tasks that a system's users can perform using the system. In this example, we will simply describe plausible use cases for the booking system, but in real developments use cases are typically identified by analysts working in consultation with the future users of the system.

The first iteration of the restaurant booking system is intended to allow users to make use of an automated booking sheet. A preliminary list of use cases for this iteration can be drawn up simply by considering what the restaurant staff should be able to do with the system when it was implemented. The major tasks to be supported include those on the following list.

1. Record information about a new booking ('Record booking').
2. Cancel a booking ('Cancel booking').
3. Record the arrival of a customer ('Record arrival').
4. Move a customer from one table to another ('Table transfer').

A use case is more than simply a description of part of the system's functionality. The extra is sometimes described by saying that a use case describes what the system can do *for a particular user*: a use case describes a self-contained task that the user would recognize as a part of their normal job. If a set of use cases covers all the actions that users perform with the system, this should provide some assurance that the system's functional requirements have been fully stated.

The list above simply identifies and names some candidate use cases. A detailed description of each use case must be written, as explained in Section 4.3, in order to gain a fuller understanding of what is implied by each.

Actors

A use case, then, describes a single type of interaction between a system and its users. However, systems often have different categories of users, who are able to perform different subsets of the system's functionality. For example, multi-user systems often define a role known as the 'system administrator': this individual has access to a specialized range of functionality that is not available to ordinary users, such as defining new users, or taking back-ups of the system.

The different roles that people can fill when they interact with a system are known as *actors*. Actors often correspond to a particular level of access to a system, defined by the range of system functions that can be performed. In other cases, the actors are not so rigidly defined, but correspond simply to groups of people with different interests in the system.

In the case of the restaurant booking system, the proposed use cases fall into two main groups. The first group consists of those use cases concerned with maintaining the information about advance bookings. Customers will contact the restaurant to make or cancel advance bookings, and typically a receptionist will receive these calls and update the information stored by the booking system. We can therefore identify an actor associated with the corresponding use cases.

In the second group there are a number of tasks that will need to be performed when the restaurant is open. These include recording the arrival of customers and moving a party from one table to another in response to unforeseen operational requirements. These jobs may be the responsibility of a head waiter, say, and we can therefore identify another actor associated with these use cases.

It is important to distinguish between actors, which are constructs in the use case model, and the real users of a system. In general there is not a one-to-one correspondence between the two. In a small restaurant, for example, the same person may act as both receptionist and head waiter, perhaps by logging on to the system using passwords that give different access privileges. Conversely, there may be many real people corresponding to a single actor: a large restaurant may have a different head waiter for each room or floor in the restaurant. Actors need not even be human users. For example, the computers in a network may communicate directly with each other and remote computers may best be modelled as actors in some systems.

Use case diagrams

A *use case diagram* summarizes in graphical form the different actors and use cases in a system, and shows which actors can participate in which use cases. An initial use case diagram for the restaurant booking system, including the use cases and actors identified above, is shown in Figure 4.2.

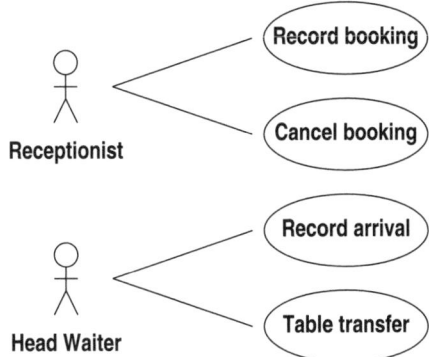

Figure 4.2 Initial use case diagram

The simplest forms of use case diagram simply show actors, use cases and the connections between them. Actors are represented by a stylized icon of a person and use cases by ovals containing the name of the use case. Where an actor participates in or can perform a particular use case, this relationship is shown by an association connecting the actor to the relevant use case.

UML allows more structure to be included in a use case diagram by defining various types of relationship between use cases and between actors. For example, it is possible to define shared behaviour that is common to more than one use case, and to formalize its inclusion in other use cases.

In practice, it is not worth spending a lot of time refining the use case diagram, however, as the additional relationships do not contribute much to later development. It is much more important to consider the details of the behaviour specified by each use case, as discussed in the next section. Additional use case diagram notation will be introduced where appropriate.

4.3 DESCRIBING USE CASES

A use case describes a whole class of interactions between a system and its users. For example, a customer who rings up the restaurant to make a booking will speak to an employee of the restaurant, who will record the booking on the system. To do this, the employee will need to act as a receptionist, even if this is not their formal job description, and interact with the system in some way. In this situation, the employee is considered to be an instance of the receptionist actor, and the interaction that takes place between them and the system is an instance of the use case.

The details of what happens in different instances of the use case can vary in many ways. For example, the receptionist will have to enter specific data for each new booking, such as the names and phone numbers of different customers, and this data will vary from instance to instance.

More significantly, things can go wrong with a use case instance, so that it fails to achieve its primary purpose. For example, if there was no suitable table available at the time the customer requested, an instance of the use case might not in fact result in a new booking being made. A complete description of a use case must specify what can happen in all possible instances of the use case.

A use case description could therefore involve a large amount of information, and some systematic way is needed to record this information. UML does not, however, define a standard way of presenting use case descriptions. Part of the reason for this is that use cases are meant to be used informally, as an aid to communication with the future users of a system, and it is important that developers should have the freedom to discuss use cases in any way that seems helpful and comprehensible to the users.

Nevertheless, it is useful to have some structure in mind when defining a use case, and in order to provide this, a number of authors have defined *templates* for use case descriptions. A template is essentially a list of headings summarizing the different items of information that could be recorded about a use case. In this chapter, the most important aspects of a use case description will be discussed informally, but a full template is presented in Appendix C.

Courses of events

A description of a use case must define the possible interactions between the user and the system when the use case is being performed. These interactions can be characterized as a kind of dialogue, in which the user performs some action on the system, which then responds in some way. This is repeated until the use case instance finishes.

A distinction can be made between a 'normal' interaction, in which the main goal of the use case is achieved without any problem or interruption, and various alternative cases, where a piece of optional functionality is invoked, or something goes wrong so that the normal case cannot be completed. The normal case is called the *basic course of events*, and the others *alternative* or *exceptional* courses of events, depending on whether they are viewed as options or errors. The central part of a use case description is an account of the various courses of events that it specifies.

In the 'Record booking' use case, for example, the basic course of events would describe the situation where a customer rings up to make a booking, there is a suitable table free at the required day and time, and the receptionist enters the customer's name and phone number and records the booking without any problem. This course of events can be presented in a slightly more structured way, to emphasize the interaction between the user's actions and the system's response, as follows.

Record booking: basic course of events

1. The receptionist enters the date of the requested reservation.
2. The system displays the bookings for that date.
3. There is a suitable table available; the receptionist enters the customer's name and phone number, the time of the booking, the number of covers and the table number.
4. The system records and displays the new booking.

It is often tempting to include interactions like 'the receptionist asks the customer how many people are coming' in a course of events. This is really contextual information, however, and not an essential part of the use case. The important thing to record is what information the user enters on to the system, not how that information was obtained. Furthermore, including contextual interactions can make use cases less reusable than they would otherwise have been, and thus make the description of the system more complex than it need have been.

For example, suppose that customers can leave requests for reservations on an answerphone when the restaurant is closed, and that these are dealt with by the receptionist at the start of each day. The basic course of events given above applies equally well whether the receptionist is talking to a customer or taking details from a recorded message, and the single use case 'Record booking' covers both cases. If the use case description contained references to the receptionist's conversation with the customer, however, it would not apply when a recorded message was being processed, and a separate use case would be required.

If there is no table available for the date and time requested by the customer, the basic course of events described above cannot be completed. What happens in this case can be described by an alternative course of events, as follows.

Record booking – no table available: alternative course of events

1. The receptionist enters the date of the requested reservation.
2. The system displays the bookings for that date.
3. No suitable table is available and the use case terminates.

This looks a bit minimal, but at least it tells us that it must be possible to interrupt the basic course of events at this point. In a later iteration, it would be possible to define additional functionality for this case, such as entering the customer's request onto a waiting list, perhaps. Notice that it is the receptionist's responsibility to identify whether or not a booking can be made; all the system can do is to check that the table is in fact available once the booking data has been entered.

Alternative courses of events describe situations that can be expected to arise as a normal part of the business operations; they do not indicate that a mistake has been made, or that an error has occurred. In other situations, it might not be possible to complete the basic course of events because of an error or oversight on the part of the user. These situations are described by exceptional courses of events.

For example, we can anticipate that many customers will request bookings when the restaurant is full; there is nothing that the receptionist can do to prevent this and so this is described by an alternative course of events. By contrast, if the receptionist by mistake tried to allocate a booking to a table that was too small to seat the requested number of diners, this might be described as an exceptional course of events.

Record booking – table too small: exceptional course of events
1. The receptionist enters the date of the requested reservation.
2. The system displays the bookings for that date.
3. The receptionist enters the customer's name and phone number, the time of the booking, the number of covers and the table number.
4. The number of covers entered for the booking is larger than the maximum specified size of the table required, so the system issues a warning message asking the user if they want to continue with the reservation.
5. If the answer is 'no', the use case will terminate with no booking being made.
6. If the response is 'yes', the booking will be entered with a warning flag attached.

The distinction between the different types of courses of events is an informal one, used to structure and clarify the overall description of a use case. All courses of events are described in the same way, and they are treated similarly in subsequent development activities. In ambiguous cases, therefore, it is not worth spending too much time deciding whether a particular situation is an alternative or an exception, say. It is much more important to make sure that a detailed description of the required behaviour is produced.

User-interface prototyping

Although the courses of events presented above describe interactions between users and the system, they do not go into detail about exactly how these interactions take place. For example, it is stated that the receptionist enters a variety of data about a new booking, but not how this is done, whether by typing it directly onto the booking sheet, filling in fields in a dialogue box, or by some other means altogether.

In general, it is not a good idea to go into details of the user interface in use case descriptions. The emphasis is on defining the overall structure of the interaction between the system and the user, and including user-interface details obscures this. Also, a user interface should be designed to be coherent and usable, and this can only be done while considering a reasonably wide range of user tasks. If use case descriptions inappropriately specify details of the user interface, it may make the job of the user interface designer harder, or require significant rewriting of the use case descriptions.

Nevertheless, it can be useful in understanding use case descriptions to have at least a broad view of what the user interface will be like. In the case of the restaurant booking system, we know that the system is intended to replace the existing booking sheets, so it is likely that the screen design will closely follow the structure of the sheets. We will assume that the screen layout will be similar to that shown in Figure 4.3.

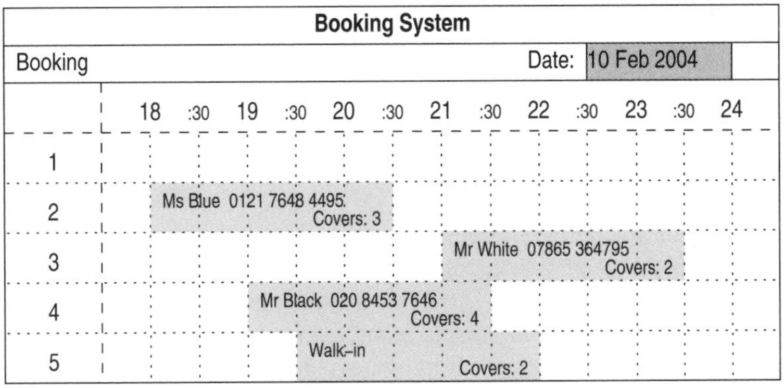

Figure 4.3 A prototype main screen for the booking system

The main body of the screen shows the bookings that have been made. Tables are listed on the left hand side of the screen, and times along the top. A booking is represented by a lightly shaded rectangle inside which the relevant data is displayed. The date of the bookings that are displayed is shown at the top of the screen.

This sketch does not specify how data is to be entered by the user. For the 'Record booking' use case, one possibility is for the user first to type the required date directly in the date box, to get a display of bookings already made for the day requested by the customer. Then perhaps a 'Record booking' option can be selected from a menu, and the booking data entered in a dialogue box. When this is completed, the display would be immediately updated to show the new booking.

4.4 STRUCTURING THE USE CASE MODEL

Once a booking has been recorded, the next significant event that must be handled is the arrival of the customer at the restaurant. This is described by the use case we have called 'Record arrival'. The basic course of events for this use case is the following.

Record arrival: basic course of events

1. The head waiter enters the current date.
2. The system displays the bookings for that date.
3. The head waiter confirms arrival for a selected booking.
4. The system records this and updates the display, marking the customer as having arrived.

An alternative course of events in this use case might occur if the system records no booking for the customer who has just arrived. In this case, a walk-in could be created if a suitable table is free.

Record arrival – no advance booking: alternative course of events
1. The head waiter enters the current date.
2. The system displays the bookings for that date.
3. There is no booking recorded on the system for the customer, so the head waiter creates a walk-in booking, by entering the time of the booking, the number of covers and the table number.
4. The system records and displays the new booking.

Comparing these courses of events with those written for the 'Record booking' use case suggests that there is a certain amount of shared functionality in the two use cases. Rather than writing out the same interactions many times, a better approach is to define the shared behaviour in one place and reference it where appropriate. The use case diagram notation defined by UML provides a number of ways in which this can be done and use of these can lead to a simpler and better structured use case model.

Use case inclusion

Perhaps the most obvious redundancy in the courses of events described so far is that they all begin with an actor entering a date and the system responding by displaying the bookings that are recorded for that date. It would be helpful if this common functionality could somehow be reflected in the structure of the model, so that it did not have to be written out repeatedly.

In fact, it is quite plausible that this interaction could form a complete use case. For example, the restaurant manager might be trying to work out how many waiting staff to employ on a given night, and simply looking at the bookings that have been made for that date might be a good way of estimating how busy the restaurant is likely to be. Given the current model, however, this could not be done, as examining the bookings for a given date can only be carried out as part of another use case.

This argument suggests that a new use case should be defined corresponding to the task of displaying the bookings for a given day. This use case could be performed by anybody working for the restaurant, so either actor could be mentioned in the following description of the basic course of events.

Display bookings: basic course of events
1. The user enters a date.
2. The system displays the bookings for that date.

The relationship between this new use case and the use cases already described can be characterized by saying that the interactions in the 'Display bookings' use case are *included* whenever one of the other use cases is performed.

This relationship needs to be made clear both in the use case descriptions and on the use case diagram. In a use case description, inclusion of another use case can be stated informally, as in the following version of the basic course of events for the record booking use case.

Record booking: basic course of events (revised)

1. The receptionist performs the 'Display bookings' use case.
2. The receptionist enters the customer name and phone number, the time of the booking, the number of covers and the table reserved.
3. The system records and displays the new booking.

The relationship between one use case and another that it includes is shown on a use case diagram by a dashed arrow, known as a *dependency*, connecting the two, labelled with a *stereotype* specifying the kind of relationship depicted. Figure 4.4 shows an 'include' dependency between the 'Record booking' and 'Display bookings' use cases.

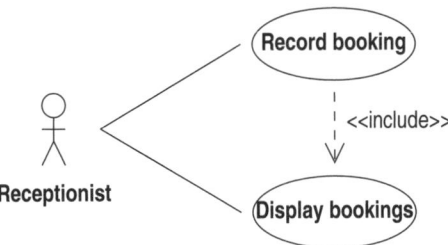

Figure 4.4 Use case inclusion

Notice that in addition to the include dependency, Figure 4.4 contains an additional association linking the actor to the 'Display bookings' use case. This specifies that this use case can be performed by the receptionist independently of making a new booking.

Actor generalization

The use case diagram in Figure 4.2 could easily be updated to include the new 'Display bookings' use case. Because both the receptionist and the head waiter can perform the new use case, the diagram would include an association to it from each actor.

These associations represent the same relationship, however, as we are assuming that anybody can display the bookings for a given date. Rather than showing what is essentially the same relationship twice, we can simplify the diagram by defining a new actor to represent what the receptionist and the head waiter have in common. Figure 4.5 shows this new actor, called 'Staff' as it represents the capabilities shared by all the restaurant's staff. The existing actors are related to the new one by *generalization*, indicating that they are viewed as special cases, defining additional properties only shared by a subset of the staff.

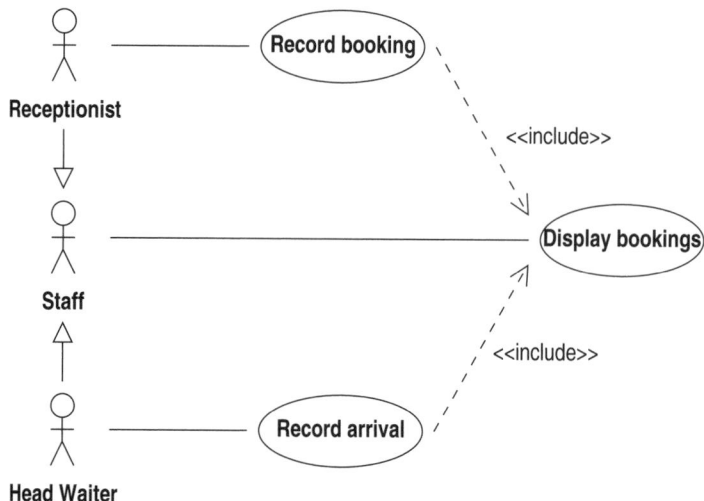

Figure 4.5 Actor generalization

The meaning of generalization between actors is that specialized actors can participate in all the use cases that are associated with the more general actor. Figure 4.5 therefore specifies that both receptionists and head waiters can perform the 'Display bookings' use case. In addition, further responsibilities can be assigned to the specialized actors. Figure 4.5 specifies that only the receptionist can record bookings, and only the head waiter can record arrivals, as defined in the original model in Figure 4.2.

Use case extension

The alternative course of events for the 'Record arrival' use case states that if the system records no booking for a customer, the head waiter can represent the fact that they are eating at the restaurant by creating a walk-in booking. It is probably better to represent recording a walk-in as a separate use case, however, as walk-ins will usually be made for customers who have never made an advance booking, and the use case will need to be performed independently of the 'Record arrival' use case.

The basic course of events for a 'Record walk-in' use case would be triggered by someone arriving to eat in the restaurant without a reservation. Its structure is very similar to that of the 'Record booking' use case, differing only in the amount of detail that is recorded. The basic course of events could be described as follows.

Record walk-in: basic course of events

1. The head waiter performs the 'Display bookings' use case.
2. The head waiter enters the time, the number of covers and the table allocated to the customer.
3. The system records and displays the new booking.

However, there now appears to be considerable overlap between the description of the alternative course of events for the 'Record arrival' use case and this new use case. It is natural to ask if this could be removed by relating the two use cases in some way, perhaps by means of the include dependency introduced above.

The include dependency is inappropriate in this case, because the interactions specified in 'Record walk-in' are not performed every time 'Record arrival' is performed. Rather, there is a kind of optional relationship between them: the 'Record walk-in' use case will only be performed in some cases of 'Record arrival', namely when there is no booking recorded for the customer, there is a suitable table free and the customer still wants to eat at the restaurant.

UML describes this situation by saying that in certain circumstances, the 'Record arrival' use case can be *extended* by the 'Record walk-in' use case. This can be shown on the use case model by means of a dependency labelled with the stereotype 'extend', as shown in Figure 4.6. Notice that the dependency goes in the opposite direction from an include dependency, pointing from the extending use case to the one being extended.

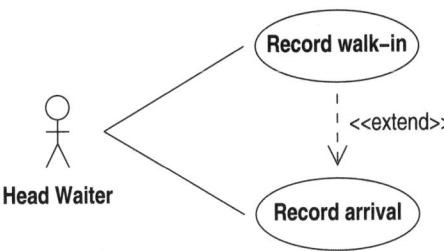

Figure 4.6 Use case extension

The distinction between include and extend dependencies is rather subtle, and there has been much debate about what exactly the two stereotypes mean. The use case model is used less formally than other UML models, however, and it is usually not worth spending too much time worrying about the details of relationships between use cases. The aim is to clarify the requirements of the system, and this is better achieved by writing use case descriptions that make clear what happens in each use case.

4.5 COMPLETING THE USE CASE MODEL

The remaining two use cases shown in Figure 4.2 can be dealt with easily. The basic course of events for cancelling a booking, for example, might be specified as follows.

Cancel booking: basic course of events

1. The receptionist selects the required booking.
2. The receptionist cancels the booking.
3. The system asks the receptionist to confirm the cancellation.

4. The receptionist answers 'yes', so the system records the cancellation and updates the display.

This course of events does not spell out in detail how the user will accomplish these tasks. As mentioned above, the details of the user interface are best specified later, when a good understanding of the functionality of each use case has been gained.

A further advantage of being unspecific is that it leaves open the possibility that the system might provide more than one way of accomplishing the task. For example, one way to cancel a booking might be through a menu option which brings up a dialogue box where identifying details of the booking are entered to select it. Alternatively, clicking the right mouse button over a booking rectangle might bring up a pop-up menu including a 'cancel' option. Both these are ways of achieving the same end, namely cancelling the booking, and it is a good idea at this stage to write the use case description in a general enough way to encompass both.

There are a number of alternative and exceptional courses of events that should be considered to complete the description of this use case. For example, it is likely that the restaurant's business rules forbid cancelling a booking for some time in the past, or a booking for which the arrival of the customers has already been recorded. Specification of these alternatives is left as an exercise.

The basic course of events for the 'Table transfer' use case can also be defined independently of the details of the user interface, as follows.

Table transfer: basic course of events

1. The head waiter selects the required booking.
2. The head waiter changes the table allocation of the booking.
3. The system records the alteration and updates the display.

This use case could be invoked through a menu option, with the user filling in the new table number in a dialogue box, or perhaps the table transfer could be accomplished by dragging the booking rectangle to its new location. Alternative and exceptional courses of events can be derived from the restaurant's business rules: as with cancellations, it should not be possible to transfer a past booking to a new table, and it should not be possible to move a booking to a table that is already occupied.

When is a use case model finished?

Consideration of these last two use cases might suggest further refinements to the use case model, using the structuring mechanisms introduced in Section 4.4. For example, both cancellation and table transfer involve selecting a booking and updating some of the information that the system holds about it. Perhaps a separate use case for selecting a booking could be identified, which could then be included by both. Maybe a more general use case, 'Update booking' perhaps, should be identified, which would provide the user with a general mechanism for changing any of the data associated with a booking, such as the number of covers, or the finishing time.

Use case analysis is an informal technique, however, and after a point there are diminishing returns in spending time searching for improvements to a model. This applies in particular to the include and extend relationships: these do not usually correspond to structural properties of the design that will be produced from the use cases, and so the consequences of missing a possible dependency are not severe.

Figure 4.7 shows a complete use case diagram summarizing the decisions discussed above about the use cases in the first iteration of the restaurant booking system. This will be used as a basis for further development of this case study in subsequent chapters.

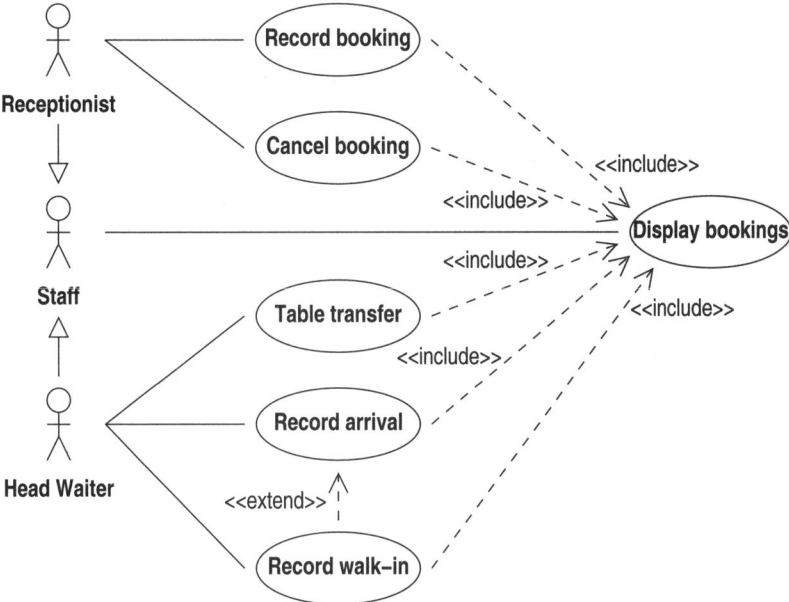

Figure 4.7 The complete use case diagram

4.6 DOMAIN MODELLING

Use cases are intended to be comprehensible to both developers and users of the system. They are therefore described using terminology taken from the business domain rather than from implementation or computer-oriented vocabularies. A useful activity that is often carried out in parallel with use case modelling is to describe systematically the business concepts that are used in the use case descriptions.

One common way of documenting this activity is by producing a class diagram showing the most important business concepts and the relationships between them. Such a class diagram is often referred to as a *domain model*. On large projects, a domain model is often produced as part of a more ambitious activity of business modelling, but smaller systems can usually be described adequately with a simple domain model.

Domain models typically do not make use of the full range of class diagram notation. The classes in a domain model usually represent entities or concepts that are significant in the real world context of the system. The data that the system must record is modelled as attributes of these classes, and a domain model also shows relationships between these concepts, using associations and generalization. Domain models do not usually contain operations: these are defined later, once the implementations of the use cases have been considered in more detail.

In the restaurant booking system the key business requirement is to record the fact that customers have made reservations, so domain modelling may start by identifying two classes, representing reservations and customers. We know that the system must record the name and phone number of each customer making a reservation, and it would be reasonable to model these as attributes of the customer class.

The fact that a customer has made a reservation could be recorded by linking the customer with the reservation; in the domain model, therefore, an association between the two classes models the fact that customers make reservations. The multiplicities on this association should specify that each reservation is made by one customer, the person whose name and phone number are recorded by the system, but that each customer may make many reservations. These modelling decisions are recorded in the diagram shown in Figure 4.8.

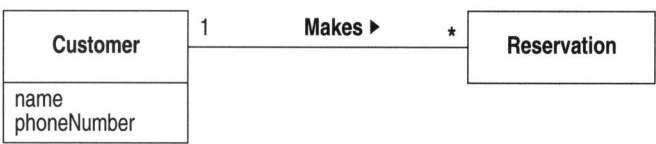

Figure 4.8 Modelling customers and reservations

There is a further relationship between reservations and customers that could be included in the domain model, however. This arises from the fact that reservations are normally made for more than one person, and that all the people eating can be described as customers of the restaurant.

Before including this relationship in the domain model, however, we should consider what information the system must maintain. The name and phone number of the person making the reservation must be recorded so that they can be contacted if there are any problems. The important thing about the people who turn up to eat, however, is simply how many there are, and it is not necessary for the restaurant to record individual details of each diner. It is probably not necessary, therefore, to link a reservation to all the customers who will be eating and instead the number of *covers* can be included as an attribute of the reservation class.

We can next consider what other information must be recorded about reservations. The date and time for which the reservation is made are straightforward properties which can be modelled as attributes. The system must also record the table that a reservation is allocated to. It is possible that this could be done by recording the table number as a further attribute of the reservation, but an alternative would be to model each table as an object in its own right, and thus introduce a table class into the domain model.

It is sometimes difficult to decide whether a particular piece of information should be included in a domain model as a class or an attribute. In the case of tables, one relevant consideration is that the restaurant needs to record additional information about each table, such as the number of people that can be seated at the table. In an object model, this information must be recorded as an attribute of a class, and a table class is a natural place to store it. Figure 4.9 shows the domain model extended to include the table class and the properties of reservations.

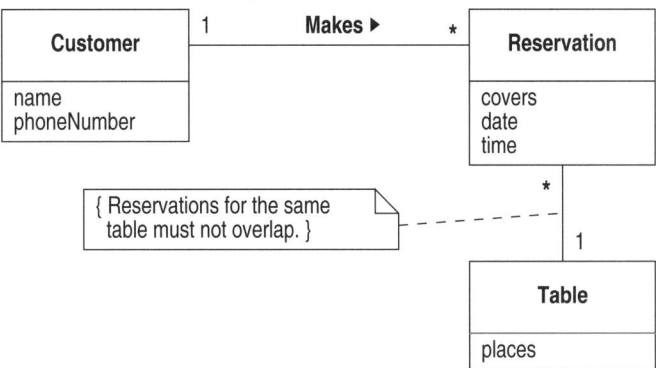

Figure 4.9 Domain model including properties of reservations

The multiplicities on the association between the reservation and table classes indicate that a reservation can only be for one table. This would seem to preclude the restaurant from taking bookings for large parties that would be seated at more than one table. We will make the assumption that in the first iteration of the development this requirement can be adequately dealt with by making multiple, simultaneous bookings for such a party, one for each table that will be occupied.

In the other direction, the multiplicity asserts that many reservations can be made for each table. This is not meant to imply that two reservations should be made for a table at the same time, but rather that the table will be assigned to different customers, on different days and at different times.

It is clearly an important business rule, however, that tables should not be double booked. This cannot be shown in the graphical notation provided by UML, and such properties are modelled by adding *constraints* to the relevant model elements. Constraints are properties that must be satisfied by all states of a system, and are discussed in detail in Chapter 12. Figure 4.9 shows an informal constraint attached to the association, ruling out the possibility of double-booking tables.

A further plausible constraint on this association would be one stating that the number of covers for a reservation can be no larger than the number of places available at the table the reservation is linked to. In most cases, this constraint will be observed, but the description of the 'Record booking' use case made clear that it is possible, in exceptional circumstances, for extra places to be made available at a table in order to seat a large party there. It would therefore not be consistent with the use case model to add a constraint ruling this possibility out.

The domain model does not yet deal with walk-ins. These share some properties with reservations, namely the basic data stored and the link with a table, but differ in that no customer information is recorded about walk-ins. This suggests that reservations and walk-ins could be modelled by defining a general class, which captures the common properties of both, and specialized subclasses to model reservations and walk-ins. This refinement to the model is shown in Figure 4.10.

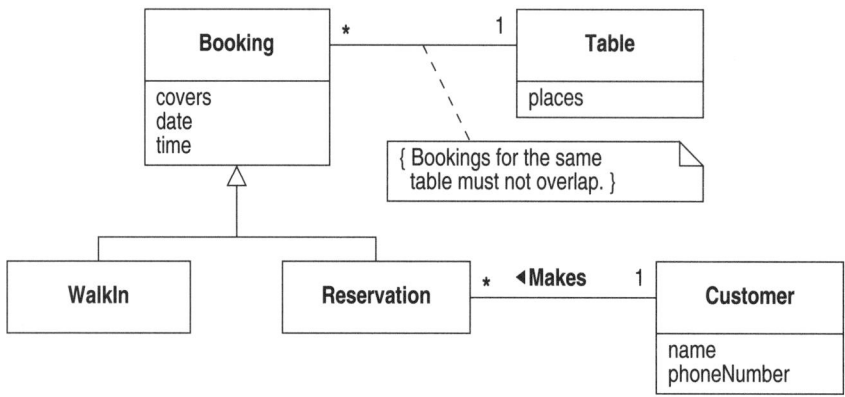

Figure 4.10 The domain model including walk-ins

It might appear that the walk-in class is redundant in Figure 4.10, as it does not add any properties to those that it inherits from the booking class. However, including it as a separate class acts as a kind of insurance against future change in the model. If it is later necessary to add a property of walk-ins to the model that reservations do not share, this could be done easily in the design in Figure 4.10. If walk-ins were simple created as instances of the superclass, however, the change involved to the model would be much more substantial.

The correctness of domain models

When a domain model is developed, it is common to come up with alternative ways of modelling certain aspects of the system, and often there appears to be no obvious reason to choose one version of the model over another. Examples of this include the treatment of table numbers and walk-in bookings in Figure 4.10. Additionally, it might be suggested that dates should be modelled with a separate class, rather than simply being an attribute of bookings.

Some models are clearly wrong, or inadequate. If the date were not included at all, the model would not be storing a crucial piece of data required by the booking system. However, it is much harder to argue for the correctness of a model, or even that one model is better than another. From the perspective of domain modelling, there does not appear to be much to choose between modelling dates as attributes or as instances of a separate class linked to the relevant bookings.

This issue can be put in perspective by considering the purpose of the domain model in a complete development. Ultimately, a designer is trying to identify sets of objects that can interact in such a way as to support efficiently the functionality that the overall system must deliver. Alternative approaches in a domain model are best judged, therefore, by the extent to which they do this.

This cannot be assessed simply by examining the domain model in isolation, however. It is necessary to consider what the model actually delivers, by seeing how interactions between instances of the domain model classes would actually support the required functionality. This is the key activity of the analysis and design workflows in the Unified Process and will be considered in the next two chapters.

4.7 GLOSSARIES

One useful outcome of domain modelling is a detailed consideration of the concepts and vocabulary that clients use in talking about the system. It is very easy to use terms ambiguously or inconsistently when writing informally about a system. For example, throughout this chapter the terms 'booking' and 'reservation' have been used interchangeably, but Figure 4.10 indicates that there is in fact a distinction to be drawn between the general notion of a booking and a reservation that is made in advance, and suggests a more careful definition of the two terms.

It is often very useful to summarize a system's core vocabulary in a series of definitions collected together into a system *glossary*. For example, the terms used so far in the development of the booking system can be listed and defined as follows.

Booking An assignment of a table to a party of diners for a meal.
Covers The number of diners that a booking is made for.
Customer The person making a reservation.
Diner A person eating at the restaurant.
Places The number of diners that can be seated at a particular table.
Reservation An advance booking for a table at a particular time.
Walk-in A booking that is not made in advance.

Ideally, once a glossary has been created, all the system documentation should be edited to make consistent use of the defined terms. In subsequent chapters, the further development of the restaurant booking system will use the terminology defined above, but editing the use case descriptions given earlier in this chapter to reflect the official definitions will be left as an exercise.

4.8 SUMMARY

- At the end of the requirements workflow, the system documentation consists of a use case model, textual descriptions of use cases, a glossary of key terms and a domain model.

- A *use case diagram* shows actors and use cases, together with various relations between them.

- A *use case* denotes a typical type of task that a user can perform with a system.

- An *actor* represents a role that a user can play when interacting with a system. Actors are associated with use cases, showing which tasks users in a given role can perform. Actors can be related by generalization, to make explicit their shared capabilities.

- One use case can *include* another: this means that the interaction specified by the included use case form part of every performance of the including use case.

- One use case can *extend* another: this means that the interaction specified by the extending use case forms an optional part of a performance of the extended use case.

- *Use case descriptions* are textual documents which describe in detail the interactions that can take place between a user and the system in performing the use case.

- Every use case description contains a *basic course of events*, describing the 'normal' progress of the use case, together with a set of *alternative* and *exceptional* courses of events.

- A *domain model* shows important business concepts, the relationships between them and the business data maintained by the system. Domain models are represented as class diagrams, typically showing classes, attributes, associations and generalizations only.

- A *glossary* defines important terms in the business domain, providing an agreed definition for each. This defines the business-specific vocabulary that should be used in use case descriptions.

4.9 EXERCISES

4.1 Suppose that the restaurant manager looked at Figure 4.2 and commented that the design was faulty because the restaurant could not afford to employ a full-time receptionist. How would you respond?

4.2 Redraw the use case diagram in Figure 4.7 without the 'Staff' actor and making no use of actor generalization. Do the two versions of the diagram describe the same facts, from the point of view of the restaurant's operations? Which diagram do you find clearer and easier to understand?

4.3 Extend the description of the 'Record booking' use case to cover the situation where the receptionist tries to double-book a particular table. Would this be an alternative or an exceptional course of events?

4.4 The system should not allow the head waiter to record an arrival for a reservation more than once. Consider ways in which the system might prevent this happening, and if necessary describe the system's response with a new course of events in the 'Record arrival' use case.

4.5 Write descriptions of any alternative or exceptional courses of events that you can think of for the 'Display bookings' use case.

4.6 Extend the description of the 'Cancel booking' and 'Table transfer' use cases to include a full list of alternative and exceptional courses of events.

4.7 Can a clear and unambiguous distinction be made between alternative and exceptional courses of events in use case descriptions? Give reasons for your answer, with examples drawn from the restaurant booking system.

4.8 Rewrite the informal use case descriptions presented in this chapter using the template discussed in Appendix C and the terminology listed in the glossary in Section 4.7.

4.9 The discussion in this chapter has said very little about how booking information can be altered. Bookings can only be cancelled, or moved to an alternative table. Extend the use case model to allow more general editing of bookings, perhaps by using a dialogue box that displays all the information held about a booking and allows suitable modifications to be made.

4.10 As it stands, the domain model would permit a party of any size to be allocated any table. Suppose that the restaurant decides to formalize the number of additional places that can be squeezed onto a table as its 'overflow capacity'. As before, the user should be asked to confirm a booking that is too large for the table, but under no circumstances should a table's overflow capacity be exceeded. Update the use case description for making a reservation to accommodate this new requirement and change the domain model appropriately.

4.11 Suppose the restaurant decides to provide designated smoking and non-smoking tables. What effect would this change in requirements have on the use case model presented in this chapter?

4.12 The discussion in this chapter has said nothing about the length of bookings: only the arrival time is entered, and we have implicitly assumed that all bookings are of a standard length. Extend the use case model to allow more flexibility in the lengths of bookings by defining a new use case to adjust the length of a booking. This could be done by entering the time explicitly or by using the mouse to change the length of the displayed booking rectangle.

4.13 In the first iteration, reservations are assigned to tables manually by the receptionist. Write use case descriptions for an increment in which the system would automatically assign a booking to a table, given information about the date and time of the booking and the number of covers.

4.14 The booking system is to be extended to support a waiting list. Customers who cannot make a reservation for the requested time should be offered the chance to be placed on the waiting list. When a table becomes available, perhaps as a result of a cancellation, the system should check whether there is anybody on the waiting list who can now make a reservation. If there is, the system sends a message to the receptionist, who then contacts the customer to see if the reservation is to be made. Extend the use case model to describe this functionality.

4.15 Consider an alternative specification of the waiting list where the system automatically alerts the customer when a suitable table is available, perhaps by sending a text message to the stored phone number. The customer then contacts the restaurant to confirm that they still want to make the reservation. Extend the original use case model to describe this functionality.

What arguments could be given, from the point of view of the restaurant's business requirements, for preferring one version of the waiting list to the other?

4.16 It might be convenient if the booking system provided an 'undo' facility, so that operations like the cancellation of a reservation or a table transfer could be quickly and easily undone. How could this feature be added to the use case model? Is 'undo' one use case, or should there be a separate use case for undoing each different kind of operation?

4.17 Consider how the system described in this chapter might be enhanced to allow a booking to be made for more than one table simultaneously. Describes the changes that would need to be made to the use case descriptions, the prototype user interface and the domain model to incorporate this requirement.

5

RESTAURANT SYSTEM: ANALYSIS

Analysis is frequently identified as a distinct stage or activity in software development, but a clear distinction between analysis and design is not always made. This is particularly so in object-oriented methods: because the same concepts and notation are used throughout development, analysis and design often seem to merge into each other. This chapter presents one view of analysis, drawn from the Unified Process, but it should be pointed out that different writers and methodologies give different accounts and in some cases do not even consider analysis to be a separate activity.

5.1 THE PURPOSE OF ANALYSIS

One way of defining the purpose of analysis is to identify what it is that is being analysed. In the context of the overall development, a plausible answer to this question is 'the system requirements'. Requirements stated in the form of use case descriptions are a valuable tool for defining a system's external behaviour, but they give no guidance about the internal structure of the system, or describe how to come up with a set of interacting objects that support the required functionality. Analysis, then, can be characterized as the task of constructing a model that demonstrates how interacting objects could deliver the behaviour specified in the use cases.

In terms of work products, typical inputs to the analysis activity are the use case and domain models. These describe structural and behavioural aspects of the system, but these descriptions are not very well integrated. The use case descriptions present the system's functionality as seen from the outside, in terms of the user's interaction with the system, and the domain model defines the relationships between the important business concepts. What is missing is an explanation of how objects representing, or derived from, the business entities can co-operate in such as way as to implement the behaviour specified in the use cases.

The analysis workflow addresses this problem by means of a technique known as *realization*. In the realization process, a high-level interaction is developed for each use case, demonstrating how the required system behaviour could be generated by means of the interaction of instances of suitable classes.

The classes in the domain model normally form a starting point for the realization of use cases, following the guideline that classes in an object-oriented system can often be derived from real-world entities. Generating the realizations invariably leads to changes in the domain model, however, and examples of this will be seen throughout this chapter. As well as the realizations, then, the analysis workflow produces an *analysis model*, a class diagram derived from the domain model but incorporating the additions and changes required to enable it to support the functionality specified in the use cases.

Use case realizations are defined in UML using *interaction diagrams*, of which there are two types. *Collaboration diagrams* were used informally in Chapter 2 to illustrate the behaviour of the stock control program. *Sequence diagrams* are an alternative type of interaction diagram and are used to document the realization of the use cases in this chapter. The two forms of diagram are more or less equivalent, providing alternative ways of presenting the same information. Sequence diagrams provide a clearer illustration of the order in which various events take place and so are often used when this aspect of an interaction is of particular importance.

The Unified Process also includes in the analysis workflow the production of an *architectural description* of the system. This documents some rather high-level decisions about the overall structure of the system, rather than the details of how individual use cases will be handled. The architectural description is described in more detail in Section 5.3.

The difference between analysis and design

The most important analysis tasks, then, are the production of use case realizations and, based on these, the evolution of the domain model into a more comprehensive class diagram. These activities are fundamental to object-oriented development, whether or not a separate analysis activity is defined.

Use case realizations could in principle be carried out in such detail that they showed every interaction and method call in the final code, and the class model would then show almost as much information as the implementations of the classes. The same techniques and notation could be used throughout, and it is therefore very difficult to give a formal definition of a point at which analysis ends and design begins. This observation underlies decisions to treat analysis and design as a single activity or to do without an explicit analysis stage altogether.

If a distinction is drawn between analysis and design, it has to be more informal, based on the different perspectives adopted rather than on any technical difference. For example, analysis is focused on the requirements of the system, whereas in design the focus shifts to the structure of the software being produced. Analysis represents the application domain in terms of the object model, whereas in design we transform the provisional analysis model into a concrete software product.

5.2 OBJECT DESIGN

In order to produce an interaction diagram that realizes a use case, the data and processing required must be divided between a set of objects that can then interact to support the functionality specified by the use case. This is typically the most difficult and creative aspect of developing an object-oriented system, because there are often many different possible design possibilities available and it is not always obvious which is the best choice.

A domain model defines a set of classes with attributes and relationships and it is tempting to think that this can serve as a basis for the design. To a considerable extent this is often the case, but the domain model has a number of limitations that need to be borne in mind.

First, the domain model shows important concepts in the application domain. It is certainly an aspiration of object-oriented design that there should be a fairly direct representation of these concepts and their relationships in the final design, but there is no guarantee that this will always be the case. At the very least, the final design will contain classes that did not appear in the domain model but have been discovered in the course of further design work, or that have no analogue in the application domain.

Second, a domain model usually does not show operations. A crucial part of developing a design, however, is to decide what processing each object should carry out, and the domain model provides no help with this. Actions in the real world are not the same as operations in the object model, so, even if actions were added to the domain model, it is unlikely that they would provide much assistance in analysis.

This section discusses a basic principle of object design, which provides some guidance on how to create good object structures. The application of this principle in the analysis of the use cases for the restaurant booking system will then be described in the remainder of the chapter.

Object responsibilities

The inspiration behind object-oriented programming is that software objects reflect the objects found in the real world, or application domain. This idea has proved very useful in motivating certain aspects of software design, particularly the static data structure of systems. However, the behaviour of software objects is not the same as that of real-world objects: objects interact by means of point-to-point communication, sending messages to each other, whereas entities in the real world are engaged in a much richer interaction with their environment and the other objects it contains.

This means that object designers cannot necessarily trust to their instincts in developing designs. What are needed are some general principles, or metaphors, which summarize the object-oriented approach and can be used to inspire and guide the creation of object designs. Perhaps the most widely used and durable metaphor used by object designers is the idea that objects should be characterized by their *responsibilities*. Objects have two basic types of responsibility: to maintain some data and to support some processing.

The data in an object-oriented system is not held in a single central data store, but instead is distributed round all the objects in the system. This can be described in terms of responsibilities by saying that each object is responsible for looking after a subset of the data in the system. The data that an object is responsible for consists not only of its attribute values, but also of the links that it maintains to other objects in the system.

The other type of responsibility that an object has is to support some processing, as defined ultimately in the methods that its class implements. The processing performed by an object typically involves carrying out some computation on the data available to the object, or co-ordinating a larger operation by sending messages to other objects and doing something with the data they return.

The metaphor of object responsibilities thus does not give an algorithm for the allocation of data and operations to an object, but it does provide a way of thinking about what an object represents and what it ought to do in the context of the system.

The metaphor on its own is not strong enough, however, as it gives little guidance on the actual allocation of responsibilities to objects. For example, there would be something odd about an object that had the responsibility to store the size of a table in the restaurant, but also update the phone number of a customer. These two responsibilities do not seem to belong together, and a system that located them in the same object would be rather difficult to understand and maintain.

The term *cohesion* is used in software design to describe the property of a set of responsibilities that seem to belong together and make up a sensible whole. An object that was responsible for maintaining table sizes and customer phone numbers would not be cohesive: these two tasks relate to quite different entities in the system and do not seem to be functionally related. It is likely, therefore, that they should be the responsibilities of distinct objects. By contrast, an object responsible for maintaining all the data about customers, and nothing else, would be described as cohesive.

A basic principle of object design, then, is that, when use case realizations are being produced, the designer should define objects and classes that possess functionally cohesive sets of responsibilities. The application of this principle is illustrated in the remainder of this chapter.

5.3 SOFTWARE ARCHITECTURE

The principle that well-defined objects should have a cohesive set of responsibilities is a very useful one, but even cohesion is a rather informal term, and it is easy to give examples of objects which could be described as highly cohesive while still being poor choices in an object design. For example, in the context of the restaurant booking system, it might be proposed that customer objects should be responsible for everything to do with customers, from displaying customer information on the screen, through maintaining and making available the name and phone number of customers, to storing this data in a relational database. In one sense, such an object would be highly cohesive, but experience has shown that incorporating such a wide range of activities in a single object does not lead to a simple and maintainable design.

As well as general principles about how objects should be designed, then, it is useful to be able to draw on past experience in design, to provide examples of which design choices work and which do not. Rather than codifying experience in abstract principles or metaphors, this approach gives very concrete examples of design strategies that have been used in the past and found to be successful. It has become customary to refer to such examples as *patterns*.

Patterns have been described at a great variety of levels, from low-level patterns that address a particular coding problem, to very high-level patterns that organize the overall structure and architecture of a system. The term *software architecture* is used to refer to a set of high-level decisions about how the system will be divided into subsystems, what the role of the various subsystems will be and how they will relate to each other. Overall strategies for handling issues such as interaction with the user or the permanent storage of data can also be described as part of the system's architecture.

A detailed discussion of software architecture is outside the scope of this book. In the remainder of this section, one specific architecture will be described, which has proved to be a suitable way to design a wide range of typical desktop applications that use a graphical user interface and provide some kind of persistent storage mechanism.

A layered architecture

The idea of defining the architecture of a system in a number of *layers* is an old one in software engineering and has been applied in many different domains. The motivation for defining layers is to allocate responsibilities to different subsystems and to define clean and simple interfaces between layers. In many ways, this can be viewed as an application of the same principles as in object design, but applied to larger components within the system.

In the architecture that will be described here, one of the fundamental ideas is to make a clear distinction between those parts of the system responsible for maintaining data and those responsible for presenting it to the user. Perhaps the earliest formulation of these ideas was the so-called 'Model–View–Controller', or MVC, architecture defined for programs written in the Smalltalk language.

It is often tempting when writing an object-oriented program to create a single class that both holds the data corresponding to some entity and also displays it on the screen. This approach appears to make it easy, for example, to update the display when the data changes: as the same object is responsible for both tasks, when its state changes it can simply update its display to reflect the new state.

However, this approach does not work well when the display consists of a complex presentation of many different objects. In order to display its state sensibly, an object may have to be aware of everything else on the screen, thus significantly increasing the complexity of the class. Further, if the user interface changes, all classes in the system would have to be changed if the responsibility for displaying data is distributed widely. To cope with these problems, the MVC architecture recommends that these responsibilities should be given to different classes, with a *model* class being responsible for maintaining the data and a *view* class for displaying it.

Designing a system in accordance with this pattern will have the effect of increasing the number of messages that are passed between objects while the system is running. Whenever a display has to be updated, for example, the view class will have to obtain the latest state of the object from the model class before displaying it.

Nevertheless, the benefits of this approach have been found to make this worthwhile. Among other things, it becomes very easy to define multiple or alternative views of the same data. By using different views, the same application could, for example, support user interfaces based on desktop PCs and on mobile phones. If the maintenance and display of data were defined in the same class, it would be much harder to separate the two and safely update the user interface code.

This principle of making a distinction between the model and the view can be applied at a system-wide level, leading to the identification of two separate layers in the architecture. Classes that maintain the system state and implement the business logic of the application are placed in an *application layer*, whereas classes concerned with the user interface are placed within a *presentation layer*.

These two layers are illustrated graphically in Figure 5.1. Each layer is represented by a *package*, shown as a 'tabbed folder' icon containing the package name. Packages in UML are simply groupings of other model elements and are used to define a hierarchical structure on models. A model can be divided into a number of packages, each of which can contain further nested packages, to any level deemed necessary or helpful. The contents of a package can, but need not, be shown inside the icon. If they are not, the package name is written inside the folder icon.

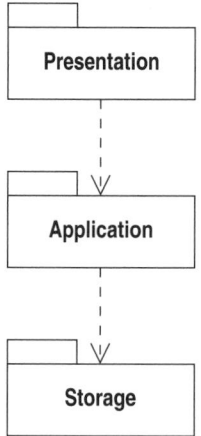

Figure 5.1 A three-layer architecture

Figure 5.1 also shows a dependency between the presentation and application layers, stating that the presentation layer depends on, or makes use of, the classes and other model elements defined in the application layer, but not vice versa. This is a typical feature of layered architectures, where 'upper' layers can make use of the features provided by 'lower' layers, but the lower layers are defined independently of any upper layers.

The asymmetry of the dependency reflects a key idea of the MVC architecture, which is that the model should be independent of the view. This reflects the observation that in many systems, the basic business logic changes much less often than the code making up the user interface. It would therefore be desirable to be able to update the view classes without affecting the model classes, and the dependency shown in Figure 5.1 reflects this requirement. For example, this approach makes it feasible to develop new interfaces for an application, perhaps to support web-based or mobile access, without making any changes to the core classes of the application.

The third layer in the architecture shown in Figure 5.1 is responsible for looking after the persistent storage of data in the system. This is an aspect of the system about which the object model says very little: object design and use case realization typically proceed as if all the required objects were held in memory and immediately available when required. In all but the simplest systems, however, this is an unrealistic assumption and some persistent data storage mechanism will be required, both to hold data that cannot fit into memory and to ensure that data is permanently stored between sessions or following a system crash, for example.

Experience has shown that it is not a good idea for application-level classes to have the additional responsibility for ensuring the persistent storage of the data that they maintain, for the same kinds of reasons that they should not be responsible for the display of that data. A common system architecture therefore locates this responsibility in a separate layer, the *storage* layer in Figure 5.1.

Based on this three-layer architecture, an alternative characterization of the difference between analysis and design can be offered. Analysis is typically concerned only with the behaviour and interaction of objects in the application layer: this level will usually be unique to each system and analysis is a way of demonstrating that the proposed system is in fact feasible. Design, on the other hand, is concerned with object design at all levels of the architecture, and in particular with the interactions between the layers. In many cases, however, the requirements of the presentation and storage layers are common to many systems and, to a larger extent than in analysis, patterns derived from previous work can be applied to produce a design.

Analysis class stereotypes

As well the distinction between model and view classes, the MVC architecture distinguishes objects whose primary role is to control complex interactions. These objects are unsurprisingly known as *controllers*. In the original MVC architecture, controllers were responsible for receiving user input and for forwarding messages both to the model objects, to update the state of the system, and to view objects to ensure that the user interface was kept up to date. Thus, in an MVC object design, individual objects can be categorized as either model, view or controller objects.

The Unified Process defines a similar categorization of objects, by distinguishing *boundary*, *control* and *entity* objects. Entity objects, like model objects in MVC, are responsible for maintaining data, but boundary and control objects are characterized slightly differently from views and controllers.

Boundary objects are those which interact with external users. They are abstractions of the user interface, handling both input and output. In MVC, user input is detected by control objects, but the handling of output is the responsibility of view objects. Control objects in the Unified Process are concerned more with controlling the interactions involved in a use case at the application level, and they do not handle input and output.

Boundary, control and entity objects are intended to be used in analysis as a way of characterizing the roles of objects in realizations, and also to provide a standard way of structuring realizations. They are ordinary classes with additional informal semantics describing their role in the system and so are represented in UML by stereotypes. The stereotypes can be written in the class icons but distinctive icons are also defined for the three types of class. These icons can replace the normal class icon, or the textual stereotype within the class icon, as shown in Figure 5.2.

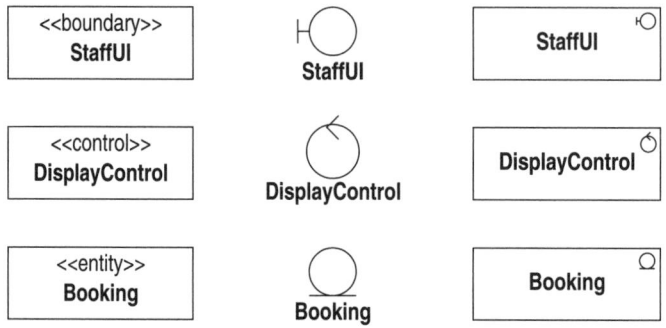

Figure 5.2 Notation for analysis class stereotypes

5.4 USE CASE REALIZATION

The simplest case in the booking system is probably the 'Display bookings' case. It is also central to the system, in that it is included by several other use cases and is responsible for updating the display that the user sees. It is therefore a sensible place to start the realization of the booking system's use cases. The interaction specified in the basic course of events is very simple: the user enters the required date and the system responds by displaying all the bookings recorded for this date.

System messages

The input that the user generates in the course of performing a use case is usually modelled by including an instance of the relevant actor in the realization to represent the user, and modelling the user's actions as messages sent from the actor instance to the system. Messages from an external user to the system are sometimes known as *system messages*, to distinguish them from the internal messages generated by the objects in the system.

The realization of the 'Display bookings' use case will therefore contain an instance of the staff actor, as any member of staff can perform this use case. The user's interaction is basically a single request, to display the bookings for a specified date. This can be modelled as a single message, with the relevant date included as a parameter of the message. In response to this message, the system responds by retrieving and displaying the bookings for the requested day, and this concludes the use case instance.

The message from the user must be sent to an instance of some class in the booking system. Often, however, a domain model such as Figure 4.10 will not include a suitable class to receive system messages. By and large, classes in a domain model represent business entities, and it is not appropriate to give such classes the additional responsibility of responding to a message from a user. This is a simple example of how analysis can lead to additions and changes to the domain model, and also of the fact that different classes have different roles to play in the overall model.

It is not entirely straightforward deciding how best to characterize the objects that receive system messages. The Unified Process defines boundary objects as being those that receive messages from the user, so it would seem to be reasonable choice to use a boundary object. However, boundary objects seem to belong to the presentation layer in the system's architecture: if we are trying to analyse the behaviour of objects in the application layer, it would seem to be misleading to use the boundary stereotype.

An alternative approach can be motivated by thinking of the role of the objects that receive the system messages. In general, there may be several system messages involved in a use case, and it is necessary to check that the user sends these correct messages in a sensible order and to co-ordinate the production of responses from the system. These are appropriate responsibilities for a control object, and for the remainder of this chapter we will characterize the objects that receive system messages as controllers.

Logically, it is possible to have a different control object for each use case, but in the case of simple systems this may not be necessary. If a single controller is used for all use cases, it can be thought of as representing the system as a whole. If it subsequently turns out that this object is unfeasibly large and uncohesive, it can be split into separate controllers.

Figure 5.3 uses a sequence diagram to show the single system message in the 'Display bookings' use case. The message is received by a controller object representing the system as a whole, and the appropriate UML stereotype is used to show this.

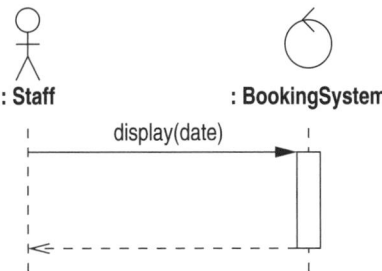

Figure 5.3 A system message

Like collaboration diagrams, sequence diagrams show how messages are passed between objects in an interaction, but the structure of the diagram is rather different. The major feature of sequence diagrams is that the passage of time throughout the interaction is represented explicitly on the diagram: normally an interaction starts at the top of the diagram and time flows down the diagram from top to bottom.

At the very top of the diagram relevant objects that exist at the start of the interaction are shown. In this case, these are an instance of the actor representing staff members and the control object. On interaction diagrams, it is common to represent these objects by *roles* rather than instances. For practical purposes, there is not much difference between the two approaches, the major difference being that, unlike instance names, role names are not underlined. Roles are explained fully in Chapter 9.

Each role or instance shown has a *lifeline*, represented as a dashed line extending below its icon. The lifeline shows the period of time during which the object exists. In this case, the staff member and the booking system objects exist at the start of the interaction and are not destroyed in the course of it, so their lifelines run from the top to the bottom of the diagram.

The interaction in Figure 5.3 contains a single system message, requesting the display of bookings for a date passed as a parameter. Messages are shown on sequence diagrams as arrows going from one object's lifeline to another. When the user interface object receives the 'display' message, a new *activation* is started, shown as an elongated rectangle on its lifeline. An activation corresponds to the period of time during which an object is processing a message. Showing activations on sequence diagrams makes it easy to see where the flow of control is within an interaction and how one message can be sent while an object is processing another.

Figure 5.3 does not show the details of how the required booking information is retrieved and displayed. At the end of the activation, a return message is shown from the user interface to the user. This does not correspond to a distinct message in the interaction, but marks the point at which the system has finished processing the user's request and control returns to the user.

Accessing bookings

The next step is to refine Figure 5.3 to show how the system actually retrieves and displays the data requested by the user. Two separate actions are involved here, namely the retrieval of the bookings for the relevant day and the update of the display to show them in place of the existing bookings, and therefore some simple control is required to ensure that these actions take place in the right sequence. Responsibility for controlling the flow of the use case has been allocated to the booking system object, which will therefore initiate these two actions.

First, we have to decide how the booking system object can get hold of the required bookings. This could be achieved by sending a message, asking for all the bookings for a given date, to an object that has the responsibility of maintaining the complete set of bookings made for the restaurant. We can then imagine various algorithms by which the required bookings could be identified.

However, no class in the design has yet been given the responsibility of keeping track of all the bookings known to the system. The booking class in the domain model is responsible for storing the information about a single booking, but we need a way of iterating across all bookings known to the system. In general, the responsibilities for maintaining individual entities and sets of entities are best given to different objects.

The only other class identified so far is the booking system controller class. However, the existing responsibility of this object is to handle system messages, which is quite different from maintaining a set of data. There would appear to be a danger of creating a rather uncohesive class if the booking system object is given both responsibilities, so it looks as if it is necessary to define a new class for maintaining the set of bookings.

In the application domain, the bookings made can be viewed as an attribute of the restaurant itself. One possible strategy, therefore, would be to introduce a new class to represent the restaurant and give this class the responsibility of maintaining links to all the bookings made, and of locating and returning particular bookings when requested. With this assumption, the use case realization for displaying bookings can be refined to the next level, as shown in Figure 5.4.

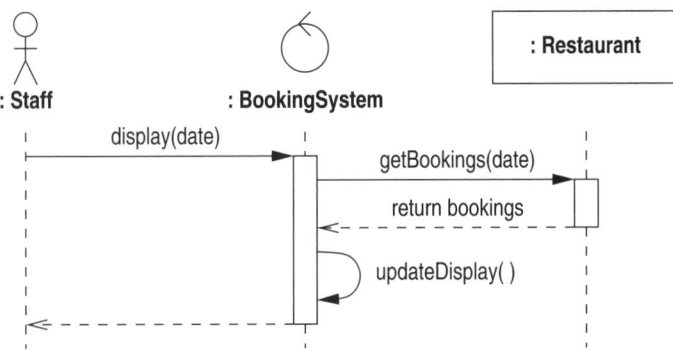

Figure 5.4 Retrieving the bookings to display

This diagram shows what the system does in response to the message from the staff member. The resulting messages are shown originating from the activation on the booking system's lifeline that corresponds to the system message, thus showing the nested flow of control that is characteristic of procedural message calls. The return message is explicitly annotated to show what data is returned.

Following this, a message is sent to update the current display. In terms of the system architecture, this message should be sent from the booking system to some class in the presentation layer, requesting that the display be updated. The 'updateDisplay' message in Figure 5.4 corresponds to a method that communicates this to the presentation layer; a mechanism by which this can be accomplished is described in the next chapter. It is likely that this method will be called on many different occasions, whenever the information to be displayed has changed.

Retrieving booking details

The remaining question to decide is how the restaurant object identifies the bookings to return. Logically, it needs to obtain the date of each booking object and return those bookings whose date matches the date supplied in the message from the actor. This interaction is shown in Figure 5.5; the asterisk before the 'getDate' message is a multiplicity, indicating that this message will in general be sent many times in this interaction, to different booking objects.

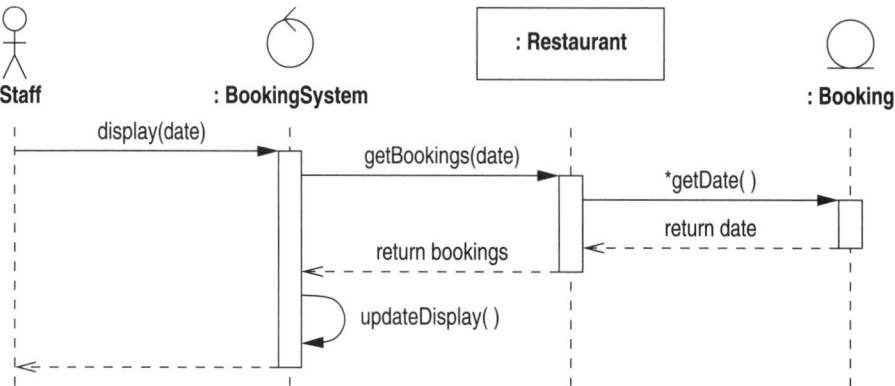

Figure 5.5 Display bookings: realization of the basic course of events

Figure 5.5 presents a complete realization of the basic course of events of the 'Display bookings' use case, at the analysis level. It does not specify everything about the interaction: for example, the data structure used to return the set of retrieved bookings is not specified, and neither is the way that the iteration through the set of booking objects is performed. This level of detail is left until the detailed design stage. The diagram does, however, outline the overall shape of the interaction and provides some reassurance that the classes identified so far are in fact capable of supporting this use case.

Refining the domain model

The process of developing the realization of the 'Display bookings' use case has resulted in the identification of two new classes and a number of messages that are passed between class instances. This information can be added to the domain model, thus beginning a process of refinement, which will transform it into a more comprehensive class diagram documenting the results of the analysis activity. Figure 5.6 shows part of an analysis class diagram, including the new classes shown in Figure 5.5.

Two new associations are shown on Figure 5.6. The first, from the restaurant class to the booking class, reflects the fact that we have given the restaurant class the responsibility of recording details of all the bookings known to the system. As bookings are represented by instances of a separate class, the only way the restaurant can keep track of them is by storing a link to each, as the association specifies.

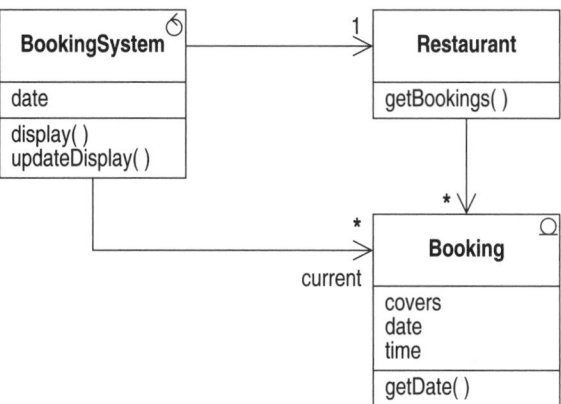

Figure 5.6 Some classes in the analysis model

There is an additional responsibility, however, to record which of the bookings are currently displayed on the screen. These are the bookings returned to the boundary object in Figure 5.5. If these were not stored once they had been displayed, then whenever the display was updated, the current bookings would have to be retrieved again from the restaurant object. An update might be required for many reasons, for example when refreshing the window after some other application had written over it, and this approach might involve a lot of unnecessary processing.

An alternative design, adopted in Figure 5.6 is to give the booking system the responsibility of remembering which bookings relate to the current day. The association between the booking system and booking classes records this information: like the restaurant object, the booking system discharges its responsibility by maintaining a set of links to the relevant booking objects. Related to this, the booking system class also records the currently displayed date, as an attribute of the class.

The messages in the sequence diagrams reappear in the class diagram as operations belonging to the various classes. The purpose of sending a message is normally to invoke a method in the object receiving the message, and this is represented by including an operation in the class that receives the message. For clarity, this operation is given the same name as the message that invokes it.

As well as maintaining information about relationships, the associations in the class diagram define 'communication channels' in the form of links between objects, along which messages can be sent. A useful consistency check, then, is to confirm that whenever a message is sent from one object to another, the class diagram records an association that can serve as a communication channel for the message.

A domain model may document relationships that are important to the real-world application, but which are not used to support message passing in the design. In many cases, such associations do not need to be implemented, or only need to be supported in the direction in which messages are sent. To document this, as a guide for subsequent implementation, navigability annotations have been added to the associations in Figure 5.6 in the directions in which messages are passed.

5.5 RECORDING NEW BOOKINGS

The process of use case realization illustrated in the previous section can now be repeated for the other use cases in the use case model, thus leading to a complete analysis model for the booking system. After displaying bookings, the next most fundamental task is probably that of creating new bookings, and this use case will be considered in this section.

As before, we do not want to model the details of the user interface at this stage. We will assume that the details required to create a new booking are gathered by some suitable element of the user interface, such as a dialogue box, and that the logical structure of the use case can be represented by a single system message from the user requesting the creation of a new booking and passing the required data as parameters.

The system message is received by the same controller object, the booking system instance, as in the previous use case. We now have to decide what object should be given the responsibility of creating the new booking object. The only two feasible choices are the booking system and the restaurant object. As the restaurant object already has the responsibility of maintaining the complete set of booking objects known to the system, it would appear that a high degree of cohesion could be maintained by also giving it the responsibility to create new bookings.

This decision is reflected in the sequence diagram of Figure 5.7, where the details of the new booking are simply passed on to the restaurant object that will actually create the new booking. As in the case of displaying bookings, the 'updateDisplay' message is sent so that the presentation layer is informed that the state of the system has changed and that relevant portions of the view need to be updated.

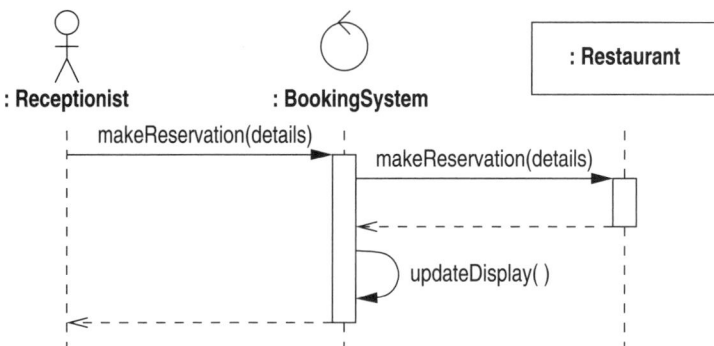

Figure 5.7 Record reservation: initial interaction

Note that, in analysis, it is quite acceptable to be unspecific about details such as parameters and data types. At some stage, a decision will need to be made about how the data relating to the new booking is represented and what parameters are passed with the system message. In analysis, however, the major concern is to demonstrate that a feasible object design can be created to support the use cases and, once this has been done, some of the details can be deferred to a later stage.

Creating new objects

To complete the realization of this use case we need to consider how the controller object responds to the 'makeReservation' message. A sequence diagram illustrating the process of creating a new reservation is shown in Figure 5.8.

Before a new reservation object can be created, it is necessary to locate the objects representing the table and customer for whom the reservation is being made. According to the domain model, each reservation object is linked to exactly one table and exactly one customer object. It would therefore be an implementation error to create a reservation that was not linked to these objects, as the system state would not be consistent with the multiplicity specifications in the domain model.

We will assume that the data passed from the user contains textual identifiers for these objects, such as a table number and the name and phone number of a customer. This data would be entered by the user when specifying the details of the new reservation. Before the reservation can be created, however, we need to locate the objects identified by this data so that the appropriate object references are available when the new reservation is created.

At this point, we must decide which object should have the responsibility of providing access to table and customer objects. As with bookings, it is natural to describe these entities as being attributes of the restaurant and so we can provisionally give the restaurant this responsibility. There is clearly a potential danger here that the restaurant object may be acquiring a rather uncohesive set of responsibilities, but for the moment there seems to be little reason to split these among distinct classes. This should be borne in mind as a potential issue for future development, however.

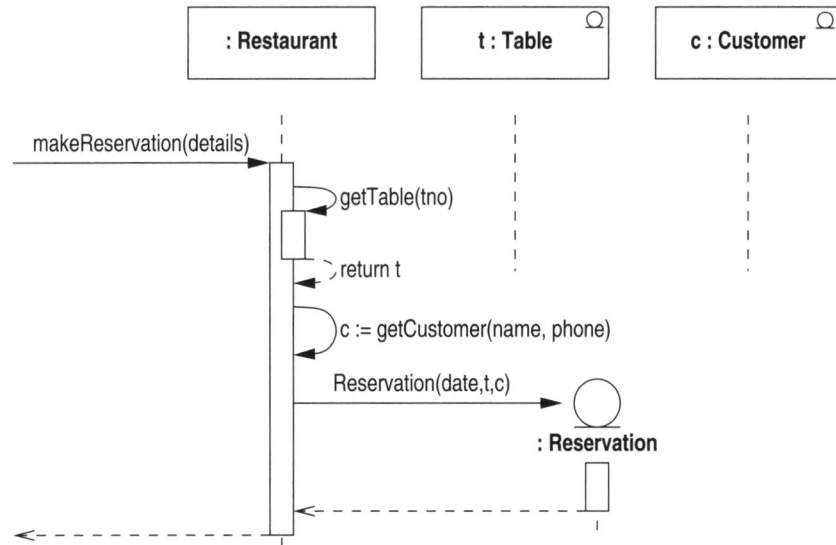

Figure 5.8 Creating a new reservation

The messages 'getTable' and 'getCustomer' return the table and customer objects, respectively, corresponding to the data passed to them as parameters. The objects returned by these messages are shown on Figure 5.8, with their lifelines truncated to avoid confusion. We are assuming that the parameters 'tno', 'name' and 'phone' can be extracted from the unspecified 'details' passed with the 'makeReservation' message.

For illustrative purposes, Figure 5.8 shows two alternative ways of showing an object calling one of its own methods. The 'getTable' message shows explicitly that a new, nested activation is created for the new message and that when it ends data is returned. The second message, 'getCustomer', is not shown with its own activation and the message itself includes the return value, using notation introduced in Chapter 2.

The new reservation does not exist at the start of the interaction, so it is not shown at the top of the sequence diagram. On sequence diagrams, new objects are shown at a point corresponding to the time at which they are created, with a lifeline continuing below them. The message that causes the creation of a new object is directed to the object itself rather than to its lifeline. These messages are usually called *constructors*, and can be shown with the optional 'create' stereotype in UML to highlight their difference from normal messages. The activation just below the new object corresponds to the execution of the constructor and it would be quite possible for messages to be sent from the newly created object at this point. Figure 5.8 assumes that constructors have the same name as their class, a convention that is followed by many languages.

Recording walk-in bookings

Walk-in bookings are created when a customer arrives to eat at the restaurant with no advance reservation. They are recorded on the system in the same way as reservations, but because they are not associated with a customer, less information is required when one is created. The realization of the 'Record walk-in' use case is left as an exercise.

5.6 CANCELLING BOOKINGS

The use case for cancelling a booking has a more complicated structure than the ones realized so far, as the user's participation in the use case consists of more than one interaction with the system. As described in Chapter 4, to cancel a booking the user must first select the booking to be cancelled, then cancel it and finally confirm the cancellation when prompted by the system to do so. A sequence diagram showing a possible realization of this course of events is shown in Figure 5.9.

This use case breaks down into two separate parts. First, the required booking is selected. There are many ways in which this could be done: perhaps the user clicks on the booking rectangle on the screen or enters some data which identifies the booking. This is realized in Figure 5.9 by a message 'selectBooking' from the user. At the analysis level, the exact nature of the information supplied by the user to identify the booking is left unspecified and the diagram simply indicates informally that sufficient is supplied to identify the required booking.

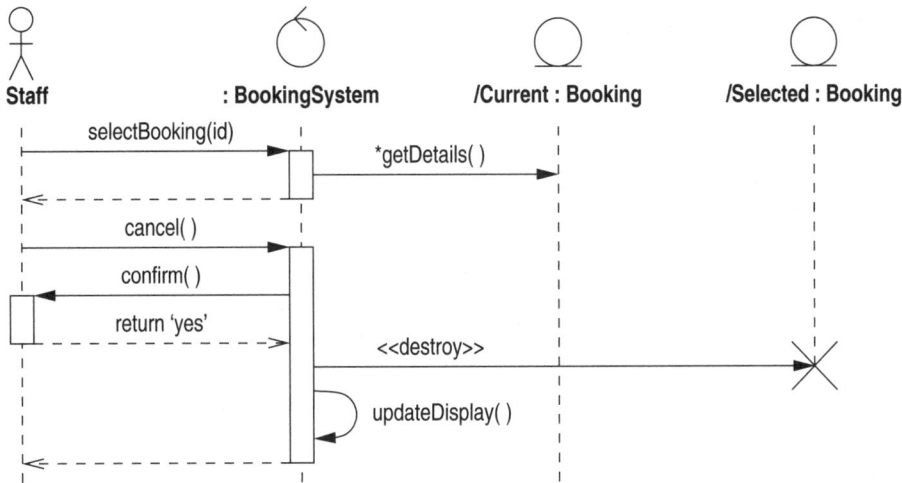

Figure 5.9 Cancelling a booking

In order to locate the required booking object, each currently displayed booking must be examined. As the booking system object already has the responsibility for maintaining this set of bookings, it is in a position to iterate directly through the bookings. The user interface checks the details of all the current bookings to see which matches the selection criterion. This is indicated by the 'getDetails' message in Figure 5.9. The multiplicity before the message indicates that it will be sent zero or more times, depending on how many currently displayed bookings there are.

In the basic course of events, we are assuming that a booking is successfully selected. As this booking is involved in the later stages of the use case, it is shown separately at the top of the diagram. *Role names* are used to distinguish the selected booking from the current bookings. A role name does not name an individual object, but describes the role that an object can play in the interaction. Each time this use case is performed, a different object may be the selected booking.

Once the required booking has been selected, and presumably highlighted on the screen in some way, the user invokes the cancel operation. The process of getting confirmation from the user is modelled by a message going from the boundary object back to the user: this may correspond to the display of a confirmation dialogue box, for example. The user is now constrained to respond to this message in some way, and the return message indicates the user's response.

Once the user's response is received, the user interface object deletes the selected booking and updates the display before the use case ends. Object deletion is indicated by a message with the 'destroy' stereotype: when an object receives such a message, its lifeline is terminated with a large 'X', indicating the destruction of the object. Notice that the form that object destruction takes may vary among programming languages and that, in languages with automatic garbage collection, no explicit method call may be required in order to delete an object.

Refining the domain model

A new responsibility is implicit in this interaction, namely the responsibility for remembering which is the selected booking. If this is not recorded somewhere, the booking system object will not know which booking to destroy. The sequence diagram in Figure 5.9 assumes that this responsibility is given to the booking system object: as that object is already responsible for maintaining the set of currently displayed bookings, this coheres well with its existing responsibilities.

This responsibility needs to be reflected in the evolving class diagram by means of an additional association between the booking system and booking classes, as shown in Figure 5.10. Notice the different multiplicities for these associations: there can be many bookings currently displayed, but at most one of these can be selected. There is an implicit constraint related to these associations, namely that the selected booking must be one of the currently displayed bookings.

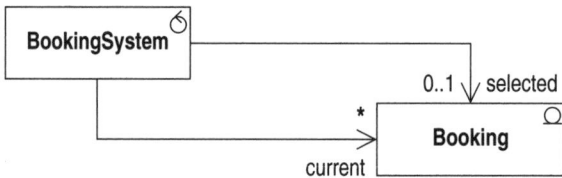

Figure 5.10 Recording the selected booking

5.7 UPDATING BOOKINGS

The structure of the 'Record arrival' use case is very similar to that of 'Cancel booking': the user first selects the required booking and then indicates to the system that the customer has arrived. A realization of this course of events in shown in Figure 5.11. Notice that the selected booking is explicitly shown as a reservation, as it makes no sense to record the arrival of a customer for a walk-in booking. In the basic course of events, we are assuming that the user does in fact select a reservation.

We are assuming that the restaurant wants to record the time at which customers arrive for reservations and so must decide what class is responsible for storing this information. For a walk-in, this information is fairly meaningless: the 'arrival time' of a walk-in booking is effectively identical to its start time. This would suggest that the most appropriate allocation of responsibility would be to make the arrival time an attribute of the reservation class.

However, it is quite possible that a user should select a walk-in booking instead of a reservation and then attempt to record an arrival time. If the walk-in class does not also support the 'setArrivalTime' operation, but the message is sent to it, a run-time error will occur. To prevent this, we must either ensure that the message is not sent to walk-in objects or make sure that the walk-in class supports the message.

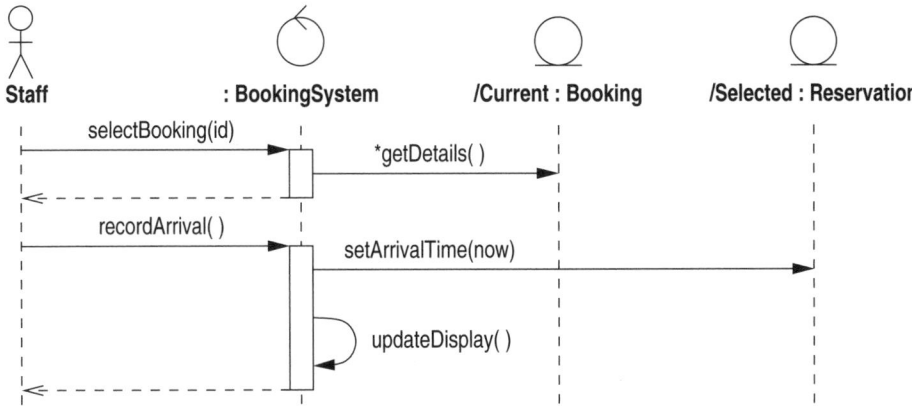

Figure 5.11 Recording a customer's arrival

The first possibility would require a run-time check to determine what subclass the selected booking belonged to. Where possible, such run-time checks are best avoided, as they lead to complex code that is hard to maintain. A better approach is to provide all the classes in the booking hierarchy with the 'setArrivalTime' operation, but to give the specific responsibility for recording the arrival time only to those classes for which it makes sense. A fragment of the class diagram illustrating this approach is shown in Figure 5.12.

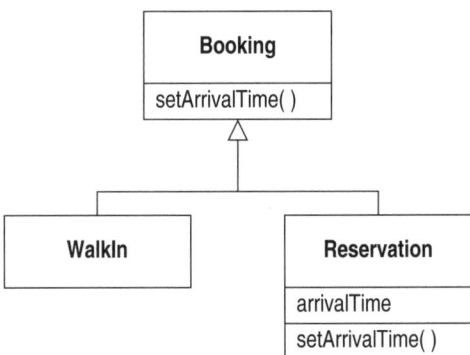

Figure 5.12 Allocating responsibility in a hierarchy

To make this a bit more concrete, imagine that an implementation provides a default implementation of the 'setArrivalTime' operation in the booking class which responds in some way to the fact that the operation has been called inappropriately. This will then be overridden in the reservation class to record the arrival time for objects of that type. In this way, the choice of appropriate behaviour for different types of booking is handled automatically by the dynamic binding mechanism, instead of being hand-coded by the programmer.

Table transfer

On the face of it, the table transfer use case might seem to have a more complex structure than those that have been considered so far. If we imagine that transfer is achieved by dragging and dropping a booking, the user will be generating a range of messages corresponding to various mouse events, and it might seem that these should be reflected in the realization of the use case.

However, as pointed out before, it is not a good idea to commit the classes in the application layer to details of a particular user interface device such as a mouse. At the analysis level, this use case is best modelled with a single system message, providing a new table identifier to be associated with the currently selected booking. This approach preserves the basic functionality of the use case, but leaves flexibility for the user interface to be designed later.

With this assumption, the structure of the 'Table transfer' use case is very similar to that of 'Record arrival' and producing a realization for it is left as an exercise.

5.8 COMPLETING THE ANALYSIS MODEL

This chapter has considered in detail only the basic course of events of each use case. Exactly the same principles can be applied to realizing the alternative and exceptional courses of action, where they add anything new to the model. In general, it is clearer to show the realization of each course of events on a different sequence diagram. UML does define notation for showing alternative flows of control on sequence diagrams, as discussed in Section 9.9, but it is usually preferable to show alternatives on separate diagrams.

Figure 5.13 shows the class diagram for the system, including the information and decisions derived in the course of carrying out realizations of the use cases. This diagram also contains information from the domain model, such as the relationships between the customer, table and booking classes and the constraint about non-overlapping bookings. Where messages are passed between instances of classes, the associations have been made navigable in the direction that the message is being sent. Other associations have, for the time being, been left without navigation annotations.

5.9 SUMMARY

- *Analysis* can be defined as the activity of representing the application domain and the system's requirements in terms of the object model.

- The basic analysis technique is the production of *use case realizations*, which demonstrate how the functionality specified in a use case could be delivered by a set of interacting objects.

- Realizations can be documented using one of the forms of *interaction diagram* defined by UML, namely *collaboration* or *sequence diagrams*.

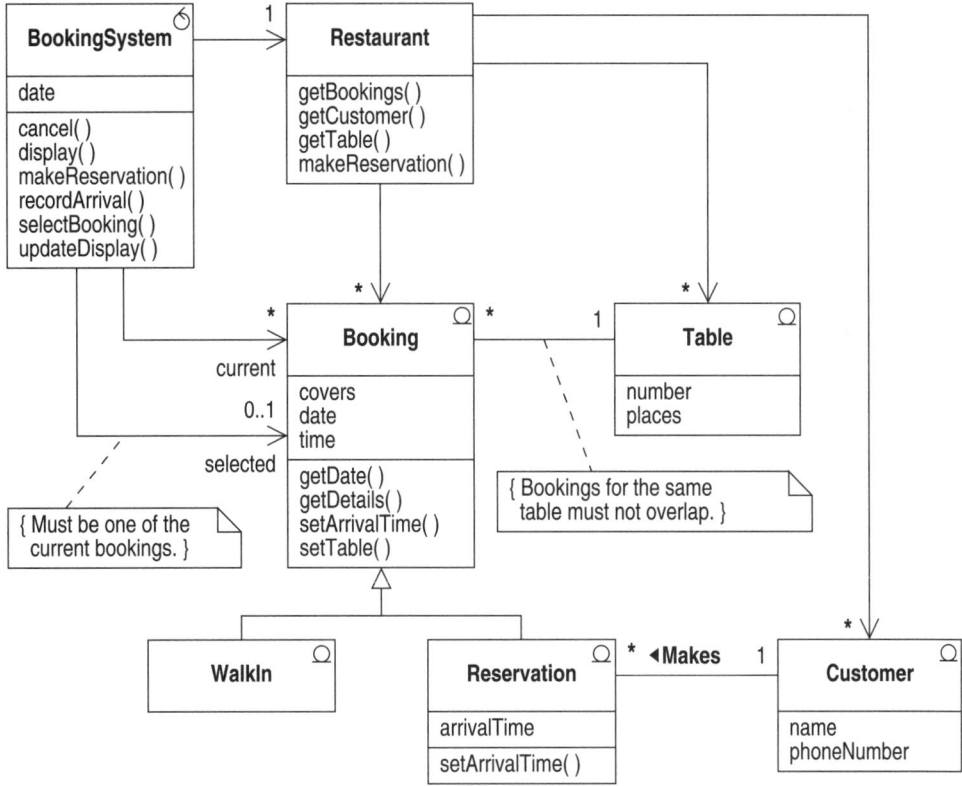

Figure 5.13 Analysis class model for the restaurant booking system

- Producing use case realizations will suggest changes to the domain model, which will evolve into a more detailed *analysis class model*.

- A central metaphor of object design is to make objects *responsible* for a subset of the data and operations in the system.

- Furthermore, an object's responsibilities should be chosen so that the object is *cohesive*: its responsibilities should be related in some way, often functionally.

- The Unified Process includes an *architectural description* as one of the products of analysis. A widely used architectural approach is to structure a system as a number of *layers*, for example, presentation, application and storage layers.

- The objects in a system can be assigned a number of *roles*, to clarify the organization of the system. UML defines class stereotypes for *boundary*, *control* and *entity* objects.

- User interaction can be shown on realizations by means of *system messages* received by control objects. There can be one control object per use case or one representing the system as a whole.

5.10 EXERCISES

5.1 The restaurant object in Figure 5.4 has not been characterized with an analysis class stereotype. Which, if any, of the stereotypes would it be appropriate to apply to the restaurant class?

5.2 In Figure 5.6, what relationship should exist between the date attribute in the booking system class and the date attributes in the bookings that the user interface is linked to via the 'current' association? Add this relationship as a constraint to the diagram.

5.3 Suppose that it was proposed to remove the date attribute from the booking system class in Figure 5.6, on the grounds that the current date could always be retrieved from one of the bookings linked by the 'current' association. How would you respond to such a suggestion?

5.4 Produce a realization for an exceptional course of events in the 'Display bookings' use cases where the date supplied by the user is invalid.

5.5 Combine Figures 5.7 and 5.8 to produce a single sequence diagram realizing the 'Record reservation' use case.

5.6 Create a sequence diagram realizing the 'Record walk-in' use case. How does it differ from that produced in the previous exercise?

5.7 Consider the 'getCustomer' message shown in Figure 5.8. If the details provided relate to a customer already known to the restaurant, the object representing that customer should be returned. If not, a new customer object should be created and returned. Show these alternatives in detail on different sequence diagrams.

5.8 Produce a sequence diagram showing a realization of the basic course of events for the 'Table transfer' use case. Assume that a table number is provided as a parameter of a system message 'transfer' and show on your diagram how the table corresponding to this number is identified.

5.9 Add details about parameters and return types, where appropriate, to the operations in the classes in Figure 5.13.

5.10 Produce realizations for the use cases defined in your answer to Exercise 4.9, allowing general editing of booking information.

5.11 Update the realizations for the 'Record reservation' and 'Record walk-in' use cases to reflect the changes made in your answer to Exercise 4.10 to allow bookings to exceed the table capacity to a limited extent.

5.12 Produce realizations for the new functionality described in Exercise 4.12, to allow the length of bookings to be altered.

5.13 Produce realizations for the use cases described in your answer to Exercise 4.13, specifying how the system automatically allocates a table to a new booking.

5.14 Produce realizations for the use cases describing how a waiting list would be operated, as described in Exercise 4.14.

5.15 Produce realizations describing how a single booking could be made for multiple tables, as described in Exercise 4.17.

6

RESTAURANT SYSTEM: DESIGN

The use case realizations produced in Chapter 5 show how the business functions of the system can be implemented with objects in the application layer. The most important design task is to extend this level of modelling to the whole system. In this chapter some basic strategies for handling input and output and persistent storage will be discussed, and the analysis class diagram will be refined so that it contains fuller information about data types, message parameters and so on. By the end of the design stage, we aim to have an understanding of the system that is detailed enough to permit implementation to begin.

In order to design these aspects of the system, we need to make some decisions about the software and hardware environment of the system. In the following two chapters we will assume that the restaurant booking system will be implemented as a single-user desktop application. We will therefore design it as a Java application with a window-based user interface. For persistency, we will assume that a relational database will be used to store permanent data about bookings, customers and so on.

6.1 RECEIVING INPUT FROM THE USER

In Chapter 5, system messages from the user were shown on the sequence diagrams as being directed to a control object representing the booking system. This is an application layer object, however, so messages will in practice not be sent directly to this object. There must be some object in the presentation layer that has the responsibility for receiving user input and forwarding requests on to the control object.

The object in the presentation layer that receives user input can reasonably be characterized as a boundary object. It represents the user interface that is presented to a particular actor. In the case of the booking system, we are assuming that all users use the same user interface, so we can name this class 'StaffUI'.

Let us assume that in order to carry out the 'Display bookings' use case, the user first selects an appropriate menu option. This causes a dialogue box to appear, in which the user enters the required date before clicking an 'OK' button to submit the request to the system. It is usually not worthwhile modelling the details of the user's interaction with standard user interface components such as menus and dialogue boxes. User interface frameworks provide reusable classes to implement these components and the details of how this is done can safely be left as an implementation issue.

What is important is the message received when the user clicks the 'OK' button to submit data entered in the dialogue box. Figure 6.1 shows the 'StaffUI' boundary object receiving this message, and then delegating the responsibility for dealing with it to the control object previously identified in the application layer. This is shown on a collaboration diagram so that the packages representing the different layers can also be shown, to clarify the system architecture. This also illustrates that packages in UML are a rather weak notion, and that links and messages can easily cross package boundaries.

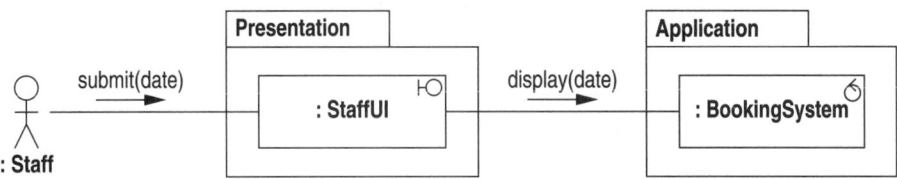

Figure 6.1 Handling a system message

In cases where the user can interact with the system by means of standard gestures such as those generated with a mouse, it is often the case that individual user interface events need to be handled by the system. In these cases the role of the boundary object is more significant.

For example, some of the use cases require the user to select one of the displayed bookings. A natural way of selecting a booking, which supports the goal of enabling direct manipulation of displayed bookings, is for the user to click on it with the mouse. This event would be detected by the user interface, and passed on to the booking system as a 'selectBooking' message, as shown in Figure 6.2.

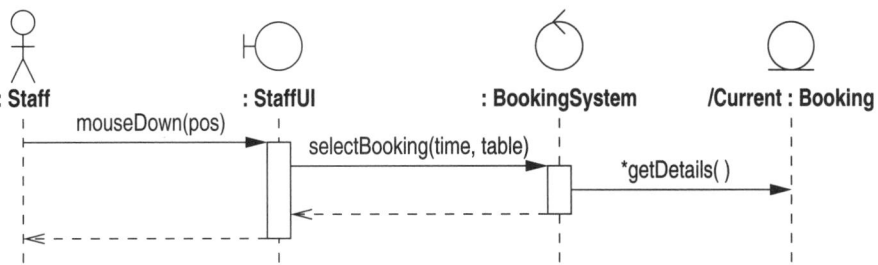

Figure 6.2 Selecting a booking

The messages in Figure 6.2 are supplied with more detailed parameter information than in the analysis model. The parameter on the mouse message represents the position, in screen co-ordinates, at which the mouse button was pressed. The application layer should not know anything about the details of the interface, however, so on the message sent to the booking system controller, the position is replaced by a table number and a time, which will enable the booking system to identify a unique booking.

This gives the user interface object the responsibility for translating mouse co-ordinates into information that is meaningful to the application. This is a reasonable decision, as the user interface object is also responsible for producing the displayed output: in order to do this, it must have mapped the table numbers and times of the bookings being displayed to the relevant screen co-ordinates, and should therefore be able to perform the reverse mapping.

Some interactions involve more than one user-generated event. For example, we would like the users to be able to move a booking from one table to another by dragging the booking rectangle from one location on the screen to another. This interaction will involve a number of user-generated events: an initial 'mouse down' message to select the required booking will be followed by a number of 'mouse move' messages and finally a 'mouse up' message will indicate that the booking has been released at its final position.

Figure 6.3 illustrates this interaction, showing that the transfer message is only sent to the booking system once the mouse button is released at the new location of the booking. This demonstrates that the correspondence between user-generated events detected by the boundary object and the system messages sent to the controller is not necessarily one-to-one. This in turn implies that some elements of control must be embedded in the boundary object, which must remember the current state of the interaction with the user and when to send a system message.

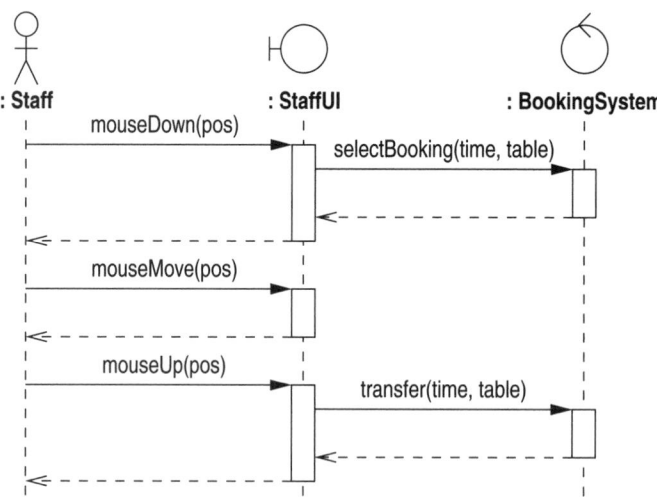

Figure 6.3 Transferring a booking to a new table

As before, this interaction assumes that the user interface object has the responsibility for translating between screen co-ordinates and the corresponding application data values. Although the use case is called 'Table transfer', the sequence diagram suggests that the additional operation of changing the time of a booking could in fact be implemented at no extra cost. In fact, implementing only table transfer might be harder, as it would be necessary to check the exceptional case where the user released the booking on a new table but at a different time. This is an example of where design-level considerations make it reasonable to revisit and alter the initial use case model. Revising the use case model is left as an exercise, however.

6.2 PRODUCING OUTPUT

The 'StaffUI' class has two distinct roles: as a boundary class, it receives messages from the user and forwards them to the controller class, but it also plays the role of a view class, in the sense of the MVC architecture described in Chapter 5. The basic responsibility of a view class is to present the application data, or model, to the user, or in other words to display the output from the system.

In general, what is required of an output mechanism is that whenever the state of the application data changes, the presentation of this data on the screen is updated so that what the user sees is consistent with the system state. The crucial thing to design, therefore, is some means whereby the view is informed of changes in the model.

One common and simple way of accomplishing this is for the view class to make periodic enquiries of the application classes, to find out if anything has changed. This technique is known as *polling*, by analogy perhaps with an opinion poll where questions are asked to find out people's views on some issue. Polling requires classes in the presentation layer to make calls on classes in the application layer, so it fits in well with the layered architecture chosen for the application.

There are a number of problems with using polling, however. For example, it is potentially expensive in terms of wasted processing time. It is likely that, with any reasonable polling rate, the system state will not change from one enquiry to another and hence that a lot of the polling activity is for nothing. More seriously, if there is a significant amount of data in the model, it can be quite a laborious task to examine it to see if anything has changed and hence if the display needs to be updated.

To avoid these problems, it might seem that a better solution would be one where the application classes inform the view classes whenever anything has changed, to that updates to the view only take place when required. This is a better solution from the point of view of object design, because it places the responsibility for triggering a view update on the classes that know just when such as update is required.

However, it is not obvious how this idea can be made to work within the constraints of the layered architecture. A fundamental principle of the two layers, inherited from the MVC architecture, is that the application layer should be independent of the presentation layer. If this is so, how can a class in the application layer inform a class in the presentation layer that a view update is required?

Applying a design pattern

This problem is typical of the situations faced by designers, and a lot of work has been put into documenting solutions to common design problems as *design patterns*. In this case, a suitable solution is provided by the *Observer* pattern defined in the influential book by Gamma *et al.* (1995). The definition of this pattern states that it is applicable:

- 'When a change to one object requires changing others, and you don't know how many objects need to be changed.
- When an object should be able to notify other objects without making assumptions about who those objects are.'

The present situation contains elements of both these conditions: we want a change in an application object to be followed by a change in the view object, and we want the application object to be able to notify the view object of this change without being dependent on the view object. The definition of the pattern is rather abstract and in this section only its application will be described.

The application of the Observer pattern to allow display updating in the restaurant booking system is shown in Figure 6.4 and the packages representing the different layers in the application are also shown. Notice that the relationships between classes that cross the package boundaries are consistent with the direction of the dependency between the two layers.

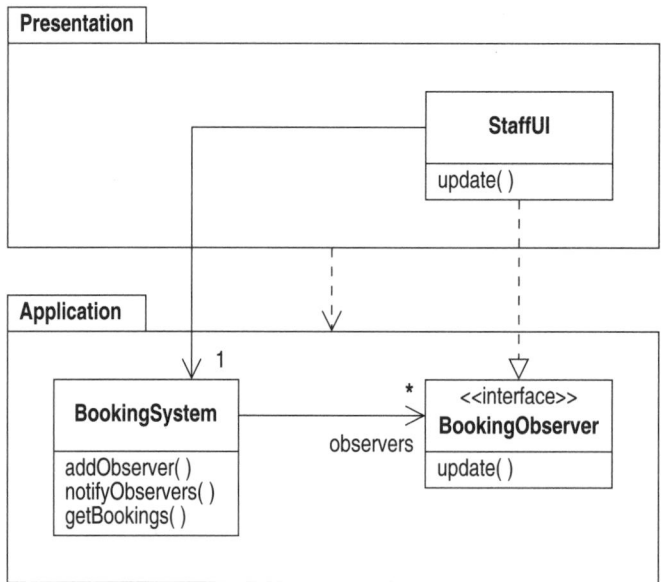

Figure 6.4 Applying the Observer pattern

As with many patterns, the solution of the problem depends on polymorphism and dynamic binding. In the application layer, an interface is defined that must be implemented by any class that wishes to be informed about relevant changes to the model. Such classes are known as *observers*. The interface is very simple, consisting of a single operation, which can be called whenever the display needs to be updated.

The booking system class maintains references to a set of observers and, when its state changes, sends the 'update' message to each observer. The observers could be of any class whatsoever, but the booking system only accesses them through this interface, defined in the application layer, so that the layered architecture of the system is preserved.

The 'StaffUI' class in the presentation layer implements the 'BookingObserver' interface. Implementation of an interface is depicted in UML by a dashed arrow with a hollow arrowhead, as shown in Figure 6.4. At system start-up, an instance of 'StaffUI' can be added to the booking system's list of observers by means of the 'addObserver' operation. Once this is done, the 'update' messages sent to the list of observers will be received by the 'StaffUI' object, thanks to dynamic binding.

Once a 'StaffUI' object receives an 'updateDisplay' message, it needs to find out what has changed. Initially, we will assume a very simple approach to this, where the boundary object simply requests from the booking system a list of all the bookings that are to be displayed and then completely refreshes the display. This rudimentary approach can be refined later if it turns out to be a performance issue.

Figure 6.5 shows the interactions that take place when the display is actually updated. In general, there will be more than one observer: the 'notifyObservers' operation in the 'BookingSystem' class simply sends the 'update' message to each, and so it replaces the 'updateDisplay' message in diagrams such as Figure 5.4. For simplicity, this message has been omitted from Figure 6.5.

Compared with the class diagram in Figure 6.4, on Figure 6.5 it looks as if the booking system and user interface objects are communicating directly with each other, and hence that an application object is dependent on an object in the presentation layer. Although the objects are communicating, however, this is only in virtue of the fact that the user interface object implements the observer interface shown in Figure 6.4. This is emphasized in Figure 6.5 by adding a role name to the boundary object.

In the context of Figure 6.5, it is probably also worth restating the responsibilities of the various objects: having a good grasp of these makes it easier to understand why the messages are the way they are. The user's request is for the bookings for a particular day to be displayed. This request is passed to the booking system object. The booking system only has the responsibility to record information about the day currently being displayed: assuming that the user has requested a different date, the information for that date must first be retrieved from the restaurant object, whose responsibility is to maintain information about all the bookings known to the system.

The user interface object's responsibility is simply to display a set of bookings, and it must request from the booking system the date and the set of bookings to display. We are not assuming that the user interface remembers these bookings, though there are potential performance improvements to be made in the future by having it cache some information about the bookings.

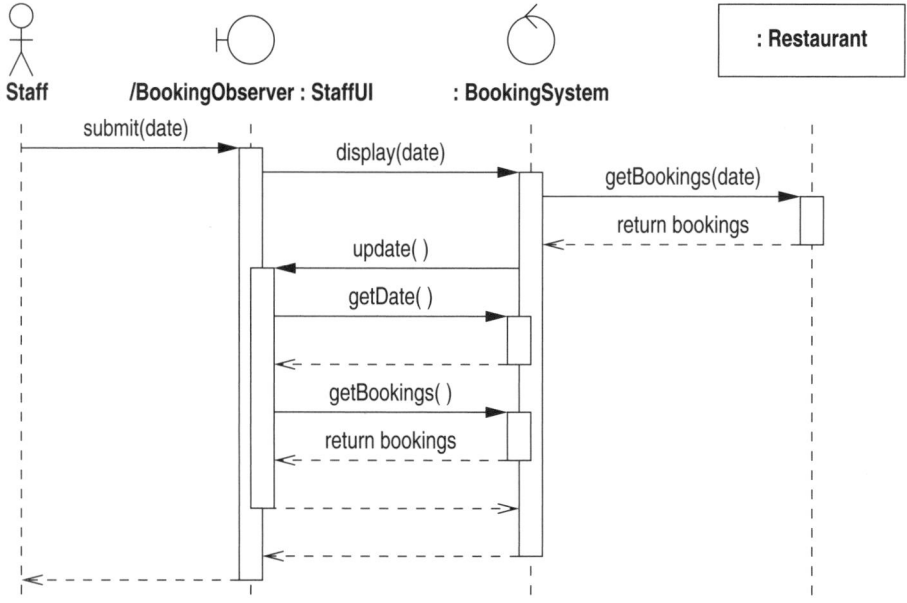

Figure 6.5 Display bookings: design view

6.3 PERSISTENT DATA STORAGE

The overwhelming majority of software systems need some way of storing *persistent* data. This term refers to data that is stored permanently in some way, so that it is not lost when the system is closed down but can be reloaded when required. In the case of the restaurant booking system, it is obviously a system requirement that booking data, for example, should be saved and reloaded on subsequent days when the system is restarted.

There are a variety of possible storage strategies that can be used to provide persistency. A simple approach is simply to write data to disc files, but in the majority of cases a database management system will be used. Although some object-oriented databases are available, the commonest database technology in use is still based on the relational model. In this section, therefore, the design will be based on the assumption that a relational database will be used to provide persistent storage.

Mixing an object-oriented program with a relational database is not a straightforward task, however, as the two technologies approach data modelling in somewhat incompatible ways. In this section, a simple approach to the problem will be outlined, but a systematic treatment of the issue is beyond the scope of this book. This section assumes a basic knowledge of relational databases and the associated terminology.

The implementation breaks down into two distinct areas. First, it is necessary to design a database schema that will allow the data held in the system's objects to be stored and retrieved. Second, the code to access the database and to read data from and write data to it must be designed.

Designing a database schema

The first step in implementing persistent data storage for the booking system is to decide what data needs to be persistent. It is clear that bookings will need to be saved across sessions, as the whole point of the system is to capture and record booking information. Along with this, the table and customer objects that bookings are linked to will also need to be persistent.

By contrast, the data stored in the booking system object, namely the date of the displayed bookings and the set of current bookings, does not need to be stored. When the system is started up, it will usually be of no interest to the user what was displayed last time the system was in use and, if bookings in general are persistent, no irreplaceable data will be lost by not storing the set of current bookings. The remaining class in the application layer, the 'Restaurant' class, does not really have any properties of its own, but acts as an interface to the system's data; provided this data is stored, it does not need to be made persistent.

These decisions can be recorded on the design class diagram using a *tagged value* in the appropriate classes. Tagged values are a way of recording arbitrary properties of model elements, in the form of name–value pairs. The tagged value 'persistence' is used to indicate whether a class is persistent or not. It has two values, the default 'transitory' for classes that are not persistent and 'persistent' for those that are. A tagged value is recorded in the form 'persistence = persistent' but in Figure 6.6, which shows the persistent classes in the restaurant booking system, the tagged value is shown in a widely-used abbreviated form.

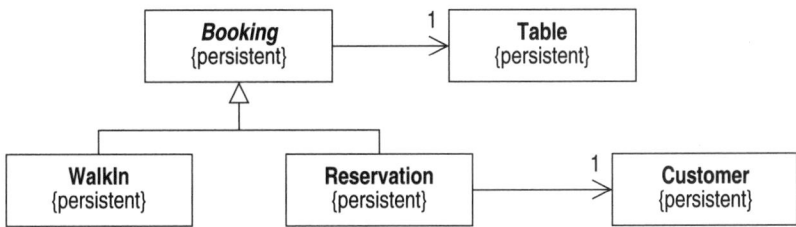

Figure 6.6 The persistent classes in the booking system

The only bookings that ever get created in the booking system are walk-ins and advance reservations, and these are stored as instances of the respective subclasses of the 'Booking' class. This means that 'Booking' is an abstract class, as shown on the diagram. It may seem a little strange to mark an abstract class as persistent, but some of the data it contains is inherited by the subclasses and so is permanently stored.

The 'persistence' tagged value can be applied to model elements other than classes, and in particular associations can be marked as being persistent. Often, however, this is left implicit on diagrams, the assumption being made that any association between persistent classes is itself persistent. In the restaurant booking system, then, the associations between bookings and tables and between reservations and customers will both be treated as being persistent.

After deciding what data will be persistent, the next step is to describe how the persistent classes and associations will be stored in the database. This requires mapping between the object-oriented data model and the storage formats used by relational databases. In an object-oriented system, data is held in a structure of interconnected objects, of various classes. In a relational database, however, data is held in *tables*, each consisting of a number of *rows*. Relationships between data are supported by having certain data items, known as *foreign keys*, appear in more than one table.

The most obvious correlation between the object design and a relational database is that both classes and tables define a particular data structure and that the instances of a class, which store actual data values, seem to correspond closely to the rows in a table. A basic strategy in mapping a class diagram to a relational database schema, therefore, is to represent each class by a table.

Generalization introduces a complication into this mapping, however, as it is a relationship between classes which has no direct equivalent in relational databases. In the implementation of the booking system, we will take advantage of the fact that the 'Booking' superclass is abstract, and hence that the instances that need to be stored will always belong to one or other of the subclasses 'WalkIn' or 'Reservation'. This means that a separate 'Booking' table is not needed in the database, provided that any inherited attributes are stored in both the 'WalkIn' and 'Reservation' tables.

The relational schema for the booking system will therefore contain four tables, one for each of the persistent non-abstract classes in Figure 6.6. The attributes of these classes, defined in Figure 5.10, will be modelled as fields in the tables. To complete the design of the relational schema, we need to consider the other main feature of the class diagram, namely the associations.

Associations are typically implemented, as discussed in Chapter 7, by having one object hold a reference to another. Such a reference clearly plays a similar role to a foreign key in database, but unfortunately the references cannot simply be stored in the database. The reason for this is that a reference is simply a representation of an object's address in memory. If an object is stored in a database and then reloaded, there is no guarantee that it will be placed at the same position in memory as it was earlier. If the earlier address is held in some other object, it is very likely that the reference will then be broken, leading to unpredictable run-time problems.

References to objects cannot, then, simply be stored in a database, but this leaves it unclear how associations are to be represented in a relational schema. However, references can be viewed as a way of storing the more abstract notion of object identity, a sort of implicit data value possessed by each object, and unique to that object. A common solution to the problem of storing associations involves making object identities explicit in the database by giving each table an additional field representing the identity of particular instances. If one object holds a reference to another, the corresponding row in the database table will store the explicit identity of the referenced object, which can then be looked up to follow the link to another object.

Following this approach, we come up with the relational schema shown in Table 6.1. This schema defines how the persistent data in the booking system will be saved in a relational database.

Table 6.1 A database schema for the restaurant booking system

Table		
oid	number	places

Customer		
oid	name	phoneNumber

WalkIn				
oid	covers	date	time	table_id

Reservation					
oid	covers	date	time	table_id	customer_id

Unlike the identities in a pure object-oriented program, which are automatically handled by the language's run-time system, this schema requires object identities to be explicitly generated and manipulated by the program. The object identifiers act as the *primary key* for each table, even in cases where there seems to be a natural key among the attributes of the class, such as the table number in the table class, and they are stored as foreign keys in other tables to represent links between objects.

Saving and loading persistent objects

Once a suitable database schema has been defined, we must define how the system will move persistent data between the database and memory. A simple approach to this deals with the data on a class-by-class basis: for each persistent class in the model, an associated *mapper* class is defined with the responsibility for storing objects in the database, and for recreating objects based on the stored data values, when requested.

In order to keep track of class instances, and to make sure that duplicate instances are not created, the explicit object identifiers introduced in the database schema need to be represented in the model. These should not be introduced directly into the application classes, however, as this would limit them to one particular strategy for persistent data storage. Instead, for each persistent class, a subclass will be defined that represents persistent objects and that adds an attribute to the class to store the explicit object identifiers.

The structure of this implementation of persistency is illustrated in Figure 6.7, which shows the two new classes defined for the specific case of the 'Table' class. Similar classes are defined for each persistent class in the model.

At run-time, the table objects created by the mapper class will include the explicit object identifiers, and therefore will be instances of the 'PersistentTable' subclass. The association between the two classes records this fact. As 'PersistentTable' is a subclass of the 'Table' class, however, this will be transparent to other classes in the application layer that expect to handle 'Table' instances.

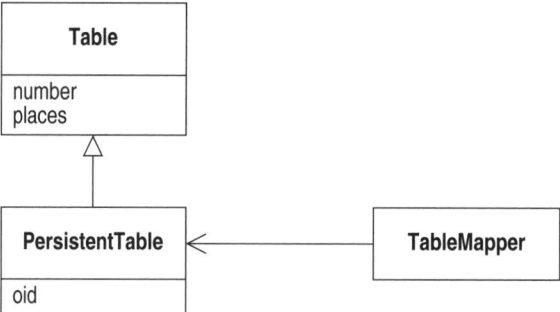

Figure 6.7 The persistency classes

Persistency and the layered architecture

Finally, we should consider how the approach to implementing persistency outlined above fits into the layered architecture of the overall system. The first point to notice is that the new 'persistent' subclasses and the mapper classes depend on the application classes that they are supporting. This means that they must be placed in the application layer, not the storage layer, as the storage layer is to be independent of the application layer.

However, the basic application classes are largely independent of the new classes. The only dependency is caused by the 'Restaurant' class, which has the responsibility for knowing about all the bookings, tables and customers known to the system. Once a persistent storage mechanism is introduced, it will not actually store these objects itself, but instead retrieve them from the database when required. In order to be able to do this, it must be linked to the various mapper classes, whose responsibility it is to create objects based on the data in the database.

The structure of the application layer can now usefully be clarified by dividing it into two subpackages, one containing the basic domain classes, and the other containing the classes required to support persistency for those classes. Assuming that the storage layer provides application-independent database services, only the persistency subpackage is dependent on the storage layer. The refined system architecture is shown in Figure 6.8, as it applies to the 'Table' class.

This design preserves the important property of keeping the core application classes independent of the strategy adopted for persistence. If a different persistent storage strategy were adopted, the classes in the 'Persistence' and 'Storage' packages would have to be altered. However, the only change that would have to be made to the domain classes would be to the 'Restaurant' class, to take into account the new mapper classes or their equivalents.

The design described in this section has been aimed at providing the simplest possible approach to persistency supported by a relational database. The detailed design could be improved considerably, however, with the overall aims of reducing dependencies between packages and moving as much code as possible into the storage layer. A more complex approach is described in the book by Craig Larman (Larman, 2002).

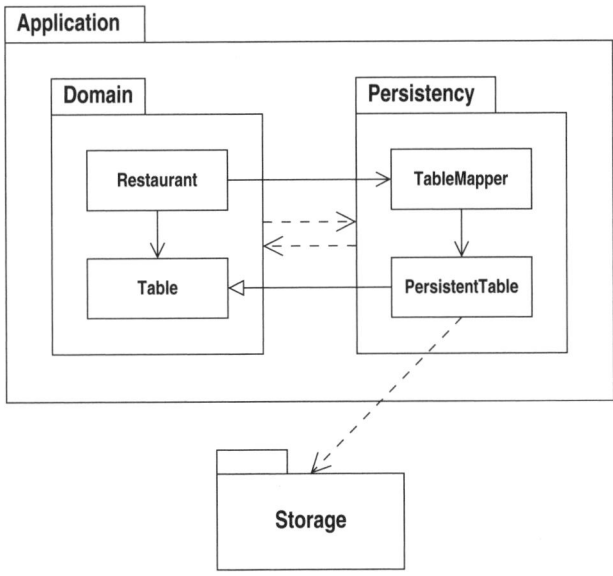

Figure 6.8 The booking system architecture including persistency

6.4 THE DESIGN MODEL

The complete design of the first iteration of the restaurant booking system has now been described. Starting from the analysis model of Figure 5.13, the elements shown in Figure 6.4 were added to support input and output, and those in Figure 6.8 to handle persistency. A complete class diagram for the system could therefore be drawn by combining and completing these three diagrams.

The resulting diagram would be rather large and complex, however, and it is unlikely that in terms of understanding the system it would add anything to the information presented on the three separate diagrams. Rather than drawing such documentation by hand, it is more useful to enter it into a tool offering support for UML. Such tools can perform useful syntactic and consistency checks on the model and make it very easy to produce a variety of diagrams very easily.

6.5 DETAILED CLASS DESIGN

As well as defining the overall structure of the designed system, a key design activity is to look in detail at individual classes. The sequence diagrams produced as realizations of the system's use cases contain the input to this activity: they define the messages that instances of classes must be able to respond to, and hence the operations that must be defined in each class. The design of individual classes proceeds by collecting all the relevant messages from the sequence diagrams, checking them for consistency and adding information about parameters and return types as necessary.

In this section, the booking system class will be looked at in detail as an example of the kind of issues that arise. A complete listing of the features of this class, together with full parameter and type information, is shown in Figure 6.9.

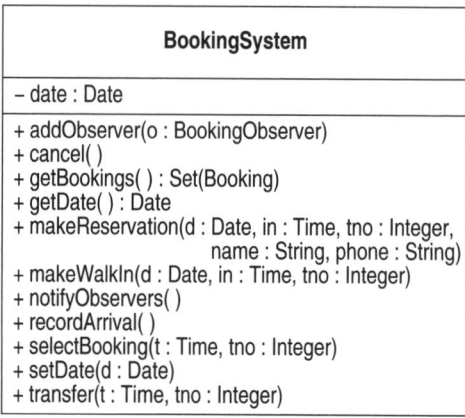

BookingSystem
– date : Date
+ addObserver(o : BookingObserver) + cancel( ) + getBookings( ) : Set(Booking) + getDate( ) : Date + makeReservation(d : Date, in : Time, tno : Integer,   name : String, phone : String) + makeWalkIn(d : Date, in : Time, tno : Integer) + notifyObservers( ) + recordArrival( ) + selectBooking(t : Time, tno : Integer) + setDate(d : Date) + transfer(t : Time, tno : Integer)

Figure 6.9 Features of the booking system class

The basic responsibility of this class is to maintain the set of current bookings, namely the ones that the user can see on the screen, and the operations that it supports are mostly operations on this set, or on the individual bookings within it. The bookings themselves are not modelled as an attribute of the class, but by means of an association between the booking system and booking classes, as shown in Figure 5.13.

As well as the bookings themselves, the class needs to record the date for which bookings are being displayed, as shown in Figure 5.6. This is stored as an attribute, and it is given the type 'Date'. This is not a built-in UML type: rather, we are assuming that a suitable type will either be provided by, or could easily be defined in, the target programming language.

This raises the following question, however: if 'Date' is going to be implemented as a class, why not show it as a class on the class diagram and model the current date as an association to this class rather than as an attribute? The answer has to do with a fundamental distinction made by both UML and object-oriented programming languages between data types and classes.

Instances of data types are 'pure values': familiar examples are the basic type provided by programming languages, such as `int` and `char`. They are not thought of as having identity, as objects do, and they can be freely copied and replicated. The same integer can exist at different locations in memory, for example, whereas each object is unique, stored at a particular location.

By using 'Date' as an attribute type rather than a class, we are indicating that dates will be treated like integers: they will be freely copied in the implementation, dates held in different objects will be able to be easily compared, and so on. As dates will most likely be implemented by a `Date` class, it would not be wrong to show it as a separate class in a class diagram, but it would not accurately reflect the planned use of dates.

In diagrams such as Figure 6.1 the 'display' message was sent to the booking system to request it to display the bookings for a particular date. Now that the mechanism for performing the display has been considered in more detail, this seems a rather inappropriate name for this operation: displaying data is a function of the presentation layer, so an operation called 'display' looks rather out of place in the application layer. This operation has therefore been renamed 'setDate'.

A number of operations in the class maintain the set of current bookings. The 'getBookings' operation returns the set of bookings. The return type indicates that a set of bookings will be returned, but does not yet specify the data structure that will be used to do this. This detail can be resolved in implementation, and the class diagram refined accordingly.

The 'makeReservation' and 'makeWalkIn' operations create new bookings and the parameters required to do this have now been spelled out in detail. It could be argued that the date parameter on these messages is unnecessary, as bookings are always made for the date currently displayed by the system. Although this is true for the system as described so far, this would be rather a fragile assumption to make: for example, the restaurant could ask for an enhancement whereby customers could make bookings by texting the details to the restaurant. In this case, the user interface would be quite different, if not non-existent, and customers could be making booking requests for any date in the future. By including the date parameter on these operations, the system is being to some extent 'future-proofed': the texting scenario could be implemented without any changes to the application layer of the system.

A further group of operations provides the functionality for selecting a particular booking and performing a variety of operations on it. A booking is selected by specifying a time and a table, and the operations 'cancel', 'recordArrival' and 'transfer' update the booking in ways specified by the various use cases that they represent.

Finally, the 'addObserver' and 'notifyObservers' operations are part of the interface defined by the Observer pattern shown in Figure 6.4. New observers can be registered with the booking system using 'addObserver' and, when the system state changes, the 'notifyObservers' operation is called to send an 'update' message to all registered observers. The 'updateDisplay' message shown in analysis diagrams such as Figure 5.4 has been replaced by the 'notifyObservers' message, in effect.

6.6 DYNAMIC MODELLING OF BEHAVIOUR

A complete design should specify both the structure and the behaviour of the classes in a system. Class diagrams define the data held by the booking system, and the way in which data items are related to each other, and therefore give a fairly comprehensive description of the static structure of a system. Some information about the behaviour of objects is defined by realizing use cases and is shown on interaction diagrams, which show the objects and messages involved in particular interactions. However, some kinds of relationships between the operations of an individual object cannot be captured on interaction diagrams.

For example, if a 'cancel' message is received by the booking system object before a 'selectBooking' message identifying the booking to be cancelled, then the system will not know which booking to cancel. Alternatively, if a booking has been cancelled, a message transferring it to another table should not be received, as this operation is not permitted on cancelled bookings. These kinds of problems cannot be dealt with on interaction diagrams, which are good for showing interactions that can be expected to take place but are not a suitable notation for specifying those that should not take place.

Message sequencing

In general, the order in which messages are sent to an object will depend on the object's environment. For example, the messages sent to the booking system depend ultimately on actions taken by the user of the system, not on any processing carried out within the system. Objects are not in general capable of dictating what messages are sent to them or when they are sent. In principle, then, we need to specify how an object might respond to any possible sequence of messages.

Interaction diagrams like the ones drawn in this chapter and in Chapter 5 illustrate in detail how an object responds to a particular sequence of messages. In interaction diagrams, however, the sequences of messages shown are examples only and it is left to the reader to generalize them appropriately. For example, in Figure 6.3 it is understood that multiple 'mouseMove' messages could occur in an interaction, depending on how often or how quickly the user moves the mouse, but that the 'mouseDown' and 'mouseUp' messages occur once only in this interaction.

Furthermore, some sequences of messages are assumed to be impossible, such as any sequence that contained two consecutive 'mouseDown' messages without an intervening 'mouseUp', but these are not explicitly ruled out by any set of sequence diagrams. A suitable design notation for dynamic modelling should state explicitly and unambiguously exactly what sequences of messages an object expects to receive throughout its lifetime.

History-dependent behaviour

Some messages have the property of eliciting a different response from an object at different times. For example, when an arrival at the restaurant is recorded, the arrival time of the booking should be appropriately set. If the same message is subsequently sent again to the same object, however, there should be no change to the object's state, as it makes no sense to arrive for a reservation more than once.

For simplicity, we are ignoring here the possibility that the first arrival time was set in error. Changing this would be better handled by means of a new use case, 'Change arrival time' perhaps. It might also seem that the user interface could prevent the message being sent twice, by disabling it somehow on the user interface. This is possible, but does not affect the general point: after all, there might be separate interfaces, such as the one provided by sending text messages to the restaurant from a mobile, on which an operation could not be disabled.

A better approach is to give an object the responsibility for checking for messages that do not make any sense in its current state. As the effect of a message can depend on what messages have been sent previously, this means that objects must in some way be aware of their *history*, or of the messages that they have already received.

Specifying behaviour

There are therefore two aspects of an object's behaviour that are not captured in interaction diagrams, but which need to be specified as part of a system's design.

1. What sequences of messages the object expects to receive.
2. How the object responds to messages, and in particular how this response depends on its history, namely the messages that it has already received.

We can specify the required behaviour by formalizing the notion that an object can be in one of a number of different *states* at different times. If we assume that objects can change state in response to receiving a message, an object's state at a given time will depend on the messages it has received up to then. Furthermore, if an object's response to a message may vary depending on its state, we will be able to specify both aspects of its behaviour described above.

The behaviour of objects can be specified using UML's *statechart* notation. A statechart is defined for a class, and specifies the behaviour of all the instances of that class. The statechart notation will be introduced informally in the following two sections by defining statecharts for two classes in the restaurant booking system.

6.7 A STATECHART FOR THE BOOKING SYSTEM

The most significant piece of state-dependent behaviour exhibited by the booking system class, as indicated above, has to do with the selection of bookings. Certain messages, such as 'recordArrival', can only be sensibly handled if a booking has already been selected. The basic dynamics of this situation are defined in the statechart in Figure 6.10.

Figure 6.10 A simple statechart

Figure 6.10 illustrates the main features of statecharts. A *state*, loosely speaking, corresponds to a period of time when an object is waiting to receive a message. States are shown as rectangles with rounded corners. *Events* correspond to the messages an object can receive. A *transition* is an arrow connecting two states and is usually labelled with the name of an event.

At any given time, an object is in one of its possible states. When it receives a message corresponding to an event on a transition leading from its current state, that transition *fires* and the object ends up in the state at the other end of the transition.

For example, assume that no booking is currently selected and the booking system is in the 'NotSelected' state shown on the left of Figure 6.10. If the interaction shown in Figure 5.11 now takes place, the booking system will first receive a 'selectBooking' message: this will cause the transition labelled with the name of that message to fire, and the booking system object will move into the 'Selected' state. A 'recordArrival' message will then be received and the transition labelled 'recordArrival' will fire. This, however, leaves the booking system in the state it was in before the message was received; in other words, the object is still selected after this message has been handled.

The other messages that only make sense when a booking is selected are 'transfer' and 'cancel'. 'transfer' behaves in the same way as 'recordArrival', but the effect of 'cancel' is slightly different. Once a booking is cancelled, it is removed from the display and deleted, so there will no longer be a selected booking. On the statechart, therefore, the transition labelled 'cancel' must move the system back into the 'NotSelected' state, as shown in Figure 6.11.

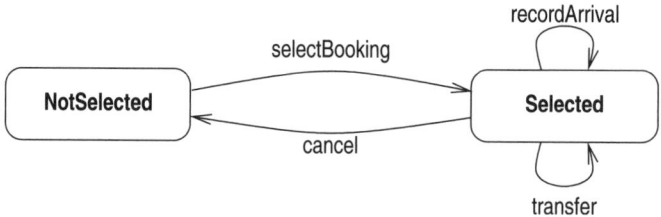

Figure 6.11 Performing an operation on a selected booking

Non-determinism

Figure 6.11 does not tell the full story about the effect of the 'selectBooking' message, but only illustrates the situation where a booking is initially selected. It will also be possible for users to select an alternative booking when one is already selected: this can be modelled by adding a transition to Figure 6.11 that loops on the 'Selected' state.

There is also the possibility, however, that receiving the 'selectBooking' message does not result in a booking being selected. This would happen, for example, if the user clicked the mouse at a screen position where no booking was displayed: the time and table parameters passed to the booking system would then correspond to no booking. Figure 6.12 illustrates all the possible effects of receiving the 'selectBooking' message, assuming that any selected booking stays selected if the mouse is clicked at an empty spot on the screen.

The looping transition on the 'NotSelected' state represents the situation where no booking is selected and the user clicks the mouse over an empty slot. In this case, the system stays in the 'NotSelected' state. By contrast, if the user clicks the mouse over a booking, the transition to the 'Selected' state fires.

Figure 6.12 Non-determinism in selecting a booking

Figure 6.12 does not make these details explicit, however, but just shows two distinct transitions from the 'NotSelected' state, with nothing to distinguish the situations in which one will fire rather than the other. A statechart with the property of leaving it ambiguous which of two transitions labelled with the same event will fire is called *non-deterministic*.

Guard conditions

In cases where genuine non-determinism exists in the system being modelled, a statechart like Figure 6.12 is quite appropriate. Most systems, however, are *deterministic*, in that receiving a given event in a given state will always lead to the same outcome. In the case of the booking system, it all depends on the parameters passed with the 'selectBooking' message: if the cursor is over a booking, the 'Selected' state will be reached; otherwise the system will remain in the 'NotSelected' state.

These facts can be shown on the statechart by adding *guard conditions* to the relevant transitions. Figure 6.13 shows how guard conditions can be specified to resolve the ambiguity in Figure 6.12. Essentially, the guard conditions incorporate the informal discussion above into a statechart, by explicitly noting the situations in which one transition rather than the other will fire.

Figure 6.13 Removing non-determinism with guard conditions

A guard condition is written in square brackets after the event label on a transition. A transition with a guard condition can only fire if the corresponding event is detected and its condition is true. In Figure 6.13 only one of the guards can be true at any time, so the non-determinism in Figure 6.12 has been removed.

Notice that no guard condition is required on the looping transition on the 'Selected' state. This is because in either case the system will remain in the state where a booking is selected: if no booking is found at the specified place, the originally selected booking will remain selected, as stated above.

Actions

If required, the fact that a new booking is selected can be recorded on the statechart by including *actions* on the appropriate transitions. Actions are written in a transition label following the event name and guard condition, if any, and prefixed with a diagonal slash. Figure 6.14 shows the statechart with actions added to highlight the cases in which a new booking will be selected.

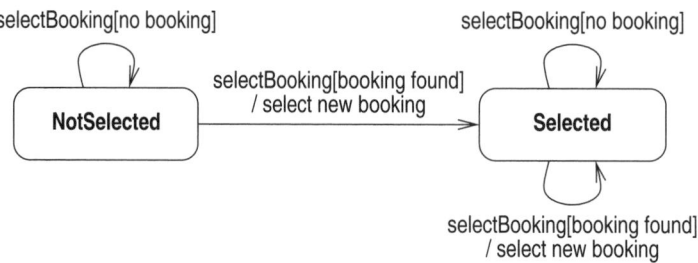

Figure 6.14 Including actions on a statechart

Composite states

With the exception of 'setDate', Figures 6.11 and 6.14 together define transitions for all the relevant operations defined in the booking system class. However, if they were all put together on a single diagram, it would be rather cluttered and hard to read, in part because of the repetition of messages, guard conditions and actions in Figure 6.14.

To enable clearer and simpler statecharts to be written, *composite states* can be used to group together related states and make explicit the behaviour that they share. Figure 6.15 shows a complete statechart for the booking system class, making use of a composite state.

The composite state is represented by the large state icon enclosing the two nested 'substates'. Transitions that are shared by both the substates are attached to the composite state: these transitions then apply to all the nested substates.

For example, Figure 6.14 shows that, no matter what state the booking system is in, if a 'selectBooking' message is received and a booking found at the cursor position, the effect is the same: the booking is selected and the booking system ends up in the 'Selected' state. This shared behaviour is shown in Figure 6.15 by means of a single transition from the composite state, having exactly the same event name, guard condition and action as the two transitions in Figure 6.14, and ending at the 'Selected' state. This single transition replaces the two identically labelled ones in Figure 6.14, but specifies exactly the same behaviour.

A transition from a composite state, then, is equivalent to a number of identically labelled transitions from each of the nested substates. This same technique is used to specify the effect of receiving a 'setDate' message: no matter what state the system is in, the effect of this is to return it to the 'NotSelected' state. Any record of a selected booking, then, is lost when a new date is entered by the user.

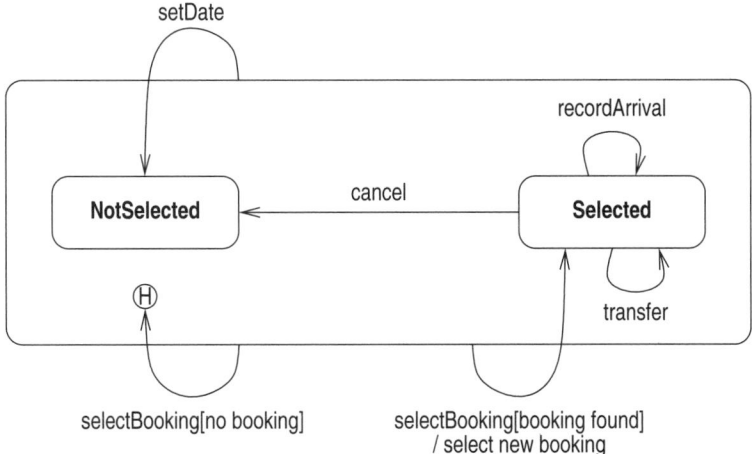

Figure 6.15 A complete statechart for the booking system class

In the case where a 'selectBooking' message is received but there is no booking to select, the situation is not quite so simple. From Figure 6.14, it can be seen that in some sense this event has the same effect in both states: the system remains in the state is was already in. It would be nice also to represent this shared behaviour with a transition from the superstate, but as the two transitions end up in different states, this cannot be done as simply as in the other cases.

For cases like this, a special *history state* can be used within a composite state, denoted by a 'H' within a circle. A history state acts as a reference to the last substate that the system was in. In Figure 6.15, if 'selectBooking' message is received but there is no booking to select, the appropriate transition from the superstate will fire, leading to the history state. The system will then end up in either the 'Selected' or 'NotSelected' state, depending on what state it was in just before following the transition.

6.8 A STATECHART FOR RESERVATIONS

The reservation class provides another example of using a statechart to summarize the behaviour of the objects of a class. Reservations do exhibit state-dependent behaviour: once an arrival has been recorded, it is not possible to cancel the booking, or to record the arrival again. A statechart summarizing this behaviour is shown in Figure 6.16.

This diagram shows two states, the 'Booked' state, corresponding to the period where the reservation has been made but the customer has not yet arrived in the restaurant, and the 'Seated' state, which is reached when the customer has arrived and their arrival time has been recorded by the system.

It is possible to change the table a reservation is allocated to at any time, as a 'setTable' transition appears on each state. If it was felt to be worthwhile, this could be replaced by a composite state and a single transition.

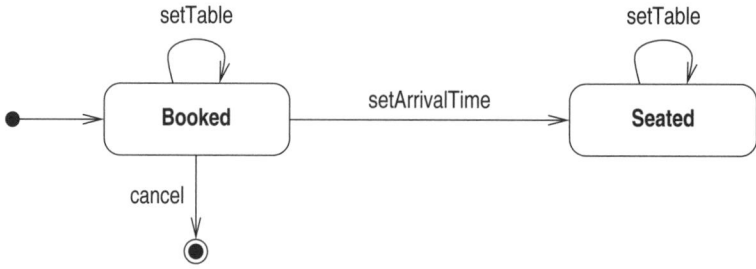

Figure 6.16 A statechart for the reservation class

Figure 6.16 also illustrates a new feature of the statechart notation, the use of *initial* and *final* states. An initial state is represented by a small black ball with an unlabelled transition to another state in the statechart. This transition corresponds to the call of a constructor for an object, and the effect is to show what state a newly created object is in. Figure 6.16 therefore specifies that when reservations are created, they enter the 'Booked' state.

A final state is represented by a small black ball with a ring round it, and corresponds to the point at which an object is destroyed. Figure 5.9 shows that booking objects are destroyed when a booking is cancelled, so the transition to the final state is labelled with the 'cancel' event. Once an arrival has been recorded, cancelling a booking is not possible, implying that the booking object is never destroyed. This might correspond to a business requirement that old booking information is archived, perhaps to be used later for management purposes.

Even though no 'cancel' transition is shown from the 'Seated' state in Figure 6.16, it is of course possible that a cancel message could be received when a reservation was in that state, perhaps because of some undetected error in the code. There are two possible responses to this situation: one would be simply to ignore the message, and the other to treat it as an error and raise an exception by some means or other.

The semantics of statecharts are that if an event is detected and there is no transition leaving the current state with that event as a label, the event is simply ignored. This makes it easier to write statecharts, because it is not necessary to include events on states where the event has no significant effect. On the other hand, it does mean that something must be added to a statechart to represent the fact that certain events must not be detected in certain states. An easy way to do this is simply to add an 'Error' state to a statechart and have the erroneous events cause a transition to the error state, where the required error handling can be defined.

When not to draw a statechart

It is not necessary to draw a statechart for every class in a system. Normally, statecharts are only drawn for classes with 'interesting' behaviour: typically, these will be classes that expect to receive messages in a certain fixed order or which exhibit state-dependent behaviour, responding to the same message in different ways at different times.

For example, it might seem that a statechart could be drawn for the customer class, to show, for example, a distinction between a customer who has a reservation made for some time in the future and one who hasn't. Differences like this between customers can certainly be identified, but from the perspective of the system they are entirely irrelevant. The operations in the interface of the customer class can be called at any time, and have the same effect at all times. A statechart for the customer class specifying this would therefore not be a useful addition to the system's design documentation.

6.9 SUMMARY

- Input to a system can be handled by a boundary object in the presentation layer, which sends suitable system messages to the controller in the application layer.

- The *Observer* pattern can be used to define a means whereby the application layer can inform the presentation layer when changes to the system state may require changes to the display.

- If persistent storage is being provided by a relational database, a schema can be created by defining one database table for each persistent class, and adding explicit object identifiers to each.

- *Mapper* classes can be defined for each persistent class, with the responsibility for saving and loading persistent objects to and from the database.

- Detailed class design carried out in the design workflow adds operations from all sequence diagrams to classes and makes properties like parameters, return types and visibility explicit.

- *Statecharts* can be used to specify the behaviour of classes that display state-dependent behaviour. They illustrate the sequences of messages that can be sent to an object and the response that an object might make to a message at different times.

- Statecharts show the different *states* that instances of a class can be in, the *transitions* they can follow in changing state and the *events* that trigger state changes. *Initial* and *final* states represent the creation and destruction of objects.

- *Guard conditions* specify when a transition is followed, and *actions* specify what an object does in response to a message received while in a particular state.

- *Composite states* can be used to simplify the structure of a statechart, by factoring out common behaviour.

6.10 EXERCISES

6.1 Rewrite the 'Table transfer' use case from Chapter 4 as a more general 'Move Booking' use case. What other changes need to be made to the system documentation as a result of this change?

6.2 If you have access to a UML tool, such as Rational Rose, create a complete design model for the restaurant booking system, incorporating all the points discussed in this chapter.

6.3 The operations of the 'BookingSystem' class in Figure 6.9 have been given public visibility. However, many of the operations do not need to be visible to the entire system, but only within the 'Domain' subpackage shown in Figure 6.8. Revise Figure 6.9 so that the only public operations are those used from outside the package and use *package visibility*, denoted by '~', for the rest.

6.4 Produce diagrams similar to Figure 6.9 for the other classes in the restaurant booking system.

6.5 Figure 5.9 shows an interaction between the user and the booking system to get confirmation of a cancellation. Is this interaction consistent with the layered architecture proposed for the booking system? If not, explain why not, and produce a revised sequence diagram showing how confirmation of a cancellation will be obtained.

6.6 Draw a statechart for the booking system class that is equivalent to Figure 6.15, but which does not use composite states. Compare your answer with Figure 6.15 from the point of view of readability.

6.7 Add an error state to Figure 6.16 to indicate that some error-handling must take place if an attempt is made to cancel a reservation that has already been seated.

6.8 Is the statechart for the 'Table' class that is shown in Figure Ex6.8 a useful piece of design documentation for the booking system? If so, complete it. If not, explain why not.

Figure Ex6.8 A proposed statechart for tables

7

RESTAURANT SYSTEM: IMPLEMENTATION

This chapter describes some aspects of the implementation of the restaurant booking system whose design has been discussed in the previous chapters. Chapter 1 explained how the semantics of the object model ensure that there are close links between designs and their implementations, and some straightforward and systematic techniques for translating UML design notations into code in an object-oriented language are illustrated in this chapter.

The booking system is representative of a large class of interactive, single-user applications that have a graphical user interface and detect user interactions by means of input devices such as a mouse and a keyboard. A large amount of low-level code is involved in any such application, to handle the detailed interactions between the application code and the input and output devices.

As this code is common to a wide range of applications, frameworks have evolved which provide standard implementations of the core input and output functionality. Rather than writing complete applications from scratch, application programmers nowadays often have only to integrate the code that implements the functionality specific to the application into a generic framework. Section 7.3 discusses the general notion of a framework, and in Section 7.4 the details of integrating the booking system into the Java Abstract Windowing Toolkit framework are presented.

7.1 IMPLEMENTATION DIAGRAMS

The documentation produced during the analysis and design activities describes the logical structure of the software application. This describes a system basically as a collection of classes, possibly subdivided into a number of packages. The dynamic behaviour of instances of the classes is further defined by means of interaction diagrams and statecharts.

When the system is implemented, these classes are represented in some way in the programming language being used. At this point, the system for the first time takes on a physical form, typically as a collection of files of source code. The source code is then compiled, generating various object, executable or library files. Finally, these files are executed on one or more processors, possibly in combination with other resources.

UML defines two types of *implementation diagram* for documenting various aspects of the physical structure of a system. *Component diagrams* document the physical components of the system and relationships between them, and *deployment diagrams* document how those components are mapped onto physical processors.

Components

Programmers typically talk as if a class and the source code implementing it were the same thing, but the distinction between the two is important. If a program is being developed to run in more than one environment, perhaps on different operating system platforms, the same class may need to be implemented in more than one way, or perhaps even in different programming languages.

To make this distinction explicit, UML defines the notion of a *component*. Components are physical entities, which represent part of a system. There are many different types of components, including source code files, executable files, libraries, database tables and so on, and stereotypes are frequently used to make explicit what kind of entity a component represents.

Figure 7.1 shows the UML notation for a component, as a rectangle with smaller rectangles embedded in its boundary. The relationship between a class and the component implementing it can be modelled with a dependency between the two. This dependency is sometimes labelled with the 'trace' stereotype, but this is often omitted if the meaning of the diagram is otherwise made clear.

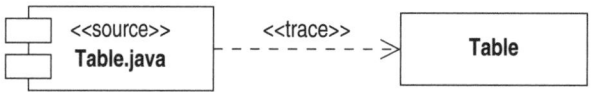

Figure 7.1 A component implementing a class

Component diagrams

The source files that make up a system can be shown on a component diagram. Component diagrams show components linked by dependencies, which typically represent the compilation dependencies between components. A compilation dependency exists between two source files if, in order to compile one, the other has to be available. This situation arises when one class makes use of another: for example, as the type of an attribute or as a superclass. Compilation diagrams therefore document the build requirements for a system and could, for example, form the input for the generation of a makefile for the system.

Figure 7.2 shows a partial component diagram for the restaurant booking system, showing the presentation layer and the domain classes in the application layer. Notice that the package structure defined in the analysis and design models is preserved in the component diagram. The diagram basically documents a one-to-one correspondence between classes and source files, as is common in Java programs, except that the classes in the booking hierarchy have been placed in a single source file.

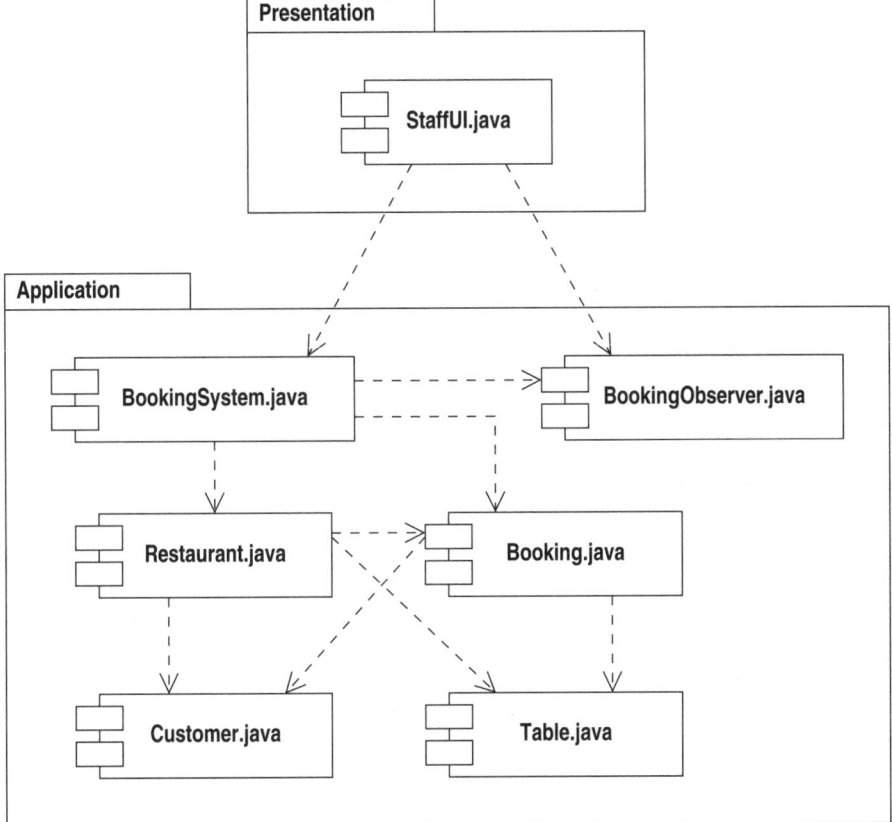

Figure 7.2 Component diagram for the booking system

Deployment diagrams

Deployment diagrams show how the components in a system are mapped onto processors when a system is deployed. The restaurant booking system is initially intended to be deployed as a single-user application running on a stand-alone PC, so the deployment diagram, shown in Figure 7.3, is rather trivial. Processing nodes are represented on deployment diagrams as cuboids and the components that are deployed on the node are shown 'inside' the cuboid.

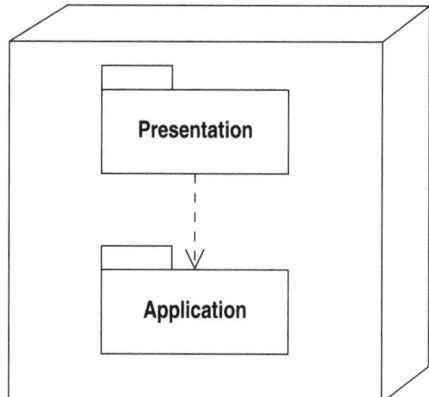

Figure 7.3 Deployment diagram for the booking system

Deployment diagrams are more illuminating when a system is being deployed across a network, when different nodes in the network can be shown in a diagram. The purpose of the diagram is then to show the physical distribution of processing across the different nodes.

7.2 IMPLEMENTATION STRATEGIES

The component diagram in Figure 7.2 shows the source files that have to be created to implement the booking system. The dependencies between the components impose certain constraints on the order in which source files can be created and tested, however, and two basic approaches to this have been described in the literature.

Top-down implementation starts with the higher-level components, and proceeds 'downwards', in the direction of the dependency arrows, through Figure 7.2. An advantage of this strategy is that the overall design of the system can be tested early on in the process. A disadvantage is that *stubs*, or temporary implementations, need to be created for lower-level classes, only to be replaced later by real implementations of these classes as development progresses.

Bottom-up implementation starts with the lower-level classes and proceeds 'up' the diagram. This approach makes the development and testing of individual components easier: when a class is implemented, all the classes on which it depends have already been implemented, so it can easily be compiled and tested without the need to develop stubs. However, the bottom-up approach runs the risk of postponing the generation of a complete executable program until quite a late stage in implementation.

A compromise between these two approaches is to adopt a more iterative approach and think of implementing use cases rather than classes. With this approach, developers implement those features of each class that are required to support a single use case, which is then fully tested. Further use cases are then implemented one by one, adding additional features to the classes as required.

7.3 APPLICATION FRAMEWORKS

An application like the restaurant booking system contains a certain amount of functionality that is specific to the application, to do with the implementation of the business objects and rules specific to the restaurant, but there is also a large amount of functionality that is shared with other applications that make use of a window-based graphical interface.

Application programmers rarely have to write code to carry out this generic, low-level functionality. Most programming languages and environments now support a significant level of reuse, making the code that handles input and output, for example, available for reuse in the form of a *framework* of classes. Typically, a framework for interactive graphical applications will support the following functionality.

1. It will manage the interactions between the application and its environment. In a windowing environment, the framework may support the creation and subsequent management of the windows used by the application. In the case of applets, the framework may provide the functionality necessary for a browser to start and stop applets running on a web page.
2. It will provide means to detect user input and present it to the application in the form of a number of standard and well-defined messages. This input may be generated directly by physical devices such as the mouse and the keyboard, or it may be mediated by user-interface 'widgets' such as menu items and buttons.
3. It will provide a library of graphics functions, which enable output to be produced, and displayed in the windows controlled by the application.

The term 'framework' is used metaphorically, but is meant to suggest two things. First, the framework code can be thought of as surrounding the application-specific code, in much the same way as a frame surrounds a picture. Second, the framework provides a complete but skeletal application that can be used as a framework on which a complete and specialized application can be built.

One visualization of the role of a framework in shielding application programmers from low-level concerns is shown in Figure 7.4. This informal diagram illustrates the way in which the framework shields an application programmer from the details of low-level application programming interfaces (APIs) used to handle input and output. It also indicates how, by providing a standard interface to this low-level functionality, a framework can be reused in many different applications.

Hotspots

This general description of the role of frameworks does not explain how a programmer can integrate application code with that provided by the framework. Object-oriented frameworks often achieve this by means of *hotspots*. A hotspot is a class in the framework that applications are meant to specialize, as shown in Figure 7.5. The dashed line in this diagram is an informal addition, which indicates the boundary between the framework classes and code specific to a particular application.

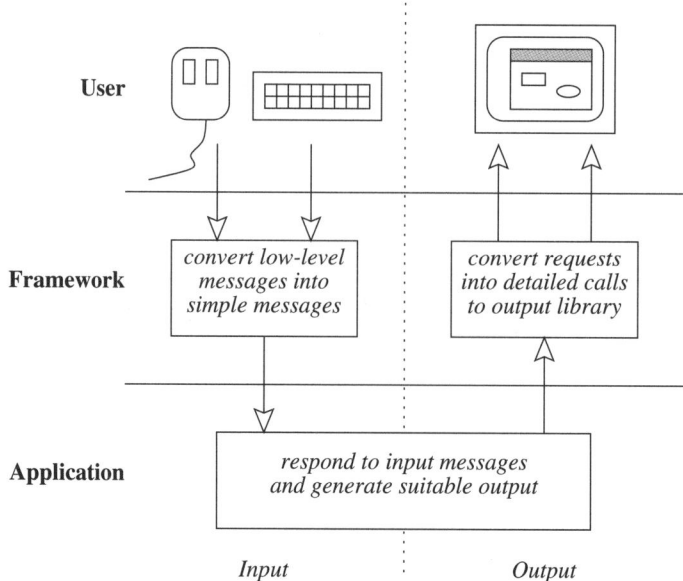

Figure 7.4 The role of a user-interface framework

Suppose that the hotspot class provides basic functionality to display a window and its contents. This functionality must be provided in all applications, and there are a number of standard situations where it is executed. For example, if the user opens another window that obscures an application window and then closes or moves that window, the contents of the application window may need to be redrawn to restore the correct display. The framework will detect these events and at appropriate times will send a message to the window class, the hotspot, instructing it to refresh its display.

In general, a hotspot class defines a number of operations, which are called by the framework at certain standard times. This situation is illustrated in Figure 7.5 by a message being sent from some other framework class to the hotspot. The basic tasks of the application programmer are to define specializations of hotspot classes and to override operations to implement functionality specific to a particular application.

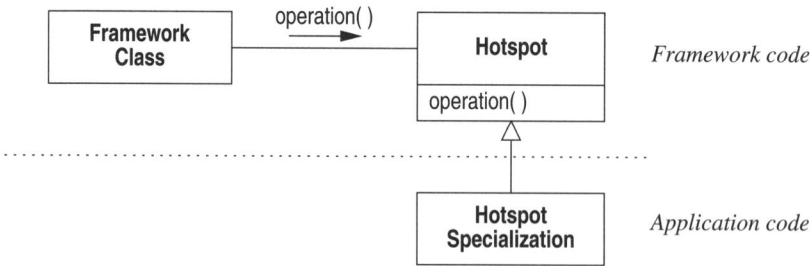

Figure 7.5 A hotspot class

An operation in a hotspot class may be abstract. Implementations of such operations must be provided by the application programmer before a complete application can be produced. In most cases, however, a sensible default implementation can be written for an operation, even if it is a trivial one which does nothing. In this case, a complete, if trivial, application can be generated from the framework and all the application programmer has to do is to override operations of interest.

Exactly which operations need to be overridden depends on the implementations provided by the framework. Figure 7.6 shows the hotspot receiving a message indicating that the user has moved the mouse. In this case, there is no default functionality that the framework can sensibly provide, so the hotspot class provides a null implementation of the operation. The application programmer overrides this operation in the specialized class and the mechanism of dynamic binding ensures that, when the framework class sends a message, the application-specific code is executed.

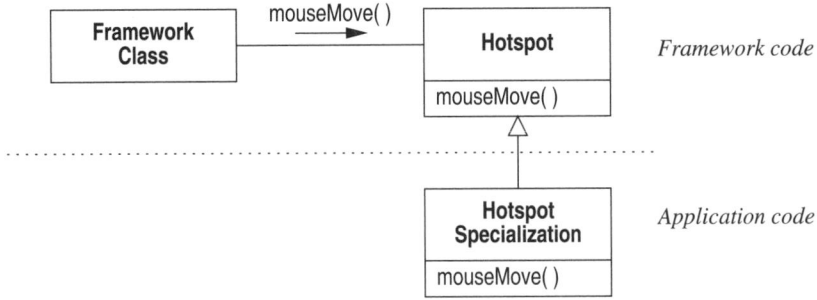

Figure 7.6 Overriding a framework operation

In other cases, it may be possible for a framework to provide a substantial default implementation of an operation. Figure 7.7 shows a situation where the framework is requesting that a window and its contents are redisplayed. In this case, the framework can supply some general-purpose code to redisplay the window background, its borders and scroll bars, and so on. This code is provided in the 'redisplay' method in Figure 7.7. The code that displays application-specific content in the window must, on the other hand, be provided by the programmer.

If the programmer provided this code by overriding the redisplay method, the generic code provided by the framework would be lost. In principle, it could be replicated in the overriding function, but this approach would remove many of the benefits to be gained from using a framework. In such cases a different mechanism is used. The hotspot class defines a second method, called 'displayContent' in Figure 7.7, whose purpose is to display application-specific content in the window. This is given a null default implementation, and it is this function that the programmer overrides.

The redisplay operation calls this additional method at an appropriate place to integrate the application-specific code into the general framework. At run-time, then, when a redisplay message is received, the hotspot 'redisplay' method is first executed; this calls the 'displayContent' method and by use of dynamic binding, the specialized method is executed.

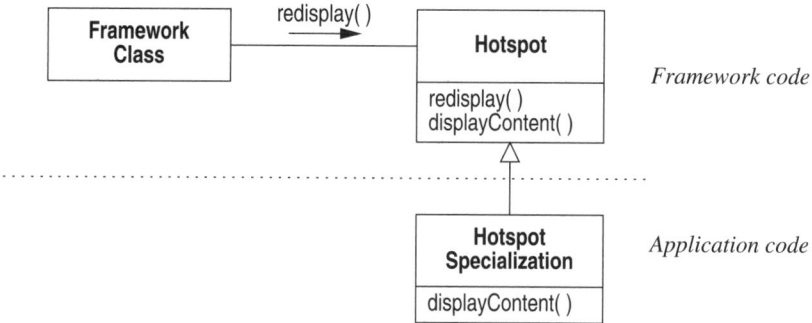

Figure 7.7 Overriding a 'callback' method

Operations like 'displayContent' in Figure 7.7 are known as *callback* or *hook* functions. They provide a technique whereby an application programmer can extend the functionality of a framework method, by redefining other operations that the framework methods calls.

Inversion of control

Use of a framework brings with it a particular style of programming, which differs from conventional styles. In the traditional model, the programmer writes a 'main program', which dictates the overall flow of control within an application. The application can be decomposed into a set of classes and functions, some of which may be provided by libraries, but essentially control remains in the hands of the programmer, who determines what the user can do when the program is running.

When a framework is used, however, this relationship is reversed, a situation often referred to as *inversion of control*. The flow of control in the program resides in the framework code, and the programmer simply provides a number of functions, which are called at certain well-defined places in the process. Control at run-time is in the hands of the user, not the programmer, whose job is to provide code that responds in a suitable way to the user's actions. For this reason, this style of programming is sometimes referred to as *event-driven*.

7.4 THE JAVA AWT FRAMEWORK

As a very simple example of the use of a framework, this section describes how the Java Abstract Windowing Toolkit (AWT) framework could be used to support the graphical user interface of the restaurant booking system as illustrated in the sketch of Figure 4.3. The structure of the interface is very conventional, consisting of a single main window with a title and a menu bar. The current date is displayed, and the remainder of the window is taken up with an area within which the current bookings are displayed, and where mouse events can be detected.

Documenting a framework with UML

Frameworks like AWT are simply libraries of Java code, and so UML diagrams can be used to document their structure and functionality. Often this can be very helpful as a way of coming to understand how a framework is put together and how to use it. For example, Figure 7.8 shows a simplified version of part of the AWT framework that is relevant to supporting the implementation of the booking system user interface.

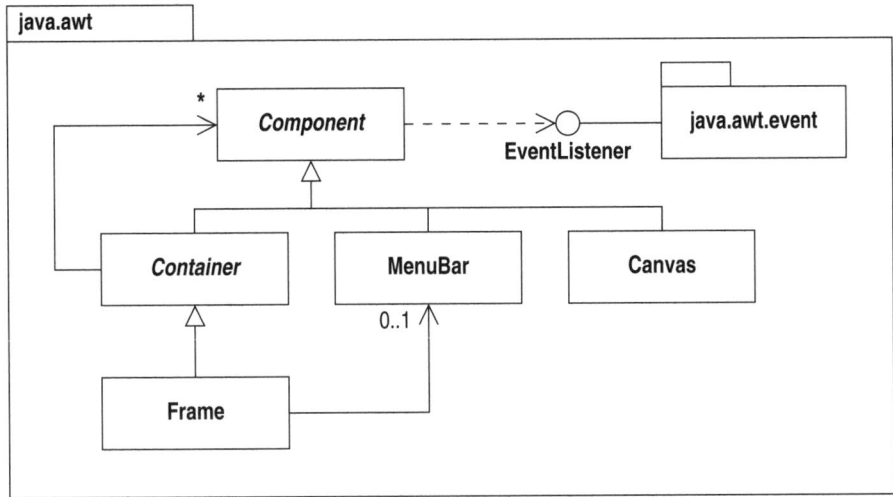

Figure 7.8 Some AWT classes (simplified)

The AWT is defined in the Java package `java.awt`, and the various AWT classes are shown within a corresponding UML package in Figure 7.8. The elements that make up a user interface are known as *components* and are defined as subclasses of the abstract class 'Component'. Some components, known as *containers*, can contain others, as shown by the association between the 'Container' and 'Component' classes.

A *frame* is a particular type of container that represents an application window, containing a title, a menu bar and various platform-specific attributes. Menu bars are defined by a separate class, and a further association records the fact that frames contain menus. A further type of component, a *canvas*, defines an area of screen on which any type of graphical output can be produced and which is capable of handling user input events. There is no predefined relationship between frames and canvases.

User-generated events are defined in a subpackage `java.awt.event`, which defines an interface, 'EventListener'. This interface is implemented by a wide variety of classes that detect various types of event. Components can have associated with them a collection of listeners, to detect events generated by the user on that component. Figure 7.8 shows an alternative notation for interfaces, a small circle attached to the component that supports the interface, with the interface name written under the circle. A dependency from the 'Component' class to the 'EventListener' interface documents the fact that a component can have attached listeners.

Integrating the booking system with the AWT framework

In order to make use of the AWT framework in the implementation of the restaurant booking system, we must locate the relevant hotspot classes within AWT that need to be specialized. The two most important of these are the 'Frame' and 'Canvas' classes.

Canvases provide the basic functionality required for the main display area of the user interface, namely the abilities to display graphical material and to detect user-generated events. In the design of the booking system, these tasks are the responsibility of the 'StaffUI' class. A sensible application choice is therefore to implement 'StaffUI' as a subclass of `java.awt.Canvas`, and to support the required functionality by redefining the appropriate methods in that class.

A canvas requires a container to place it inside, however, so in addition we need a subclass of 'Frame' to serve as the main application window for the booking system. This class has not been identified in the design so far, as the functionality it supports consists of purely generic operations, such as 'minimize window', which have not been made explicit in the booking system use cases. The new class is shown in Figure 7.9, which documents the way that the presentation layer of the booking system is integrated with the AWT framework.

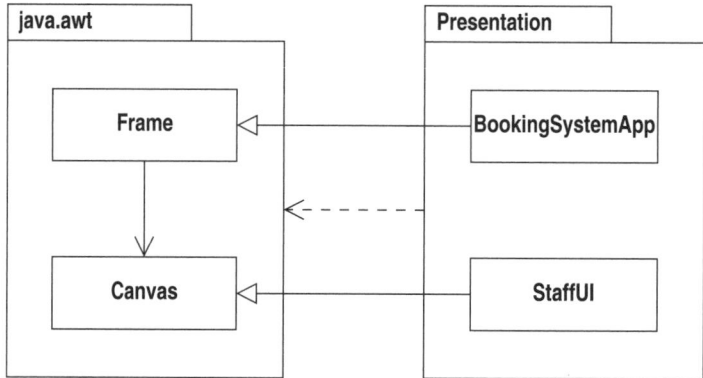

Figure 7.9 Using the AWT framework for the presentation layer

There are many more low-level details involved in the use of AWT in the booking system, but once the overall strategy shown in Figure 7.9 is grasped, these can best be understood by studying the source code of the application, available on the book's website.

7.5 IMPLEMENTATION OF CLASSES

The following sections describe some aspects of the implementation of the booking system in Java, showing how the various UML features in the design are mapped into code. The techniques presented are not the only way of carrying out such a translation, but have the advantage of being clear and straightforward, and emphasizing the close relationship that exists between design notations and programming language constructs.

Classes

Unsurprisingly, classes in a UML class diagram are implemented as classes in object-oriented languages. Figure 7.10 shows the booking class with a subset of the attributes and operations identified for it earlier in the development.

Figure 7.10 The booking class

This class can naturally be implemented as a Java class containing equivalent fields and methods. An outline of a Java class implementing the booking class as specified in Figure 7.10 is shown below.

```java
public abstract class Booking
{
  protected int covers ;
  protected Date date ;

  protected Booking(int c, Date d) {
    covers = c ;
    Date = d ;
  }

  public Date getDate() {
    return date ;
  }
  public void setArrivalTime(Time t) { }
  public void setCovers(int c) {
    covers = c ;
  }
}
```

As the booking class is abstract in the design class diagram, it is implemented as an abstract class in Java. A constructor is defined to initialize the values of the attributes, but it is declared to be protected, so that instances of the class can only be created by subclasses. Note that constructors are often omitted from class diagrams, but are required in implementations of classes. Attributes of the class are represented by fields in Java, with UML data types being translated into the appropriate Java equivalents where necessary. Operations of the class are defined as methods in Java, with appropriate, and in this case rather trivial, implementations.

The 'setArrivalTime' method only has significance for reservations. It is included in the booking superclass so that all bookings share a common interface, but a null implementation of it is provided so that the walk-in class, to which it is irrelevant, can simply ignore its existence.

When a class is implemented, the visibility of its members needs to be considered. If visibility has not been specified by the designer, a useful rule of thumb for implementing attributes and operations is to transform attributes into private fields of the implementation class, and operations into public methods of the class. This reflects a widely adopted policy on the implementation of classes, which states that a class's data should be private and only accessible through its operational interface. An exception to this rule occurs when attributes of a class need to be accessible to instances of subclasses. As in this case, attributes are often given protected visibility, as above.

Generalization

Figure 7.11 shows an example of generalization in the design of the diagram editor, where the booking class defined in Figure 7.10 is extended by two subclasses representing the two different kinds of booking.

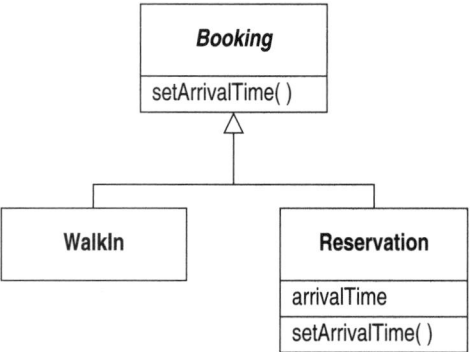

Figure 7.11 Generalization in the booking system

Generalization can be implemented using inheritance in Java. Generalization in UML permits the substitutability of a subclass instance wherever a superclass instance is expected and the inheritance of class members from superclasses, and both of these properties are preserved by the semantics of inheritance in Java, as illustrated in the following outline implementations of the 'WalkIn' and 'Reservation' classes.

```
public class WalkIn extends Booking
{
  public WalkIn(...) {
    super(...) ;
  }
}
```

```
public class Reservation extends Booking
{
  Time arrivalTime ;

  public Reservation(...) {
    super(...) ;
    arrivalTime = null ;
  }

  public void setArrivalTime( Time t ) {
    arrivalTime = t ;
  }
}
```

The implementation of the 'WalkIn' class is rather minimal here, and it might be questioned whether this needs to be defined as a separate class at all. The arguments in favour of the approach followed here are discussed in more detail in Section 14.2.

Class multiplicity

When a class has been defined, there are, by default, no restrictions on the number of instances of that class that can be created by the system. This is very often exactly what is required: for example, the booking system will need to create and manipulate many instances of the booking, table and customer classes.

In some cases, however, it is useful to state that only one instance of a class will be created: we only want one instance of the user interface and booking system classes, for example, as they play a central co-ordinating role in the system. As Figure 7.12 illustrates, this decision can be recorded by including the appropriate multiplicity in the upper right-hand corner of the class icon. Classes that should only be instantiated once are called *singleton* classes.

Figure 7.12 Notation for class multiplicity

It is possible to implement classes in such a way that only one instance of the class is ever created, and a standard method for doing this is documented in the design pattern known as *Singleton*. If a class is implemented as a Singleton, at most one instance of it will be created, and that instance can be made available to other classes as required.

The central idea behind the Singleton pattern is to make the constructor of the class inaccessible, so that classes that use the singleton class cannot create instances of the class. The singleton class stores a single instance as a static data field, and this is made available to clients through a static method that will initialize the unique instance the first time it is called. The application of this pattern to the booking system class is illustrated in the outline code below.

```
public class BookingSystem
{
  private static BookingSystem uniqueInstance ;

  public static BookingSystem getInstance() {
    if (uniqueInstance == null) {
      uniqueInstance = new BookingSystem() ;
    }
    return uniqueInstance ;
  }

  private BookingSystem() { ... }
}
```

7.6 IMPLEMENTATION OF ASSOCIATIONS

In class diagrams, associations relate classes together. Whereas all object-oriented programming languages provide direct support for the concept of a class, none of the languages in common use provide features that can be directly used to implement associations. When implementing a design, therefore, it is necessary to give some thought to the question of how associations are to be handled.

The role of associations is to define the properties of the links that connect objects when a system is running. A link asserts that one object knows of the existence and location of some other object. In addition, links serve as channels along which messages can be sent to the linked object if necessary.

This suggests that individual links between objects could be implemented using *references*. A reference, being essentially the address of an object, certainly records the object's location and identity, and by means of the reference it is possible to call the methods of the linked object, thus simulating message passing. A simple strategy for implementing an association between two classes is therefore to declare fields in each class to hold references to instances of the associated class.

Associations have certain logical properties, however, which are not explicitly handled by this rather simplistic approach and which need careful consideration in the implementation of associations. These properties are briefly considered in the remainder of this section. A more systematic treatment of various methods for implementing associations is given in Chapter 13.

Bidirectionality

Associations and links connect classes and objects, respectively, but, unless navigability annotations are used, place no restriction on the direction in which the connection can be traversed. For example, a link in a collaboration diagram can serve as a communication channel between two objects, and messages can be sent in either direction along this channel, as required by the needs of the design. This property is often expressed by saying that associations and links are *bidirectional*.

References, on the other hand, are *unidirectional*. If an object *x* holds a reference to object *y*, this gives *x* access to *y* and the ability to call the member functions of *y*, but gives *y* no knowledge at all of *x*. To implement a bidirectional link two references are required, one from *x* to *y* and the other from *y* back to *x*. To illustrate the difference, Figure 7.13 shows links between three objects contrasted with the references that would be required to implement the links in both directions. References are distinguished from links by means of an arrowhead, which shows the direction of access.

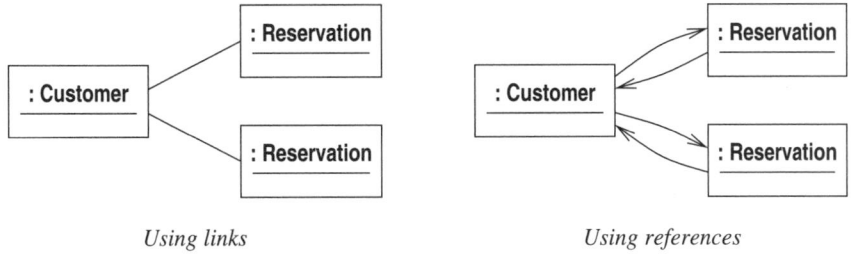

Using links   *Using references*

Figure 7.13 Implementing bidirectional links with references

Although it is certainly possible to implement links as pairs of references in this way, there are a number of good reasons why this is undesirable and should be avoided if possible. First, in order to support a cyclical structure of references, the relevant class declarations must be mutually referring. This can only be achieved at the cost of increasing the coupling between the two classes, with a detrimental effect on the simplicity and maintainability of the resulting code.

Second, the two references implementing a link must be kept mutually consistent throughout the lifetime of the link. They must be created and destroyed together, and must not be altered independently. Programming with references is an error-prone area, however, and doubling the number of references required increases the potential problems. Even if a safe scheme for maintaining references is defined and consistently adhered to, there may be a significant overhead involved in maintaining both references.

Unidirectional implementation of associations

Fortunately, it is often not necessary to implement an association in both directions, depending on the dynamic properties of the system. It may turn out, for example, that messages are passed from reservation to customer objects, but never in the other direction. In order to support this, it is clearly necessary for a reservation to hold a reference to its customer, but there may be no immediate benefit to be gained from having each customer object hold references to its reservations.

The implementation of associations can therefore be simplified by providing references only in the directions in which the associations are actually used. In practice, it turns out that relatively few associations need to be supported in both directions. For example, in the first iteration of the booking system, messages are passed from reservation objects to customers, but never from a customer to a reservation.

We can therefore decide, for the purposes of simplifying the implementation, only to implement this association in the direction from reservation to customer. This decision can be added to the class diagram in the form of a navigability annotation, as shown in Figure 7.14.

Figure 7.14 Making an association unidirectional

A simple unidirectional implementation of this association might use a data member to store the reference to the linked customer in the reservation class. This is shown below, along with the code in the constructor for initializing this reference.

```
public class Reservation
{
  private Customer customer ;

  public Reservation( Customer c )
  {
    customer = c ;
  }
}
```

By choosing to implement the association in one direction only, we are making a tradeoff between present ease of implementation and future modifiability. It is now impossible to traverse the association in the direction from customers to reservations. Any future change to the system that makes it desirable to retrieve all the reservations that a particular customer has made, for example, will now be much harder to implement than it would have otherwise have been, because we will have to add back in the ability to traverse the association in the reverse direction.

Implementing multiplicity constraints

When an association is implemented with references, the information that the class diagram contains about the multiplicity of the association is not always automatically preserved. For example, the association in Figure 7.14 asserts that each reservation object is always associated with exactly one customer object. A reference in Java, however, can always take on the value null, which refers to no object. If this is the case at any time the system is running, therefore, the system will be inconsistent with the multiplicity specified for the association.

The multiplicity constraint can only be preserved by adding code that will at suitable places explicitly check that a null value is not being stored in the variable. For example, the code below throws an exception if an attempt is made to create a reservation without associating with it a customer object.

```
public class Reservation
{
  private Customer customer ;

  public Reservation( Customer c )
  {
    if (c == null) {
      // throw NullCustomerException
    }
    customer = c ;
  }
}
```

A related issue with multiplicity occurs if the association specifies a multiplicity greater than one, as in the example shown in Figure 7.15. The problem here is that a single variable, obviously, cannot hold references to more than one linked object.

Figure 7.15 A one-to-many association

In order to implement a one-to-many association, a class must define not a single reference variable, but a suitable data structure to hold an unspecified number of references. In Java, the Vector class is often an appropriate and simple choice, as a vector can grow to accommodate as many data values as required. Outline code for the 'BookingSystem' class that adopts this strategy is shown below.

```
public class BookingSystem
{
  private Vector current = new Vector() ;

  public void addBooking(Booking b) {
    current.addElement(b) ;
  }
}
```

7.7 IMPLEMENTATION OF OPERATIONS

Class diagrams contain static information, which can be implemented by translating it into structural features of the implementation, such as definitions of classes and their members. They also contain definitions of the operations in each class, but do not describe the processing carried out by each operation. This dynamic information is contained in the interaction diagrams produced as use case realizations, and in some cases summarized on a class-by-class basis in statecharts.

When an operation is implemented, the interaction diagrams showing correspond-ing messages should first be collated. These diagrams show which other messages are sent while the operation is being executed, and hence which other class methods should be invoked by the implementation of the operation. If different interaction diagrams show different behaviour, suitable control structures must be implemented to discriminate between the different situations involved. Alternatively, if a statechart exists for the class in question, it may be possible to use this as a guide for implementing the operations in the class, as explained below.

Implementation of statecharts

Statecharts provide dynamic information about how an object behaves during its lifetime. This information can readily be translated into code, being reflected in the implementation of class methods, which need to be aware of the current state of the object when they are called in order to determine how to react.

As with class diagrams, it is desirable to use a systematic approach to translate the information contained in statecharts into code. This section uses the statechart for the booking system class, shown in Figure 6.15, to illustrate a possible approach.

The basic idea underlying the approach is to keep an explicit record of the current state of the booking system in a field defined in the booking system class. The statechart defines two distinct states, 'NotSelected' and 'Selected'. These states are defined as constants in the booking system class, and a 'state' field holds the value corresponding to the current state of the system.

Figure 6.15 does not specify an initial state for the system, but it is reasonable to assume that when the system is started, no booking is selected, and hence the state variable should be set to 'NotSelected'. The partial class definition below shows this, together with the definition of constant values representing the two states.

```
public class BookingSystem
{
  final static int NotSelected = 0 ;
  final static int Selected  = 1 ;
  int state ;

  BookingSystem()
  {
    state = NotSelected ;
  }
}
```

Messages sent to the booking system have the potential to elicit different behaviour at different times, depending on the system's current state. This property can be reflected in the implementation of the class by structuring every method as a switch statement. The switch statement has a case for each possible value of the state variable, and the code for each case specifies what to do if the message is received when the system is in that particular state.

If this convention is followed, every method in the booking system class will have the form specified by the following template. In some methods many of the cases may be empty; nevertheless, including them all makes the structure of the implementation clear and consistent, and easy to modify.

```
public void operation()
{
  switch (state) {
    case NotSelected:
      // Specific actions for 'Not Selected' state
      break ;
    case Selected:
      // Specific actions for 'Selected' state
      break ;
  }
}
```

Much of the specific behaviour implemented in each of the different cases can be derived directly from the actions included on the statechart or from the sequence diagrams that illustrate the external behaviour of the various operations. The details of this implementation are best studied in the code of the restaurant booking system. A more detailed explanation of this approach to the implementation of statecharts is given in Section 13.7.

7.8 SUMMARY

- Much software development now takes place in the context of an *application framework*. Frameworks provide semi-complete, generic applications and shield programmers from low-level APIs.

- An object-oriented framework will typically define a number of *hotspot* classes. To develop applications, programmers must specialize these classes and override various operations to provide application-specific functionality.

- The diagram editor can be implemented as a Java applet by specializing the `Applet` and `Canvas` classes from the Java APIs.

- Classes in a design map naturally onto classes in a Java implementation, and generalization maps to inheritance.

- Programming languages contain no feature with the same properties as associations. Associations can be implemented by means of fields in a class holding references to instances of the association class.

- Statecharts can be used to guide the systematic implementation of the operations in a class, by making the states explicit in the implementation.

7.9 EXERCISES

7.1 Examine the code for the booking system, available from the book's website, and draw a complete component diagram for the system, extending Figure 7.2.

7.2 Suppose that the restaurant deploys the booking system on a number of PCs, each linked to a single machine on which a shared database of booking information is maintained. Draw a deployment diagram illustrating this new configuration.

7.3 Suppose that the restaurant enhances the booking system so that booking information can be displayed on hand-held devices linked by a wireless network to a PC running the application layer. Draw a deployment diagram illustrating this configuration of the system.

7.4 Figures 7.5, 7.6 and 7.7 bend the rules of UML slightly, by including messages on class diagrams. For each of these diagrams, draw a corresponding sequence diagram showing an instance of the framework class and an instance of the hotspot specialization together with the messages that would be sent in each interaction.

7.5 Examine the code of the restaurant booking system, and produce an extended version of Figure 7.9 which documents all the classes in the presentation layer of the system and their relationships with the `java.awt` package.

7.6 Extend the implementation of the booking system to support the general editing of bookings, as described in your answers to Exercises 4.9 and 5.10.

7.7 Extend the implementation of the booking system to support the handling of overlarge bookings on tables, as described in your answers to Exercises 4.10 and 5.11.

7.8 Extend the implementation of the booking system to allow the lengths of bookings to be adjusted, as described in your answers to Exercises 4.12 and 5.12.

7.9 Extend the implementation of the booking system to allow the automatic allocation of tables to bookings, as described in your answers to Exercises 4.13 and 5.13.

7.10 Extend the implementation of the booking system to support the functionality of a waiting list, as described in your answers to Exercises 4.14 and 5.14.

7.11 Extend the implementation of the booking system to allow bookings to be made for more than one table, as described in your answers to Exercises 4.17 and 5.15.

8

CLASS AND OBJECT DIAGRAMS

Static models of a system describe the structural relationships that hold between the pieces of data manipulated by the system. They describe how data is parcelled out into objects, how those objects are categorized and what relationships can hold between them. They do not describe the behaviour of the system, nor how the data in a system evolves over time. These aspects are described by various types of dynamic model.

The most important kinds of static model are *object diagrams* and *class diagrams*. An object diagram provides a 'snapshot' of a system, showing the objects that actually exist at a given moment and the links between them. Many different object diagrams can be drawn for a system, each representing the state of the system at a given instant. An object diagram shows the data that is held by a system at a given moment. This data may be represented as individual objects, as attribute values stored inside these objects or as links between objects.

One aspect of understanding a system is knowing which object diagrams do and which do not represent possible valid states of the system. For example, consider the two object diagrams shown in Figure 8.1, which depict student and module objects in a hypothetical university record system.

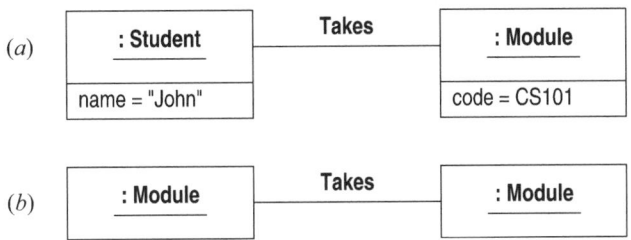

Figure 8.1 (*a*) Valid and (*b*) invalid object diagrams

Figure 8.1(*a*) shows a situation where a particular student is taking a module. Assuming that one of the responsibilities of the system is to record which students are taking which modules, this object diagram represents a legitimate state of the system. There will undoubtedly be times when the particular link shown in Figure 8.1(*a*) does not exist. It may even be the case that throughout the whole time that the system is running, this particular configuration of objects never occurs. It does, however, represent a situation that could occur, if the facts about the real world demanded it.

The case is different with Figure 8.1(*b*). It does not make sense for one module to take another, and so in the context of a university record system this diagram is simply meaningless. We cannot ask whether the situation it depicts is true or not, as it fails to depict a meaningful situation at all.

It is not possible, however, to specify a system by explicitly considering all the possible object diagrams and classifying them as legal or illegal, as there are simply too many of them. A more general method is required for specifying the properties that must hold of any object diagram that purports to represent a legal state of the system. UML uses *class diagrams* for this purpose.

A class diagram acts as a kind of specification for a system and, among other things, states what kinds of objects can exist, what data they encapsulate and how objects in the system can be related to each other. A suitable class diagram for the student record system, for example, would make clear that Figure 8.1(*a*) represents a possible state of the system but Figure 8.1(*b*) does not.

This chapter describes the features of UML's class diagrams and explains how class diagrams are used to specify certain structural properties of software systems. The examples used in this chapter are artificial to the extent that they discuss the static structure of systems without any reference to the processing that this structure is supposed to support. This simplification is of benefit when introducing the details of the notation, but should not be taken as a realistic illustration of how class diagrams are used and developed. As the examples in Chapter 5 indicate, class diagrams are often developed hand in hand with interaction diagrams, which help in identifying the classes required in a system.

8.1 DATA TYPES

In common with many programming languages, UML defines a number of primitive *data types* and also provides a mechanism whereby new types can be defined. Data types represent simple, unstructured kinds of data such as numeric, character and Boolean values. Data types are commonly used to specify the type of an attribute or an operation parameter in a class.

Instances of data types are called *data values*. Data values differ from objects in that they have no notion of identity. For example, two separate occurrences of the integer 2, stored at different locations, would be regarded as the same data value and if tested for equality would return the value 'true'. Two objects, on the other hand, are always regarded as distinct, even if their states are identical.

The data types available in UML fall into three categories. First, there are a number of predefined types, principally integers, strings and Boolean values. The UML notation defining these types is shown in Figure 8.2, although in practice only the names are used in type expressions. The values of these types are not defined in UML, but are assumed to be understood.

Figure 8.2 Predefined data types in UML

Data values are unstructured, so data types define no attributes or operations. Pure functions can be defined for data types, however: they can return data values, but cannot update their arguments.

Data types can also be defined as *enumerations*, which are essentially the same as the enumerated types provided in many programming languages. The values of an enumeration are a set of named *enumeration literals*. Boolean values are represented by a predefined enumeration, shown in Figure 8.2. The literals of this type are the two values 'true' and 'false'. User-defined enumerations can be defined by listing the enumeration literals in the lower compartment of the icon, as shown in Figure 8.3.

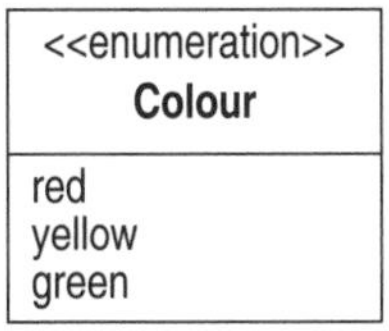

```
<<enumeration>>
     Colour
─────────────────
red
yellow
green
```

Figure 8.3 A user-defined enumeration

Finally, models can use *programming language data types*. These allow the types from a specific programming language to be used in UML. This is useful when reverse engineering a class diagram from code or when implementating a design, when it may be necessary to specify that pointer or array types, for example, are to be used.

Multiplicity

There are a number of places in UML where it is necessary to state how many times a given entity can occur in some context. These are represented by *multiplicities*. A multiplicity is a set of integer values; each member of the set represents one possibility for the number of occurrences of the entity being specified.

Multiplicities are defined as a data type in UML and are represented using *multiplicity ranges*. A range consists of a pair of integers separated by dots, such as '0..9'. The special symbol '*', meaning 'unlimited', can be used to represent a range that is not bounded above.

The range '0..100' therefore represents all the whole numbers from '0..100' inclusive, whereas the range '0..∗' represents all the non-negative integers. A multiplicity range where both ends are the same number, such as '1..1', is represented by the single number '1'.

In general, a multiplicity is given by a list consisting of number ranges and individual numbers, preferably arranged in ascending order. For example, suppose that a given entity is optional but that if it is present there must be at least three of them. This multiplicity could be represented as '0, 3..∗'.

8.2 CLASSES

A basic technique for simplifying the description of an indefinitely large number of objects is to classify similar objects into groups. Objects that share certain properties and behaviour are grouped together, and for each group a *class* is defined. The class does not describe particular properties of individuals, but specifies the common features that are shared by all the objects in the group.

For example, Figure 8.1 shows objects representing students and modules in a hypothetical university record system. In such a system the same pieces of information, such as a name and an address, would be stored about each student, while the actual data values stored would vary from student to student. By defining a student class we can specify once and for all the structure of the information that the system will store about students.

The same goes for operations: the operation of changing an address, for example, is potentially applicable to any student or, in other words, each student object must provide this as one of its operations. By describing the operation as part of the student class, we specify its applicability to all student objects.

In UML a rectangular box is used to represent a class graphically. The name of the class is written in a bold font at the top of the box. The way in which the properties of the objects of the class can be shown is described in the following sections. In many cases, however, it is sufficient simply to include the class name in the icon.

The individual objects, whose structure is described by means of a class, are known as the *instances* of the class. Alternatively, objects can be described as 'belonging to a class'. Every object is an instance of some class. This is an essential part of the object's definition and, among other things, determines what data will be stored in that object.

To emphasize the relationship between class and instances, UML represents objects with the same kind of icon as classes. The class name is preceded by a colon and underlined and, in addition, instances may be named. Figure 8.4 shows a 'Student' class and two of its instances.

The dashed line is known as a *dependency*, and is the notation used by UML to denote a unspecified sort of relationship between two model elements. The label, or *stereotype*, attached to the dependency gives an indication of what particular relationship is being depicted. In Figure 8.4, the 'instanceOf' dependency states that an object is an instance of a particular class.

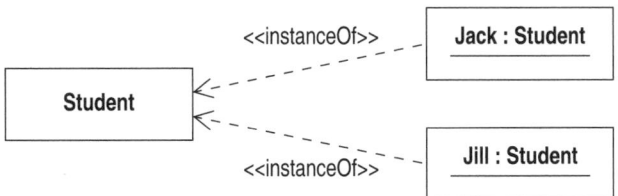

Figure 8.4 A class and its instances

The fact that an object is an instance of a particular class is already expressed by the use of the class name in the label of each object, however, so the notation shown in Figure 8.4 is rarely used. In fact, class and object icons do not in normal circumstances appear together on the same diagrams.

Class multiplicity

The concept of multiplicity can be applied to classes: the multiplicity of a class specifies the number of instances of the class that can exist at any one time. The default multiplicity for a class is 'zero or more', implying that there is no restriction on the number of instances that can be created. This default multiplicity does not need to be shown on a diagram.

In some cases, however, it is desirable to specify certain limitations on the number of instances that can exist at any given time when the system is running. To enable this, classes can contain a multiplicity annotation, in the top right-hand corner of the class icon. The most common use for this notation is to specify that a class is a *singleton* class, which can only have one instance. For example, a student record system might need to record certain information about the university itself and thus define a class in which to store this information. As the system is entirely internal to a single university, however, it would not make sense to have more than one instance of this class. This constraint is expressed in the class symbol shown in Figure 8.5.

Figure 8.5 A singleton class, showing class multiplicity

8.3 DESCRIBING OBJECTS WITH CLASSES

Every object contains certain pieces of data and a number of operations to process this data. All the objects of a given class contain the same data items, though with differing actual values, and the same operations. This common structure is defined by a number of *features* in the class to which the objects belong, including *attributes*, which describe the data items found in its instances, and *operations*.

Attributes

An attribute is a description of a data field that is maintained by each instance of a class. Attributes must be named. In addition to the name, other pieces of information can be supplied, such as the type of the data described by the attribute or a default initial value for the attribute. Attributes are shown in a separate compartment in the class icon, beneath the name. If the attribute type is shown, it is separated from the name by a colon and initial values follow an equals sign. In the early stages of design it is very common to show nothing more than the name of the attribute, however. The notation for attributes of a class is illustrated in Figure 8.6.

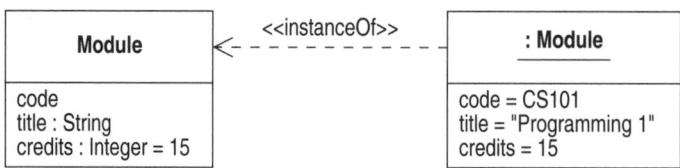

Figure 8.6 Attributes and attribute values

Figure 8.6 shows a class representing modules with attributes to model the code number, name and number of credit points of a module. An instance of the class is also shown, illustrating the way in which attribute values are specified in object icons. The first attribute, named 'code', represents the identifier used within the university to refer to the module. No type is specified for this attribute, indicating that no decision has yet been made about how to store this code as a concrete piece of data.

Data types can be used to show the types of attributes. Classes are not normally used as attribute types. For example, if a model had classes defined to represent students and modules, it might be tempting to show a module that a student is taking as an attribute within the student class with type 'module'. A better way to model this situation would be to use an association between the student and module classes, as described in Section 8.4.

The attributes shown in Figure 8.6 have *instance scope*, meaning that each instance of the class can store a distinct value for the attribute. Some data describes not individual instances, however, but the collection of all current instances. For example, we might want to record the total number of modules known to the system. One way of doing this is shown in Figure 8.7.

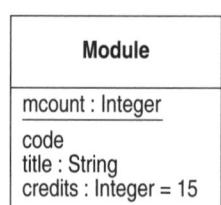

Figure 8.7 An attribute with class scope

An underlined attribute, such as 'mcount' in Figure 8.7 is said to have *class scope*. This means that there is a single copy of the attribute, which is accessible to all instances of the class. Attributes with class scope correspond to static, or class, variables in programming languages.

Attributes can also have an explicitly defined multiplicity. The default multiplicity for an attribute is 'exactly one', implying that each instance of the class stores exactly one value for each attribute. In some cases, this default is not appropriate, however. Suppose that the module class was extended with an attribute to record the date of an examination to be held at the end of the module. As some modules may not have such an examination, this attribute is optional in the sense that some instances of the class need not store a data value for it. This can be shown by adding a multiplicity specification after the attribute name, as shown in Figure 8.8.

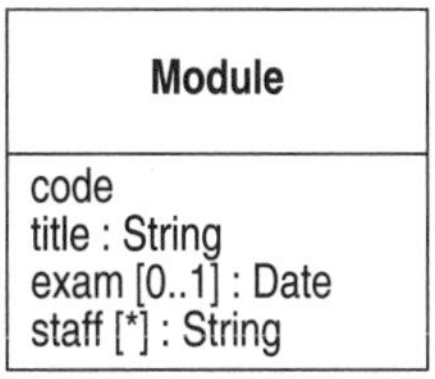

```
+--------------------------+
|          Module          |
+--------------------------+
| code                     |
| title : String           |
| exam [0..1] : Date        |
| staff [*] : String       |
+--------------------------+
```

Figure 8.8 Attribute multiplicity

Figure 8.8 also shows an attribute *staff* with a multiplicity of 'many', which is intended to store the names of the staff members involved in the delivery of the module. An attribute with a multiplicity greater than one is in many ways equivalent to an array, and this could also be specified directly by using a programming type.

Operations

As well as attributes, operations can be shown in class icons. These operations are those that are provided by every instance of the class; the module class, for example, might provide operations to set and retrieve the module title and to enrol a student on the module. Operations are shown in a separate compartment at the bottom of the class icon, as shown in Figure 8.9. Either or both of the attribute and operation compartments can be omitted from a class icon, and empty compartments are not shown.

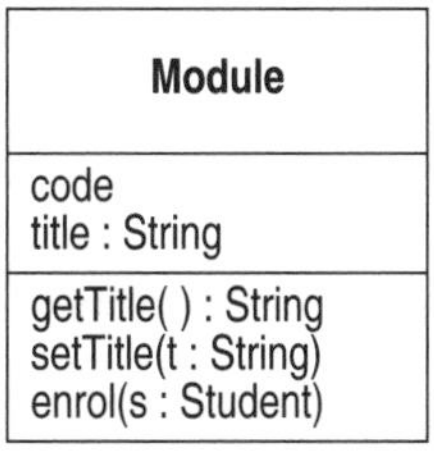

```
+--------------------------+
|          Module          |
+--------------------------+
| code                     |
| title : String           |
+--------------------------+
| getTitle( ) : String     |
| setTitle(t : String)     |
| enrol(s : Student)       |
+--------------------------+
```

Figure 8.9 A module class with attributes and operations

Operations are named and in addition can have arguments and return results, like functions in programming languages. The parameter and return types of operations can be either names of data types, as used for specifying attribute types, or names of classes. As with attributes, all the information apart from the operation's name is optional. As little or as much information can be provided as is appropriate at the stage that the development process has reached.

It is very common for operations to be omitted in class diagrams. The reason for this is that it is difficult to decide what operations a class should provide when the class is considered in isolation. The necessary operations are discovered by considering how the system's global behaviour is implemented by the network of objects making up the system. This analysis is performed when constructing the dynamic models of the system and only towards the end of the design process would it be possible to compile a complete definition of the operations of a class.

The operations in Figure 8.9 have instance scope. This means that they apply to individual instances of the class and can only be called once an instance has been created. Operations with class scope can also be defined; these operations can be called independently of any instance of the class, but as a result they only have access to attributes that also have class scope. Figure 8.10 shows an operation that returns the number of instances of the module class currently existing.

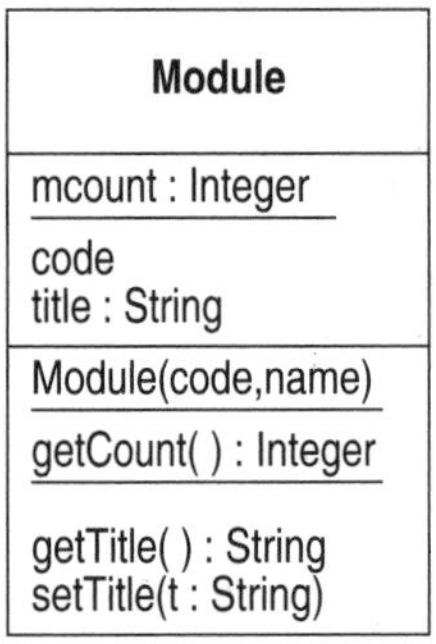

Module
mcount : Integer
code title : String
Module(code,name)
getCount( ) : Integer
getTitle( ) : String setTitle(t : String)

Figure 8.10 An operation with class scope

Constructors, the operations that create new instances of a class, also have class scope in UML, even though they have slightly different properties from other operations. A constructor is shown in Figure 8.10, following the common convention that the constructor has the same name as the class.

Identitifying objects

In Chapter 2, the notion of *object identity* was introduced as an essential part of the object model. An object's identity is an implicit property of the object, which distinguishes it from all other objects in the system. In an object-oriented programming language, an object's address in memory, which cannot be shared with any other object, is often used as an implementation of its identity.

Object identities are not represented by a UML data type, and therefore cannot be made explicit in a model. In particular, an object's identity is quite distinct from any of the attributes of the object. It is quite possible for two different objects to have the same values for all of their attributes, as shown in Figure 8.11, and yet still be distinct objects, distinguishable by their different identities.

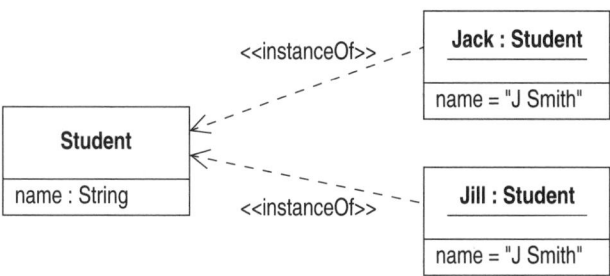

Figure 8.11 Distinct objects with equal state

Within a model, object identities can be represented textually by an 'object name' prefixed to the class of the object, such as 'Jack' and 'Jill' in Figure 8.11. Object names are quite distinct from any attributes the object may have, however.

In many cases, of course, objects do have identifying attributes. Students, for example, may have unique identification numbers that are allocated when they enrol for a course. The identification number is a real world piece of data, printed on a student's ID card. It is therefore quite appropriate for it to be included in the model as an attribute of the student class, as shown in Figure 8.12. Such attributes do not replace identities, however: each instance of the 'Student' class will have both an identity and an explicit id number. Also, notice that this diagram does not make it explicit that every instance of the class should have a distinct identification number.

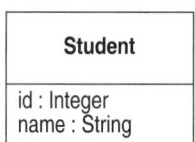

Figure 8.12 A class with an identifying attribute

Visibility of features

Each feature in a class can have a *visibility* associated with it, which specifies the extent to which the feature is available to other classes. Unless method bodies are being defined, the notion of visibility has little application in a design language. The notation does allow the corresponding properties of a programming language class to be defined explicitly, however, and the meaning of the UML visibility symbols is essentially derived from the equivalent notations in languages such as Java and C++.

UML defines four levels of visibility, namely *public*, *protected*, *private* and *package*. Private features can only be used in the class owning the feature, protected features can also be used in descendents of the owning class and public features can be used in any class. Features with package visibility can be used by other classes within the same package as the owning class.

Visibility is denoted graphically by a symbol before the feature name, as shown for example in Figure 2.1. Public visibility is denoted by '+', protected by '#', private by '-' and package by '~'. The UML specification gives tools the freedom to define their own symbols to represent visibilities. There are no default values defined for visibilities, so if they are not shown on a class they are assumed to be undefined. A common rule of thumb, however, is to assume that attributes are private, or protected if they are to be used in descendent classes, and that operations are public.

8.4 ASSOCIATIONS

The previous section explained how the different kinds of objects found in a system can be described by classes. The other major structural feature of object diagrams is the existence of links between objects. In the same way that similar objects are grouped together and described by a single class, related links are described by a single construct, known as an *association*.

A link between two objects models some sort of connection between the linked objects, such as a student taking a particular module. Normally, the idea expressed by a link can be described as a more general relationship between the classes involved. In this case, the relationship is that it is possible for students to take modules. It is this more abstract relationship that is modelled by an association.

An association therefore involves a number of classes and models a relationship between the classes. Associations are represented in UML as lines joining the related classes. For example, Figure 8.13 shows an association modelling the fact that companies employ people.

Figure 8.13 An association modelling employment

The association is labelled with a name, 'WorksFor', which is shown near the middle of the association. Association names are often chosen so that, when taken in conjunction with the names of the related classes, something approaching a sensible English sentence describing the association is produced. In this case, the association represents the fact that people work for companies.

The small triangle next to the association name indicates the direction in which this sentence should be read. It is necessary in this case because the inverse association, that companies work for people, is a sensible, but quite distinct, relationship and it is necessary to distinguish the two.

Links

The existence of an association between two classes indicates that instances of the classes can be linked at run-time. Figure 8.14 shows an example of a link specified by the association in Figure 8.13. Links can be labelled with the relevant association name, underlined to emphasize that the link is an instance of the association.

Figure 8.14 An instance of the employment relationship

Properties of association ends

Apart from its name, most of the information about an association is defined at its ends, where it meets a class. Each association end can be labelled with a *role name*. Role names are chosen to describe the objects at one end of an association as seen from the perspective of the other end. For example, a person working for a company would naturally describe the company as their employer, and this would be a suitable role name for the 'Company' end of the association. Similarly, the other end could be labelled with the role name 'employee'.

Each end of an association can also be given a multiplicity. This multiplicity specifies how many objects an instance of the class at the other end of the association can be linked to. Figure 8.15 shows the 'WorksFor' association with role names and multiplicity annotations added. The diagram specifies that a person works for exactly one company and that a company can have zero or more employees.

Figure 8.15 Annotation of association ends

As this example suggests, multiplicity annotations can be read in conjunction with role names, or with the names of associated classes, to give a fuller description of the relationship being modelled by the association. The precise meaning of multiplicity annotations, however, is to do with the number of links that can exist at a given time.

For example, the association in Figure 8.15 specifies that any given instance of the Person class must be linked to exactly one instance of the Company class. It follows that the situation shown in Figure 8.16 is illegal on two counts: first, because the object representing Jack is simultaneously linked to two company objects and, second, because the object representing Jill is not linked to any company object.

The diagram in Figure 8.15 also asserts that a company object must be linked to zero or more person objects. In fact, this places no restriction at all on the number of links a company object can have.

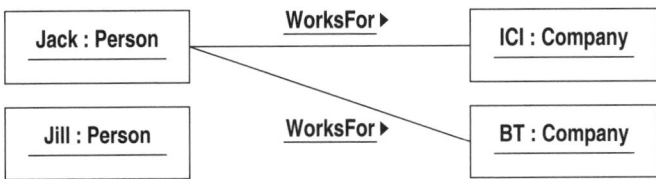

Figure 8.16 Violations of the multiplicity specification

There are many similarities between the attributes of a class and the far ends of the associations connected to it. For example, both a person's name and the company they work for are pieces of data about that person that a system may have to record, and it is natural to view both as being properties of that person. In UML it is customary to model a property whose values belong to a data type as an attribute and one whose values are instances of another class as an association, but this should not obscure the commonalities between the two notions.

A further similarity is that association ends, like attributes, can have visibility annotations attached to them, written before the role names. The visibility symbols and their meanings are the same as those defined for attributes. Association ends can also be defined to be of class scope, if necessary.

Navigability

The idea of navigability was introduced in Chapter 2, where it was used to record the fact that certain links in the system could only be traversed, or messages sent, in one direction. This was shown by means of arrowheads on the links, and the same arrowheads are used on the corresponding association.

An association with no arrowheads, such as the one in Figure 8.13, is normally assumed to be navigable in both directions. (Notice that the triangle defining the direction in which the association name should be read has nothing to do with navigability, which is defined by arrowheads on the association itself.) If it was subsequently decided that there was no need for employee objects to explicitly store a reference to the related company object, say, the association might be redefined to be navigable in only one direction, as shown in Figure 8.17.

Figure 8.17 An association navigable in one direction only

This does not change the meaning of the association: the system still relates employee objects to the companies they work for. It does imply, however, that it will not necessarily be straightforward to find out which company a given person works for, and also that messages cannot be sent directly from a person to a company using instances of this association.

Different types of association

The general UML notation allows an association to connect any number of classes, as discussed in Section 8.10. In practice, however, the majority of associations used are *binary*, connecting only two classes. In principle, any situation can be modelled using only binary associations, and binary associations are more easily understood and implemented in conventional programming languages than those involving larger numbers of classes.

Binary associations often connect two different classes, but there are also many situations where objects can be linked to other objects of the same class. These situations are modelled by using a *self-association*, a binary association of which both ends are attached to the same class. Figure 8.18 shows an example of a self-association on the 'Person' class and some possible links derived from it. A link between two objects represents the fact that one person is the manager of the other.

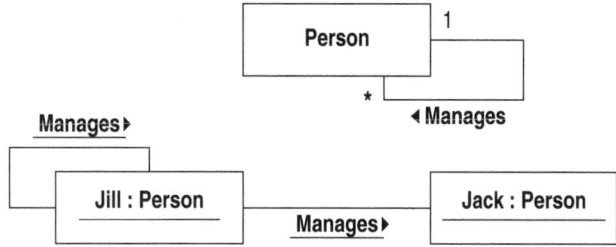

Figure 8.18 A self-association on a class

The 'Manages' association states that every person has exactly one manager. This includes the possibility of certain people, like Jill in Figure 8.18, being their own manager. In general, a self-association leaves open the possibility of objects being linked to themselves. If this does not make sense for a particular association, it can be ruled out using an explicit constraint.

Labelling associations

In general, multiplicity information should be shown on associations, but association names and role names are optional. The designer can choose the level of detail necessary to make a diagram easily comprehensible.

One situation where some textual labelling is required is where there is more than one association between the same pair of classes. In this case, labels are required to clarify the associations, and to ensure that the correct multiplicity is understood for each association. Figure 8.19 shows an additional association between the person and company classes, showing that people can be customers as well as employees of companies. Notice how the designer here has made the decision that one role name is sufficient labelling to make the meaning of each association clear.

Role names are also very helpful in distinguishing between the two ends of a self-association, as shown in Figure 8.20.

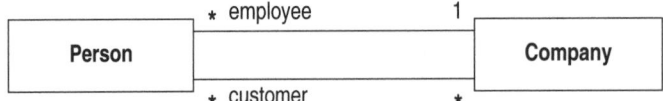

Figure 8.19 Distinguishing between pairs of associations

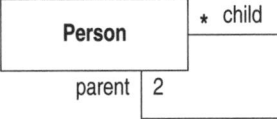

Figure 8.20 Distinguishing the ends of a self-association

Reifying associations

Consider the association 'WorksFor' as defined in Figure 8.15 and suppose that a person is employed twice by the same company, in two different roles. An object diagram attempting to show this situation is given in Figure 8.21: perhaps Jill is employed as a lecturer during the day, for example, but has to work as a part-time bar attendant in the evenings to make ends meet.

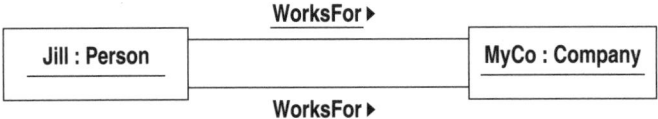

Figure 8.21 Being employed by the same company twice

It is not obvious whether the situation depicted in this object diagram is actually permitted by the 'WorksFor' association. The multiplicity of the association states that Jill can only work for one company, but it could be argued that the diagram in Figure 8.21 preserves this property. Jill may have two contracts, but they are with the same company, 'MyCo', so technically she only works for one company. On the other hand, Jill possesses two 'WorksFor' links: this seems to allow for the possibility of working for more than one company, even though in this particular case both links shown are to the same object. This might suggest that the situation depicted is only accidentally consistent with the multiplicity in Figure 8.15, and hence that the situation depicted is illegal.

The answer depends on exactly how UML defines links. Links are normally understood to be simple *tuples* of objects, like a set of co-ordinates or a line in a relational database table. In the case of a binary association, this means that a link is nothing more than the pair of objects connected by the link, such as the pair '(Jill, MyCo)'. This further implies that the two links in Figure 8.21 are identical, because they link the same pair of objects, and so the diagram could not be used to record two different contracts of employment. If this was the intention of the diagram, it is at best misleading, as it suggests that there are two distinct links between the objects.

Links, then, do nothing more than record whether or not a particular relationship holds between two objects. There cannot be two links that are instances of the same association linking the same pair of objects, and some other way must be found of modelling situations like the one in Figure 8.21.

We need a way of telling the two links apart, even though they share the same properties. This would be possible if links had identity, like objects, but tuples are simply identified by their components and so have no identity as such.

One solution, however, is to replace the links by objects, which do have identity. To do this, we need to come up with a plausible class whose instances correspond one-to-one with the links we wish to depict. For example, Jill might sign different contracts for each of her jobs. If this was so, a class representing contracts could replace the simple 'WorksFor' relationship, as shown in Figure 8.22.

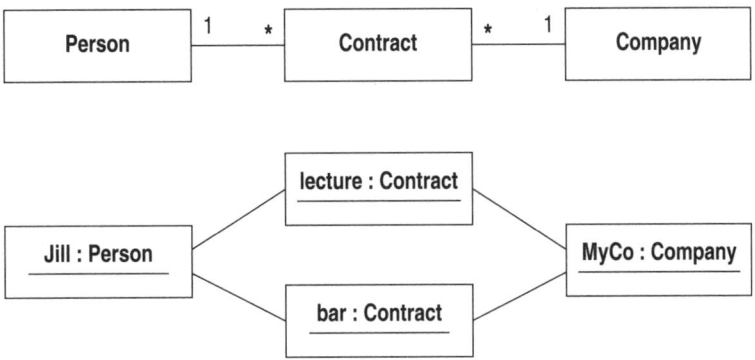

Figure 8.22 Resolving multiple links with an intermediate class

The term *reification* is sometimes used to refer to this technique of replacing an association with a class. As well as allowing multiple links, the technique allows information about the relationship, such as the salary paid on a particular contract, to be stored as attributes of the new intermediate class.

Reification can change the meaning of a model, however. In the new model a person can hold multiple contracts, but there is nothing to prevent those contracts being with two or more distinct companies. This situation was not permitted with the original 'WorksFor' relationship, which only allowed a person to work for a single company. The restriction could be conveyed by adding an explicit constraint to Figure 8.22, as explained in Chapter 12.

Reification is often used in database design to remove many-to-many relationships from models. For each many-to-many relationship a new link class is introduced and the many-to-many relationship replaced by two one-to-many relationships, as in the transition from Figure 8.15 to Figure 8.22. There is no particular requirement to remove many-to-many relationships in UML, however, and reification is normally carried out only when it is necessary to produce a more accurate model.

8.5 GENERALIZATION AND SPECIALIZATION

It is very common for an application to contain a number of classes that are closely related. Either the classes may share a number of properties and relationships or it may seem natural to think of them as representing different varieties of the same thing. For example, consider a bank that offers its customers a variety of accounts including current accounts, deposit accounts and an online account. One important aspect of the bank's operations is the fact that a customer can hold a number of accounts, which may be of different types. A class diagram modelling this is given in Figure 8.23.

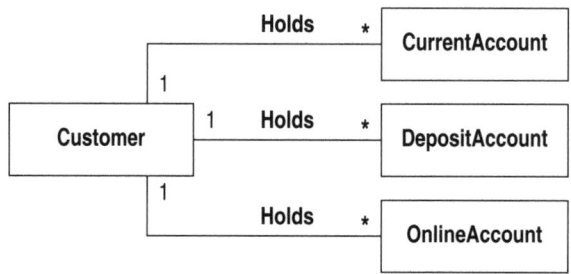

Figure 8.23 A class diagram modelling bank accounts

There are a couple of significant problems with this model, however. First, there are too many associations in the model. From a customer's point of view, holding an account is a simple relationship, which is not significantly affected by the fact that different kinds of account can be held. Figure 8.23, however, models this with three distinct associations, thus destroying the conceptual simplicity of the model. Worse still, if a new type of account were added, a new association would also have to be added to the model to allow customers to hold accounts of the new type.

Second, the different kinds of account are modelled as completely separate classes. Nonetheless, they will probably have a large amount of common structure, as they are likely to define many similar attributes and operations. It would be highly desirable if our modelling notation could provide a way of explicitly showing this common structure.

These problems can be overcome by making use of the notion of *generalization*. This concept is provided by all object-oriented design notations and is intimately related to the programming language concept of inheritance. Use of generalization will permit the model shown in Figure 8.23 to be redrawn in such a way as to meet both the objections discussed above.

Intuitively, what is going on in this example is that we have a general notion of what an account is and what is involved in holding an account. In addition to this, we can imagine a range of different kinds of accounts like the ones listed above, which, despite their differences, share a significant amount of functionality. We can formalize this latter intuition, by defining a general 'Account' class to model the things that accounts of all kinds have in common, and then show the classes representing particular types of accounts as *specializations* of this general class.

Generalization is therefore a relationship between classes, in which one class is identified as a general class and a number of others as special cases of it. Figure 8.24 shows a general 'Account' class together with the three classes representing the specialized types of account mentioned in Figure 8.23. Generalization is represented by an arrow pointing from a specialized class to the general class. If there are many specialized classes, a separate arrow can be drawn from each; alternatively, they can be merged into a single arrow with multiple 'tails', as in Figure 8.24.

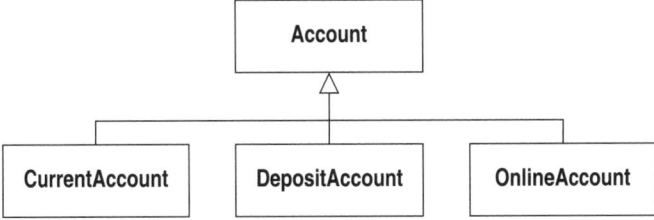

Figure 8.24 Bank account classes using generalization

The more general class is referred to as the *superclass* and the specialized classes as its *subclasses*. The term 'generalization' implies a perspective where one is moving from subclass to superclass, trying to create a more general class to represent some common features of a set of classes. Moving in the other direction, it is sometimes more natural to think of creating a set of subclasses reflecting special cases of a class. This process is known as *specialization* and this is sometimes used as an alternative name for the generalization relationship.

Generalization is purely a relationship between classes and does not specify any sort of link or relationship between instances of those classes. Role names, multiplicities and visibility symbols are therefore not applicable to generalizations. The only label that can be attached to a generalization relationship is a *discriminator*, which describes the property that distinguishes the various subclasses. A possible discriminator for the generalization in Figure 8.24 might be the rather uninformative 'account type'. Discriminators are rarely used in simple cases of generalization, however, where they add little to the information conveyed by the diagram.

The meaning of generalization

A common account of the meaning of generalization is that it represents a classification relationship between classes, and in particular the relationship expressed by the phrase 'is a kind of'. So the fact that we can correctly say, for example, that 'a current account is a kind of account' indicates that the classes are appropriately linked by a generalization relationship, as in Figure 8.24.

This definition gives a rather informal explanation of generalization, however, based on properties of the real-world entities being modelled. It suggests when it might be appropriate to use generalization in modelling, but a more precise account is needed of what generalization means when it is used in a model.

Within UML, generalization is explained by the notion of *substitutability*. This means that in any context where an instance of a superclass is expected, an instance of a subclass can be substituted for it without any problems. We can make use of substitutability to simplify the diagram in Figure 8.23, replacing the three associations by one, as shown in Figure 8.25. Intuitively, this diagram states that customers can hold any number of accounts, and also that those accounts can be of a variety of different types, as defined by the subclasses.

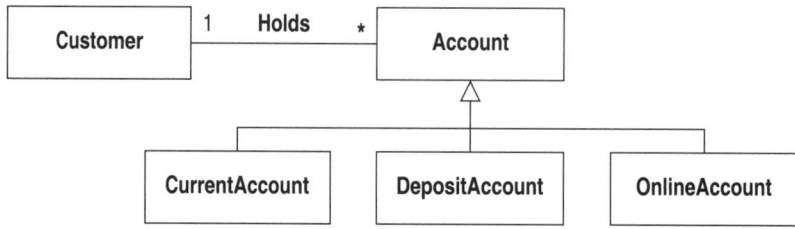

Figure 8.25 A single relationship of 'holding an account'

This works as follows. The association in Figure 8.25 implies that instances of the 'Customer' and 'Account' classes can be linked at run-time. Because of substitutability, the 'Account' instance in any of these links can be replaced by an instance of any of the subclasses of 'Account'. This process of substitution might lead to links such as those shown in Figure 8.26, where customers are linked to the various accounts that they actually hold.

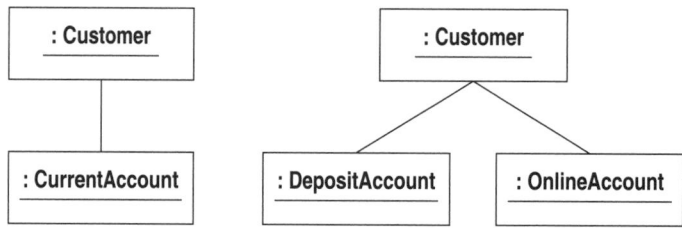

Figure 8.26 Holding a variety of accounts

Comparing Figures 8.25 and 8.26, it is apparent that in some circumstances it is possible for two objects to be linked, even though there is not an association connecting precisely the two classes that they belong to. This is possible provided that there is an association connected to superclasses of the linked objects. In other words, the link between the customer and current account objects in Figure 8.26 is an instance of the association between the customer and account classes in Figure 8.25.

This phenomenon is one form of *polymorphism*. Polymorphism means 'many forms' or 'many shapes', and is a pervasive feature of object-oriented programming languages. In this case, the 'many forms' referred to are the various subclasses of the account class.

Abstract classes

Superclasses are often introduced into a model to define the shared features of a number of related classes. Their role is to permit the overall simplification of a model, through use of the principle of substitutability, rather than to define an entirely new concept. As a result, it is not uncommon for there to be no need to create instances of the root class of a hierarchy, as all the objects required can be more precisely described as instances of one of the subclasses.

The account hierarchy provides an example of this. It is likely that in a banking system, every account must be either a current account, a deposit account or one of the other specialized types of account. This means that there are no instances of the root account class, or more precisely, that no instances of the 'Account' class should be created when the system is running.

A class, such as 'Account', which has no instances of its own is called an *abstract class*. Abstract classes are denoted in UML by writing the class name in a sloping typeface, as shown in Figure 8.27.

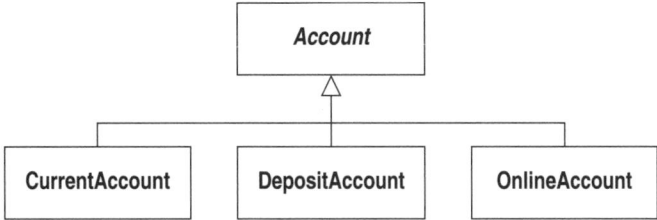

Figure 8.27 The account hierarchy with an abstract root class

It should not be thought that abstract classes, because they have no instances, are redundant and can be removed from class diagrams. The role of an abstract class, or of a root class in a hierarchy generally, is to define the common features of all its descendants. This can contribute significantly to the production of clear and well-structured class diagrams. Also, root classes define a common interface to all classes in a hierarchy, and use of this common interface can greatly simplify the programming of client modules. Abstract classes can provide these benefits just as well as concrete classes with instances.

Generalization hierarchies

If required, specialization can be carried out to more than one level. Figure 8.28 shows an example of this where the bank has introduced two distinct types of current account: a personal account for individual customers and a business account for companies. As a result, undifferentiated current accounts are no longer available and so this class has been redefined to be abstract. The three dots in the diagram are called an *ellipsis*, and they indicate that there may be other subclasses in addition to those shown, in this case the online account class shown earlier.

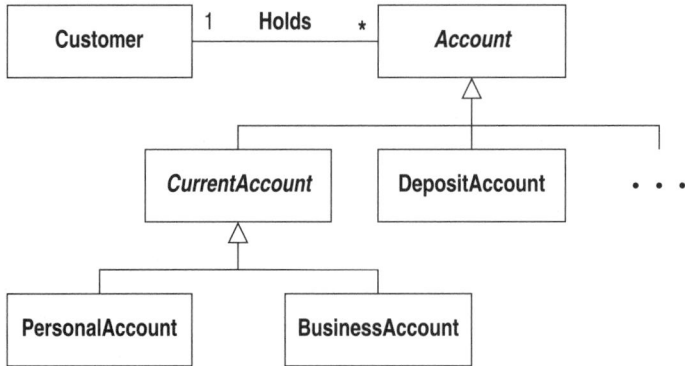

Figure 8.28 A generalization hierarchy

In Figure 8.28 the current account class is a subclass of 'Account', but a superclass of 'PersonalAccount'. The terms 'subclass' and 'superclass' are therefore relative terms, describing the role a class plays within a particular generalization relationship, rather than any intrinsic property of the class itself.

Such a hierarchy can be developed to as many levels as required. The *ancestors* of a class in the hierarchy are all the classes found by traversing the hierarchy towards the top. Its *descendants* are those found by going downward in the hierarchy from the class. 'Up' and 'down' here mean 'towards more general classes' and 'towards more specialized classes' respectively. Although hierarchies are often drawn so that general classes come above their subclasses, there is nothing in the notation that demands this. The superclass is always the one pointed to by the generalization relationship.

Substitutability applies to all descendent classes, not just to immediate subclasses. A customer holding an account could, consistently with Figure 8.28, hold a personal account and a deposit account, as both these classes are descendents of the top-level account class. This means that when new subclasses are added to the hierarchy, they immediately become available for use with the 'Holds' association. This would not have been the case with the original model in Figure 8.23, where a new account class would also have required the definition of a new association.

This ability to add functionality in new subclasses and to make it available without requiring that other parts of the system be modified is one of the great strengths of the object-oriented approach to program design. The principle of substitutability, as expressed by generalization in UML, is what makes it possible.

8.6 INHERITANCE OF ATTRIBUTES AND OPERATIONS

A consequence of the principle of substitutability is that an instance of a class must have all the properties specified by its ancestor classes. If this was not the case, an attempt to make use of one of the missing properties would fail and the object could not be substituted for a superclass object.

Inheritance is the process by which properties of a class are automatically defined for all descendent classes. In the previous section, the property of interest was the ability to participate in links specified by a given association. Other properties of classes include the possession of various attributes and operations, and these are inherited by subclasses in much the same way as in object-oriented programming languages.

More precisely, all the attributes and operations defined in the ancestors of a class are also features of the class itself. This provides the means whereby common features shared by a number of classes can be defined in one place and yet made available in a number of different classes. To illustrate inheritance, Figure 8.29 shows part of the account hierarchy with attributes and operations added.

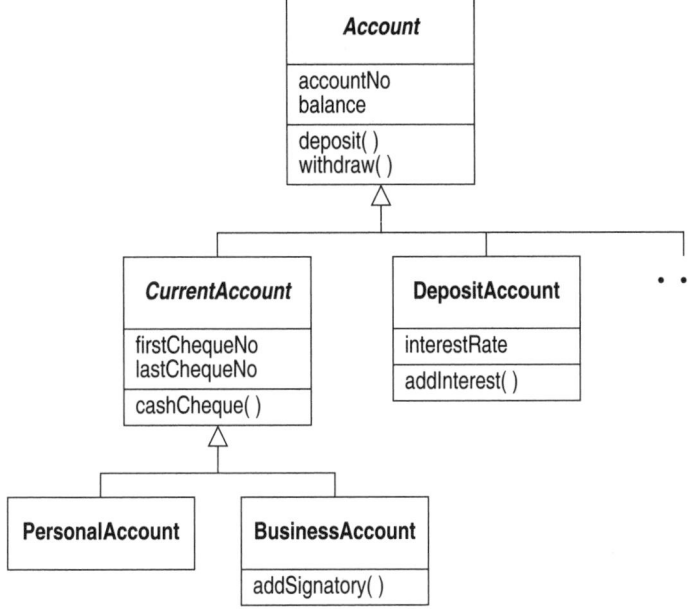

Figure 8.29 Account hierarchy with inheritance

This diagram states that all accounts have account number and balance attributes, and operations to deposit and withdraw amounts of money. These features are defined in the root class 'Account', but as a result of inheritance are implicitly present in every other class in the hierarchy.

Inheritance, therefore, means that features shared by more than one class do not have to be written out in full in each class, but can be moved up the hierarchy to the appropriate superclass. In general, this has the effect of avoiding repetition and making hierarchies clearer and easier to read.

Notice that in many programming languages, the term 'inheritance' is used to refer to the relationship between classes known as 'generalization' in UML. UML reserves the term for the specific mechanism described above, which is a consequence of the use of generalization.

Adding features in subclasses

Subclasses are often distinguished from their superclass by the fact that they need to define additional features supporting their own particular specialized behaviour. For example, suppose that current accounts provide a cheque book facility. To implement this, instances of the current account class keep a record of the range of cheque numbers that have been issued for a given account. In addition, an operation is provided to draw a cheque against the account.

Business accounts are a further specialization of current accounts, distinguished by the fact that they are held by companies rather than by individuals. For a business account, it may be necessary to record the signatories of the account, namely the people who are permitted to sign cheques, and an operation is provided to add a new signatory to an account.

Additional attributes and operations supporting these requirements are shown in Figure 8.29. The full list of features defined for any class can be obtained by combining the inherited features with those defined in the class itself. For example, the attributes of the business account class are 'accountNo', 'balance', 'firstChequeNo', and 'lastChequeNo', and the operations supported by the class are 'deposit', 'withdraw', 'cashCheque' and 'addSignatory'.

Overriding operations in subclasses

The examples above have shown how, in the context of an inheritance hierarchy, a class can be defined by specifying the new attributes and operations that it requires in addition to those inherited from its ancestors. It frequently happens, however, that instead of simply adding a new operation, a class requires a modified version of an operation that it has inherited.

For example, suppose that whenever a deposit or a withdrawal is made from an online account an email message is sent to the account holder to confirm the details of the transaction. To implement this, the online account class will have to redefine the deposit and withdraw operations to include this new functionality. Figure 8.30 shows the overriding of these two operations, together with the attribute storing the customer's email address.

When a class provides a redefinition of an inherited operation, it is said to *override* the inherited feature. Overriding is indicated by simply writing the name of the overridden operation in the subclass that redefines it, as shown in the online account class in Figure 8.30. Notice that it is not necessary to do this simply to indicate that a feature is inherited from a superclass.

Abstract operations

Some abstract classes include operations for which an implementation cannot be given at that point in the hierarchy. For example, a classic example of generalization is shown in Figure 8.31. This hierarchy represents various shapes that might be defined in a graphics system.

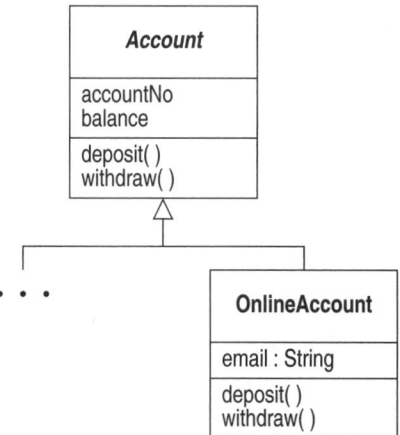

Figure 8.30 Partial account hierarchy, overriding the 'deposit' and 'withdraw' operations

The root class 'Shape' will define properties common to all shapes, such as a position, and also the operations that all shapes must provide, such as an operation to draw the shape. 'Shape' is an abstract class, however, as it is impossible to have a shape that is not either a triangle, a circle or some other specific kind of shape. Furthermore, it is impossible to give an implementation of a general draw operation for shapes. Each subclass needs to define this operation for itself, by invoking the appropriate graphics primitives. Nevertheless, the draw operation should be part of the shape class, to indicate that it is provided by all descendants of 'Shape'. To indicate that it is unimplementable, it is written in a sloping font, as shown in Figure 8.31.

Such an operation is known as an *abstract operation* and any class containing an abstract operation must be an abstract class. An abstract operation must be overridden in descendant classes by a non-abstract operation, as shown in Figure 8.31. Any class that does not either contain or inherit an operation which overrides an inherited abstract operation is itself an abstract class.

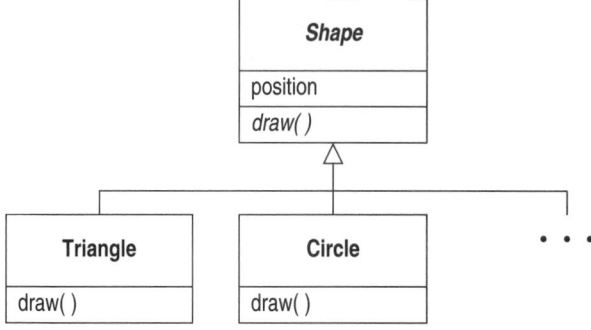

Figure 8.31 Hierarchy of shapes, with abstract class and abstract operation

8.7 AGGREGATION

Associations can be used to model any sort of relationship between objects, and the name of the association gives information about precisely what relationship is being modelled. UML singles out one particular relationship for special treatment, however, namely the 'part of' relationship that holds between objects when one is a part of another or, inversely, when an object consists of a collection of other objects.

Aggregation is the term used in UML for this relationship. An aggregation is simply a special case of an association, symbolized by adding a diamond to the association end next to the class representing the object that 'contains' the objects at the other end. Figure 8.32 shows a typical example of aggregation, in which the parts of an electronic mail message are defined to be a header, a body and number of attachments.

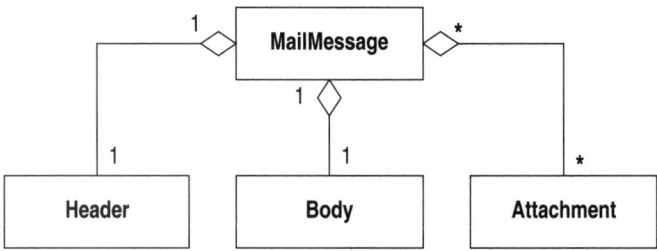

Figure 8.32 An example of aggregation

As Figure 8.32 shows, multiplicity annotations can be used on aggregation relationships in exactly the same way as on normal associations. As well as indicating the different number of headers, bodies and attachments in a single message, the multiplicities specified in Figure 8.32 also show that, unlike headers and bodies, an attachment can be a part of more than one message simultaneously.

The meaning of aggregation

In cases like this, the use of aggregation achieves little more than suggesting informally that objects of one kind form part of objects of another kind, in some sense. It imposes no constraints on a model in addition to those already implied by the use of an association and, if there is any doubt about the applicability of aggregation, a good rule is simply to leave it out.

One case where aggregation does have a useful role to play is if the objects in a system are arranged, at run-time, in a hierarchical manner. An example of this was given in the stock control system discussed in Chapter 2. In that system, a general notion of a component was defined: a component could be either a single part or an assembly consisting of a number of subcomponents. The class diagram in Figure 2.12 defined the relationships between these classes. However, object structures such as the ones shown in Figure 8.33, where all the links are instances of the 'Contains' association, are perfectly legal instances of the model of Figure 2.12.

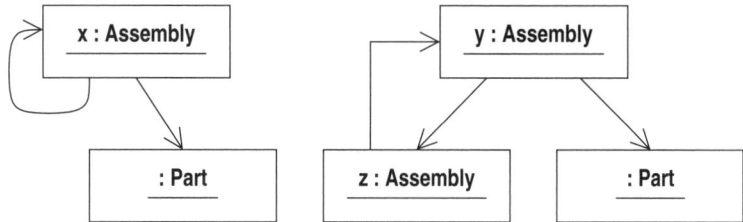

Figure 8.33 Cyclical object structures

The problem with the object structures shown in Figure 8.33 is that they show an assembly that is a part of itself, directly or indirectly. This is not a meaningful notion when applied to physical objects such as parts and assemblies, and it also means that any operation that traverses the part hierarchy will loop. These problems can be removed by the use of aggregation, as shown in Figure 8.34, which adds an aggregation symbol to the association originally defined in Figure 2.12.

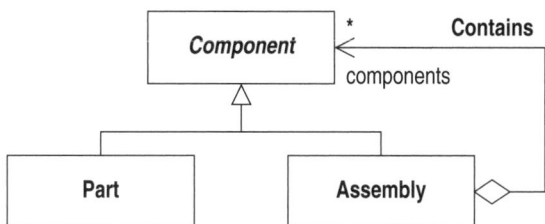

Figure 8.34 Specifying acyclic structures

Aggregation has two formal properties which mean that the object structures in Figure 8.33 are not legal instances of the class diagram in Figure 8.34. The first property is *antisymmetry*, which simply means that a link which is an instance of an aggregation cannot be used to link an object to itself. This rules out the first situation shown in Figure 8.33 where the assembly named 'x' is linked to itself.

The second property is *transitivity*: this is based on the observation that if A is a part of B and B is a part of C, then A is also a part of C. More formally, if object A is linked to B and B to C by links that are instances of the same aggregation, then A should also be thought of as linked to C.

These properties of aggregation work together in the following way to rule out the second possibility shown in Figure 8.33. As 'y' is linked to 'z', and 'z' to 'y' (by a different link), the property of transitivity implies that 'y' should be thought of as being linked to itself. However, this is ruled out by antisymmetry so the configuration depicted cannot be a legal state of the system.

Aggregation therefore has a useful role to play in specifying that legal states of a system should not include cyclical object structures. However, these formal properties of aggregation do not necessarily have anything to do with the intuitive idea of a relationship between wholes and parts.

For example, the ancestor relationship has the properties of transitivity and antisymmetry: one's ancestors' ancestors are also one's own ancestors, and nobody can be one of their own ancestors. These constraints could be documented by using aggregation, as shown in Figure 8.35, but the informal reading of this, suggesting that people are parts of their ancestors, makes little sense.

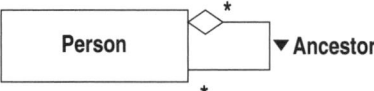

Figure 8.35 The applicability of aggregation

It should be noted that the properties of antisymmetry and transitivity described above only apply in cases where the aggregation enables objects to be linked to instances of their own class. This will happen when the aggregation is a self-association, like the ancestor relation, or where a generalization enables recursive object structures to be created, as with assemblies. In cases of whole–part relationships between different classes, such as those illustrated in Figure 8.32, aggregation specifies little more than a straightforward association would.

8.8 COMPOSITION

Composition is a strong form of aggregation in which the 'part' objects are dependent on the 'whole' objects. This dependency manifests itself in two ways. First, a 'part' object can only belong to one composite at a time and, second, when a composite object is destroyed, all its dependent parts must be destroyed at the same time.

In the example of the email message given in Figure 8.32, it might be reasonable to model the relationships between a message and its header and body as composition relationships, as it is likely that neither a header nor a body exist once a message has been deleted, and while they exist they belong to a single message. As shown in Figure 8.36, the notation for composition is similar to that for aggregation, except that the diamond at the 'whole' end of the relationship is solid.

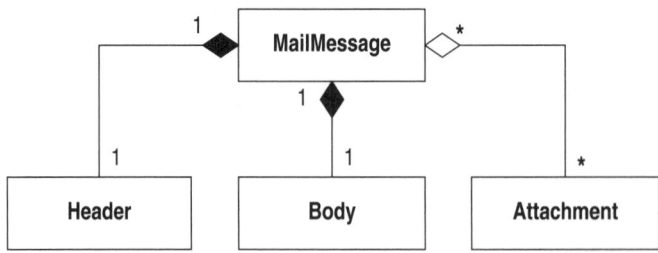

Figure 8.36 The use of composition

The relationship between a message and its attachments is unlikely to be correctly modelled using composition, however. First, it may be that an attachment can belong to more than one message at the same time and, second, it is likely that attachments can be saved, and therefore that they will have a lifetime that exceeds that of the message to which they are attached.

This basic notion of composition is not strong enough to enforce certain natural properties of composite objects, however. For example, consider the class diagram in Figure 8.37, which gives a simple model of certain aspects of a computer. It states that a computer is a composition of a processor and a number of ports, and that the ports must be connected to a processor, but it does not specify the natural constraint that a port and a processor that are connected together must belong to the same computer. An instance diagram showing a port as a part of one computer, but linked to the processor of another, would be a legal instance of this class diagram.

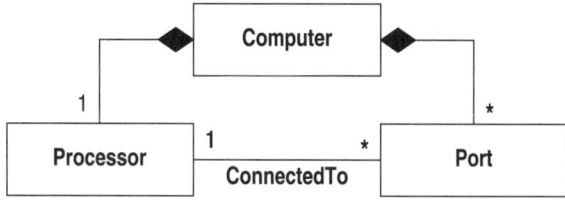

Figure 8.37 The structure of a computer

To model this situation more accurately, we need a way of stating that the association between ports and processors should be included in the composition, so that only objects belonging to the same composite can be linked. This can be depicted by using an alternative graphical notation for composition, which places the classes and associations that form part of the composite inside the class icon for the computer, as shown in Figure 8.38. Notice that the multiplicities that were associated with the composition relationships in Figure 8.37 are now shown as class multiplicities on the nested classes.

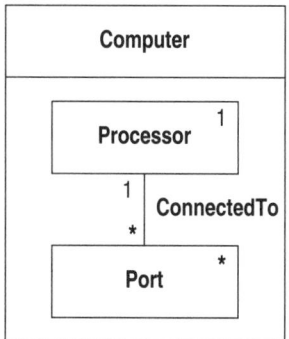 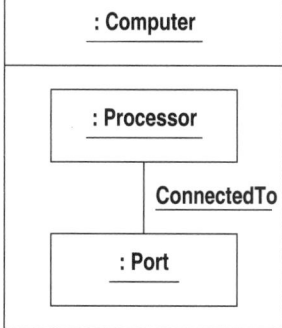

Figure 8.38 The computer as a composite object

Figure 8.38 also shows an instance of the computer, as a *composite object*: by physically including the 'ConnectedTo' link in the object, the diagram makes the constraint that port and processor must belong to the same computer visually clear.

In Figure 8.38, the classes and association that make up the parts of the composite object are shown in the compartment of the class icon that normally contains attributes. Attribute values share with the parts of composites the properties that they can only belong to one object at a time and are destroyed when that object is destroyed; they can almost be considered as a special case of composition.

There are of course cases where it is desirable to link parts of different composites. For example, consider a number of computers linked together into a network. The physical linkage might be accomplished by connecting pairs of ports, and this could be modelled by means of an association on the port class in the class diagram.

If this association were drawn entirely within the 'Computer' composite object box, however, this would imply that ports could only be connected if they belonged to the same computer. If we are trying to model a network, however, this is clearly not what we want, as the whole point of the model is to show links between different computers. To show this possibility, the association for linking ports has to be drawn in such a way that it passes outside the composite object box, as shown in Figure 8.39. This means that the ports linked by the instances of the association can belong to different composite objects, as required.

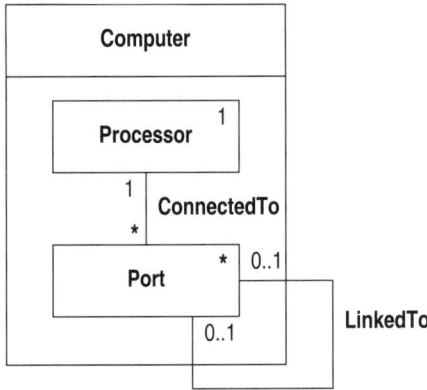

Figure 8.39 Connecting computers together

8.9 ASSOCIATION CLASSES

Attributes describe properties of the instances of a class. A student class might have an attribute 'name', for example, and then every student object would contain a data value giving the name of the student. Sometimes, however, it is necessary to record information that seems to be more naturally associated with the link between two objects than with either of the objects considered individually.

Consider, for example, the association between students and the modules they take shown in Figure 8.40 and assume that the system needs to record all the marks gained by students on all the modules that they are taking. The class diagram notation introduced so far does not enable us to model this situation very easily.

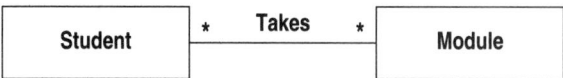

Figure 8.40 A simple model for recording exam results

It is not sufficient to add a 'mark' attribute to the student class, as students in general take many modules and therefore it will be necessary to record more than one mark for each student. An attribute that allowed a set of marks to be stored would get round this problem, but would not preserve the information about which mark was gained for which module. This problem in turn might be addressed by associating with each mark some kind of module identifier. This would be a poor idea, however, as it would duplicate some of the information modelled by the existing association and, by storing module data in the student object, introduce potential problems of consistency.

Because each module can be taken by many students, the same problems arise if we consider storing the marks that students receive for a module in the module object itself. It therefore appears that students' marks cannot naturally be stored in either of the classes in this model.

One possible approach to this problem is to consider associating data with the link between two objects rather than with either of the individual objects. Intuitively this is an attractive proposal: students only get marks when they take modules, and this is precisely the relationship modelled by the links.

Association classes provide a means of associating data values with links. An association class is a single model element in UML, one which has all the properties of both an association and a class. In particular, an association class can, like an association, connect two classes and yet at the same time have attributes, like a class, to store data belonging specifically to the link.

Figure 8.41 shows an association class enabling the mark a student receives for a module to be stored. This replaces the association 'Takes' defined in Figure 8.40. The association class is shown as an association and a class icon, linked by a dashed line. Both components must have the same name, which, to remove the redundancy, need not be shown on both. The choice of whether to label the association class with a verb, in the style of an association, or with a noun, in the style of a class, is left to the discretion of the designer, but will often depend on whether the label is written in the class icon, or near the association.

Association classes share all the properties of both associations and classes, so when a student's mark is recorded, there will be both a link between the student and the module objects and, associated with this link, an instance of the 'Takes' class in which the mark will be recorded as the value of an attribute. This model therefore allows a single mark to be recorded every time a student takes a module, as originally required.

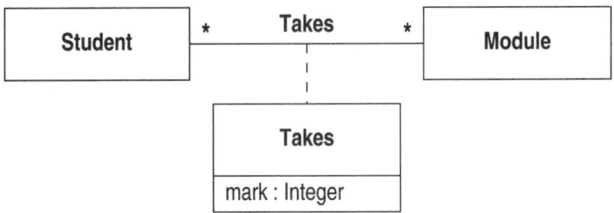

Figure 8.41 Using an association class to store marks

An alternative way of storing students' marks would be to use the technique of reification, discussed in Section 8.4. To do this, the association in Figure 8.40 would be replaced not with an association class, but with a new class and a pair of associations. An instance of the intermediate class should be created each time a student attempts a module, and provides a place to record the mark that they receive. The 'Attempt' class is shown in Figure 8.42, along with the associations that link it to the student and module classes.

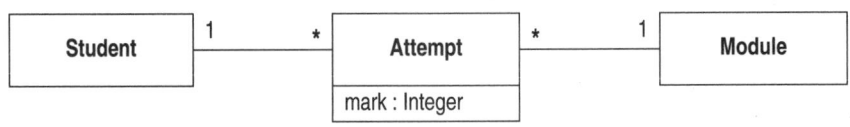

Figure 8.42 Using reification to store marks

The models shown in Figures 8.41 and 8.42 are not completely equivalent, however. The major difference concerns the number of links there can be between a particular student and module. Suppose, for example, that students were allowed to retake modules that they had failed. The system might then be required to record data about all the attempts that a student has had at a module.

The model in Figure 8.42 can handle this new requirement without modification. This model allows any number of 'Attempt' objects, each recording a distinct mark, to be linked to the same student and module. This is not possible with the association class shown in Figure 8.41, however. It shares with the equivalent association the property that only one link can exist between a given student and module, and so the model would have to be changed to accommodate the new requirement.

This example demonstrates that association classes have all the properties of ordinary associations. They also share all the properties of classes, and in particular the ability to participate in further associations.

Suppose, for example, that the system had to be further enhanced to support the production of mark sheets listing all the students taking a module with the marks they gained. For every student that takes a module, there is a single instance of 'Takes', recording their mark, so a natural way of modelling the mark sheet is by means of an association linking a mark sheet class to the 'Takes' association class containing the marks, as shown in Figure 8.43.

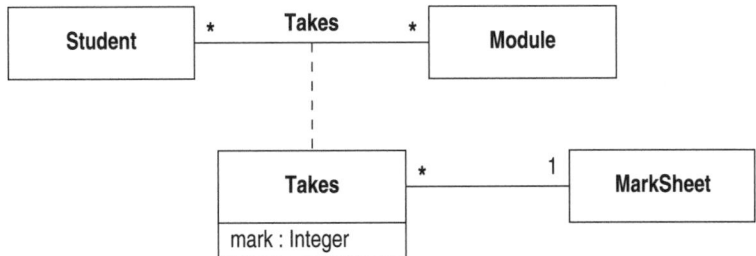

Figure 8.43 An association class participating in an association

8.10 N-ARY ASSOCIATIONS

All the associations illustrated so far have been binary, linking exactly two classes. The concept of an association is more general than this, however, and in principle any number of classes can be connected by an association. For example, yet another way of modelling the situation described in the previous section, where we need to record the attempts that students make at modules, would be to use a ternary association, as shown in Figure 8.44.

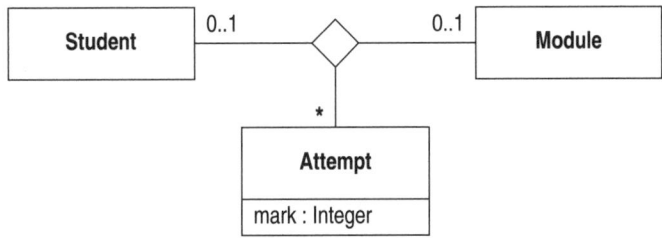

Figure 8.44 A ternary association

The term *n-ary association* is used to refer to a general association linking any number of classes, and *ternary* refers to an association linking exactly three classes. N-ary associations are depicted with a diamond linked to each of the classes participating in the association. There is an association end at each of the classes, where many of the normal properties of association ends can be recorded, including role names, multiplicity annotations and navigability arrow heads. Aggregation and composition cannot be used with n-ary associations, however.

The meaning of the multiplicity annotations is rather more complex for a general n-ary association than for a binary association. The multiplicity at a given association end defines the number of instances of the class at that end that can be linked to a tuple of instances, one from each of the other ends of the association. For example, the 'many' multiplicity in Figure 8.44 specifies that each pair of student and module objects can be linked to zero or more 'Attempt' objects. Like Figure 8.42, this allows a student to have multiple attempts at a module.

By changing the multiplicity, however, we can impose the restriction that a student can only have one attempt at a given module. In this case, a pair consisting of a student and module object should be linked to at most one 'Attempt' object, and this could be specified by changing the multiplicity at the 'Attempt' end of the association to '0..1'.

The multiplicity of '0..1' by the 'Module' class, say, can be interpreted in a similar way. It states that any given pair consisting of a student and an attempt object will be linked to at most one module object. This formalizes the requirement that an attempt object holds the mark for just one module. The optional multiplicity is required here: the model should not require a pair of unrelated student and attempt objects to be linked to a module.

8.11 QUALIFIED ASSOCIATIONS

Consider the following example, based on certain details of a Unix-like file system. The file system contains a number of files, which are known to the system by means of a unique internal identifier quite distinct from any file name seen by the user. From the user's point of view, files can be named and placed in directories. A file can appear in more than one directory, and a different name can be given to a file each time it appears in a directory. A file can even appear in a single directory more than once, provided that a different name is used for each occurrence, thus giving users many ways to access the same file. Within a directory each name can only be used once. The same name can be used in many directories, however, and need not identify the same file in each case.

The basic relationship between files and directories can therefore be modelled by a many-to-many association: a directory can hold many files and a file can appear in many directories. The name by which a file is known is not an attribute of the file object: files do not have unique names, but instead a name is assigned each time a file appears in a directory. The name of a file is therefore an attribute of the link between a file and a directory, and it is therefore natural to attempt to model the situation using an association class containing the file name, as shown in Figure 8.45.

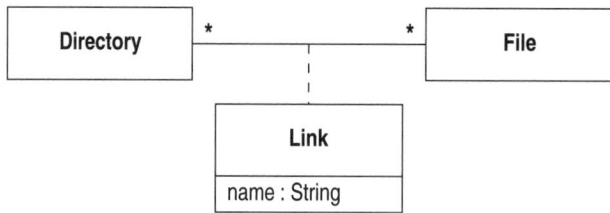

Figure 8.45 A simple model of Unix file names

There are two ways in which this diagram is an inaccurate reflection of the facts of the situation, however. First, it does not express the fact that file names must be distinct within a directory. It would be quite possible according to the model for all the files linked to a particular directory to have the same value for the 'name' attribute.

Second, Figure 8.45 does not allow for the possibility of multiple links between the same file and directory. A given file can appear in a directory more than once, under different names. As discussed in Section 8.4, however, the semantics of associations only permit one link between a given pair of objects.

Both problems can be resolved by using a *qualifier*, as shown in Figure 8.46. Qualifiers are used in cases where some piece of information can be used as a key to uniquely identify one out of a set of objects. The relevant properties of a key are that in a given context each key value can appear only once, and must somehow identify a single object, which is described by the key. In this example, the file name acts as a key. A context is provided by a directory, within which a key value (file name) can only appear once. Each file name in a directory names a unique file.

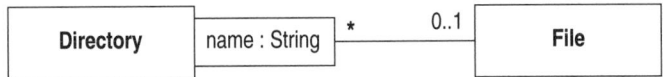

Figure 8.46 Modelling file names with a qualifier

An attribute of an association class that has properties which enable it to act as a key is known in UML as a *qualifier*. Qualifiers are written in a small box next to the class that defines the context within which values of the qualifiers pick out objects. The association line is connected to the qualifier box rather than the class, as shown in Figure 8.46, and the normal range of multiplicity symbols can be used at that end of the association.

Part of the meaning of Figure 8.46 is the same as that of Figure 8.45, namely that files and directories are connected by a many-to-many relationship of containment, and that a name is given to each occurrence of a file in a directory. The association in Figure 8.46 does not look like a many-to-many relationship, however: the multiplicity at the file end is 'optional', not 'many'. To clarify the sort of situation that a qualified association models, Figure 8.47 shows some qualified links between objects, consistent with the association shown in Figure 8.46.

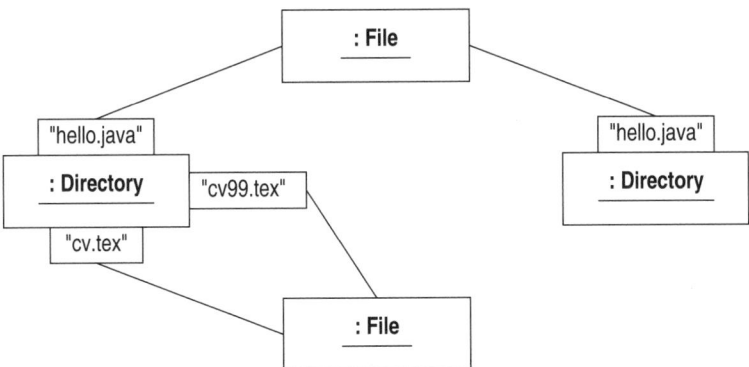

Figure 8.47 Qualified links between objects

Intuitively, the meaning of a qualified association is that instances of the class with the qualifier maintain a mapping from qualifier values to instances of the class at the other end of the association. In this case, each directory will maintain a mapping from file names to file objects.

The values of the qualifier, the file names, are written in boxes adjoining the directory object in the same way as the qualifier adjoins the class, and the links end at these boxes, not at the object itself. The optional multiplicity in Figure 8.46 refers to the fact that at most one file can be linked to each qualifier value, because file names must be unique within a directory. This still defines a many-to-many relationship between directories and files, however, because many file names can be attached to a single directory object, as shown in Figure 8.47.

The diagram also shows how a single file can appear under the same name in different directories, or more than once in the same directory, under different names. In this case, then, use of a qualifier has resolved both of the problems identified with the initial model in Figure 8.45.

Qualifiers and identifiers

Qualifiers are often used in connection with attributes, which serve to identify objects in the real world. For example, Figure 8.48 shows part of a student registration system where students are known to the university and each student is given a unique identification number.

Figure 8.48 An identifying attribute

This model does not make it clear that the identification number for every student is unique, however. To include this constraint on the diagram, it would be normal to rewrite the attribute as a qualifier on the university class, as shown in Figure 8.49.

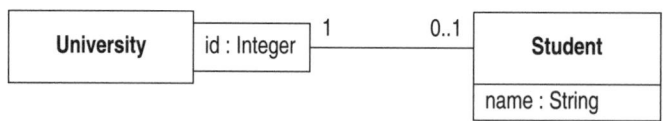

Figure 8.49 Identifiers as qualifiers

Because of object identity, it is never necessary to introduce attributes containing unique identifiers into a data model simply to distinguish different instances of a class. Where they exist in the real world, however, they should be included and can often be modelled using qualifiers.

8.12 INTERFACES

An interface in UML is a named set of operations. Interfaces are used to characterize the behaviour of an entity such as a class or a component. Interfaces in UML can be thought of as generalizing the notion of interface as found in Java. The notation for an interface uses the same graphic symbol as a class, but includes a stereotype to identify the classifier as an interface, as Figure 8.50 shows.

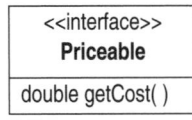

Figure 8.50 An interface

Generalization relationships can exist between interfaces, where one interface is defined as a specialized 'subinterface' of another. The relationship between interfaces and classes is one of *realization*, where a class implements an interface. This means that the class declares, or inherits from other classes, all the operations that are defined in the interface. Figure 8.51 shows the notation for realization, stating that the catalogue entry class from the stock control example realizes the 'Priceable' interface defined in Figure 8.50.

Figure 8.51 A class realizing an interface

An alternative notation for realization is shown in Figure 8.52. The interface is represented by a small circle, labelled with the name of the interface, and is linked by a line to the class that is realizing it.

Figure 8.52 An alternative notation for realization of an interface

One useful application of the interface notation is to show explicitly which features of one class another makes use of. Figure 8.53 shows that the part class depends only on the cost function defined in the catalogue entry class. The dependency between the class and the interface symbol means that the class makes use of the operations specified in that interface.

This information can alternatively be attached to the role name at one end of an association. Using this notation, Figure 8.54 shows the same information as Figure 8.53. The interface is here being used as an *interface specifier*, to assign a 'type' to the role name. This type indicates which features of the class adjacent to the role name are used as a result of the association shown.

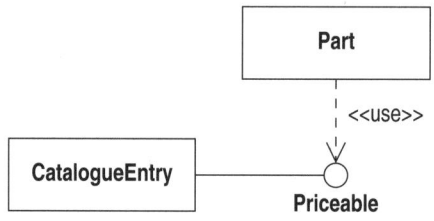

Figure 8.53 Dependency on an interface

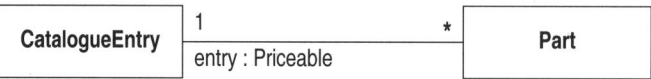

Figure 8.54 Using an interface specifier

8.13 TEMPLATES

A template is a parameterized model element. A familiar example of the use of templates is to define container classes. A container class is a data structure such as a list, set or tree that can hold many data items. The code that defines the data structure is independent of the actual type of data that is stored, but languages without templates make it difficult to express the required level of generality.

For example, suppose that a class has been written to implement a list of integers. This could be reused to provide a list of strings by physically copying the source code and editing it to refer to strings rather than integers. A major problem with this approach, however, is that there are now two copies of the code to maintain, and any modification to the data structure code will have to be made in multiple places.

The traditional object-oriented solution to this problem is to define data structures that can hold objects of a root class in the class hierarchy. Java uses the `Object` class for this purpose, and data structures such as vectors are defined to hold references to instances of `Object`. As every class in Java is a descendant of `Object`, this means that, by virtue of polymorphism, any type of data can be stored in the data structure.

A limitation of this approach is that it does not ensure that data of the correct type is stored in a data structure. Careless programming could lead to unexpected data types being stored in the vector and, because knowledge of the run-time type of the objects in the vector is lost, this kind of error can be hard to recover from. Practical uses of classes like `Vector` make use of wrapper functions to guarantee that all objects inserted in the vector are of a single class, and so can be safely cast back to their original type when they are removed from the vector.

The solution to this problem using templates takes a different approach. By using template classes, for example, programmers can define a data structure that stores elements of an undefined type T, say. To use such a data structure, a programmer has to specify what type to substitute for T in an application of the data structure. This process is very reminiscent of ordinary parameter binding, so type parameters like T are known as *template parameters*.

A template class in UML is notated like an ordinary class, except that the template parameters are shown in a dashed rectangle in one corner of the class icon, as shown in Figure 8.55. A class that is formed from the template can be shown as being dependent on the template, and the 'bind' stereotype on the dependency gives information about the binding of the template parameters.

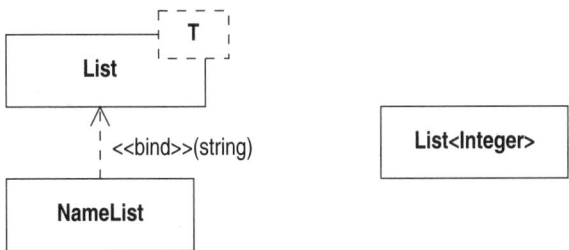

Figure 8.55 Notations for template classes

Figure 8.55 also shows the notation for denoting an 'anonymous' instantiation of the template, where the new class is not given its own name but simply referred to as a 'list of integers', say. This notation is identical to that employed in C++.

8.14 SUMMARY

- Static models describe structural relationships between the data in a system. Object diagrams show the objects that exist at a particular time, and the links between them.

- UML defines a number of standard *data types* and permits user-defined *enumerations*. *Data values*, the instances of data types, differ from objects in that they do not possess identity.

- Class diagrams show the general properties that a system's data must satisfy at all times. Given a class diagram, we can decide whether or not an object diagram represents a possible state of the system being specified.

- Classes describe the different kinds of object in a system. As well as a name, classes have attributes and operations that describe the state and behaviours of the objects which are instances of the class, namely those objects described by it.

- Links between objects are defined by associations on a class diagram. Associations show which classes can be connected by a given kind of link and how many objects a given object can be linked to. This information is given by means of multiplicity annotations. Associations can be labelled and have a role name at each end.

- *Generalization* defines a relationship between classes where any instance of one class, the subclass, can be substituted for, or treated as if it was, an instance of another class, the superclass. A given class can have any number of mutually exclusive subclasses. This process can be carried out as often as required, giving rise to generalization hierarchies.

- The attributes and operations of a superclass are *inherited* by its subclasses. Subclasses can define additional attributes and operations to express their specialized properties. If necessary, the definitions of inherited operations can be overridden in a subclass.

- An association to a class can be instantiated by links to instances of any of its subclasses. This leads to polymorphism, where a single association can in fact specify links between objects of different classes.

- *Abstract classes* are classes that are intended to have no instances. They represent a partial concept and are introduced to help structure a generalization hierarchy.

- *Aggregation* is a specialized form of association intended to capture the semantics of the whole–part relationship. Aggregation can be used to prohibit loops and cycles in object diagrams.

- *Composition* represents a stronger form of aggregation where the lifetimes of instances of one class are contained within those of another.

- In some cases, information in a class diagram is better thought of as belonging to a link than to an individual object. This can be modelled by making use of *association classes*. Association classes share the properties of both associations and classes, and can participate in further associations if required.

- *Qualified associations* can be used in the situation where a piece of data acts as a key with which objects of an associated class can be retrieved.

- *Interfaces* define sets of operations that can be supported by classes. A class that supports the operations in an interface is said to *realize* the interface.

- Classes can be parameterized, leading to the definition of *template classes*. Template classes provide reusability, by binding arguments to the template parameters.

8.15 EXERCISES

8.1 Draw UML class and object icons representing each of the following. Where appropriate, use enumerations and programming language types to specify attribute types.

(*a*) A class representing positions, with attributes giving the x and y co-ordinates of a point. Also show two instances of this class, the origin, with co-ordinates $(0, 0)$, and the point $(100, -40)$.

(*b*) A class representing a counter with operations to set or reset the counter to zero, to increment and decrement the value stored by a specified amount and to return the current value.

(*c*) A class representing a switch that can be turned on or off.

(*d*) A class representing traffic lights, with attributes to record which colours are currently illuminated.

8.2 Define multiplicities for the following associations:

(*a*) 'Has on loan', linking people to books in a library system.

(*b*) 'Has read', linking people to books.

(*c*) 'Is occupying', linking chess pieces to squares on a chess board.

(*d*) 'Spouse', linking class 'Person' to itself.

(*e*) 'Parent', linking class 'Person' to itself.

8.3 In Figure Ex8.3, state which of the object diagrams are legitimate instances of the class diagram given. Assume that all links in the object diagrams are instances of the association in the corresponding class diagram. If an object diagram is not a legitimate instance, explain why not.

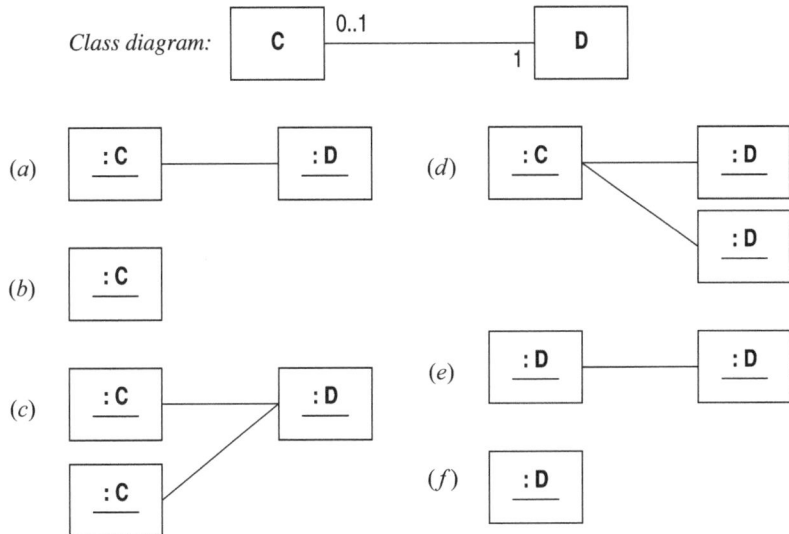

Figure Ex8.3 An 'optional' association and some candidate object diagrams

8.4 Repeat the previous question for the diagrams given in Figure Ex8.4.

8.5 Companies may employ many people, and people may work for many companies. Each company has a managing director and every employee in a company has a manager, who may manage many subordinate employees. Add suitable labelling to the class diagram in Figure Ex8.5 to make this intended meaning clear.

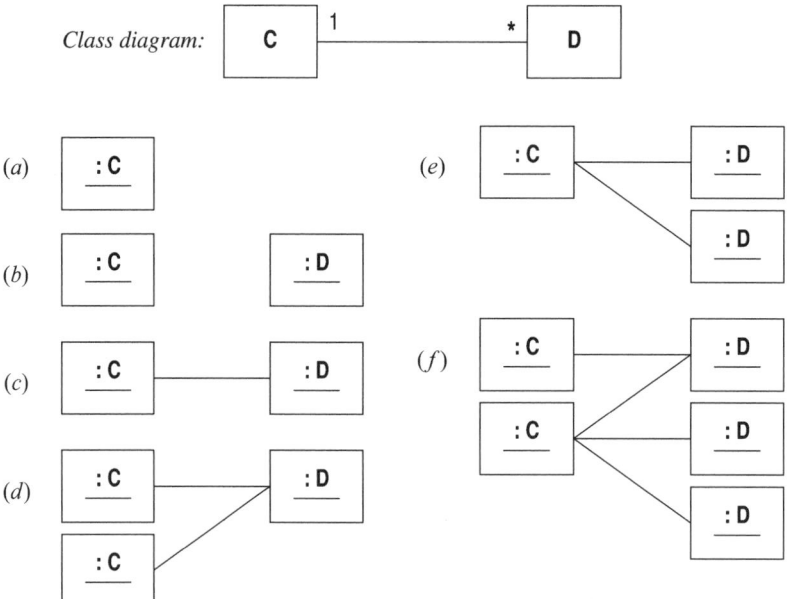

Figure Ex8.4 A 'many' association and some candidate object diagrams

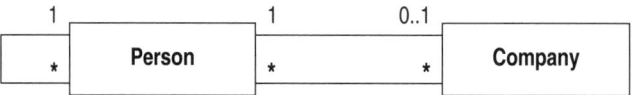

Figure Ex8.5 Associations related to employment

8.6 Suppose you are writing a program to maintain family trees.

(*a*) Would the class diagram in Figure 8.20 be a suitable model for storing information about people's ancestors? If not, explain why not and make appropriate changes to the diagram.

(*b*) Extend the diagram so that it can store information about marriages. Your model should be able to record not only marriages, but also divorce and remarriage, possibly to the same person.

8.7 Amend Figure 8.22 so that Jill's job titles and salaries are recorded by the model. As well as updating the class diagram, amend the object diagram showing this information for the two contracts shown.

8.8 In Figure Ex8.8, state which of the object diagrams are valid instances of the class diagram given. If an object diagram is not a valid instance, explain why not.

8.9 What would be the consequences of omitting the abstract draw operation from the shape class in Figure 8.31? Would this be a failure of substitutability, or is some other principle involved here?

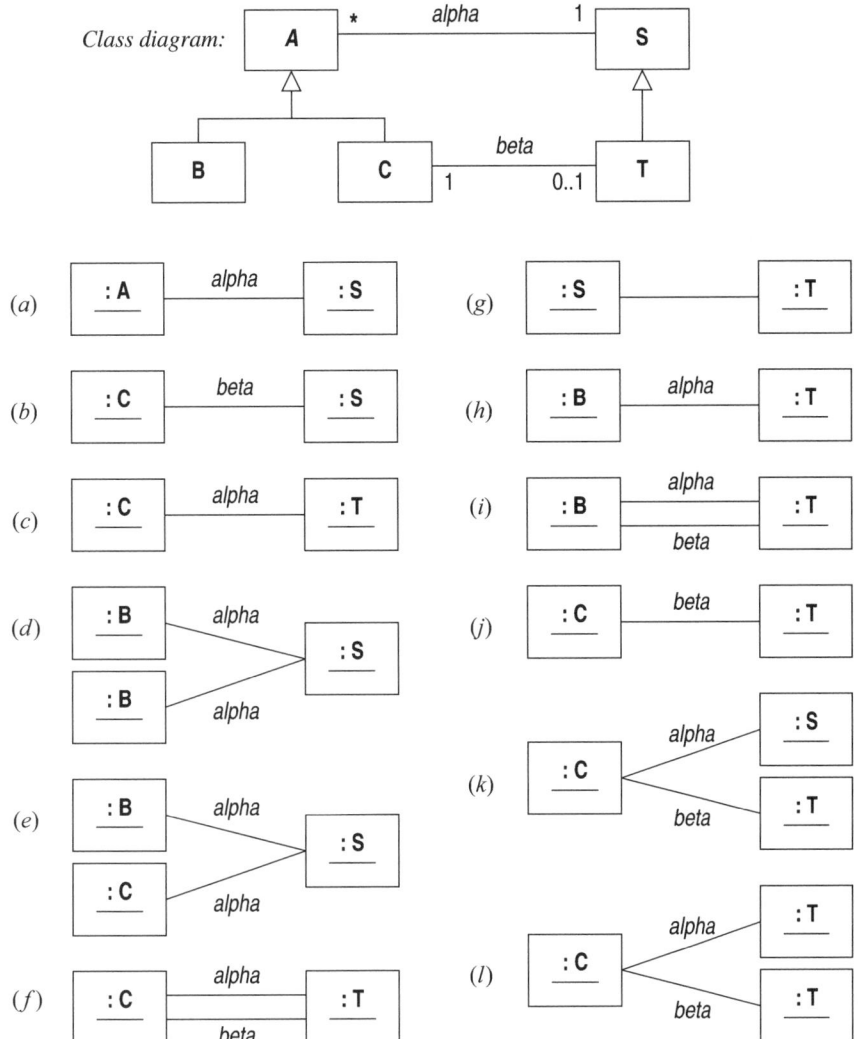

Figure Ex8.8 Generalizations and candidate object diagrams

8.10 Does the association in Figure 8.20 have the properties of antisymmetry and transitivity? Could it correctly or usefully be shown as an aggregation?

8.11 Redraw the class diagram of Figure 8.36 using the 'nested class' form of the composite notation. Draw a composite object showing a message with its header and body, and with two attachments.

8.12 Draw an object diagram that is an instance of Figure 8.37 and shows a port that is a part of one computer, but is connected to the processor of another.

8.13 Does the diagram in Figure 8.44 specify that each instance of the 'Attempt' class is linked to exactly one student and one module? If not, can the multiplicities on the association be changed to require this?

8.14 Extend the model in Figure 8.15, showing employees working for companies, so that it can store an employee's salary (*a*) as an attribute and (*b*) using an association class. What arguments could be made in favour of each of these alternative models?

8.15 Draw a class diagram summarizing the following facts about a library. Discuss your design decisions, and any limitations of your model.

> For each book held by the library, the catalogue contains the title, author's name and ISBN number of the book. There may be multiple copies of a book in the library. Each copy of a book has a unique accession number. There are many registered readers belonging to the library, each of whom is issued with a number of tickets. The system records the name and address of each reader and the number of tickets that they have been issued with. Readers can borrow one book for each ticket that they possess and the system keeps a record of which books a reader has borrowed, along with the date by which the book must be returned.

8.16 Figure Ex8.16 models some aspects of a file system in which directories can contain files and subdirectories. The file system consists of a single root directory and all its contents. Users can own directories and files, read files and have a home directory.

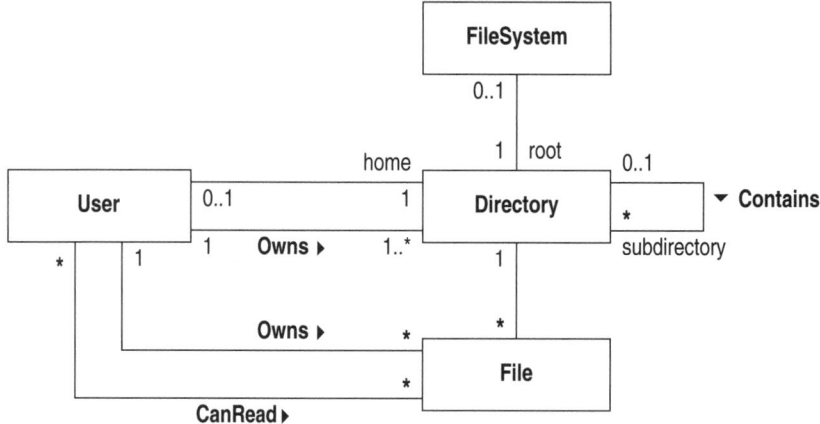

Figure Ex8.16 A class diagram for a file system

    (*a*) Draw an object diagram corresponding to this class diagram, showing the file system, a user object corresponding to your account, your home directory, a subdirectory called `mail`, a file called `.login` in your home directory and a file called `message1` in the `mail` directory.

    (*b*) The specification of the file system could be made more Unix-like if a new class 'Node' were introduced. This is a superclass of 'File' and 'Directory'. Redraw the class diagram using this new class to *reduce* the number of associations in the diagram.

(*c*) Does the introduction of the 'Node' class have any effect on the object diagram you drew for part (*a*)?

(*d*) Consider whether composition or aggregation could correctly be used in these diagrams.

8.17 Here is an extract from the documentation of a drawing tool for graphical workstations.

> The objects in the package are divided into *primitive objects* and *compound objects*. The primitive objects are: *arc*, *ellipse*, *polyline*, *polygon*, *box* and *text*.
>
> A primitive object can be moved, rotated, flipped vertically or horizontally, copied or erased. The *text* primitive may not be flipped.
>
> A compound object is composed of primitive objects. The primitive objects that constitute a compound cannot be individually modified, but they can be manipulated as an entity; a compound can be moved, rotated, flipped vertically or horizontally, copied or erased. A compound that contains any boxes may only be rotated by 90 degrees.

Based on this description, draw a class diagram using generalization to show the relationships between the various different kinds of graphical object in the drawing package. Discuss the limitations of your model and any significant design decisions that you make.

8.18 A customer places an order with a supplier. The order is for various numbers of different kinds of parts; the distinction between different kinds of parts can be ignored for the purposes of this exercise. An order consists of a number of order lines; each line specifies a particular part from the supplier's catalogue and says how many are to be ordered. In response to an order, the supplier makes up a delivery, consisting of all the ordered parts. Describe this situation in a class diagram and discuss the possible use of aggregation in your diagram.

8.19 The UK banking system consists of a number of banks. Each bank has a number of branches, each identified by a unique sort code. Banks maintain accounts, each with a unique account number; in addition, each account is held at a particular branch of the bank. Some accounts allow cheques to be written; each cheque is identified with a cheque number.

Draw a class diagram to represent this information, paying particular attention to the use of qualified associations. Explain any assumptions or design decisions that you make.

8.20 Based on the following description of part of the syntax of a programming language, construct a class diagram showing the structure of programs written in the language.

> A *module* consists of a collection of named *features*. A feature can either be a *variable*, a *routine* or a nested module. Routines consist of a *declaration part* and a *statement part*. Features local to the routine can be declared in the declaration

part, and the statement part consists of a non-empty sequence of statements. Statements can be *loops*, *conditionals* or *assignments*, and each assignment contains a reference to the variable that is being updated.

8.21 Draw a class diagram modelling the system described in the following:

A company has decided to computerize the circulation of documents round its offices, and to do this by installing a network of *electronic desks*. Each desk provides the following services:

- A *blotting pad*, which can hold a document that the user is currently working on. The blotting pad provides basic word-processing facilities.
- A *filing cabinet*, which models a physical filing cabinet. It is divided into drawers, and each drawer is divided into folders. Documents can be stored either in drawers or in folders within drawers.
- A *mail service*, which allows the user to communicate with other users on the network. Each desk is provided with three *trays*, corresponding to the IN, OUT and PENDING trays in traditional offices. The network will automatically put new mail in a user's IN tray, and periodically take documents from the OUT tray and mail them to their recipients.

Documents can be moved between the mail trays and the blotting pad, and between the blotting pad and the filing cabinet. There is no provision to move documents directly between the trays and the filing cabinet. Only one document can be on the blotting pad at any given time.

8.22 Many programming languages define a notion of *scope*. Every identifier is declared within some scope, and it is an error to declare two or more identifiers with the same name in the same scope. Scopes can be nested, however, and an identifier can be defined in an inner scope with a name that has been used in an outer scope. Draw two class diagrams modelling these facts about scopes and identifiers, one using qualifiers and one not. Compare the two resulting diagrams and decide which is the more accurate representation of the situation being described.

8.23 Construct a class diagram summarizing the aspects of the window manager described below:

When you are running the system, your work takes place on the *desktop*, the screen space occupied by the window manager. At any time you will be running a number of applications; each application will be displayed on the desktop either as an icon or in an application window. The control application starts when the window manager is started up; terminating this application terminates the current session.

As you work with applications, two kinds of windows appear on your desktop: application windows and windows contained within the application windows, often known as *document windows*. All windows contain a title bar, maximize and minimize buttons, a control-menu box and optionally horizontal and vertical scroll bars. In addition, application windows contain a menu bar; operations chosen from the menu bar can affect either the application window or any of the document windows contained within it.

8.24 Users of a network are authorized to use certain workstations. For each such machine, they are issued with an account and password. Draw a class model describing this situation and discuss any assumptions that you make.

8.25 Imagine a library full of books. Each book contains a bibliography; each bibliography consists of a number of references to other books. Typically, a book will be referred to in many places and therefore a reference can appear in more than one bibliography.

Draw a class diagram for this situation and discuss the possible uses of aggregation in the diagram.

8.26 Construct a class diagram for the Electronic Noticeboard (EN) system described in the following:

> The EN is a system designed to facilitate communication between a group of users of a computer system. It enables notices to be posted that all users can read and permits discussions to take place between the users.
>
> When a user logs on to the EN, they are presented with a user workspace that contains two main areas, the *noticeboard* and the *discussion groups*. The user has to choose which area they want to access; it is possible to move freely between the areas at any later stage.
>
> The noticeboard contains a list of notices, and a user can choose between reading any of the existing notices and adding a new notice to the noticeboard. A notice must have an expiry date; after that date it will be archived and will no longer appear on the standard noticeboard. By default, all notices appear to all users until their expiry dates; however, a user can choose to remove specified notices from their private view of the noticeboard, although this is not recommended.
>
> The system also maintains discussion groups, each dealing with a particular topic. Each discussion consists of a number of contributions. Users can choose which, if any, of the discussions they wish to read. By default, only unread contributions in a particular discussion will be presented to the user. A discussion is started when a user posts an initial contribution. Other users can respond to this by posting *followup contributions*, which in turn can generate further followups. If a followup is deemed to have moved sufficiently far away from the original topic of discussion, it can be identified as the initial contribution of a new discussion group; it will then be accessible through both the old and new groups.
>
> All notices and contributions are archived, together with their date and, in the case of contributions, a record of the contributions, if any, that they are following up.
>
> A user starting a new discussion can specify that only a subset of the registered users of the EN can access the group. It is possible to allow users to have read-only, read–write or no access to a group. By contrast, all notices are readable by all users. A user can only read an archived contribution if they had read access to the group to which it was originally posted.

8.27 Construct a class diagram based on the information contained in the following description of the `info` system provided with the Emacs text editor. Where appropriate, give justifications for the design decisions you make.

> The `info` system in Emacs provides a simple hypertext reading facility enabling on-line documentation to be browsed from within the editor. The `info` system consists of a number of *files*, each roughly corresponding to a single document. Each file is divided into a number of *nodes*, each node containing a small amount of text describing a particular topic. One node in the system is identified as the *directory* node: it contains information about the files available in the `info` system and is presented to the user when the system is started.
>
> Nodes are connected together by *links*: each link connects two nodes, and operations are provided enabling the user to move from one node to another via a link: in this way it is possible to browse through the complete document. There are three important kinds of links, called *up*, *next* and *previous* links: the names imply that the nodes in a document will be structured in a hierarchical manner, but this is not enforced by the system. In addition to links, a node can contain a *menu*. A menu consists of a number of entries, each of which connects to another node in the system.
>
> When the system is running, a record is kept in a *history list* of all the nodes that have been visited, thus enabling users to retrace their path through the document.

9

INTERACTION DIAGRAMS

A complete model must describe both the static and dynamic aspects of a system. Static models, such as class and object diagrams, describe the objects in a system, the data each object contains and the links that exist between them, but they say very little about the behaviour of these objects.

When a system is running, objects interact by passing messages, as explained in Chapter 2. Interactions occur when a use case is executed, for example, or when an operation in a class is called. The messages that are sent determine the system's behaviour, but they are not shown on static diagrams such as class diagrams.

This chapter describes the diagrams that are used in UML to describe interactions, namely *collaboration diagrams* and *sequence diagrams*. These two types of diagram provide alternative ways of expressing much the same information, and they are collectively referred to as *interaction diagrams*.

9.1 COLLABORATIONS

Although the most important thing about an interaction is the messages that make it up, these cannot be specified without knowing what objects are involved in the interaction and how they are related. A *collaboration* defines a set of objects that are related in such a way as to support a given interaction. An interaction diagram consists of a collaboration together with the messages that make up the interaction itself. These messages will be passed between the objects in the collaboration.

Collaborations are often defined by simply using an object diagram showing a particular set of linked objects. An interaction can then be shown by adding messages to this object diagram. For example, consider an operation in a banking system which transfers funds from one account to another. Each time this operation is invoked, a certain amount of money is withdrawn from one account and deposited in another.

This transaction is illustrated in the object diagram shown in Figure 9.1. This shows two account objects, together with an object representing the bank that removes money from one account and deposits it in the other.

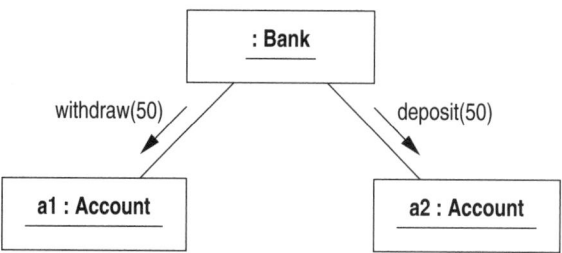

Figure 9.1 A transfer between two bank accounts

Although diagrams like this are often used to explain how particular operations might be implemented, Figure 9.1 in fact only shows one particular transfer between the two specific accounts 'a1' and 'a2'. There are a number of reasons why this use of object diagrams is unsatisfactory as a general method for specifying interactions.

First, 'a1' and 'a2' are not the only objects that funds can be transferred between. Although it is unlikely that anyone would draw this conclusion from Figure 9.1, a more general specification should make it explicit that any account object can participate in a transfer, either as the account from which money is taken or that in which it is deposited, and that the messages it sends and receives will vary from case to case.

Second, an object diagram shows a fixed number of objects, and the links between them. On the different occasions that an operation is called, however, both the number of objects involved and the pattern of links between them may vary, and the interaction that is generated will vary accordingly. For example, an alternative form of the transfer operation might allow money to be withdrawn from one account and shared out between a number of other accounts. A specification of an operation should state in a general way what will happen in these different cases, rather than showing a few examples and leaving it up to the reader to infer what will happen in other cases.

Third, some operations may exhibit different functionality on separate occasions; in this case perhaps no transfer is made when the account from which money is withdrawn would become overdrawn as a result. In general, this implies that the course of an interaction may be affected by properties of the data stored in objects. Different possibilities could be shown on separate object diagrams, but it would be preferable to have a notation that can show alternative possibilities on a single diagram rather than having to draw a set of illustrative examples.

In order to achieve the required generality, collaborations in UML in general do not show individual objects, but rather the *roles* that objects can play in the interaction. An object diagram used to illustrate a collaboration is known as a *collaboration instance set*. Among other things, the use of roles in collaborations makes it clear that different objects can be involved in the interaction at different times.

9.2 CLASSIFIER ROLES

In general, then, collaborations describe not individual objects, but the *roles* that objects play in an interaction. Each role describes a particular way in which an object can participate in an interaction. For example, each transfer of funds involves two account objects, but they participate in the transaction in different ways. One has money withdrawn from it and the other has money deposited in it.

This can be specified by defining two roles for this transaction, which might be called the 'debtor' and 'creditor' roles. A general description of the transaction can then be given by saying that money is taken from a debtor account and transferred to a creditor account. Whenever a fund transfer takes place, an account object is assigned to each role, one being the debtor and one being the creditor.

The roles that objects can play in interactions are called *classifier roles*. Figure 9.2 shows a collaboration corresponding to the object diagram in Figure 9.1, with classifier roles in place of actual objects. A classifier role has a name and a *base class*, shown in a rectangular icon, separated by a colon.

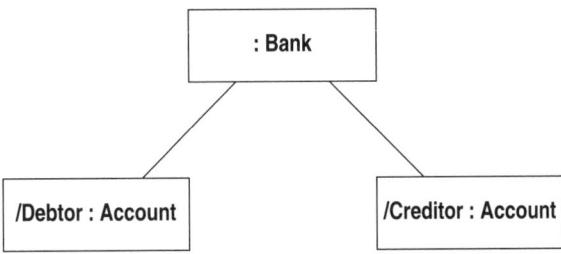

Figure 9.2 A collaboration with classifier roles

The notation for classifier roles is clearly related to that used for objects and classes. A classifier role can be given a name, prefixed by a diagonal slash; if the name is omitted, the colon must be included to distinguish a role from a class. The name and class of a role are not underlined: this signifies that a classifier role is not an instance, but a more general notion, which can itself have objects as instances.

The relationship between roles and the objects that actually take part in interactions is rather like the relationship between variables and numbers in mathematics. To work out how much energy is contained in 3 grams of matter using the formula $E = mc^2$, for example, the value 3 must be substituted for the variable m. In the same way, to derive the object diagram in Figure 9.1 from the collaboration in Figure 9.2, actual objects are substituted for the classifier roles in the collaboration. At different times, of course, different objects could be substituted for the same role, or the same object in different roles, depending on the exact transfers that are being carried out.

Objects that are to play a particular role in an interaction must be instances of the role's base class or one of its descendant classes. In a given interaction, however, an object playing a particular role will not normally make use of all the features provided by the base class of the role.

For example, a creditor account in a transfer will receive deposit messages, but not withdrawals. In principle, it would be possible to specify a role without naming a base class, simply by listing the features that objects playing that role must possess. UML does not allow this flexibility, however: the only way of specifying the properties of a classifier role is by naming a base class.

The distinction between objects and classifier roles is not always clearly made in the literature on UML. In particular, interactions are often shown on object diagrams, rather than collaborations. In these cases, the objects shown are sometimes described as 'prototypical' objects. It is understood that other objects can be substituted for such a prototypical object in various circumstances, in much the same way as objects can be substituted for roles. In practice, this causes little confusion, but in order to differentiate the two concepts, roles and objects will be clearly distinguished in this book.

9.3 ASSOCIATION ROLES

Classifier roles in a collaboration are connected by *association roles*. An association role connecting two classifier roles indicates that objects playing those roles can be linked to each other, and hence exchange messages, in interactions based on the collaboration. Unlike classifier roles, association roles are rarely labelled with role names.

One way in which objects can be linked is for there to exist an association defined between their classes. In this case the association is said to be the *base association* of the association role. A possible base association for the association roles in Figure 9.2 is shown in the class diagram in Figure 9.3.

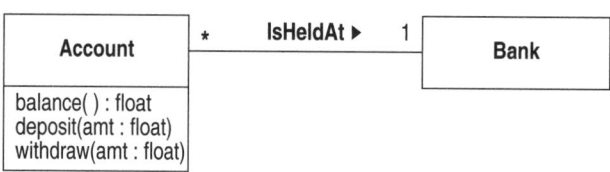

Figure 9.3 A base association

When objects are substituted for the classifier roles in Figure 9.2, the links connecting the bank object to the account objects are instances of the 'IsHeldAt' association. In some situations, however, objects can communicate even if they are not linked by an instance of an association, and these alternatives also need to be shown on collaborations. They are distinguished from normal association roles by the use of stereotypes.

Association role stereotypes

An association between two classes implies that instances of the classes can be linked and messages sent between them. An association implies a fairly permanent connection between objects, however, often implemented as a data member or as a field within a class.

There are other situations in which objects are able to communicate and in these circumstances they are also described as being linked. UML distinguishes the following different ways in which one object can gain access to another in such as way as to be able to send messages to it.

1. One object can be passed to another as a parameter of a message. In programming languages, this is often implemented by passing a reference to the object. In this case the object receiving the message knows the identity of the parameter object, and can in the method body send messages to that object. Such a link is temporary, because it is only available while the operation is executing.
2. Implementations of operations can create local instances of any class, and then send messages to these objects during the execution of the operation. Again, a link corresponding to a local variable only lasts for the duration of an operation call.
3. If any global variables exist and are visible, an object can send messages to an object stored in such a variable.
4. An object can always send messages to itself, even though no explicit 'link to self' is defined. In programming languages, this capability is provided by defining a pseudo-variable called `this` or `self`.

These kinds of link are important in collaborations because during the execution of an operation messages are often sent to parameter objects, local variables and to the object executing the operation itself. Association roles can be labelled with one of the following stereotypes to indicate the type of link that they support: 'parameter', 'local', 'global', 'self' and 'association'. The first four correspond to the types of link listed above. The 'association' stereotype indicates that a link is an instance of a genuine association; it is the default case and can be omitted.

For example, suppose that statements are to be printed for bank accounts. This might be implemented by the bank object passing the relevant account objects to a separate object, which would prepare the required statement and, in the course of doing this, find out the current balance of the account. Figure 9.4 shows this interaction: because an account is passed as a parameter to the statement object, the association role connecting the two roles has the appropriate stereotype at one end.

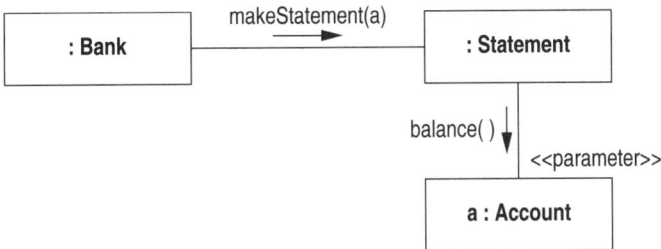

Figure 9.4 A stereotyped association role

9.4 INTERACTION DIAGRAMS

Two kinds of diagram are defined in UML for showing interactions, sequence diagrams and collaboration diagrams. Collaboration diagrams show classifier and association roles, and superimpose messages on association roles, as shown in Figure 9.4. Sequence diagrams show classifier roles only, but make the sequencing of messages very clear. In different circumstances, one or other form of diagram may be preferable.

As well as showing sequences of messages, both types of interaction diagram can explicitly show the creation and deletion of objects, iterated and conditional message passing, and objects sending messages to themselves. The major difference between the two forms of diagram is the way they show the order in which messages are sent.

Sequence diagrams

A sequence diagram showing the same interaction as Figure 9.4 is given in Figure 9.5. The classifier roles involved in the interaction are displayed at the top of the diagram, but association roles are not shown. The vertical dimension in a sequence diagram represents time and the messages in an interaction are drawn from top to bottom of the diagram, in the order that they are sent.

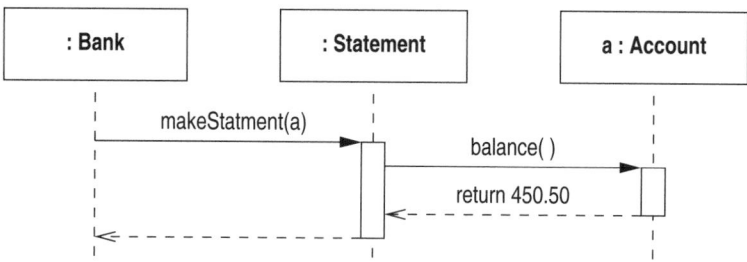

Figure 9.5 A simple sequence diagram

Each role has a dashed line, known as its *lifeline*, extending below it. The lifeline indicates the period of time during which objects playing that role actually exist. In Figure 9.5 all objects exist throughout the entire interaction, but examples where objects are created and deleted during an interaction will be examined later.

Messages are shown as arrows leading from the lifeline of the sender of the message to that of the receiver. When a message is sent, control passes from the sender of the message to the receiver. The period of time during which an object is processing a message is known as an *activation* and is shown on a lifeline as a narrow rectangle whose top is connected to a message.

When an object finishes processing a message, control returns to the sender of the message. This marks the end of the activation corresponding to that message and is marked by a dashed arrow going from the bottom of the activation rectangle back to the lifeline of the role that sent the message giving rise to the activation.

The messages shown in Figure 9.5, with a solid arrowhead, denote *synchronous* messages, such as normal procedure calls. These are characterized by the fact that processing in the object that sends the message is suspended until the called object finishes dealing with the message and returns control to the caller. UML includes notation for other types of messages, but this will not be considered further here.

In the course of processing a message, an object may send messages to other objects. These messages are depicted as arrows from the activation corresponding to the first message to the lifeline of the receiver, where they give rise to a second activation. Assuming that a conventional procedural flow of control is being modelled, the period of time occupied by this second activation will be 'nested' within the period of time occupied by the first activation, as shown in Figure 9.5.

It is optional whether or not to show activations and return messages on sequence diagrams, but including them helps to clarify the flow of control within an interaction. Arguments passed with a message are shown in conventional functional style. Data values returned to the sender of a message are shown on the return messages at the end of an activation.

Collaboration diagrams

A collaboration diagram corresponding to the sequence diagram in Figure 9.5 is shown in Figure 9.6. With the exception of the notation used to show return values and the sequencing of messages, it is identical to the diagram shown in Figure 9.4.

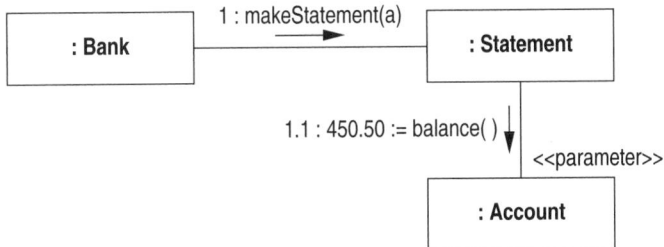

Figure 9.6 A simple collaboration diagram

Unlike sequence diagrams, collaboration diagrams show association as well as classifier roles. As a result, message sequencing cannot be shown graphically and messages are numbered to indicate the order in which they are sent. Messages can be numbered sequentially, but more commonly a hierarchical numbering scheme is used. Figure 9.6 shows a very simple example of this, where the messages are not numbered 1 and 2, as might have been expected, but 1 and 1.1.

The rationale for hierarchical numbering is to enable the numbering of messages to reflect the structure of nested activations that is made explicit on sequence diagrams. The correspondence between the two notations is shown schematically in Figure 9.7. This diagram shows the messages on an abstract sequence diagram labelled with the numbers they would have on an equivalent collaboration diagram.

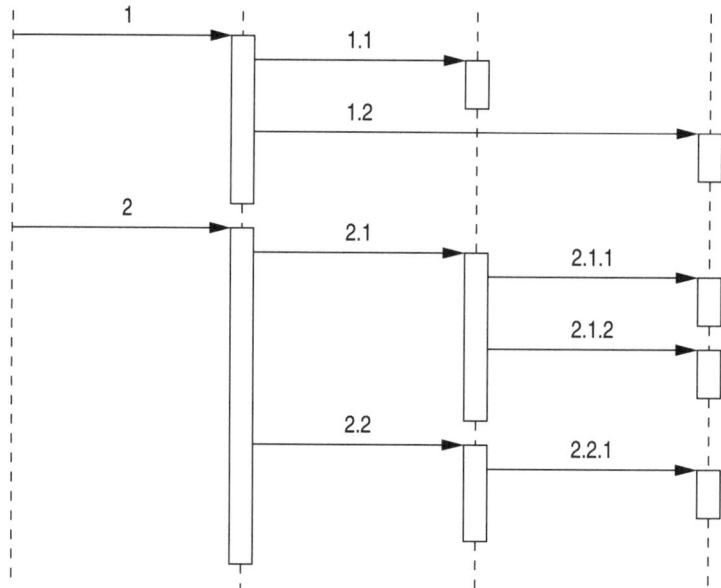

Figure 9.7 The hierarchical numbering of messages

Numbers are assigned to messages in Figure 9.7 in the following way. Within each activation, messages are numbered sequentially starting from 1. This includes messages sent from the leftmost lifeline in the diagram. Each activation can be identified with the number of the message that gave rise to it. For example, the activation that starts when message number 2.1 is received should be thought of as being activation number 2.1.

A unique label can then be generated for each message by adding the number of the message to the end of the number of the activation sending the message, with a dot to separate the numbers and to reflect that another level of nesting of control flow has been initiated. For example, the two messages sent by activation 2.1 are labelled as 2.1.1 and 2.1.2 respectively.

With practice, information about activations can be read off collaboration diagrams fairly readily by interpreting the message numbers in this way. Most people find the graphic representation given by sequence diagrams easier to read, however, and this is a major factor in the popularity of this form of diagram.

Collaboration diagrams do not include return arrows at the end of activations, as these would complicate the diagram to an unacceptable extent. Data that is returned from a message is prefixed to message name, and separated from it by the assignment symbol ':='.

The major advantage that collaboration diagrams have over sequence diagrams is that they clearly specify the mechanism used to support each message, by suitably labelled association roles as shown in Figure 9.6. As sequence diagrams do not show association roles, it is important to check that messages are not sent where there is no suitable link between objects to support the message.

9.5 OBJECT CREATION

Suppose that the stock control program from Chapter 2 is to be extended with the capability to store details about orders. For the purposes of this example, an order will be defined to consist simply of a number of order lines, each of which specifies a certain number of parts of a particular type. Figure 9.8 shows a class diagram summarizing the necessary facts about orders.

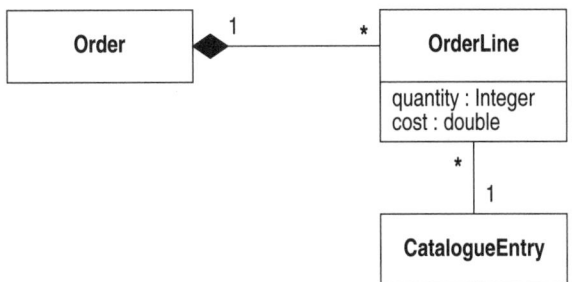

Figure 9.8 Orders in the stock control system

The relationship between orders and order lines is one of composition, because we assume that when an order is destroyed all lines on that order are also destroyed. This is a characteristic application of the semantics of composition, as explained in Section 8.7. The cost attribute of the order line class records the total cost of parts ordered on that line; it should be computed when an order line is created, by multiplying the cost recorded in the catalogue entry object by the number of parts ordered.

Let us assume that to create an order line, a client object must send a message to an order specifying the part and the quantity to be ordered. A new order line object will then be created and added to the order. A sequence diagram illustrating this interaction is shown in Figure 9.9.

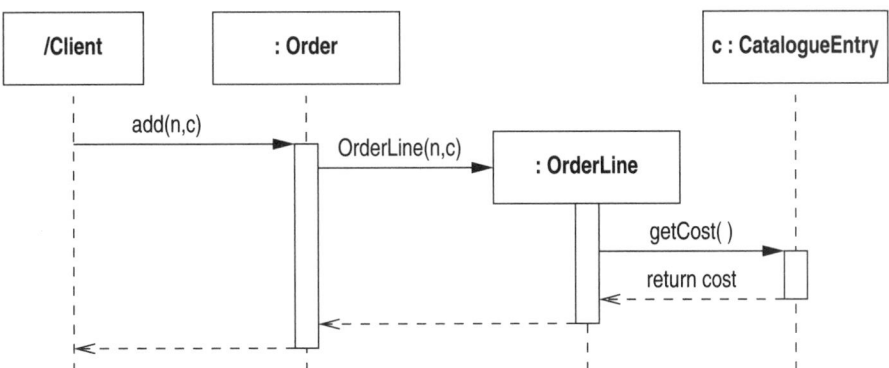

Figure 9.9 Object creation on a sequence diagram

The new order line object is created in response to a message labelled 'add' sent from the client to the order. The parameters of this message supply the number of parts to be added and the catalogue entry object corresponding to the required parts.

In response to this message, an order object creates a new order line object and the constructor call creating this object is shown as the next message in the interaction. On a sequence diagram, the classifier role representing a new object is drawn at a position corresponding to the time at which the new object is created and the message that creates the new object is shown terminating at the role symbol, not on a lifeline as with normal messages. Sequence diagrams thus show very graphically when new objects are created in the course of an interaction.

The activation immediately below the order line icon in Figure 9.9 corresponds to the execution of the object's constructor. The diagram shows that during the construction of order lines the cost of the relevant parts is retrieved from the catalogue entry object that was passed as a parameter. This value will be used in the initialization of the order line's 'cost' attribute. At the end of this activation, control returns to the order and the order line's lifeline continues as normal.

In the course of this interaction two new links are created, one linking the order line to the order that contains it and one linking the order line to its catalogue entry object. These links correspond to the associations shown on Figure 9.8. They cannot be shown in Figure 9.9 because association roles are not depicted on sequence diagrams. Figure 9.10 shows the same interaction on a collaboration diagram, including the two new links.

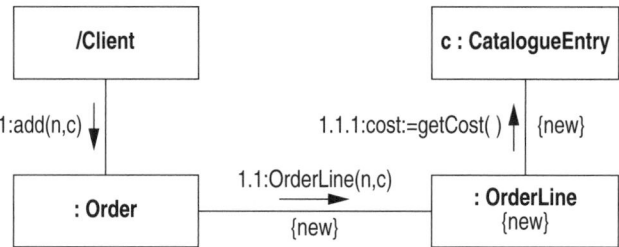

Figure 9.10 Object creation on a collaboration diagram

Collaboration diagrams cannot explicitly show the time at which a new object is created. In order to distinguish elements that are created during the course of an interaction from those that existed at the start, classifier and association roles corresponding to new objects and links are annotated with the property 'new'.

9.6 OBJECT DESTRUCTION

The converse of the creation of new objects is object deletion. Suppose that order lines are removed from orders when a client sends a 'remove' message to the order. A sequence diagram showing object deletion is illustrated in Figure 9.11. Messages that cause the destruction of objects are labelled with the stereotype 'destroy'. The lifeline of the object destroyed terminates in a large cross.

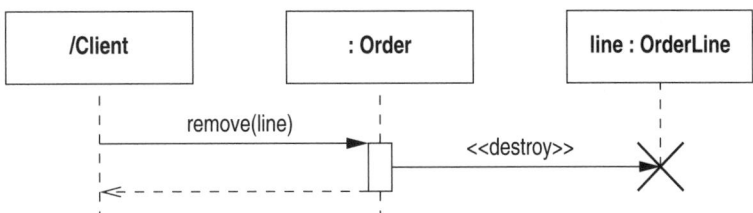

Figure 9.11 Object deletion on a sequence diagram

As with object creation, collaboration diagrams cannot explicitly show the time at which an object is destroyed. Instead, the object and any links that are destroyed are labelled with the property 'destroyed', as shown in Figure 9.12. If an object is created and destroyed in the course of a single interaction, it can be labelled on a collaboration diagram with the property 'transient'.

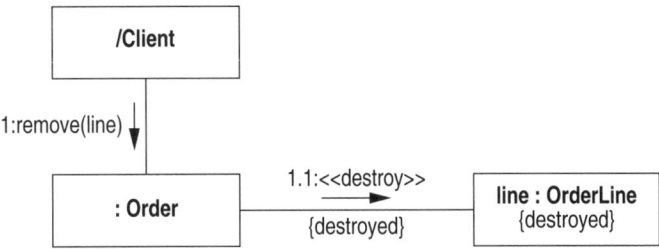

Figure 9.12 Object deletion on a collaboration diagram

9.7 ROLE MULTIPLICITY AND ITERATED MESSAGES

In many cases, the number of objects playing a particular role can vary from one interaction to another. For example, consider the interaction in Figure 9.13 describing how to find the total value of an invoice.

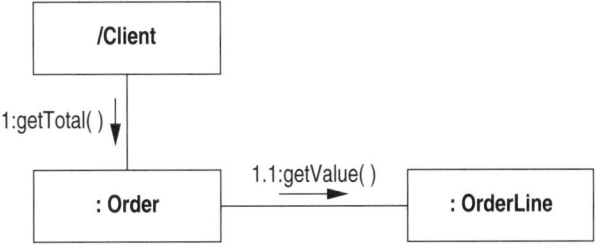

Figure 9.13 Finding the total value of an invoice

The multiplicity properties on the class diagram in Figure 9.8 state that each order can contain zero or more order lines. In the general case, we would expect that there will be more than one order line on an order, and hence the 'getValue' message on Figure 9.13 would be sent more than once in an interaction, depending on how many order lines there were at any given time. The possible iteration of this message is not explicitly shown, however.

Multiplicity can be shown on classifier and association roles in a collaboration, in the same way as on classes and associations. Multiplicity on a classifier role, for example, specifies the number of instances that can play that role in an interaction. This notation is rarely used, however, and it is more common to show that a message can be sent more than once in an interaction by adding a *recurrence* to the message itself. Figure 9.14 shows both a multiplicity in the role representing order lines and a recurrence on the message being sent to this role.

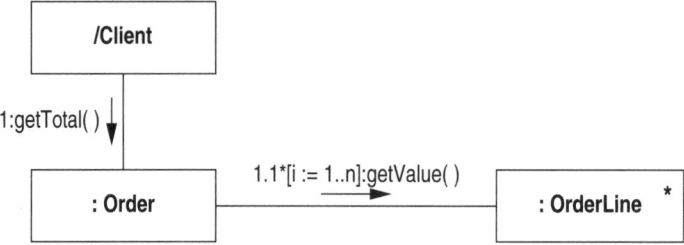

Figure 9.14 An iterated message in a collaboration

A recurrence consists of an asterisk written after the message number, possibly followed by an iteration clause. The iteration clause specifies the details of the iteration and can be omitted if the intention is simply to show the potential repetition of a message. UML does not specify the syntax used to specify a recurrence and a suitable programming language notation is commonly used. Recurrences can be used on both collaboration and sequence diagrams.

9.8 MULTIOBJECTS

An alternative way of showing multiplicity information associated with a classifier role is to use a *multiobject*. Rather than representing a role that can be played by many objects, a multiobject represents a collection of objects of the base type of the multiobject. The effect of this is, for many purposes, equivalent to specifying a role with a multiplicity of zero or more. The notation for a multiobject is shown in Figure 9.15.

The distinction between a multiobject and a role with multiplicity is rather subtle. It has to do with the fact that an object that can hold zero or more links to other objects usually does so in virtue of being linked to a suitable data structure, such as a list or a vector. Figure 9.16 shows a pedantically complete collaboration, which depicts all the objects that might actually exist in the situation shown in Figure 9.15.

Figure 9.15 Showing multiplicity with a multiobject

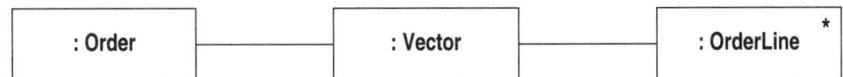

Figure 9.16 Multiplicity with an intermediate data structure

As well as being time-consuming to write, and unnecessarily complicated to read, a diagram like Figure 9.16 represents a premature commitment to a particular data structure class. At an early stage of design, it may not be appropriate to specify what data structure will be used to hold a collection of links. Figure 9.15, then, can be viewed as an abbreviation of Figure 9.16, which removes this premature commitment.

Technically, then, a multiobject represents a single object, namely a collection of objects of some other sort. It follows that a multiobject is a suitable target for messages that perform some operation on a set, such as finding a particular element within the set. For example, suppose in the example of Figure 9.15 that it was necessary to locate the order line corresponding to a particular type of part. We will assume that there is at most one order line per order for a given type of part. An interaction to accomplish this is shown in Figure 9.17.

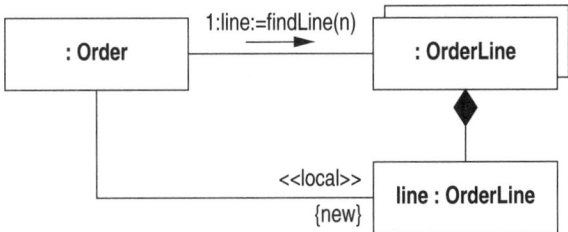

Figure 9.17 Finding a specific order line

Figure 9.17 shows an order object sending a message to a collection of order lines, asking for the line that corresponds to the catalogue entry with part number 'n'. As the multiobject represents only a single object, the collection of lines rather than the lines themselves, this message should not be marked as an iterated message.

Figure 9.17 also shows the order line that is returned by the 'findLine' message as a separate symbol, distinct from the multiobject and labelled to indicate that it is the same object that was returned by the 'findLine' message. To indicate that it is not a new object, but merely one of the order lines represented by the multiobject, it is linked to the multiobject with a composition link, thus indicating that it is part of the set of order lines represented by the multiobject. The order object creates a new link to this line in a local variable.

If an object wants to send a message to all the objects represented by a multiobject, it cannot in principle do so directly. As the multiobject represents the single object containing the other objects, a single message should be sent to it. Some form of iteration will have to take place to get the message to all the objects represented.

However, it would complicate diagrams unnecessarily to show interactions in such detail, and so the convention is frequently adopted that an iterated message to a multiobject, such as the one shown in Figure 9.18, is understood as being an abbreviation for the more complicated processing that would be involved in iterating through all the objects in a multiobject and sending a message to each one individually. This diagram is therefore essentially an alternative form of Figure 9.14 that arguably makes the iterated message sending more graphic.

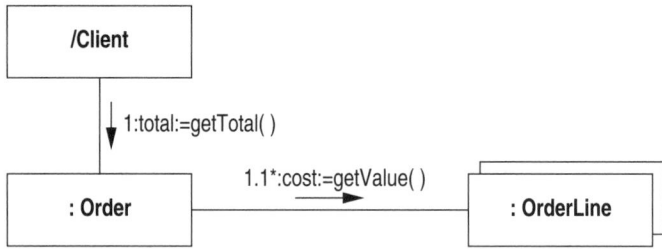

Figure 9.18 Finding the total cost of an order

9.9 CONDITIONAL MESSAGES

The notation discussed so far in this chapter does not enable any variations in the course of an interaction to be shown. Both collaboration and sequence diagrams provide means for showing *conditional* message passing or, in other words, messages that are only sent under certain circumstances. Together with the notation for iterated message passing, this in principle allows interaction diagrams to show the design of an algorithm in full detail, though in most cases this flexibility is not used because of the complexity of the ensuing diagrams.

To illustrate the simple notation for conditional messages, consider the following scenario. Suppose that stock levels for parts are held in catalogue entry objects and that, when a message is received to add a new order line to an order, the order object should first check that sufficient parts of the requested type are in stock before creating the new order line object and adding it to the order. This interaction can be illustrated by the sequence diagram in Figure 9.19, an extension of that shown in Figure 9.8.

To show that the message creating the order line object will only be sent under certain circumstances, a *condition* is attached to it. This consists of a Boolean expression written in square brackets. If the condition evaluates to true at the point in the activation when the message is reached, the message will be sent. Otherwise, control will jump to the point following the return message corresponding to the message bearing the condition.

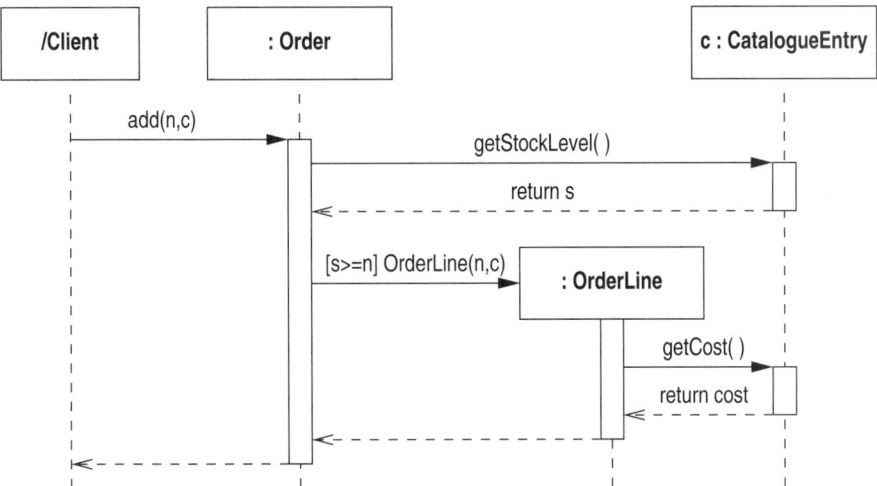

Figure 9.19 Conditional messages on sequence diagrams

Exactly the same notation can be attached to messages in collaboration diagrams, as Figure 9.20 shows. As with the sequence diagram above, this is an extension of the interaction shown in Figure 9.9.

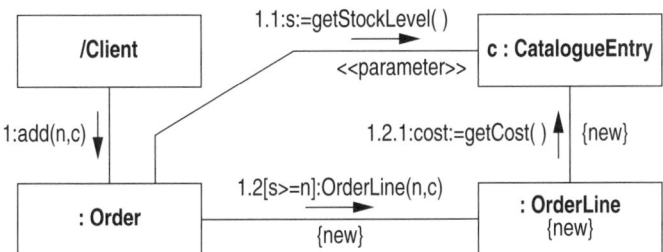

Figure 9.20 Conditional messages on collaboration diagrams

Figures 9.19 and 9.20 illustrate the situation where a particular message may or may not be sent, depending on the state of the system at the time of dispatch. A more general form of conditionality allows alternative courses of action to be followed in different circumstances; perhaps, if the stock level is sufficiently high, the interaction proceeds as shown in Figures 9.19 and 9.20 but, if not, a message is sent to the catalogue entry object asking it to restock the given type of part.

This kind of interaction can be shown explicitly on sequence diagrams but not on collaboration diagrams. The notation is illustrated in Figure 9.21, largely for the sake of completeness. In most cases the visual complexity of this notation will interfere with the ability of the diagram to communicate the details of the interaction to readers, and alternative forms of documenting the design of the algorithm would be used.

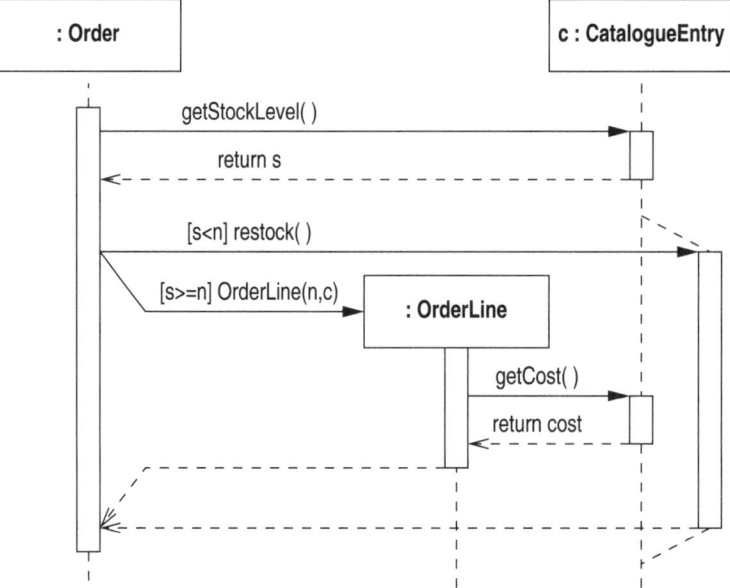

Figure 9.21 Alternative messages on a sequence diagram

Unlike Figure 9.19, the sequence diagram in Figure 9.21 shows an alternative message at the point where the new order line object is created. The new message has the opposite condition to the first, namely that the stock level is too low to permit the order to be made. Only one of the two messages will be sent as the interaction proceeds, and this is shown by having both originate from the same point.

Each time the flow of control reaches this point in the interaction, one or other of the messages will be sent. Later in the interaction there is a point where the two branches rejoin; after this point the interaction continues in a normal sequential manner. The join of control following the fork is shown by the meeting of the two return messages that correspond to the branching messages.

The catalogue entry object will receive different messages depending on which branch is executed. It would not be correct to show all these messages arriving at one lifeline, as this would imply that all messages were received in a single interaction. Instead, the lifeline of the catalogue entry object branches, reflecting the fork of control in the order object. Messages from one alternative are sent to one branch of the lifeline and those from the other to the other branch.

As well as a fork of control, the diagram now contains a branching lifeline, as the history of a catalogue entry object in the course of the transaction now contains alternative possibilities. Reading from top to bottom of the sequence diagram in Figure 9.21, only one branch of the lifeline will be followed in any one interaction. One unsatisfactory feature of this notation is that the condition that causes this branching is not associated with the lifeline itself. This can rapidly lead to obscurity in diagrams that are more complex than Figure 9.21.

9.10 MESSAGES TO SELF

Occasionally it can be useful to show explicitly the messages that an object sends to itself. Often such messages can be thought of as internal details of the object's implementation, but sometimes showing them can clarify the description of an algorithm. This is particularly true if further messages are sent to other objects as a result of the message that the object sends to itself. In this case, showing all the messages is necessary for understanding the details of the nesting of activations within the interaction.

As with messages to other objects, a message that an object sends to itself gives rise to a new activation, but in this case the new activation takes place in an object that already has a live activation. On a sequence diagram, the recursive nature of this new activation is shown by superimposing the new activation on top of the original one, as shown in Figure 9.22.

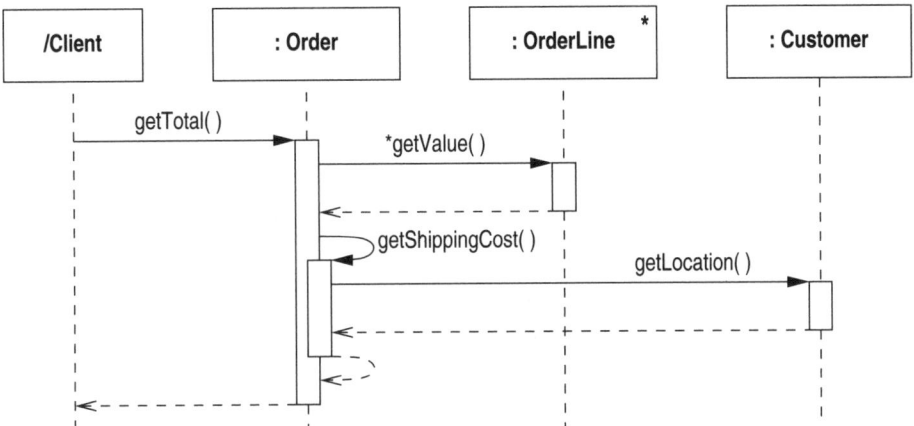

Figure 9.22 A recursive activation

The interaction in Figure 9.22 shows how the total cost of an order is calculated. First, the cost of each order line is obtained and then the order object sends itself a message to calculate the shipping costs of the order. In programming terms, this would correspond to the decision to implement this functionality as a separate method within the order class, as it may need to be called from more than one place.

In response to this message, a further message is sent to the customer object linked to the order, to find out the address of the customer from which, presumably, the cost of delivering the order can be calculated. This message is sent from the nested activation, making the flow of control from message to message completely explicit. At the end of the nested activation a return message is shown looping back to the activation that was responsible for sending the message.

Recursive activations are not shown so explicitly on collaboration diagrams but, as with normal activations, each recursive activation gives rise to an extra level of hierarchy in the numbering of subsequent messages and in this way the dependency of one message on another is kept clear.

Figure 9.23 shows the same interaction as Figure 9.22, but on a collaboration diagram. Notice that an association role labelled with the 'self' stereotype is used as a vehicle for a message sent by an object to itself.

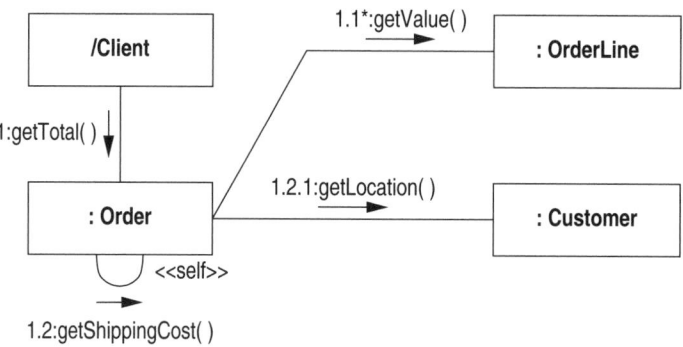

Figure 9.23 A message to self on a collaboration diagram

In Figures 9.22 and 9.23 nested activations have been shown arising from an object sending a message to itself. There is no reason in principle why a nested activation should not arise from a message sent from a different object, in the situation where object A sends a message to object B and in the course of responding to that message object B sends a message back to object A. An example of this sort of interchange between objects is shown in Figure 6.5.

9.11 SUMMARY

- *Interactions* define part of a system's behaviour as a set of messages passed among a set of collaborating objects. The objects involved in an interaction are known as a *collaboration*.

- Collaborations can be defined at the *instance level*, when they show individual objects, or at the *specification level*, when they show the *classifier roles* that objects can play in an interaction.

- *Association roles* connect classifier roles in collaborations and indicate how objects can be linked, and hence exchange messages, in interactions.

- Association roles can correspond to associations in the class model, but various types of transient link between objects can also be specified, to model the sending of messages to local variables and operation parameters.

- UML defines two types of diagram for showing interactions, *collaboration diagrams* and *sequence diagrams*. Both forms depict objects or classifier roles, and the messages that are passed between them.

- Collaboration diagrams depict association roles as well as classifier roles. A hierarchical numbering scheme has to be used in order to clarify the sequencing of messages.

- Sequence diagrams do not depict the association roles involved in an interaction. The sequencing of messages is shown very clearly, as arrows between objects' lifelines, with time flowing down the diagram.

- Both types of interaction diagram can show object creation and destruction and, in order to clarify the details of an algorithm, an object sending a message to itself. In this latter case, an additional recursive activation is generated.

- Like class diagrams, collaborations can contain multiplicity annotations which specify the number of objects that can participate in interactions. Collections of objects can also be shown using *multiobjects*.

- Conditions can be used on interaction diagrams, to show either the optional sending of messages or alternative flows of control.

9.12 EXERCISES

9.1 Suppose that in a banking system a transfer is carried out in the following way: a transfer object is created to control the interaction, and the two accounts and the amount to be transferred are then passed as parameters to a 'doTransfer' method in the transfer object. Draw a collaboration diagram, based on Figures 9.1 and 9.2, illustrating this interaction. Draw a sequence diagram showing the same interaction and discuss which is the most suitable diagram in this case.

9.2 Draw a schematic collaboration diagram showing the same structure of interactions as the sequence diagram shown in Figure 9.7.

9.3 Redraw Figure 9.14 as a sequence diagram, showing the recurrence on the message.

9.4 Draw a sequence diagram corresponding to Figure 9.17 and comment on the relative usefulness of the two forms of diagram in this case.

9.5 After reading Chapter 14, redraw Figure 14.22 as sequence diagrams and comment on the relative strengths and weaknesses of the two forms of diagram in this case.

9.6 Many word processors, graphical editors and similar tools provide *cut*, *copy* and *paste* operations by means of some kind of a clipboard facility. At run-time suppose that such a system consists of an instance of an 'Editor' class linked to a number of instances of an 'Element' class. Elements are the items manipulated by a tool, such as words or shapes. Some of the elements may have been *selected* by the user. The editor is also linked to an instance of a 'Clipboard' class, which in turn maintains links to all the elements that have been placed on the clipboard. An element cannot simultaneously be displayed by the editor and on the clipboard.

(*a*) Draw a collaboration showing a configuration where there are several elements displayed by the editor and one element on the clipboard. Assume that the selected elements are identified by an additional link from the editor.

(*b*) Draw a sequence diagram showing what happens when the editor receives a *cut* message from a client. The effect of this is that all the currently selected elements are moved to the clipboard.

(*c*) Draw a sequence diagram showing what happens when the editor receives a *paste* message from a client. The effect of this is that all the elements on the clipboard are moved back to the editor.

(*d*) Draw a sequence diagram showing what happens when the editor receives a *copy* message from a client. The effect of this is that all the currently selected elements are copied to the clipboard. Assume that elements implement a 'clone' operation, which returns an exact copy of the element.

(*e*) Draw equivalent collaboration diagrams for each of your answers.

9.7 The code below shows a class `DataSet`, which provides basic statistical functionality on a set of data, and a class `ExamMarks`, which uses `DataSet` to store and work out the average of a set of exam marks. The main function shown reads in two marks and uses `ExamMarks` to store them and print out the average. Draw a sequence diagram showing the interaction that takes place when the main function executes.

```
class DataSet
{
  private float data[] ;
  private int items ;

  public DataSet() {
    data = new float[256] ;
    items = 0 ;
  }

  public void addDataPoint(float d) {
    data[items++] = d ;
  }

  public float mean() {
    float total = 0 ;
    for (int i = 0; i < getSize(); i++) {
      total += data[i] ;
    }
    return total / getSize() ;
  }

  public int getSize() {
    return items;
  }
}
```

```
class ExamMarks
{
  private DataSet marks ;

  public void enterMark(float m) {
    if (marks == null) {
      marks = new DataSet() ;
    }
    marks.addDataPoint(m) ;
  }

  float average() {
    return marks.mean() ;
  }
}

public class Average
{
  public static void main(String args[]) {
    ExamMarks exam = new ExamMarks() ;
    exam.enterMark(56) ;
    exam.enterMark(72) ;
    System.out.println(exam.average()) ;
  }
}
```

10

STATECHARTS

In an interaction, an individual object may be sent one or more messages, and these messages are received in a particular order. In other interactions, however, the same object may receive quite different messages. The order in which particular messages are sent to the object may also vary from case to case, depending on the details of each interaction. By considering all the possible interactions that an object could participate in, we can see that an object may have to respond sensibly to a very wide range of sequences of messages throughout its lifetime.

We have seen in Chapter 8 that object diagrams are not used to specify all the possible states of a system: first, there are simply too many states to document exhaustively and, second, as well as knowing what the possible states are, we need to know which states are impossible, or illegal. For exactly the same reasons, sequence and collaboration diagrams are not used to describe all the possible interactions that an object can participate in.

In both cases, the solution is the same, namely to use a more abstract form of notation that allows the system to be specified, and not just illustrated. In UML, a behavioural specification of an object is given by defining a *state machine* for the object. A state machine specifies an object's responses to the events it might detect during its lifetime. In UML, state machines are normally documented in a type of diagram known as a *statechart*.

Interaction diagrams and statecharts present two complementary views of the dynamic behaviour of a system. Interaction diagrams show the messages passed between the objects in the system during a short period of time, often the duration of a single user-generated transaction. These diagrams must therefore depict a number of objects, namely those that happen to be involved in that particular transaction. A statechart, on the other hand, tracks an individual object throughout its entire lifetime, specifying all the possible sequences of messages that the object could receive, together with its response to these messages.

10.1 STATE-DEPENDENT BEHAVIOUR

Many objects exhibit *state-dependent behaviour*. Loosely speaking, this means that the object will respond differently to the same stimulus at different times. For example, consider the behaviour of a simple CD player, which consists of a drawer to hold the CD, if any, that is currently being played and an interface consisting of three buttons labelled 'load', 'play' and 'stop'. The load button causes the drawer to open if it is currently shut and to shut if it is open. The stop button causes the player to stop playing. If the stop button is pressed when no CD is playing, it has no effect. Finally, the play button causes the CD contained in the drawer to be played. If it is pressed when the drawer is open, the drawer shuts before playing starts.

This CD player exhibits state-dependent behaviour in at least two ways. For example, when the drawer is open, pressing the 'load' button shuts it and when it is shut, pressing 'load' causes it to open. Furthermore, if a CD is playing, pressing the stop button causes playing to stop, but, if no CD is playing, this action has no effect.

In this example we can identify at least three distinct states that the CD player can be in. The different effects of pressing 'load' indicate that we need to distinguish an 'open' and a 'closed' state, and the different effects of pressing 'stop' suggest that there is a third state, which might be labelled 'playing' and which is distinct from either of the first two states. It is also noteworthy that the CD player may change state in response to events. For example, pressing the 'load' button repeatedly will cause the CD player to switch between the open and closed states.

Agreeably enough, the three states in this example correspond to observable differences in the physical state of the CD player, but this will not always be the case. The fundamental principle for distinguishing states is that an object in a particular state will respond differently to at least one event from the way in which it responds to that event in other states. States thus identified may or may not correspond to easily detectable external features of the object.

The notion of state used in behavioural modelling should be distinguished from that discussed in Chapter 2, where an object's state was defined to be the aggregate of the values of its attributes at a given time. The behavioural notion of state is wider than this: it is perfectly possible for an object's attributes to differ at two different times and yet for it to be in the same behavioural state. An example of this is provided by the 'closed' state of the CD player: the presence or absence of a CD in the drawer can be considered to be different attribute values of the CD player, yet in either case we can still consider the player to be in the closed state.

The identification of behavioural states is not a rigorous process. States are distinguished by the fact that the object may respond differently to events when in different states, but what counts as a relevant difference in response is to some extent a question of judgement. The important properties of behavioural states are, first, that an object has a number of possible states and it is in exactly one of these states at any given time. Second, an object can change state and, in general, the state it is in at a given time will be determined by its history. Finally, depending on its state, an object may exhibit different responses at different times to the same stimulus.

10.2 STATES, EVENTS AND TRANSITIONS

Statechart diagrams, usually simply called *statecharts*, show the possible states of an object, the events it can detect and its response to those events. In order to construct a statechart for an object, therefore, we must first establish, at least provisionally, what states it can be in and what events it can detect. For the example of the CD player, we have identified the open, closed and playing states which will serve as a basis for developing a statechart.

In software terms, it is common to assume that the events detected by an object are simply the messages sent to it. It is not necessary to be so specific when starting a design, however: all that is required is the more general notion of an object being able to detect an external event. In the case of the CD player, the external events that can be detected are simply the pressing of the three buttons. A state machine for the CD player will therefore involve at least three events, 'load', 'play' and 'stop'.

In general, detecting an event can cause an object to move from one state to another. Such a move is called a *transition*. For example, if the CD player is in the open state, pressing the load button will cause the drawer to shut and the CD player to move into the closed state. The basic information shown on a statechart is the possible states of the entity and the transitions between them, or in other words the way that detecting various events causes the system to move from one state to another.

A statechart describing a basic model of the CD player is shown in Figure 10.1. The states of the system are shown as rounded rectangles, with the name of the state written inside them. State transitions are shown by arrows linking two states. Each such arrow must be labelled with the name of an event. The meaning of such an arrow is that if the system receives the event when it is in the state at the tail of the arrow, it will move into the state at the head of the arrow. It follows that events will normally appear on a state diagram more than once, as it will be possible for the object to detect the same event in many different states.

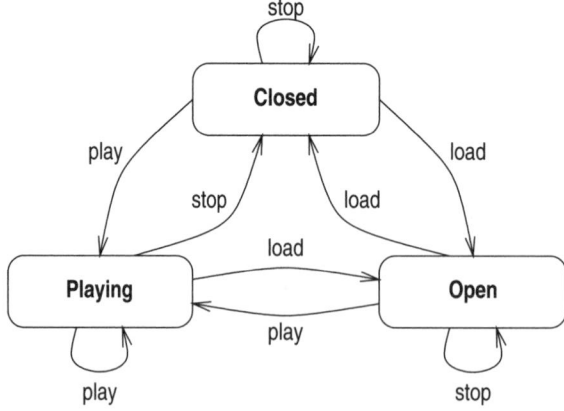

Figure 10.1 A simple state machine for a CD player

In Figure 10.1, every state has three arrows leaving it, one for each event detectable by the CD player. This kind of completeness is not an essential property of state machines but simply reflects the fact that the user of the CD player can press any of the three buttons at any time. If an event does not cause a change of state, the corresponding transition simply loops on a state. An example of this is the transition that shows what happens when the play event is detected and the CD player is already in the playing state. Such transitions are referred to as *self-transitions*.

Events, like messages, can carry data with them, written in parentheses after the message name. None of the events in the CD example need to carry additional data, but examples of this will be seen in the example considered in Section 10.10.

Execution of state machines

A simple state machine, such as the one shown in the statechart in Figure 10.1, can be thought of as 'executing' in the following manner. At any given moment the object is in exactly one of the states shown on the diagram. This is known as the *active state*. Any outgoing transaction from the active state is a candidate for *firing*. For example, if the active state of the CD player is the 'open' state, the transitions that are candidates for firing are the self-transition on that state, the transition labelled 'load' leading to the closed state and the transition labelled 'play' leading to the playing state.

The events that can cause transitions to fire are known as *triggers*. When an event is detected, an outgoing transition from the active state that is labelled with the name of that event will fire. The state at the other end of the transition that fires then becomes the active state and the process repeats, with the difference that the candidates for firing are now the outgoing transitions from the new active state.

If no outgoing event from the current state is labelled with the name of the event detected, the event is simply ignored. No transition is fired and the current state remains active. If it is necessary to specify that it is an error for a particular event to be detected while a state is active, an error state can be defined and a transition added, leading to the error state and labelled with the name of the prohibited event.

10.3 INITIAL AND FINAL STATES

The diagram in Figure 10.1 describes the functioning of the CD player when it is in use, but it does not say what happens when the machine is switched on and off. We will assume that when the machine is switched off it exhibits no behaviour and that when it is powered on it always goes straight to the closed state.

We can show this latter behaviour by adding an *initial state* to the state diagram; initial states are shown as small black disks. A transition leading from an initial event shows the state that the object goes into when it is created or initialized. An initial state for the CD player is shown in Figure 10.2 with a transition showing that the player is always in the closed start after being switched on. Notice that no event should be written on a transition from an initial state.

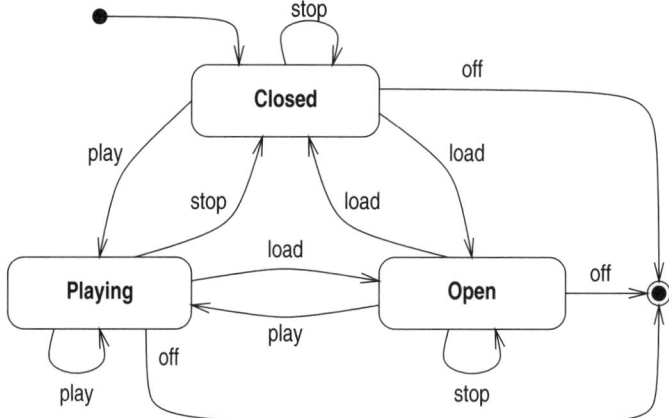

Figure 10.2 Initial and final states

As well as an initial state, a state diagram can show a *final state*. This represents the state reached when an object is destroyed, switched off or otherwise stops responding to events, and it is shown by a small black disk within a larger circle. In general, a final state can be reached from many different states. In the case of the CD player, the event that causes the final state to be reached is the player being switched off. We can model this as a new event called 'off'. The machine can be switched off at any point, so the final state is linked to all the other states by a transition labelled with the 'off' event.

The meaning of the final state depends on the nature of the object being described by the statechart. If a software object, an instance of a class, reaches its final state, it will literally be destroyed: its destructor, if it has one, will be called and the memory it occupies will be retrieved.

However, Figure 10.2 clearly should not be interpreted as saying that the CD player is physically destroyed each time it is switched off: such a design would be unlikely to make it to market. What is really being modelled is the behaviour of the software that controls the CD player: when it is switched off the control program is terminated and the machine will not respond to any events until it has been switched on again.

10.4 GUARD CONDITIONS

The statechart in Figure 10.2 gives an oversimplified description of the behaviour of the CD player. One problem is that the player does not always go into the playing state when the play button is pressed. It will do so if there is a CD in the drawer when the event is detected, but otherwise the drawer will simply shut, if it is not already shut, and the player will go into the closed state. This means that an accurate model should contain two transitions labelled 'play' from both the closed and open states. Which transition is actually followed on any given occasion will depend on the contents of the drawer at that time.

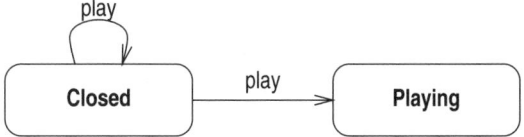

Figure 10.3 Two possible outcomes of pressing 'play'

Figure 10.3 shows the two possible outcomes of pressing the play button when the drawer of the CD player is closed. This is an example of a *non-deterministic* statechart. The diagram shows that two possible transitions can be triggered by a play event, but does not explain when one will fire rather than the other.

There is nothing wrong with non-deterministic diagrams in principle, but if the system being modelled is in fact deterministic, a non-deterministic diagram must be leaving out some information about the system. In the case of the CD player, there is no real non-determinism when the button is pressed, as the subsequent behaviour of the player is determined by the contents of the drawer. A more accurate model should remove the non-determinism present in Figure 10.3 by showing what causes one transition to be followed rather than another.

This information can be shown on the statechart by adding *guard conditions* to the play transitions, stating the circumstances under which the transitions will fire. Guard conditions are part of the specification of a transition and are written in square brackets after the event name that labels the transition. Guard conditions are often written in informal English, as here, but if desired a more formal notation can be used, such as the OCL language described in Chapter 12.

Figure 10.4 shows the statechart for the CD player extended to include guard conditions that differentiate the full and empty states of the drawer. For simplicity, the initial and final states, which are not relevant to the current discussion, have been omitted from this diagram.

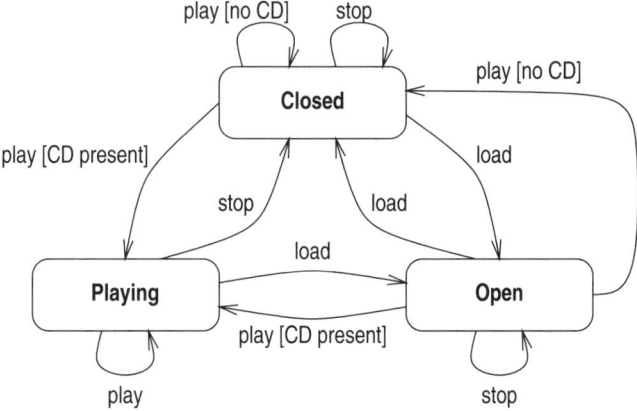

Figure 10.4 Using guard conditions to distinguish transitions

The effect of the guard conditions on the execution of a state machine is as follows. When an event is detected, any guard conditions on transitions that are labelled with the name of that event are evaluated. If a transition has a guard condition, it can only fire if that transition evaluates to true. If all guard conditions evaluate to false and there are no unguarded transitions, the event will be ignored.

If more than one transition has a guard condition that evaluates to true, exactly one of them will fire. In this case, non-determinism has been reintroduced into the state machine; normally guard conditions on a set of outgoing transitions are chosen so that no more than one of them can be true at any given time.

For example, suppose that the CD player is in the open state and the play button is pressed. The first thing that will happen is that the drawer will close; this is necessary so that the machine can detect whether or not a disk is present. It is important to notice that at this point, despite the fact that the drawer is closed, the CD player is not in the closed state. It is still in the open state, evaluating the guard conditions on the play transitions to see which transition should fire. This illustrates a point made earlier, that the states in the CD player's state machine do not necessarily correspond exactly to the physical states of the CD player.

If a CD is present, the transition leading from the open to the playing state will fire. The state machine moves directly from the open to the playing state and does not, even temporarily, pass through the closed state. If it did, it would have to detect a second event to fire a transition to move it to the playing state. Only a single event, however, the pressing of the play button, is necessary to move it from the open to the playing state. The physical fact of the drawer closing can be modelled on the statechart, if desired, as an *action*, as described in the next section.

10.5 ACTIONS

Statecharts can show what an object does in response to detecting a particular event. This is shown by adding *actions* to the relevant transitions in the diagram. Actions are written after the event name, prefixed by a diagonal slash. Figure 10.5 shows the statechart for the CD player with actions added to show the points at which the drawer is physically opened and closed.

Actions can either be described in English, in pseudo-code or by using the notation of the target programming language. Transitions often carry both conditions and actions. If this is the case, the condition is written immediately after the event name, followed by the action.

Actions are thought of as short, self-contained pieces of processing, which take an insignificant time to complete. The defining characteristic of an action is that it is completed before the transition reaches the new state. This implies that an action cannot be interrupted by any other event that might be detected by the object, but must always run to completion. Actions that are not atomic in this sense, or processing that is carried out while an object is in a given state, can be described by *activities* instead of actions, as described in Section 10.6.

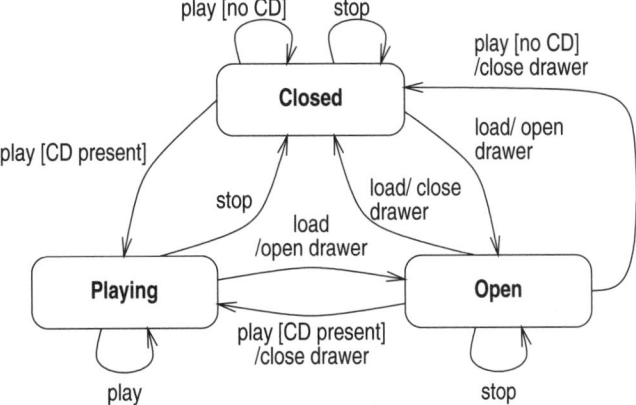

Figure 10.5 Actions for manipulating the drawer of the CD player

Entry and exit actions

Suppose that every time the play button is pressed with a CD in the drawer, the playing head of the CD player positions itself at the start of the current track. This could be shown on the statechart by writing a suitable action on every transition labelled 'play' that leads to the playing state. However, this is rather clumsy and redundant, and the same effect can be achieved more economically by including an *entry action* in the playing state, as shown in Figure 10.6.

Entry actions are performed every time a state becomes active, immediately after actions on transitions leading to the state have completed. For example, if the CD player was in the open state and the play button was pressed, the drawer would close and the transition to the playing state would fire. As a result of this, the playing state would become active and the entry action in the playing state would immediately be executed.

States can also be provided with *exit actions*, which are performed whenever a transition is fired to leave the state. The exit action in Figure 10.6 states that whenever an action is performed that causes playing of a CD to stop, the first thing to happen is that the playing head of the CD player is raised.

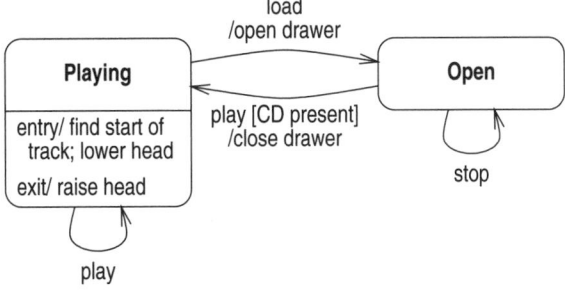

Figure 10.6 Entry and exit actions

Notice that self-transitions count as changes of state. When a self-transition on a state fires, the state temporarily ceases to be active and is then reactivated. This means that when a self-transition is followed, first the exit and then the entry action of the state are executed, if they exist. In Figure 10.6 this means that the effect of pressing the play button when a CD is being played will be to reposition the playing head at the start of the current track, thereby restarting the track. This behaviour is in fact exhibited by many CD players.

10.6 ACTIVITIES

Obviously, when it is in the playing state, the CD player is doing something, namely playing the current track of the CD. Extended operations that take time to complete can be shown as *activities* within states. Like actions, activities are written inside the state, prefixed with the label 'do' as shown in Figure 10.7.

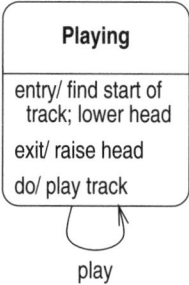

Figure 10.7 The activity of playing a track

The distinction between actions and activities is that, unlike actions, which are thought of as being instantaneous, activities take place over an extended period of time. When a state becomes active, its entry action is performed and then its activity begins, and the activity continues to run throughout the period when the state is active.

Entry actions must be completed before the object can respond to any events. Activities, on the other hand, can be interrupted by any event that causes an outgoing transition from the state containing the activity to fire. For example, the activity of playing the track would be interrupted and terminated if a 'stop' event was detected before the track finished. When a transition leaving a state fires, execution of the activity is interrupted before the exit action is performed.

Completion transitions

As well as being interrupted by events, some activities will come to an end of their own accord. For example, this will happen to the activity in the playing state in Figure 10.7 when the end of the track is reached. In some cases the termination of an activity causes a state transition, and the statechart should specify what state becomes active next.

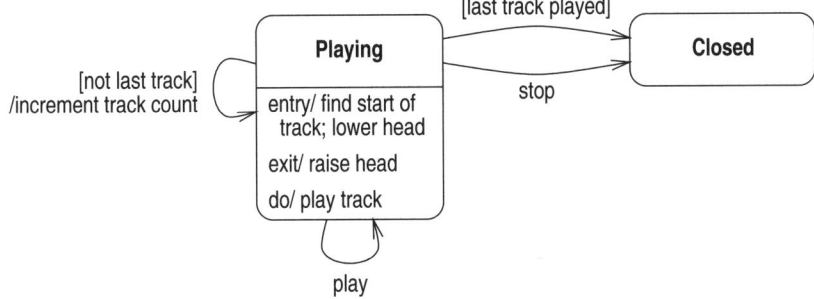

Figure 10.8 Completion transitions

This can be done by means of a *completion transition*. Completion transitions are transitions that have no event labels. They can be triggered when a state's internal activity terminates normally without being interrupted by an external event. Figure 10.8 shows the playing state of the CD player with two completion transitions, one leading from the playing state to the closed state, and one self-transition on the playing state.

While the CD player is playing, the user can press either the play or stop button to interrupt the current track. If neither of these events is detected, the current track will eventually come to an end. In this case, there is no external event to detect, so the only candidate transitions for firing are the completion transitions. What happens next will depend on whether the track that has just finished was the last track on the CD.

The completion transitions have guard conditions to distinguish between these two cases. If the last track has just finished playing, the transition leading to the closed state will fire and the CD player will stop playing altogether. Otherwise, the self-transition will fire: the track counter will be incremented, the playing state will be re-entered and the CD player will begin to play the next track on the CD.

Internal transitions

Self-transitions count as changes of state so, as explained above, if either of the self-transitions in Figure 10.8 fires, the activity in the playing state will be terminated, if necessary, and the exit action of the state executed before the state is re-entered, its entry action executed and its activity restarted.

Sometimes it is necessary to model events that leave an object in the same state, but without triggering a change of state and the execution of entry and exit actions. For example, suppose the CD player has an 'info' button, which when pressed causes the time remaining on the current track to be displayed. This should happen without interrupting the ongoing playing of the track.

This can be modelled as an *internal transition* within the playing state. Internal transitions are written inside the state, labelled with the name of the event that causes them, as shown in Figure 10.9. Unlike self-transitions, internal transitions do not cause a change of state and therefore do not trigger entry and exit actions.

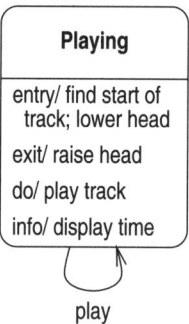

play

Figure 10.9 A state with an internal transition

10.7 COMPOSITE STATES

Figure 10.5 is rather cluttered and hard to read, and there is a certain amount of redundancy in it, with certain transitions occurring more than once in a virtually identical form. If statecharts are to be usable in practice for complex systems, some method of simplifying diagrams is required. One such technique is provided by allowing a state to contain a number of *substates*. The substates are grouped together in the enclosing state because they share certain properties, which can more concisely be represented as properties of a single 'superstate'.

One property that states can share with other states is their behaviour or, in other words, the transitions that they participate in. For example, when the CD player is in the open or closed state, its response to a play event with a CD in the drawer is the same, namely to move to the playing state and to play the CD. Slightly less obviously, the response is the same even if there is no CD present: the player ends up in the closed state. This may or may not involve a change of state, depending on whether the drawer was originally open or closed, but the net effect of the event is the same.

Figure 10.10 shows a statechart for the CD player that uses a superstate to factor out this common behaviour. A new state called 'Not Playing' has been introduced and the open and closed states now appear as substates of this new state. The not playing state is known as a *composite state* consisting of the two nested substates.

This new state exists only to group together related states and does not introduce any new behavioural possibilities for the CD player. Composite states have the following properties. First, if a composite state is active, exactly one of its substates must also be active. So in Figure 10.10, if the CD player is not playing, it must also be in either the open or closed state.

Second, an event that is detected while an object is in a composite state can trigger outgoing transitions from either the composite state itself or from the currently active substate. For example, suppose that the CD player is in the closed state. If a load event is detected, the transition leading to the open state will fire and the open state will become active. This is an internal transition of the not playing state, however, and so it remains active, but with a different active substate.

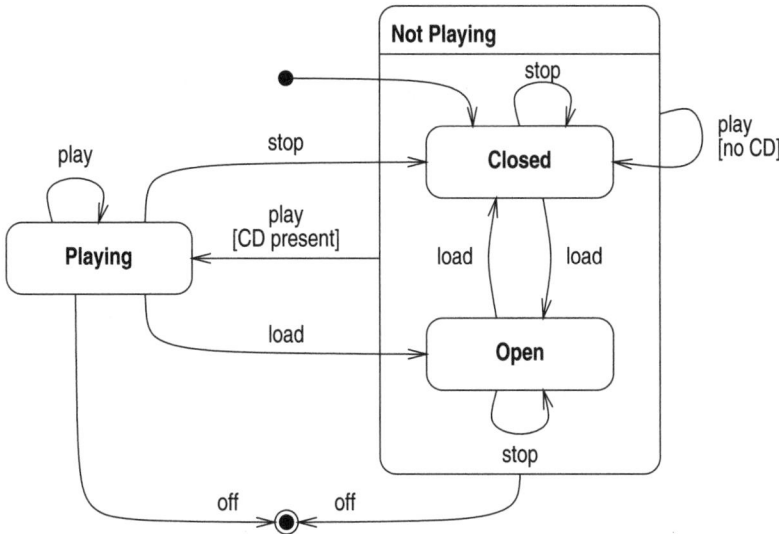

Figure 10.10 The CD player using substates

Suppose, on the other hand, that a play event is detected. There are no outgoing transitions labelled 'play' leaving the closed state, but there are such transitions leaving the not playing state. As this state is also active, these transitions will be enabled and, depending on whether there is a CD in the drawer or not, one or other of them will fire. If a CD is present, the playing state will become active. If not, the closed state will become active, but by means of a self-transition leaving the not playing state.

Substates are perfectly normal states, and transitions to them can freely cross the boundary of the superstate. The stop and load transitions from the playing state in Figure 10.10 illustrate this property. They now cross the boundary of the not playing state, but have not altered in form or meaning from Figure 10.5. Transitions can also connect substates within a single superstate, as the load transitions between the open and closed states demonstrate. Finally, transitions can go from a substate to a state outside the superstate, although Figure 10.10 does not contain an example of this.

Properties of composite states

The nested states within a composite state form a sort of 'sub-statechart' and, in addition to normal states, a composite state can contain initial and final states. An initial state in a composite state shows the default substate that becomes active if a transition to the composite state terminates at the boundary of the composite state. A final state in a composite state indicates that ongoing activity within the state has finished. Arrival at a final state enables completion transitions from the composite state to fire.

Composite states can also have entry and exit actions of their own. These are activated in exactly the same way as with simple states whenever the state becomes, or ceases to be, active.

For example, suppose that pressing a pause button on the CD player causes playing to be interrupted. When the button is pressed again, playing continues from the position where it was paused; in other words, unlike the situation where the play button is pressed, the track is not restarted. The statechart in Figure 10.11 models this behaviour.

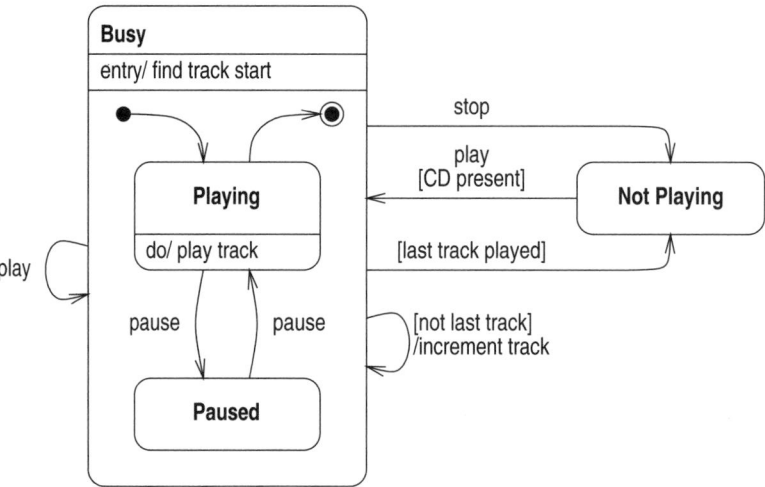

Figure 10.11 Modelling the pause button

This diagram can best be understood by following through some sequences of events in detail. Suppose that the CD player is in the not playing state and the play button is pressed with a CD in the drawer. The transition labelled 'play' will fire, making the state labelled 'busy' the active state. As a result the entry action of the state is performed and the start of the current track located. This transition does not specify which substate of the busy state becomes active, however, so the internal transition from the initial state to the playing state fires, making the playing state active. As a result, the activity of playing the current track starts.

If the user does nothing to interrupt this, at the end of the track the completion transition from the playing state to the final state within the busy state will fire. This is the normal behaviour when a state's activity terminates. This in turn triggers a completion activity from the composite state. Assuming that there are more tracks to play, the self-transition on the busy state will fire, the track counter will be incremented, and the busy state will be re-entered. As before, this will cause the start of the new track to be located and playing of it to start.

Now suppose that the user presses the pause button before the end of the track. This will interrupt the activity of playing the track and cause the transition to the 'paused' state to fire. When the user presses pause again, the transition leading back to the playing state will fire and the activity of playing the track will restart. In this case, however, all the transitions have been internal to the busy state and so the entry action of locating the start of the track will not have been triggered. The playing head will therefore not have been moved and playing will restart from the point of interruption, as required.

10.8 HISTORY STATES

Suppose that the behaviour of the CD player is as described in Figure 10.11, and that the user presses the play button when the CD player is in the paused state. This will fire the self-transition labelled 'play' on the busy state, so the paused state will be exited and the busy state re-entered. The entry action will cause the start of the track to be found and, as the self-transition only leads to the composite state, the transition from the initial state will be followed, leaving the machine in the playing state, playing the CD.

Suppose, however, that the actual behaviour exhibited by the CD player is different, and that pressing the play button when the CD player is paused restarts the track, but leaves the player in the paused state. The user has to press the pause button again before playing will restart. One way of modelling this would be to replace the self-transition on the busy state labelled 'play' by two self-transitions, one on the playing state and one on the paused state.

However, it would be possible to avoid replicating transitions if a transition to a composite state could 'remember' which substate was active last time the composite state was active and automatically return to that substate. If the CD player is playing, it should carry on playing from the start of the track if 'play' is pressed, but if it is paused, it should stay paused until the pause button is pressed again.

This effect can be achieved by the use of a *history state* as shown in Figure 10.12. History states are represented by a capital 'H' within a circle and can only appear inside composite states. A transition to a history state causes the substate that was most recently active in the composite state to become active again. Now, if 'play' is pressed when the CD player is paused, the self-transition on the busy state will be followed, terminating at the history state. This will cause an implicit transition to the last active substate, which in this case was the paused state, as required.

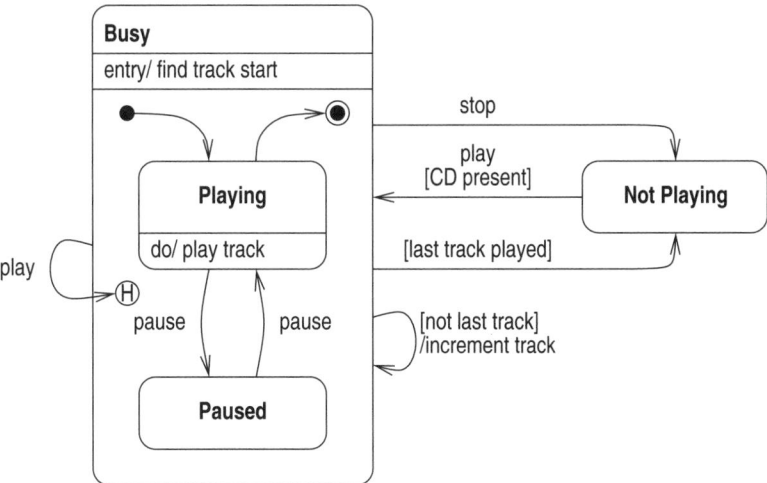

Figure 10.12 A history state

If the stop button was pressed when the CD player was paused, followed by 'play', Figure 10.12 specifies that the player would revert to the playing state. If it was required that it should still be paused, even if playing had been stopped and restarted, this could be modelled by extending the end of the play transition from the boundary of the busy state to the history state.

This raises the question of what would happen if the history state was the first substate of the busy state to be made active: in this case there would, by definition, be no history to remember. In this case we must specify a default state that will be made active. This is done by drawing an unlabelled transition from the history state to the required default, which in this case would be the playing state.

10.9 SUMMARY OF THE CD PLAYER

Figure 10.13 shows a complete statechart describing the behaviour of the CD player, incorporating many of the points that have been discussed in this chapter. This diagram has been derived by combining Figures 10.10 and 10.12. An initial state has been added to the 'not playing' state, and also an additional history state to indicate that pressing the stop button while no CD is being played has no effect and does not cause the player to change its state.

Further extensions and modifications to this diagram are suggested as exercises at the end of this chapter.

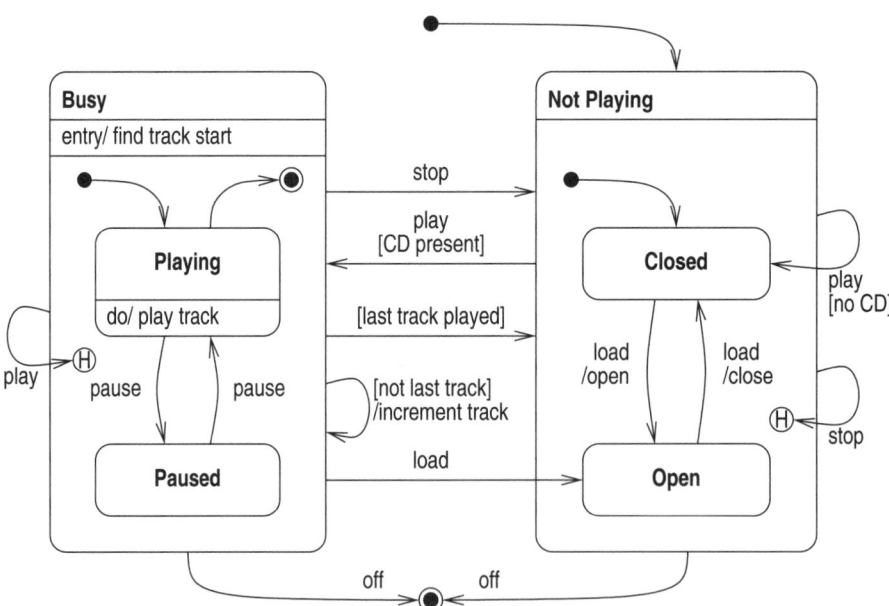

Figure 10.13 Complete statechart for the CD player

10.10 DYNAMIC MODELLING IN PRACTICE

This section illustrates a process that can be useful for constructing a statechart, and in so doing explains how information derived from interaction diagrams can be used to derive statecharts. The example used is the automatic ticket machine described in the following paragraphs.

The ticket machine can accept money and other input from a passenger, and at the end of a successful transaction issues the requested ticket and any necessary change. When no transaction is in progress the machine displays either the message 'Exact money required' or 'Change available'. The message displayed determines whether the next customer must enter exactly the amount of money required to pay for the ticket selected, or whether the machine is able to give change when more money than necessary is entered.

The interface of the machine consists of a number of buttons, each corresponding to a given type of ticket. If the user presses one of these buttons, the machine displays an amount of money to be entered, namely the cost of the ticket. As the user enters money into the machine, the amount displayed is reduced by the amount that the user entered. As soon as an amount of money greater than or equal to the cost of the ticket has been entered, one of two things can happen. If the machine originally displayed the 'Change available' message, the required ticket together with any necessary change will be issued. If the 'Exact money required' message was displayed, a ticket will only be issued if the user entered exactly the amount of money requested. If the user has entered too much money, all the money entered will be returned.

At the beginning of the transaction, the user has the option of entering money before selecting a ticket type. If when a ticket is finally selected, enough money has already been entered to pay for it, a ticket and change will be issued as in the previous case. If the money entered is less than the cost of the selected ticket, the machine will display the remaining cost and will carry on as in the previous case.

In any event, if no input is received from the user in any period of 30 seconds, the transaction will be terminated and any money that has already been entered will be returned to the customer. A 'cancel' button is also available to enable the user to terminate a transaction explicitly.

State machines and event sequences

A statechart summarizes all the possible sequences of events that an object can receive. It can sometimes be rather difficult to identify all the states that are necessary to model the object's behaviour accurately, however. The technique presented here avoids this difficulty by considering only one sequence of events at a time and gradually building up a complete description of the required statechart.

Individual sequences of events can be obtained from interaction diagrams. The messages arriving at an individual object, when arranged in the order in which the object receives them, make up such a sequence. On the statechart for that object, it must be possible to trace a path corresponding to each such sequence of events.

When constructing a statechart we can start by taking a single sequence and defining a simple statechart which represents that sequence only. Further sequences of events can then be integrated into this preliminary statechart and in this way a complete diagram can be built up in a step-by-step manner.

The remainder of this section will illustrate this process for the example of the ticket machine. A number of typical transactions involving the ticket machine will be considered and a complete statechart will be gradually built up. Formal object interaction diagrams will not be drawn, as there is only one object involved in these transactions, namely the ticket machine itself, and the only messages sent are a sequence of events generated by the user.

Selecting a ticket before paying

Suppose that a user first selects a particular ticket type and then enters three coins, one after the other. The total value of the three coins amounts to more than the cost of the ticket, so the machine issues the ticket and the required change, and returns to an idle state waiting for the next transaction. A sequence of four events is received by the machine in this case: a 'ticket' event is followed by three 'coin' events. Each of these events has associated data giving the cost of the selected ticket and the value of each coin entered, but we will ignore this detail for the moment.

A very simple statechart can be drawn for any individual sequence of events simply by assuming that every event corresponds to a transition between two states; in effect we place states at the beginning and end of the sequence, and also between each pair of events. In the current case we end up with the statechart shown in Figure 10.14. As this is only a preliminary diagram, no attempt has been made to label the states.

Figure 10.14 Preliminary statechart for the ticket machine

Although this statechart is an accurate model of the single sequence of events considered, it requires some restructuring before it will serve as an adequate foundation for the statechart of the ticket machine. First, Figure 10.14 defines only one transaction, whereas the ticket machine is capable of carrying out repeated transactions, one after the other. To model this, we can unify the first and last states of Figure 10.14. As these states represent the situation where no transaction is in progress, we will label this new state 'Idle'.

Second, the number of coins entered in the sample transaction above is essentially arbitrary. Any number of coins could be entered in a transaction: the precise number required depends on the cost of the selected ticket and the value of the coins that are entered. Some kind of loop is required to show the possibility of entering an arbitrary number of coins. This can be achieved by combining the three intermediate states of Figure 10.14 into a single state with a self-transition.

A refined version of the statechart for this initial transaction, which incorporates these modifications, is shown in Figure 10.15. This consists of only two states, derived from the initial five states of Figure 10.14 as explained above. The machine starts off in the idle state and, when the user selects a ticket, the transition leading to the 'paying for ticket' state is followed. When coins are subsequently entered, one of two things can happen. If the total amount of money entered is enough to pay for the selected ticket, the transition back to the idle state is followed. If, on the other hand, more money is required, the self-transition on the paying state is followed and further coins must be entered to continue the transaction.

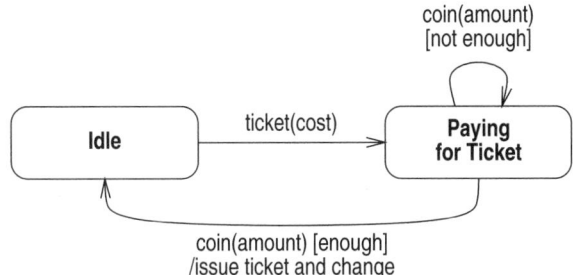

Figure 10.15 A more refined statechart

Figure 10.15 uses several features of the statechart notation introduced earlier to clarify the behaviour of the machine in this transaction. First, parameters are attached to the various messages to transmit the cost of the ticket and the value of each coin to the machine. Second, there are two transitions labelled with the 'coin' event leaving the paying for ticket state. They are distinguished by means of an informal guard condition that checks whether enough money to pay for the selected ticket has been entered. Finally, the actions performed by the machine if enough money has been entered are also shown on the transition leading back to the idle state. In this example, we are assuming that the machine is able to issue the required change.

Paying before selecting a ticket

We have now dealt with one possible transaction and constructed a preliminary statechart. The next step is to consider a second transaction and to integrate it as far as possible into the existing statechart, extending the statechart where necessary.

As well as initially selecting a ticket, the specification of the ticket machine also allows the user to enter money before selecting the required ticket. The sequence of events corresponding to this transaction starts with a number of coin events and, when a ticket event is received, the ticket and change are issued and the transaction finishes. We can assume that the transaction starts in the idle state already identified in Figure 10.15. There is a problem with the first event, however, as Figure 10.15 contains no transition labelled 'coin' leading from the idle state. We therefore need to extend the statechart with a suitable transition, leading to a new state.

As in the previous case, any number of coins can be entered, and we can model this by means of a self-transition on this new state. Finally, a ticket event will be received and the machine will issue the ticket and change and return to the idle state. Figure 10.16 shows the statechart with these additions.

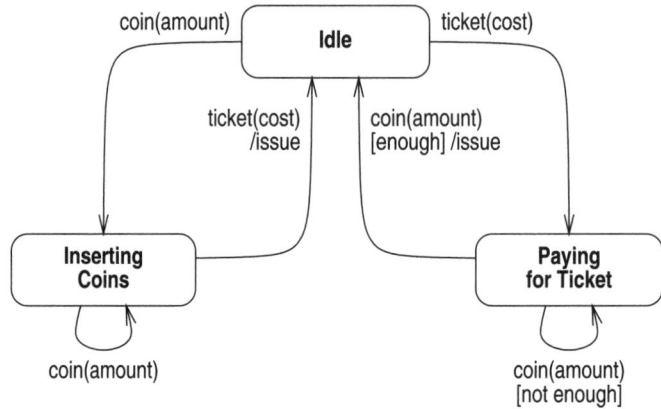

Figure 10.16 Incorporating a second transaction

Integrating the transactions

The two transactions considered so far are mirror images of each other. In the first, the ticket type is selected before any coins are entered and, in the second, after all the coins have been entered. The specification of the ticket machine allows for a third possibility, however, where some coins are entered before the ticket type is selected, but then further coins need to be entered to make up the cost of the ticket. This possibility is not catered for on Figure 10.16: once coins have been entered, selection of a ticket type returns the state machine to the idle state, leaving no possibility of continuing the transaction by entering more coins.

What is required is an additional transition labelled 'ticket' leading from the 'Inserting Coins' state of Figure 10.16. This transition should be differentiated from the existing one by means of a condition. The necessary condition is the same as the one that distinguishes whether insertion of a coin causes the machine to return to the idle state when the user is paying for a ticket, namely whether enough money has been entered to pay for the selected ticket or not.

This new transition could lead to a new state: to meet the specification of the ticket machine, the new state would have to allow for coins to be entered until the value of the ticket had been reached, whereupon the ticket would be issued and the machine would return to the idle state. This is precisely the behaviour provided by the existing 'Paying for Ticket' state, however, so the new transition can be defined to arrive at this state, as shown in Figure 10.17. The names of the states have been changed to reflect the relevant difference between them more accurately, which is simply whether or not the user has selected the ticket type.

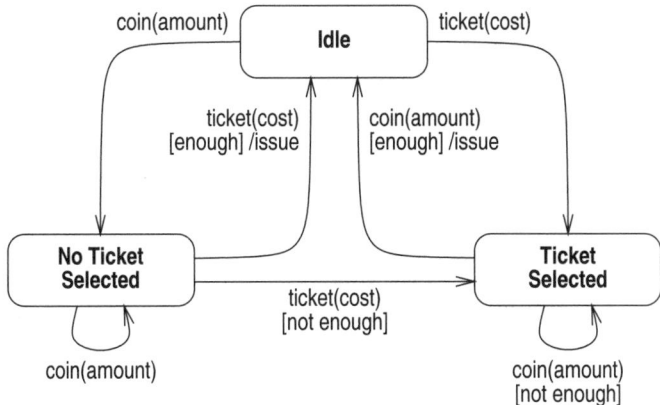

Figure 10.17 Integrating the two transactions

The statechart in Figure 10.17 summarizes all the possible sequences of events that the user can generate in the course of a transaction that terminates in the issue of a ticket, in the sense that any given sequence of events corresponds to a connected path through the statechart. In a transaction, any number of coins can be entered, the ticket type can be selected once and these events can take place in any order.

Users of the ticket machine will not always behave in such a sensible manner, however. It is easy to imagine a user selecting a ticket type, then having second thoughts and selecting an alternative type before entering any coins. The statechart of Figure 10.17 does not allow for this possibility. Once a ticket type has been selected, the machine enters the 'ticket selected' state, and there are no 'ticket' transitions out of this state. There seems to be a contradiction here between what the user can in fact do and what the statechart specifies.

One way of explaining this kind of phenomenon is to note that, although the user can in fact press the ticket selection buttons repeatedly, this does not necessarily mean that 'ticket' events are received by the machine. It might be the case, for example, that the ticket selection buttons are deactivated once the 'Ticket Selected' state is entered, and only reactivated when the idle state is reached again.

If this is not the case, some explicit account of additional ticket events will need to be given in the statechart. This could be achieved in a number of ways, perhaps by introducing an error state if such events are to be disallowed, or a self-transition on the 'Ticket Selected' state if they are permitted. In a realistic example, of course, the choice between these options would be governed by the actual behaviour of the ticket machine being modelled.

Figure 10.17 accurately models the basic behaviour of the ticket machine. To complete the model it is necessary to show the alternative ways in which transactions can be terminated, namely by pressing the cancel button or by a timeout, and also the alternative behaviour in the situations where the machine requires that the exact cost of tickets is entered. Before completing the ticket machine statechart, the notation required to model these features will be introduced.

10.11 TIME EVENTS

If no input is received from the user for 30 seconds, the ticket machine will time out: the current transaction will be terminated, and any money entered will be returned to the customer. A time out should be modelled by a transition, as it will change the state of the ticket machine from an intermediate state in a transition back to the initial idle state. However, it is not obvious what event should label such a transition: the whole point, after all, is that such a transition has to fire precisely when no event is detected.

UML defines special *time events*, which can be used in these cases. Figure 10.18 shows a transition that will fire 30 seconds after the 'no ticket selected' state is entered. This can be understood by imagining that an implicit activity of each state is to run a timer, which is reset every time the state is entered. An outgoing transition from a state that is labelled with a time event will fire as soon as the timer has been running for the period of time specified in the time event. In Figure 10.18, notice that the timer is reset every time a coin is entered, because a self-transition counts as a change of state and triggers a state's entry actions.

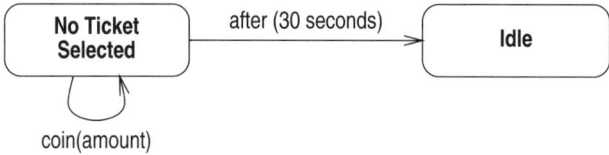

Figure 10.18 A time event

Following the keyword 'after', any period of time can be given as a parameter. An alternative form of time event consists of the keyword 'when' followed by a specified point in time. This defines a transition that will fire when the specified time is reached.

10.12 ACTIVITY STATES

In Figure 10.17, two separate transitions lead back to the idle state after a transaction has been successfully completed. In each case it is necessary to check whether the machine is able to return any change that is required. If it can, the change and the ticket should be issued and, if not, the money entered should be returned.

This behaviour could be represented by a pair of transitions with appropriate guard conditions and actions, but these would have to be repeated on each route back to the idle state. To avoid this repetition, an *activity state* can be used to simplify the structure of the statechart, as shown in Figure 10.19.

An activity state represents a period of time during which an object is performing some internal processing. As such, it is shown on a statechart as a state that contains only an activity. In Figure 10.19, as soon as a customer's input to a transaction is complete, the activity state becomes active, corresponding to the machine working out whether it is capable of returning the change required to complete the transaction.

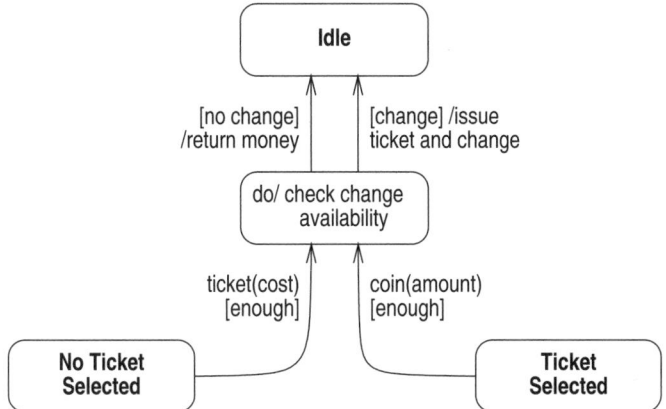

Figure 10.19 An activity state

The internal processes represented by activity states often cannot be interrupted by external events, and in these cases the only transitions leaving an activity state will be completion transactions. In Figure 10.19 there are two such transitions, differentiated by guard conditions that state whether or not change is available. In each case, these transitions also carry an appropriate action.

Activity states should be used sparingly on statecharts, as the purpose of a statechart is usually to show the response of an object to external events and not to model internal processing in detail. On occasion, however, activity states can be useful, as in Figure 10.19, as devices to simplify the structure of a statechart.

10.13 SUMMARY OF THE TICKET MACHINE

Figure 10.20 shows a complete statechart for the ticket machine. It incorporates the various points made in the preceding sections, and also shows the effect of the user pressing cancel in the middle of a transaction.

To reduce the number of transitions required to specify the interruption of a transaction by either a time out or a cancellation, a composite state has been included in Figure 10.20. It is intended to correspond to the period of time during which a transaction is in progress.

10.14 SUMMARY

- *Statecharts* provide a specification of the behavioural aspects of objects that can be illustrated on interaction diagrams.

- Statecharts show the *events* that an object can detect throughout its lifetime, and its responses to those events.

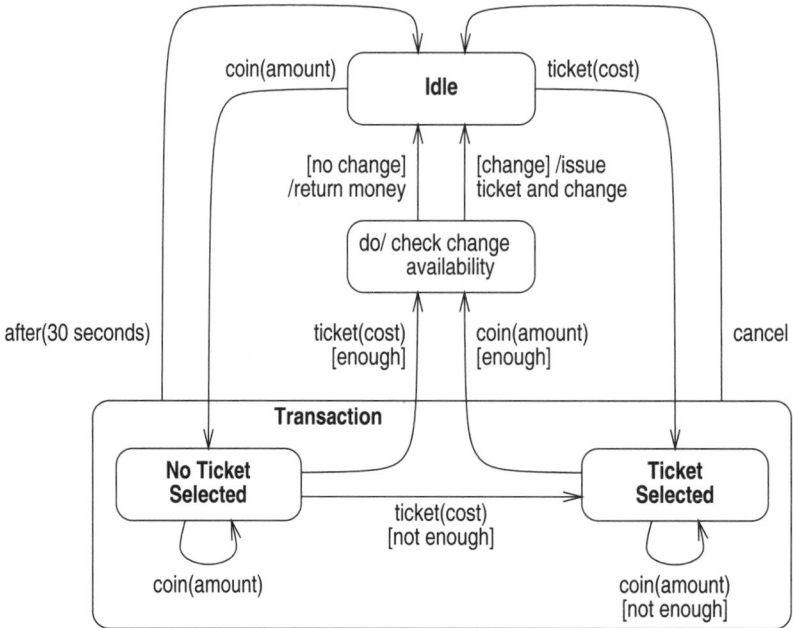

Figure 10.20 Complete statechart for the ticket machine

- In general, objects exhibit state-dependent behaviour. States are distinguished by the fact that the detection of an event can have a different effect, depending on what state the object is in.

- The detection of an event can cause a *transition* to fire, where an object moves from one state to another.

- *Guard conditions* can be used to specify which one out of a set of transitions actually fires on a particular occasion.

- *Actions* specify the response of an object to an event. Entry and exit actions on states are equivalent to actions on all incoming and outgoing transitions, respectively.

- States can include *activities* that take place throughout the time that an object is in that state. Activities can be interrupted by user-generated events. If an activity terminates without interruption, a completion transition out of the state will be followed.

- *Composite states* can be used to simplify complex statecharts. A transition from a superstate applies equally to all of the nested substates. The effect of a transition to a superstate is specified by means of an initial state within the superstate.

- Statecharts can be developed by considering individual sequences of events, derived from object interaction diagrams, in turn. First, a simple statechart is developed to model one such sequence and then this is extended where necessary by considering additional sequences.

10.15 EXERCISES

10.1 What state is the CD player specified in Figure 10.13 in after the following sequences of events are detected? Assume that a CD is always present when tested for.

(*a*) Initialize, load.
(*b*) Initialize, load, play, stop.
(*c*) Initialize, load, play, pause, play
(*d*) Initialize, play, stop, load.
(*e*) Initialize, load, pause, play.

10.2 This question refers to the dynamic model of the CD player given in Figure 10.13. Suppose that the player is turned off when it is in the open state, with no CD in the drawer and the drawer open, and is then immediately powered on again. What state is the CD player in after these operations? What is the physical condition of the drawer of the CD player? What will happen if the user now presses the load button? What buttons would the user have to press in order to close the drawer of the CD player?

10.3 Draw a revised version of Figure 10.12 modelling the requirement that the CD player should remain paused even when 'stop' and then 'play' are pressed.

10.4 Is a default transition required from the history state in the not playing state in Figure 10.13? If not, why not? If so, which substate should it go to?

10.5 The description of the CD player in this chapter has left vague the details of how it records which is the current track. Assume that the CD player has an attribute called the 'track counter', which behaves as follows.

When no CD is in the drawer, the track counter is set to zero. When a CD is detected, the track counter is set to 1; this happens when the drawer is physically closed following the detection of either a load or play event. The track counter determines which track start is located, and hence which track is played, whenever the busy state is entered.

Two buttons, labelled 'forward' and 'back', allow the user to adjust the track counter manually. If no CD is in the drawer, these buttons have no effect. Otherwise, pressing 'forward' increments the track counter and pressing 'back' decrements it. Pressing either of these buttons when the CD player is in the busy state causes the playing head to move immediately to the start of the requested track.

Extend the statechart in Figure 10.13 so that it models this behaviour.

10.6 In the ticket machine example of Section 10.10, suppose that the ticket selection buttons are deactivated once a ticket type has been selected and only reactivated at the end of a transaction. In addition, suppose that once enough money has been entered to pay for the required ticket, the coin entry slot is closed and only reopened once any ticket and change have been issued. Use entry and exit actions to show this behaviour explicitly on the statechart of Figure 10.20.

10.7 Redraw Figure 10.20 with the activity state removed and compare the resulting statechart with Figure 10.20 from the point of view of clarity and comprehensibility.

10.8 Alter the statechart of Figure 10.20 so that the availability of change is checked at the start of a transaction and a suitable message displayed, as specified in Section 10.10.

10.9 Redraw the statechart given in Figure Ex10.9, removing all the composite states and replacing all transitions to and from the composite states with equivalent transitions between the remaining states.

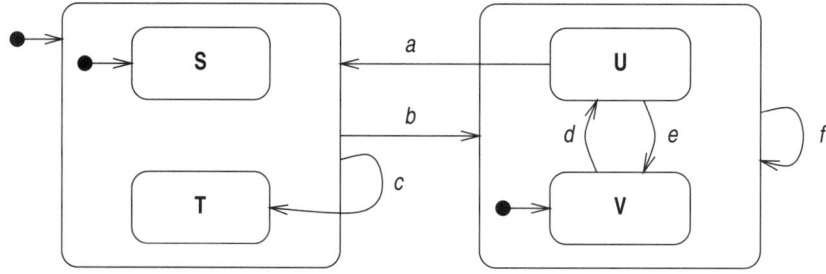

Figure Ex10.9 A statechart using nested states

10.10 Demonstrate that the two statecharts in Figure Ex10.10 are not equivalent in meaning by finding a sequence of events that is accepted by one but not by the other. Assume that sequences start from the initial state shown.

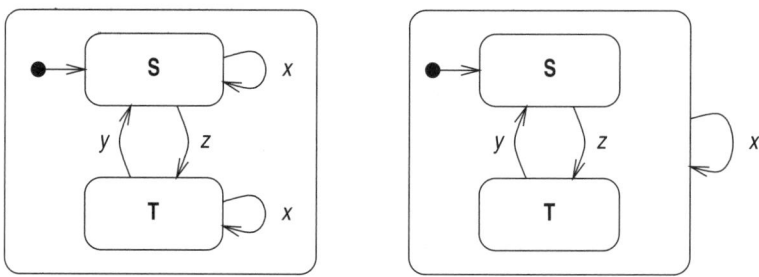

Figure Ex10.10 Two non-equivalent statecharts

10.11 The lights in a lecture theatre are controlled by a panel of three switches, labelled 'On', 'Off' and 'Dim'. 'On' switches the lights on to their full brightness and 'Off' switches them off. There is also an intermediate level of brightness, used when slides and other projected material are being shown. The 'Dim' switch reduces the lighting level from full to this intermediate level; full brightness can be restored by pressing the 'On' switch again. Draw a state diagram modelling the behaviour of the lighting system in this lecture theatre.

10.12 A window in a window management system on a computer can be displayed in one of three states: *maximized*, where it takes up the entire screen; *normal*, where it is displayed as a bordered window with a given size and position on the screen; and *iconized*, where it is displayed as a small icon. When a window is opened, it will be displayed as a normal window, unless *minimize on use* has been selected, in which case it will be displayed as an icon. A normal window and an icon can be maximized; a maximized window and a normal window can be minimized or reduced to an icon. Maximized windows can be restored to their normal size and icons can be restored to the size they had before they were minimized. Icons and normal windows can be moved and normal windows can also be resized. No matter how it is displayed, a window can always be closed. Draw a state diagram expressing these facts about the display of windows.

10.13 A description of the behaviour of an automated telling machine (ATM) is given below. Produce a state diagram describing its behaviour. List any assumptions you have to make as a result of ambiguity, unclearness or incompleteness of the description.

A user begins a transaction at the ATM by entering a bank card. If the card is readable by the machine, the user is prompted to enter their personal identification number (PIN). Once this number has been entered, a menu is presented to the user containing the following options: show account balance, withdrawal with receipt and withdrawal without receipt. If the user selects one of the withdrawal options, they are prompted to enter an amount of money to withdraw; the amount entered must be a multiple of 10.

The user's PIN is validated when the ATM sends the details of the transaction to the bank's remote computer. If the PIN is invalid, the user is given the option of re-entering it and the selected transaction is retried. This is repeated if the new PIN is also invalid. Once three invalid PINs have been entered, the transaction is terminated and the user's card is retained by the machine.

If a valid PIN is entered, further processing depends on the transaction type selected. For a 'show balance' transaction, the balance is displayed on the screen, and, after they have confirmed this, the user is returned to the transaction menu. A withdrawal transaction may fail if the user has exceeded the amount of money that can be withdrawn from the account; in this case an error message is displayed and, after confirmation, the user is returned to the transaction menu. Otherwise, the user's card is returned and the money is issued, followed by the receipt if required.

At any point where user input, other than a simple confirmation, is required, a 'cancel' option is provided. If this is selected, the user's card is returned and their interaction with the ATM terminates.

10.14 A simple digital watch consists of a display showing hours and minutes separated by a flashing colon and provides two buttons (A and B), which enable the display to be updated.

(*a*) To add two to the number of hours displayed, the following actions should be performed, where button B increments the hours display:

Press A; press B; press B; press A; press A.

Draw a simple statechart showing precisely this sequence of events.

(*b*) In the above interaction, the hours displayed could be incremented by any required number, and the whole interaction could be repeated as often as required. Redraw the statechart to incorporate these generalizations.

(*c*) To increment the number of minutes displayed by the watch, button A can be pressed twice, followed by repeated presses of button B, each of which increases the minutes displayed by 1. Draw a complete statechart for the watch, incorporating updates to both the hours and minutes displayed. Give the states in your statechart meaningful names and add appropriate actions to any transition labelled 'press B'.

(*d*) The watch is subsequently enhanced to incorporate an alarm and the following interaction is proposed as a way of setting the time of the alarm:

Press A; press A; press B (repeatedly); press A; press B (repeatedly); press A.

The intention is that the user presses button A twice in quick succession, like a 'double click' with a mouse. Explain how this proposal would introduce non-determinism into the statechart for the digital watch. Show how you could remove the non-determinism by introducing an extra state into the statechart.

10.15 Draw a statechart summarizing the information given in the following description of some of the events that can arise in the life cycle of a thread in Java.

When a thread is created, it does not start running immediately, but is left in the *New Thread* state. When the thread is in this state, it can only be started or stopped. Calling any method besides *start* or *stop* makes no sense and causes an exception to be raised.

The *start* method causes system resources to be allocated to the thread and calls the thread's *run* method. At this point the thread is in the *Running* state.

A thread becomes not runnable if either its *sleep* or *suspend* methods are called. The *sleep* method has a parameter specifying the length of time the thread should sleep for; when this time has elapsed, the thread starts to run again. If the *suspend* method has been called, the thread only runs again when its *resume* method is called.

A thread can die in two ways. It dies naturally when its *run* method exits normally. A thread can also be killed at any time by calling its *stop* method.

11

COMPONENT DIAGRAMS

In the literature on object-oriented design, great emphasis is placed on the *logical* design of programs. From this perspective, a program consists of a collection of classes related primarily by association and generalization, and the behaviour of the system is encapsulated in the operations defined in the classes. As described in Chapter 2, running programs are viewed as being collections of interacting objects, and to a great extent the notations described in Chapters 8, 9 and 10 can be explained and understood in terms of this run-time model.

This account provides a complete computational model in terms of which all the behaviour of a system can be specified. However, the classes in a design also have a parallel *physical* existence. They are first implemented in the target programming language and stored as files of source code. Subsequently, these source files are compiled to produce files of object code, which themselves can be interpreted by the Java run-time system, perhaps, or in other languages linked with other files to produce a file of executable code.

Object-oriented design notations originally concentrated on documenting the logical structure of object-oriented programs. As UML has evolved, however, it has also introduced notation intended to capture more of the physical properties of software. The physical design of a system can be shown in UML using *implementation diagrams*. Two kinds of implementation diagram are defined: component diagrams show dependencies between the various components that make up the system, and deployment diagrams show how components are located in the deployment environment.

This chapter describes features of UML that relate primarily to the physical structure of programs. These aspects of UML are currently less well developed than its logical core: the notations are still evolving rapidly and are used in a variety of frequently inconsistent ways by different authors. For the most part, they are to be understood not in terms of the logical object model of Chapter 2, but in terms of an abstract account of the physical properties of software.

11.1 DEPENDENCIES

Like all the diagrams defined by UML, implementation diagrams are graphs, showing entities of various sorts and the relationships between them. Many of the relationships on implementation diagrams are depicted using *dependencies*, although the use of dependencies is not restricted to these diagrams.

Dependencies are really defined in UML by what they are not: a dependency depicts a relationship between model elements that is not an association or a generalization or realization relationship. Figure 11.1 illustrates the notation for a dependency, as a dashed arrow between two model elements.

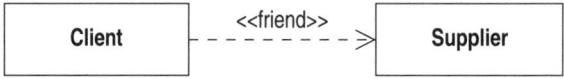

Figure 11.1 A dependency between two classes

The model element at the tail of the dependency is known as the *client* and the element at the head as the *supplier*. Because the notion of a dependency is so general, most dependencies are labelled with a stereotype giving some indication of what relationship is being modelled. UML defines a number of predefined stereotypes, but others can be defined for particular modelling needs.

In order to illustrate the wide applicability of the dependency notation, Figure 11.1 represents the 'friend' relationship that can hold between two classes in C++. This is a language-specific notion that states that one class can have access to the properties of another, irrespective of their visibility or access levels. This relationship does not correspond to anything in the object model and so has to be represented by a dependency. UML borrows the keyword 'friend' from C++ to denote this relationship.

The meaning of dependencies

In earlier chapters, a wide range of dependencies have been introduced as required, in order to meet various modelling needs. These have included, for example, the 'include' and 'extend' relationships between use cases in Figure 4.7, the relationship between an object and the class it is an instance of in Figure 8.4, and the relationship between a class derived from a template class and the template itself in Figure 8.55.

These different relationships have very little in common with each other. All that can be said in general is that the presence of a dependency between two elements indicates that the client in some way requires the presence of the supplier element and cannot function, or be fully defined or implemented, in the absence of the supplier. As the name suggests, the core meaning is that the client *depends* in some way on the supplier.

It is quite common to see unlabelled dependencies drawn between model elements. In such cases, this is meant to model a general notion of one element 'using' another, with the exact nature of the relationship made clear, hopefully, from the context. Such general dependencies are often labelled with the stereotype 'use'.

A usage dependency models the fact that one component makes use of the services provided by another and cannot function correctly in their absence. Particular cases where dependencies can arise are considered in detail below. One consequence of a usage dependency is that when a component is modified, any other components that depend upon it may also have to be modified, as there is in general no guarantee that those aspects of the component that give rise to the dependency have not been changed.

Usage dependencies are transitive: if a component A depends on B and B depends on C, then A also depends on C, as shown in Figure 11.2. It is common not to show the indirect derived dependency between A and C, however.

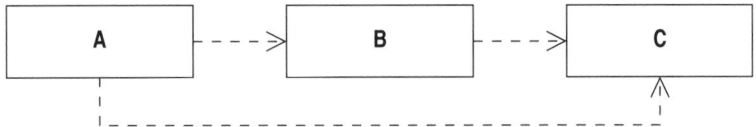

Figure 11.2 The transitivity of usage dependencies

11.2 COMPONENTS AND ARTEFACTS

The basic unit of physical design is normally taken to be not a class, but a *component*. This term has been defined in many different ways, but a component is usually taken to be a physical entity, such as a binary file, which can be deployed as part of a system. One of the motivations for defining components is to enable a style of software construction where systems can be built by assembling components and replacing one component with an alternative, or improved, implementation. To enable this, components are defined to support certain interfaces.

The definition of 'component' in UML largely reflects these issues. A component is defined to be a deployable and replaceable part of a system, which encapsulates some implementation details and also exposes certain interfaces.

In the context of Java programming, a class file, produced as a result of compiling a file of Java source code, would appear to fit the definition of a component. A class file is a physical file that can be deployed as part of a system and, if the source code is updated, can be replaced by a recompiled version. It encapsulates the implementation of the class or classes it contains and supports an interface defined by the methods of the class.

Figure 11.3 illustrates the basic notation for a component. Assuming that the 'Part' class from the stock control system in Chapter 2 is defined in a source file `Part.java`, Figure 11.3 shows the class file that would be generated by compiling this class.

The component is labelled with the name of the file it represents, not simply the class defined within it. The small rectangles on the left-hand side of the icon represent the interfaces exposed by the component: they cross the component boundary, indicating that the only way the internal details of the component can be accessed is through its interface.

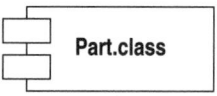

Figure 11.3 UML notation for a component

Artefacts

By contrast, the source file itself, Part.java, does not seem to meet the definition of a component. Many software systems are deployed without including the source code, often because of its commercial value. The source code, being a compile-time rather than a run-time entity, is not, in one sense at least, a part of the system and so cannot really be said to encapsulate implementation details, or expose interfaces.

A more natural view is that the source code is an *artefact* out of which a component, the corresponding class file, can be built. UML defines artefacts to be physical pieces of information, primarily files of various sorts and also database tables. The notation for artefacts, illustrated in Figure 11.4, depicts an artefact by a simple rectangle, with a stereotype denoting the type of the artefact depicted.

Figure 11.4 A source file as an artefact

However, a word of caution must be introduced here. The notion of artefact is a fairly recent introduction to UML and is not used widely in the literature. Before the introduction of artefacts, components provided the only way of modelling any physical entity and source files are commonly represented by components with a suitable stereotype, as shown in Figure 11.5.

Figure 11.5 A source file as an component

A further issue is that with the introduction of artefacts, the notion of a component in UML appears to have become more abstract. As artefacts represent files, the class file in Figure 11.3 could be represented by an artefact. Components are viewed as being *implemented* by a number of artefacts, so Figure 11.3 could be more pedantically expressed as a component 'Part' implemented by the class file Part.class, as shown in Figure 11.6.

For the remainder of this chapter, we will adopt the convention of showing all physical entities as components, as shown in Figures 11.3 and 11.5, partly to avoid the potential confusion caused by the similar forms used for class and artefact icons. This is an area of UML where notational conventions are not yet strongly established, however, and not too much weight should be attached to this decision.

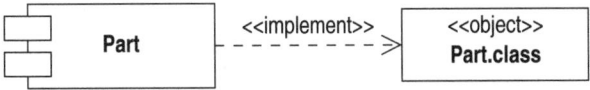

Figure 11.6 A component and an artefact implementing it

11.3 COMPONENT DIAGRAMS

Component diagrams, then, basically show components and the relationships between them, modelled by dependencies. As components can be related to other model elements, such as artefacts and even classes, and expose interfaces, model elements other than components can also appear on component diagrams.

Component diagrams can be used for a wide range of purposes and do not have a simple logical characterization in the same way that class diagrams or statecharts have. The component diagram notation itself is very simple, compared with these other forms of diagram: the difficulty in physical modelling comes from the range of situations that have to be characterized, not from the complexity of the notation used.

The following section illustrates the physical relationships that are of interest in the context of developing stand-alone applications in an object-oriented language such as Java or C++, and shows how they can be represented in UML. Section 11.5 then considers a more substantial application of component diagrams, to show the compilation dependencies between the components in a system.

11.4 SOME COMMON PHYSICAL RELATIONSHIPS

The notions of component and artefact, and dependencies between them, can be used to model a wide range of relationships between the entities that arise in software development. In this section, the process of transforming a logical design into a physical system will be loosely followed, and the work products and processes involved will be modelled using the UML notation for component diagrams.

Source code

Perhaps the most familiar physical operations on software are those involved in writing and building programs. For example, consider the simple task of implementing a class defined in a design model that specifies its attributes, operations and other properties. The first implementation step is to represent this logical information as a file of source code in the chosen implementation language.

Source files can be represented as artefacts, as shown in Figure 11.4, or components, as shown in Figure 11.5. These diagrams do not, however, make explicit the relationship between the source file and the class being implemented. Commonly, the source file is given a name derived from the name of the class, but this is only a convention. In cases where more than one class is implemented in a single file, the convention breaks down.

The relationship can be shown explicitly using a dependency, as shown in Figure 11.7. This shows that the source file is dependent on the logical class: if the design model changes, the source code will need to be updated to take the changes into account. The 'trace' stereotype denotes a dependency between two model elements that represent the same concept, but in different models or at different levels of abstraction.

Figure 11.7 Implementing a class in Java

Different programming languages have different mechanisms for making references between different files of source code. In Java, for example, references to other files in the same package are resolved automatically by the compiler, but, if a program refers to classes defined in a different package, this reference has to be made explicitly in an `import` statement such as the following.

```
import java.util.* ;
```

This creates a dependency between the source file and the package that is imported, as shown in Figure 11.8. Again, the direction of the dependency indicates that, if the imported package changes, this could potentially have an effect on the programs that import it.

Figure 11.8 Modelling the Java 'import' relationship

By contrast, in C++ the source code for a class is typically divided into two source files, a *header* file containing the class interface, loosely speaking, and an *implementation* file containing the definitions of the methods, or *member functions*, of the class. Header files are physically included in implementation files when compilation is taking place, and this relationship can be modelled as a dependency between components, as shown in Figure 11.9.

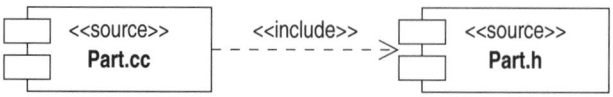

Figure 11.9 File inclusion in C++

Compilation

Once the source code has been written, the next development activity is typically to compile it, thereby generating files of object code in some form or other. In Java, these take the form of class files, which can then be interpreted by the Java virtual machine.

There is clearly a dependency between the source and object files in this situation, as any change to the source code will mean that it must be recompiled and the object code regenerated. This dependency is shown in Figure 11.10.

Figure 11.10 Compiling a file of Java code

Archive files and libraries

In some systems, collections of object files are collected together for deployment in the form of archives, or libraries of code. For example, in the Java environment, applications are often distributed in the form of JAR files, each containing a number of class files, possibly among other things.

In this situation, the archive file is naturally modelled as a component, but, unlike the other components we have seen so far, this is a component that contains other components. This can be notated by showing the components representing the class files inside the icon representing the JAR file, as shown in Figure 11.11, which shows a JAR file containing all the class files for the stock control example of Chapter 2.

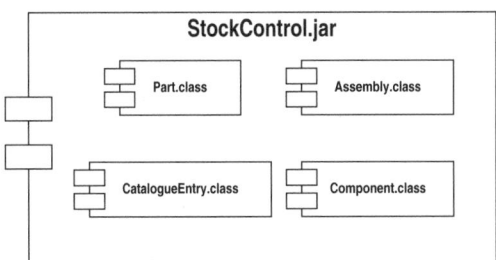

Figure 11.11 A JAR archive and the contained class files

11.5 COMPILATION DEPENDENCIES

This section examines a typical application of a component diagram, to illustrate the compilation dependencies between classes, where changes to one file may require others to be recompiled.

The organization of the code of a system into source files and the dependencies between these files can have a significant effect on certain of its non-functional qualities, particularly testability and maintainability. As properties of the logical design of a program can affect its physical design, it is important for developers to be aware of the ways in which logical design can affect physical design, in order to be able to avoid these problems.

A minimal approach to physical design would be to put the code for the entire system into a single source file. This would result in large source files, which could not easily be read or maintained. Even worse, any change to the program, however trivial, would mean that the entire program had to be recompiled. This can lead to a significant wastage of time, particularly on large projects, where the cost of compilation can be a significant factor in the overall cost of development.

If the text of a program is divided between a number of source files, however, the effect of a change can be limited to the recompilation of a small part of the program. This practice brings great benefits in terms of making the program easier to read and maintain, and also shortens development time.

When a change is made, the files that have been affected obviously need to be recompiled. In addition, however, other files containing code that relies on aspects of the changed files may also have to be recompiled. Examples of such *compilation dependencies* are shown below, but it is clear that, if such dependencies can be kept to a minimum, recompilation time after a change will also be shortened.

There are many different ways in which a program can be split into files, however, and some are better than others. Many of the problems that arise stem from cyclic dependencies between classes that refer to each other, as in the following simple example.

```
public class X          public class Y
{                       {
  private Y theY ;        private X theX ;
  ...                     ...
}                       }
```

These classes are mutually dependent, each requiring the other to be available before it can be compiled, executed or tested. A number of problems can arise from such pairs of dependent classes, including the following.

1. The classes cannot be tested independently.
2. To understand one class fully, it is also necessary to understand the other.
3. This situation can lead to significant added complexity in coding, particularly in deciding a policy for the creation and destruction of objects belonging to these two classes.

For these reasons it is usually worthwhile trying to avoid this kind of dependency between classes. This section examines where dependencies between classes come from, and how to document them using UML's component diagrams.

Where dependencies come from

In general, dependencies between components derive from properties of the logical design of the system. For example, a generalization relationship between two classes generates a corresponding dependency between the classes, as shown in Figure 11.12.

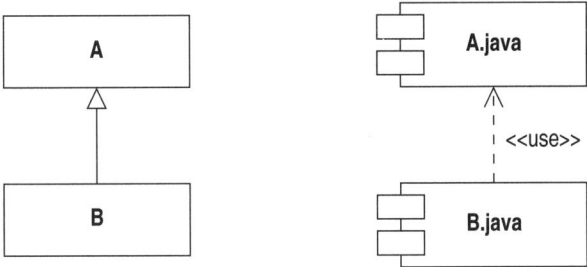

Figure 11.12 A dependency based on generalization

The reason for this is that subclasses in general expect to have access to and to make use of the features that are inherited from their superclasses. There is therefore a usage dependency from subclass to superclass. A further symptom of this is that changes to superclasses may in general affect the subclass, if any features inherited from the superclass have been altered.

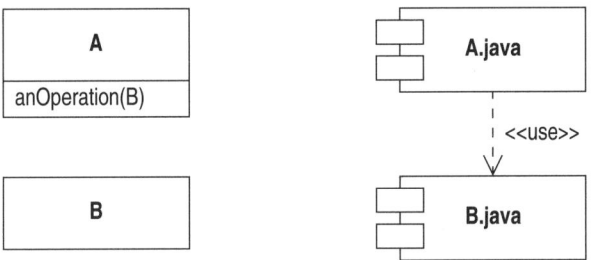

Figure 11.13 A uses B in its interface

Another source of dependencies is where a class B, say, is used in the interface of an operation of class A, as shown in Figure 11.13. The manifestation of this dependency in source code is shown below.

```
public class A
{
  public void anOperation( B theB ) {
    ...
  }
}
```

This form of dependency is sometimes known as 'using in the interface' because, in this case, the parameters of a public method form part of the interface of the class A. The expectation in this case is that the implementation of the operation will make use of features defined in the interface of class B, and any change to this interface may affect the implementation of this operation.

A third source of dependencies is where a class A contains an attribute whose type is that of another class. In UML, classes are not generally used as attribute types, so this form of dependency will normally arise from the implementation of a navigable association, as shown in Figure 11.14.

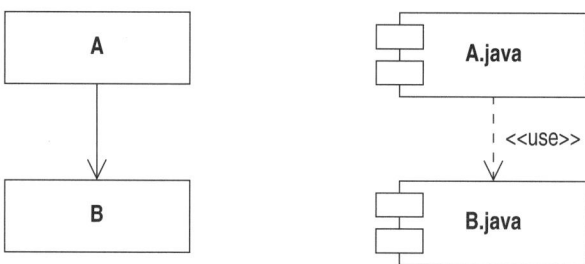

Figure 11.14 A uses B in its implementation

An example of this type of dependency, sometimes known as 'using in the implementation', is shown below. In general, class A may make use of any feature in the interface of class B, and be vulnerable to changes in that interface.

```
public class A {
  private B aLink ;
  ...
}
```

Dependency graphs

Once the dependencies between the components in a system have been identified, they can be presented in a *dependency graph* showing the components and the usage dependencies between them. For example, Figure 11.15 shows the dependency graph for the stock control program discussed in Chapter 2. A dependency graph is not a special form of UML diagram, however, but merely an application of the component diagram notation to show information for a particular purpose.

Physical hierarchy

The graph in Figure 11.15 was drawn with all the dependencies pointing downwards. This suggests that components with no dependencies are in a sense simpler, or at a lower level, than those with many dependencies.

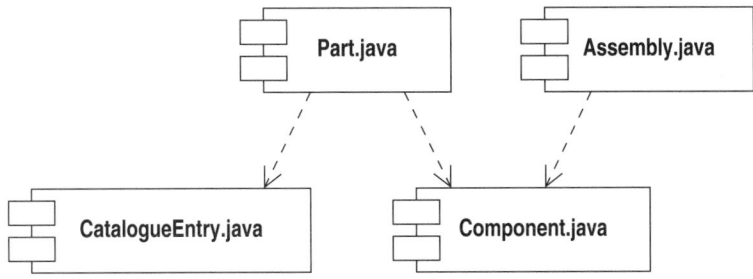

Figure 11.15 The dependency graph for the stock control program

Where possible, the design of systems ought to be carried out in such a way that the dependency graph contains no cycles or loops. In other words, we want to avoid the situation where a pair of components have a mutual dependency, as shown in Figure 11.16.

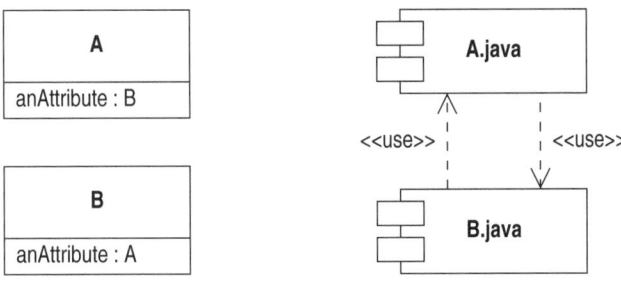

Figure 11.16 A dependency cycle

If a system has a non-cyclic dependency graph, its components can be visited 'bottom-up' in such a way that it is only necessary to consider one new component at a time. This is important for testing purposes: it means that the system can be tested incrementally, one component at a time. It also has benefits for understanding the program: in learning a new system it is only necessary to consider one new component at a time.

11.6 COMPONENTS AND INTERFACES

An important feature of components is the fact that they can support a number of interfaces. Exactly how this is done will depend of the nature of the component, but in the simple case of a component that represents the compiled form of a Java class, the interfaces supported by the component will simply be those implemented by the class itself.

For example, in Figure 8.53, the 'CatalogueEntry' class was shown as providing an interface called 'Priceable'. Because of this, the component representing the class file for this class can be shown to support the same interface, as shown in Figure 11.17.

Figure 11.17 A component supporting an interface

11.7 SUMMARY

- UML defines notation for documenting the *physical* aspects of a system's structure as well as its logical structure.

- *Components* are deployable and replaceable parts of a system, which encapsulate implementation and expose interfaces.

- Many of the artefacts that make up a system have been modelled as components, including source and object files, though UML also defines a notion of *artefact* to model entities such as files and database components.

- *Component diagrams* show components and dependencies between them. They can be used for a variety of purposes, such as showing the compilation dependencies between source files in a system.

- Compilation dependencies are generated by a number of design features, such as generalization and one class using another in its interface or its implementation.

- A guideline for physical design is to avoid, or minimize, cycles in the graph of compilation dependencies.

11.8 EXERCISES

11.1 Is there anything specifically object-oriented about the notions of component and dependency? How much of the material in this chapter about component diagrams would apply to a non-object-oriented language, such as C?

11.2 Which of the dependencies discussed in this chapter are transitive?

11.3 In Java, a class is implemented in a single source file, as illustrated in Figure 11.7. In C++, however, at least two files of source code are normally used. Lakos (1996) defines a component for C++ to consist of a pair of source files, a header file and an implementation file. Draw a component diagram which documents the relationships between this notion of component, the source files involved and the class that is implemented in the source files.

11.4 Compare the dependency graph in Figure 7.2 with the logical design of the booking system and identify what features of the design give rise to the compilation dependencies shown.

11.5 By extending Figure 7.2, draw a complete dependency graph for the restaurant booking system, based on the code available from the book's website.

11.6 What criticism could be levelled at the design fragment shown in Figure Ex11.6?

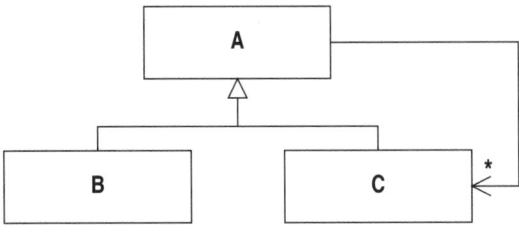

Figure Ex11.6

12

CONSTRAINTS

Much of the notation introduced so far in this book has been graphical. Icons are used to represent important concepts and many properties of the system are represented by connecting these icons in certain ways. For example, a line connecting two rectangles denotes an association between two classes and specifies how instances of those classes can be linked together. Text on diagrams is used to name and label model elements, and to add specific annotations, such as multiplicities or guard conditions.

Graphical notations are well suited for displaying structural aspects of systems, but less effective for documenting detailed properties of model elements or the restrictions that might be placed upon them by relevant business rules. These additional properties can be added to a model in the form of *constraints*. A constraint is an assertion about one or more model elements, which states properties that must be satisfied by all legitimate states of the system.

For example, suppose that a bank is introducing a new type of savings account, which pays a preferential rate of interest. However, the balance of the account must remain within the range £0 to £250,000 and a deposit or withdrawal that would take the balance outside this range will be rejected. A class representing savings accounts is shown in Figure 12.1, with the constraint represented informally in a note.

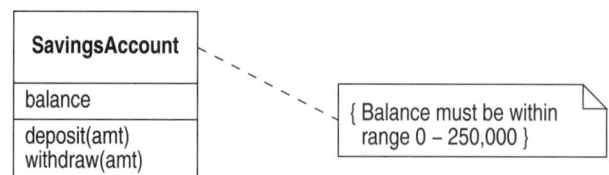

Figure 12.1 A constrained savings account

Constraints are written in UML in braces '{' and '}' in or near the model element that they describe. They can be placed inside a note and connected to the model element they describe with a dashed line.

A constraint states a property that can either be true or false. For example, given any instance of the account class in Figure 12.1, it will either be true or false that the value of the balance attribute falls within the stated range. A system must make sure that all its constraints are true. If the balance of an account fell below zero, for example, this would indicate that an error had occurred and the system would be in an illegal state.

UML defines standard constraints for a handful of common situations. More general constraints can be written either in informal English, in a more formal constraint language, or even using the notation of the target programming language. UML defines a constraint language, called the *Object Constraint Language* or OCL, and this chapter describes the most important features of this language and gives examples of their use.

12.1 STANDARD CONSTRAINTS

The UML specification defines a number of *standard constraints* applying to various model elements. For example, links and instances, or the corresponding roles, on interaction diagrams can be described as 'new', 'transient' or 'destroyed', as in Figures 9.10 and 9.12, to describe aspects of their lifetime within a particular interaction.

These constraints are rather unusual, in that they appear to describe general properties of the constrained elements rather than stating an assertion that can be true or false of a particular system state. The standard constraints defined for associations, however, are more conventional.

The xor constraint

The xor constraint can be applied to two or more associations and is useful where a class participates in all the constrained associations. It is used to state that instances of the common class can participate in only one of the constrained associations at any given time. Figure 12.2 shows an example that uses the xor constraint to specify that the bank's customers cannot hold both a savings account and a deposit account at the same time. Notice that the multiplicity of the constrained associations must include the zero case.

The subset constraint

The subset constraint on associations is used in examples in the UML specification and elsewhere, but is not formally defined as a standard constraint. This constraint can be applied to pairs of associations that link the same classes and states that the set of links which are instances of one association must be a subset of those of another. The constraint is shown by joining the associations with a dependency arrow to which the constraint is attached.

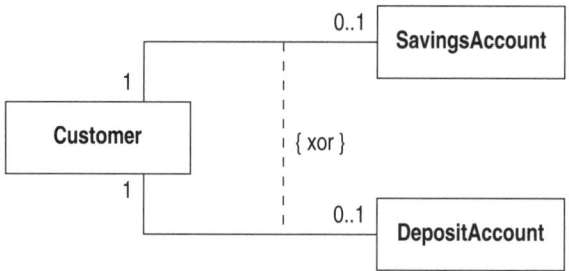

Figure 12.2 The xor constraint

Figure 12.3 shows an example of the use of the subset constraint, taken from the UML specification. It shows two associations specifying who are the members and chairs of committees. Without the constraint, it would be possible for an instance of this diagram to state that someone was the chair of a committee without at the same time being a member of it. The subset constraint rules out this possibility by asserting that any pair of objects linked by the 'ChairOf' association must also be linked by the 'MemberOf' association.

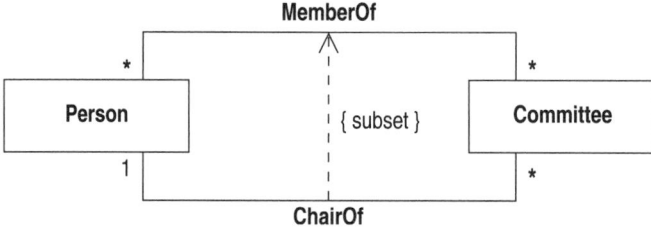

Figure 12.3 The subset constraint

12.2 THE OBJECT CONSTRAINT LANGUAGE

The standard constraints are useful, but in order to handle constraints in general, more flexibility is required. For example, consider the object diagram in Figure 12.4, which shows an unlikely situation in a banking application, where the holder of a debit card is not the same person as the holder of the account to which the debit card belongs. We would like to define a constraint on the model to rule out this situation, but this cannot be done using the simple xor and subset constraints defined above.

Stated informally, the constraint that needs to be added to rule out this situation is that all debit cards must be held by the person who holds the account the card belongs to. Informal constraints are perfectly adequate in some cases, but it is often very difficult to state a complex condition clearly and unambiguously in English. Even in this relatively simple case, the sentence stating the constraint is rather convoluted and its meaning is perhaps not obvious at a first reading.

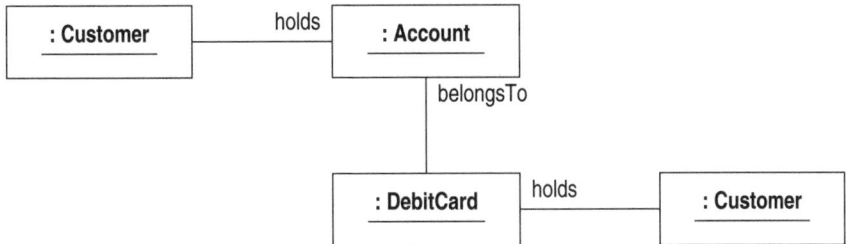

Figure 12.4 An unlikely situation

To address these problems, a wide range of formal specification languages have been developed by computer scientists. Because of their use of mathematical symbolism, these languages can appear to be rather unapproachable. OCL, the Object Constraint Language, is an attempt to provide a usable, text-based formal specification language for writing constraints that apply to UML models.

In the example above, the required constraint could be specified as a property of the debit card as follows. Imagine taking an arbitrary debit card instance: it is linked directly to the customer who holds it, but also indirectly to another customer instance. This second customer object can be retrieved by following a link to the account the card belongs to and then to the holder of that account. Once we have retrieved these two customer objects, we can state the content of constraint easily: it is simply that in both cases we must arrive at the same customer object.

This example suggests that a constraint language such as OCL should provide three essential capabilities.

1. The ability to specify which model element is being constrained. This is known as the *context* of the constraint and is discussed in Section 12.3.
2. The ability to navigate through a model to identify other objects that may be relevant to the constraint being defined. This is done by means of *navigation expressions*, which are discussed in Section 12.4.
3. The ability to make assertions about the relationships between the context object and any objects retrieved by means of navigation expressions. These assertions are similar to the Boolean expressions used in programming languages but, as discussed in Section 12.6, they are more expressive.

12.3 THE CONTEXT OF A CONSTRAINT

Every OCL constraint has a *context*, which relates the OCL expressions to the model element being constrained. The context of an OCL constraint can either be a class or an operation. Constraints can be shown on diagrams or written in a separate textual document attached to the model, and, depending on which style is used, the means for associating a constraint with its context will vary.

If a constraint is shown on a diagram, it can be placed in or near the symbols on the diagram that represent its context. For example, if the context is a class, the constraint can be placed inside the class icon. Figure 12.5 shows the account class from Figure 12.1 with a constraint added to specify that an account's balance must fall within the specified limits.

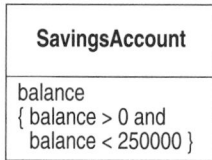

Figure 12.5 A simple constraint

Constraints can also be shown as notes attached to the appropriate model elements, as shown in Figure 12.1. It is purely a question of presentational style which method of presenting a constraint is chosen.

Instead of being shown on a diagram, constraints can be presented in a purely textual form. In this case, the context needs to be explicitly noted. Constraints start with a *context declaration*, consisting of the keyword `context` followed by the name of the class or operation being constrained. An alternative way of writing the constraint shown in Figure 12.5 is the following.

```
context SavingsAccount inv:
    self.balance > 0 and self.balance < 250000
```

The keyword `inv` states that the constraint is an *invariant*. Class invariants state properties that must be true of the attribute values at all times, in this case that the value stored in the balance attribute must be greater than £0 and less than £250,000. Other types of constraints are discussed in Section 12.7.

The term `self` in this constraint refers to the current context object. Its presence is optional, as constraints are always evaluated in this context anyway. Its use can make constraints easier to read, however, and it will often be inserted in constraints in the remainder of this chapter.

This constraint also illustrates the OCL notation for accessing the features of an object, namely to write the feature name separated by a dot from an expression which denotes the object. This notation is clearly chosen to resemble the notation used in languages such as Java and C++ for accessing features of classes.

The constraint notation allows two further variations. An alternative name can be provided for the context object and the constraint itself can be given a name. This would make it easy to refer to particular constraints in a complex model. If the constraint above was named 'account limits' and the context object called 'acc', it could be rewritten as follows.

```
context acc : SavingsAccount inv accountLimits:
    acc.balance > 0 and acc.balance < 250000
```

12.4 NAVIGATION EXPRESSIONS

The use of constraints is not limited to stating class invariants. As the discussion in Section 12.1 illustrated, some constraints place restrictions on the relationships between several model elements. In order to do this, OCL must provide ways of referring to the elements that are involved in a given constraint.

Informally, the required elements are identified by starting from a context object and then following links to gain access to other objects. As this process involves traversing part of the network of objects, the expressions that denote objects are known as *navigation expressions*.

The class diagram in Figure 12.6 will be used to illustrate the OCL notation for forming navigation expressions. This diagram models some of the information that might be maintained by a personnel department in a large company. The company is modelled as an aggregate of a number of departments. Each employee in the company is allocated to a department. A self-association on the employee class shows who in the company is managed by whom. A qualified association allows individual employees to be accessed by a unique payroll number.

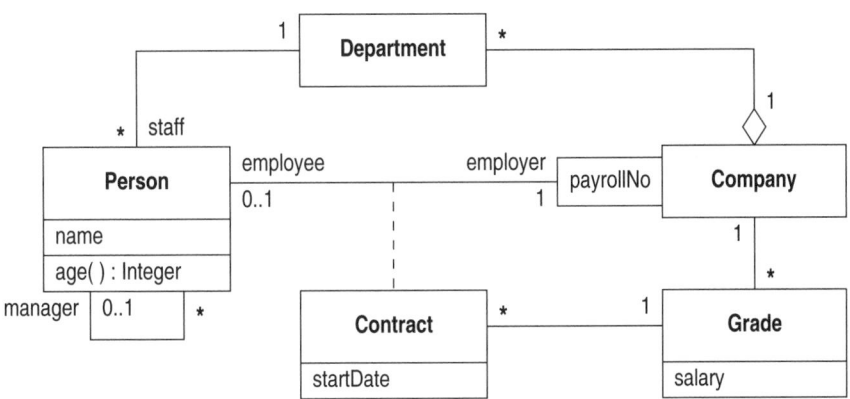

Figure 12.6 A simple model of a personnel system

The association between the person and company classes represents the relationship of a person working for the company. Further details about an employee's contract of employment are recorded by defining this relationship as an association class, 'Contract'. This class records the date on which the employee started work and maintains an association with a 'Grade' class, instances of which record the salary associated with a particular grade within the organization.

Following links

The basic form of navigation involves following links from one object to another. Every link is an instance of some association, so navigation is specified by identifying the associations that are to be traversed.

Navigation across an association is shown by writing the role name from the far end of the association end after the name of the context object, using the dot notation for attributes that was shown above. The value of such an expression is taken to be the set of objects that are currently linked to the object through the specified link.

For example, given the classes and associations shown in Figure 12.6, the following navigation expression denotes the set of employees working in the department at the time the expression is evaluated.

```
context Department inv:
    self.staff
```

If an association has no role name, the name of the class at the further end of the association is used instead, with a lower-case initial letter. For example, the following expression refers to the set of all departments in the company. This example also illustrates that there is no difference between aggregations and ordinary associations as far as navigation expressions are concerned.

```
context Company inv:
    self.department
```

The class name cannot be used in this way if there is any danger of ambiguity, for example if there are two associations between a pair of classes. In this case, suitable role names must be added to the association ends to allow the required navigation expressions to be formed unambiguously.

Objects and collections

A navigation expression denotes the objects that are retrieved by following the specified links from the context object. Depending on the multiplicities of the associations traversed, however, the number of such objects may vary.

For example, both the expressions above will in general retrieve more than one object, namely all the staff in a department and the set of departments in a company. In contrast, the following expressions, which denote the department and manager of the employee, cannot return more than one object, given the definition of the relevant associations. The second may return no objects, in the case that a person has no manager.

```
context Person
    inv: self.department
    inv: self.manager
```

In general, in OCL a navigation expression that returns more than one object is said to return a *collection*, whereas others simply return single objects. As OCL allows single objects to be treated as collections wherever necessary, the simplest approach is to think of every navigation expression as denoting a collection of objects. The detailed properties of collections are important in some situations, however, and they are discussed further in Section 12.5.

Iterated traversal

Navigation expressions are not limited to following a single association. More complex paths through a diagram can be described by writing a sequence of role or class names, separated by dots. For example, the following expression is one way of denoting all the people who work for the company.

```
context Company inv:
    self.department.staff
```

We can think of expressions like this as being evaluated in a step-by-step manner. First, the collection consisting of all the departments in the company is retrieved. Then, for each of these departments, the collection of all the people working in the department is retrieved. These collections of people are then merged together to form a large collection containing everybody who works for the company. This large collection is the value returned by the expression.

Traversing qualified associations

Qualified associations can be used in navigation just as well as ordinary ones, but they provide an additional capacity for locating individual objects. When navigating towards the qualifier, there is no difference between a qualified and an unqualified association. For example, the following expression denotes the company that a person works for.

```
context Person inv:
    self.employer
```

When navigating in the opposite direction, however, the qualifier provides a way of picking out a particular employee whose payroll number is known. The following expression denotes the employee, if there is one, whose payroll number is 314159.

```
context Company inv:
    self.employee[314159]
```

This notation can be freely combined with subsequent navigation or selection of attributes. For example, the following expression returns the manager of the employee with payroll number 314159.

```
context Company inv:
    self.employee[314159].manager
```

It is possible to traverse a qualified association without supplying a value for the qualifier, in which case all the linked objects are returned. For example, the following expression denotes the collection of all the company's employees.

```
context Company inv:
    self.employee
```

Using association classes

We can navigate from an instance of an association class to the objects at the ends of the association, using role names or class names as normal. For example, the following expression denotes the set of all employees at a particular grade.

```
context Grade inv:
    self.contract.employee
```

To navigate in the other direction, the name of the association class can be used like a role name to direct the navigation. For example, the following expression denotes the grade of a particular employee.

```
context Person inv:
    self.contract.grade
```

12.5 OCL DATA TYPES AND OPERATIONS

An OCL navigation expression, then, can denote either an individual object or a collection of objects. This section summarizes the different data types defined in OCL and discusses some of the operations provided on each. A summary of OCL types and operations can be found in Appendix B.

Basic types

To describe data items, OCL defines the basic types `Boolean`, `Integer`, `Real` and `String`, together with a number of operations defined on elements of these types. These basic types are fairly standard, and will not be discussed further here.

Curiously, the UML specification does not make explicit the relationship between the basic types of OCL and the UML data types. In particular, 'Real' is not defined as a standard UML data type. It is reasonable to assume, however, that the types are for practical purposes the same, otherwise it would be awkward to use the values of attributes in writing constraints, for example.

Model types

Any class defined in a UML model can be used as a type in OCL constraints. Types derived in this way are known as *model types*. Model types have associated with them a number of *properties* derived from features of the UML model. First, every attribute of a class defines a property. Second, there is a property corresponding to the far end of every association connected to the class. The name of the property is the role name at the far end of the association, if it exists, or the name of the associated class. Finally, query operations on a class give rise to properties. The restriction to query operations arises because evaluating an OCL expression must not change the state of the model.

Property values are denoted in OCL by writing the property name after an expression designating an object of the model type, separated by a dot. For example, the first of the following expressions denotes the age of an employee and the second denotes the employee's salary.

```
context Person
    inv: self.age()
    inv: self.contract.grade.salary
```

In these examples, properties are applied to expressions denoting single objects. If a property is applied to a collection, this is treated as a shorthand notation for the collection containing the property values for every object in the original collection. For example, the following expression denotes the collection consisting of the names of the employees belonging to a particular department.

```
context Department inv:
    self.staff.name
```

Enumerations defined in the UML model can be used in constraints, and enumeration literals are written prefixed by the name of the enumeration. For example, a constraint specifying that a particular traffic signal could only be red or green could be written using the enumeration defined in Figure 8.3 as follows.

```
context Signal inv:
    colour = Colour::red or colour = Colour::green
```

Collections

Suppose that in the organization described by the model in Figure 12.6, an operation is to be defined enabling departments to calculate their salary bill. One way of doing this would be to form a collection containing the grade objects corresponding to each staff member in the department and then to add up the values of the salary attribute in each of these to arrive at the total. It would be natural to write the following navigation expression to represent the collection of grade objects for the employees in the department.

```
context Department inv:
    self.staff.contract.grade
```

However, consider what would happen if the department contained two or more employees at the same grade. If this was the case, the same grade object would be reached many times, once for each employee at that grade. The question now arises, how many occurrences of the grade object will there be in the collection returned by the navigation expression above?

The answer to this question could make a big difference to the total salary bill that is calculated. If the collection is like a mathematical set, in which duplicate objects cannot appear, each grade object will appear only once, no matter how many employees the department contains at that grade. If this is the case, the total salary that is calculated will obviously be too low. What is required instead is a form of collection that can contain duplicate items, so that grade objects can be stored once for each employee at that grade and the correct salary bill worked out. Such a collection is known as a *bag*.

To cope with situations like this, OCL defines three different types of collection: sets, bags and sequences. A given object cannot appear more than once in a set, whereas bags and sequences can contain duplicates. In addition, the elements in a sequence are ordered.

Navigation expressions can give rise to collections whenever an association permitting a multiplicity greater than one is traversed. Navigation from a single element always gives rise to a set, because of the semantics of associations. If a duplicate arises, this would be because the original object was linked to the same object more than once, which is not permitted in UML. Navigation from a set, using the shorthand notation described above, in general gives rise to a bag of objects, however.

In the constraint above, then, navigation starts from the context object, an instance of the department class. Applying the 'staff' property to this individual produces a set of 'person' objects, and applying the 'contract' property to this set gives rise to a bag of contract objects. Finally, the grade of each of these contracts is retrieved, resulting in a bag of grades from which the total salary bill could be calculated.

In this case, then, the semantics of OCL ensure that the expression returns the required collection. Suppose, on the other hand, that the requirement had been to print a report listing the different grades that were represented in the department. In this case, a set would have been the preferred type of collection, as we do not care how many employees there are at each grade. To deal with this situation, OCL provides an operation, described below, which converts a bag to a set.

Operations on collections

OCL defines a number of operations on collections. One of these is an operation `sum`, which adds together all the elements in the collection and returns the total. Using this operation, the total salary bill for a department could be defined as shown below. The symbol '->' is used in OCL to indicate that a collection operation is being applied.

```
context Department inv:
    staff.contract.grade.salary->sum()
```

Another useful operation returns the size of a collection. This could be combined with the `asSet` operation, which converts a bag to a set, to return the number of distinct grades that are represented within a department, as follows.

```
context Department inv:
    staff.contract.grade->asSet()->size()
```

All the navigation expressions we have considered so far have returned a collection consisting of all the objects that are available as a result of the specified navigation. Sometimes, however, it is necessary to consider only a subset of the objects returned. For example, a particular constraint might apply not to all the employees in a company, but only to those whose salary is greater than £50,000.

This particular example could be handled if it was possible to form a new collection by picking out the required employees from the larger collection returned by a simple navigation. OCL provides the operation `select` on collections to perform such tasks. Here, for example, is a navigation expression returning the collection consisting of all employees in a company with a salary greater than £50,000.

```
context Company inv:
    self.employee->select(p:Person |
        p.contract.grade.salary > 50000)
```

This expression starts with a simple navigation which retrieves all the company's employees, returning a set of employee objects. The select operation is then applied to this set. This applies a Boolean expression to each object in the set, selecting only those for which the expression is true. The set of these selected objects is returned as the result of the whole expression.

The notation for the select operation includes the declaration of a 'local variable', which provides a context for navigation in the Boolean expression. In this case, the intermediate collection formed is a collection of instances of the model type `Person`, so a variable of this type is defined and used as the context object in the following expression. The declaration of this variable and its use at the start of the nested navigation is often unnecessary, as the type of the objects in the intermediate collection can be worked out from the first part of the expression.

The result of a select operation is a collection that can perfectly well serve as a basis for further navigation. For example, the expression below retrieves the managers of the highly paid employees and also illustrates the omission of the local variable in the select operation.

```
context Company inv:
    employee->select(contract.grade.salary > 50000).manager
```

Another useful operation on collections is the `collect` operation. This takes a navigation expression as its argument and returns a bag consisting of the values of the expression for each object in the original collection. For example, the following expression returns the ages of all the employees in a department. As with the select operation, the local variable is optional, but is included here for clarity.

```
context Department inv:
    staff->collect(p:Person | p.age())
```

The collect operation is not limited to calling operations from the model, but can perform additional calculations if required. For example, the following expression uses a collect expression to calculate the company's salary bill after applying a 10% pay rise to all employees.

```
context Company inv:
    contract.grade->collect(salary * 1.1)->sum()
```

A particularly simple form of the collect operation collects together the values of a single attribute belonging to all the objects in a collection. In this case, a natural shorthand form, which has already been used earlier in this chapter, is permitted. The following two expressions are equivalent ways of returning the names of all the employees in a department.

```
context Department
    inv: self.staff->collect(name)
    inv: self.staff.name
```

12.6 CONSTRAINTS

Navigation expressions allow us to write expressions that pick out some of the data stored in a model. As such, they may prove useful as the foundation for a UML-oriented query language, but they do not by themselves allow us to state desired properties of the data. This is the role of constraints, which in OCL are constructed by combining navigation expressions with various Boolean operators.

This section describes the various forms that constraints in OCL can take. These can be classified into three main groups. First, there are a number of basic properties that can be used to form simple constraints. Second, these constraints can be combined with a range of Boolean operators to express more complex properties. Finally, there are what might be called 'iterative constraints': these apply a constraint to all the elements of a collection and correspond to the quantifiers of first-order predicate logic.

Basic constraints

The simplest forms of constraints are those formed by using relational operators to compare two data items. In OCL, both objects and collections can be compared for equality or inequality using the operators '=' and '<>' respectively and the standard operators are available for testing numeric values. Examples of these have been given earlier, in Section 12.3.

Given the ability to write navigation expressions that refer to arbitrary data items in a model, quite a wide range of properties of models can be formalized using nothing but tests for equality and inequality.

For example, the constraint that the department an employee works for should be part of the same company that the employee works for can be reformulated as an assertion that the same company object is reached by navigating either directly from the employee to the company or indirectly from the employee to the department and from there to the company. The equivalence between the results of these two navigations can be expressed as follows.

```
context Person inv:
    self.employer = self.department.company
```

Equality tests apply to objects and collections, but there are in addition a number of basic constraints that only apply to collections. For the most part, these are generalizations of some of the basic properties of sets that are familiar from elementary mathematics.

For example, it is possible to test whether a collection is empty by using the constraint isEmpty, although strictly speaking it is unnecessary, as the assertion that a collection is empty is the same as the assertion that its size is equal to zero. Universal properties of a model, such as the assertion that all employees are aged 18 or over, can often be formalized by defining a collection that contains all the exceptions to the property and asserting that it is empty. The following constraints illustrate two equivalent ways of doing this.

```
context Company
    inv: employee->select(age() < 18)->isEmpty
    inv: employee->select(age() < 18)->size = 0
```

Two operations allow constraints to be written which make assertions about the membership of collections. The includes operation is true if a specified object is a member of a collection. For example, a rather basic integrity property of the system is that every employee's grade is one of the set of grades linked to that employee's company, as expressed by the following constraint.

```
context Person inv:
    employer.grade->includes(contract.grade)
```

The includesAll operation is similar, but takes a collection as its argument rather than a single object. It therefore corresponds to a subset operator for collections. As in the previous example, a common use for this operation is to make basic assertions about consistency between various associations in a model. The following OCL constraint states that the staff of a department are all employees of the company the department belongs to.

```
context Department inv:
    company.employee->includesAll(staff)
```

Combining constraints

Constraints can be combined using the Boolean operators `and`, `or`, `xor` and `not`. These operators have the standard meanings; an example of a constraint using `and` is the class invariant given in Section 12.3.

OCL differs from most programming languages in defining a Boolean operator representing implication. For example, suppose the company has a policy that every employee over the age of 50 must receive a salary of at least £25,000. This could be described in OCL as follows.

```
context Person inv:
    age() > 50 implies contract.grade.salary > 25000
```

Iterative constraints

Iterative constraints resemble iterative operators such as `select` in that they are defined over collections and return a result that is determined by applying a Boolean expression to every element in the collection. Rather than returning a new collection, however, they return a Boolean value that depends on the results obtained for each individual element.

For example, the operator `forAll` returns true if the specified Boolean expression is true for every member of the collection it is applied to and otherwise it returns false. A simple use of `forAll` is the following OCL constraint, which states that there is at least one employee appointed at every grade in the company.

```
context Company inv:
    self.grade->forAll(g | not g.contract->isEmpty())
```

Complementary to `forAll` is the operator `exists`, which returns true if the Boolean expression is true for at least one of the elements in the collection and false if it is false for all elements of the collection. A simple use of `exists` is the following OCL constraint, which states that every department has a head, in the sense of an employee in the department who has no manager.

```
context Department inv:
    staff->exists(e | e.manager->isEmpty())
```

It is easy to assume that it is necessary to use `forAll` in order to write a constraint that applies to all instances of a class. In fact this is not the case, as constraints on classes apply to all instances of that class. For example, the following constraint states that for every grade in the company, the salary for that grade is greater than £20,000.

```
context Grade inv:
    salary > 20000
```

This example shows that in simple cases there is no need to form an explicit collection in order to assert that a given property is true of all the instances of a class. Nevertheless, such a collection can be formed if necessary. OCL defines an operation `allInstances`, which is applied to the name of a type and, as the name suggests, returns the collection consisting of all the instances of that type. Using this operation, the simple constraint above could be rewritten in the following way.

```
context Grade inv:
    Grade.allInstances->forAll(g | g.salary > 20000)
```

In this simple case the use of `allInstances` makes the constraint more complex than necessary. There are situations where it is necessary, however. One common example is when a constraint has systematically to compare the values of different instances of a class. For example, the following constraint asserts that no two grades have the same value in their salary attributes.

```
context Grade inv:
    Grade.allInstances->forAll(g : Grade |
        g <> self implies g.salary <> self.salary)
```

This constraint implicitly applies to every instance of the grade class; as always, the context object is referred to by the term `self` in the constraint. The constraint compares the context object with every instance of the class, by iterating through the collection formed by applying `allInstances`. The second line of the constraint states the condition being tested, namely that two distinct instances of the class cannot define the same salary level.

12.7 STEREOTYPED CONSTRAINTS

Constraints are commonly used to state properties of a class and its operations that cannot be represented graphically. These properties include limitations on the possible states of instances of the class and certain aspects of the operations defined in the class.

Applied systematically, constraints of these types provide a general method of specifying properties of classes. This approach is quite widely used in formal specification languages, and even in programming languages such as Eiffel, and to support it UML defines stereotypes identifying the different uses of constraints.

Class invariants

A class invariant is a property of a class that is intended to be true at all times for all instances of the class. In a sense, all the constraints given earlier in this chapter can be viewed as invariants, as they state desired properties of class instances. However, the term 'invariant' is commonly used to refer only to constraints that restrict the possible values of a class's attributes.

For example, in Figure 12.1 a constraint was used to specify that the balance in a savings account had to be in the range £0 to £250,000. This is a typical example of a simple class invariant and it can be written either as the simple constraint shown below or as a stereotyped constraint, as shown in Figure 12.7. The use of notes tends to clutter up a class diagram, so in many cases the textual form may be preferable, but the difference between the two ways of representing the invariant is merely stylistic.

```
context SavingsAccount inv:
      balance > 0 and balance < 250000
```

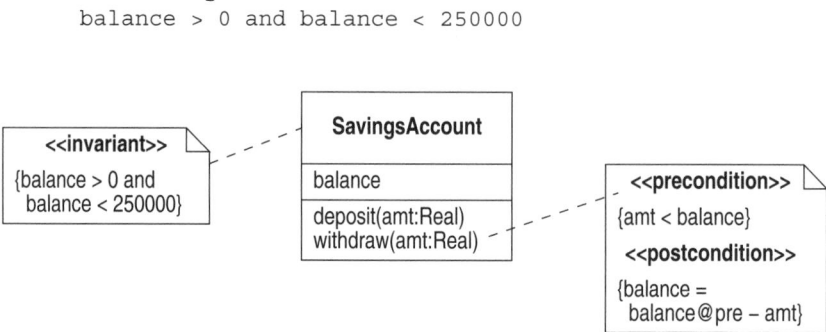

Figure 12.7 Class specification using stereotyped constraints

Preconditions and postconditions

Defining an invariant for a class provides no guarantee that the operations of the class will ensure that the invariant is maintained. If the withdrawal operation on the savings account class allowed any amount of money to be withdrawn, for example, the invariant stating that the balance had to be greater than zero could easily become invalid.

Preconditions and *postconditions* are special constraints that can be written for operations. As the names suggest, a precondition is something that must be true just before an operation is called and a postcondition is something that must be true just after the operation has completed. These constraints should be written in such a way that if they are both true at the appropriate time, the invariant of the class will still be true when the operation has completed.

A precondition is usually expressed as a constraint relating the attributes of a class instance and the actual parameters of the operation being specified. For example, if the withdrawal operation on savings accounts is not to cause the account to become overdrawn, the amount being withdrawn must be less than the current balance of the account. Stated formally, this is the precondition of this operation and is shown in Figure 12.7, identified by a stereotype.

Postconditions typically specify the effect of an operation by comparing the attribute values before and after execution of the operation. In the case of the withdraw operation, the postcondition is that the balance should have been reduced by exactly the amount specified in the actual parameter of the operation. This constraint is also shown in Figure 12.7, identified by the appropriate stereotype.

The formal statement of the postcondition introduces a slight notational problem. The name of an attribute in a constraint denotes the current value of that attribute. Postconditions are evaluated after the execution of an operation and so the attribute 'balance' in the postcondition of the withdraw operation denotes the balance after the withdrawal has been made. To state the postcondition formally, we need to compare this with the value of the attribute before the operation was called. As Figure 12.7 shows, this value is identified in OCL by writing the notation @pre after the attribute name.

Operation specifications can be written textually as well as being shown in a diagram. In this case, however, the context of the constraint is not an object of a given class, but an operation. Also, the labels pre and post are used to identify the stereotyped roles played by these constraints. The constraints below are equivalent to those shown in Figure 12.7 and illustrate this notation.

```
context SavingsAccount::withdraw(amt : Real)
    pre: amt < balance
    post: balance = balance@pre - amt
```

Design by contract

A specification of an operation using preconditions and postconditions is sometimes thought of as establishing a kind of contract between the caller of the operation and its implementation. In this model, the caller of an operation has the responsibility to ensure that the operation is not called with parameter values that would make the precondition false. The implementation makes a corresponding guarantee that, if the precondition is true, any alteration to the object's state will be such as to ensure that the postcondition is true when the operation terminates.

If both sides of this contract are satisfied, the class invariant will be maintained. This raises the question of what should happen if the contract breaks down: the situation is different depending on whether it is the precondition or the postcondition that fails.

An operation has no control over the parameter values that are passed to it. If it is called with invalid parameters, there may be no way that it can ensure that its postcondition is satisfied on completion. This situation is often thought of as a run-time error, similar to the error that occurs when an attempt is made to divide by zero. When a precondition is not satisfied, the state of the system becomes undefined and the operation may exhibit any behaviour.

It is common for operations that have preconditions to check that the precondition is satisfied before continuing with the body of the operation. If it is not, suitable action can be taken; perhaps an exception may be thrown. In general, drawing attention to the error is a better strategy than carrying on regardless and possibly letting the system's data become corrupted.

If a precondition is satisfied, on the other hand, the only way that a postcondition can fail to be satisfied is if there is an error in the implementation of the operation. In these cases, the remedy is simply to correct the programming error.

12.8 CONSTRAINTS AND GENERALIZATION

Generalization relationships do not give rise to any navigable relationships between objects, and so they do not feature explicitly in constraints. There are some cases, however, where generalization can complicate the writing of constraints by requiring the constraint to make reference to the run-time types of the objects involved.

Consider the basic polymorphic situation shown in Figure 12.8, where a customer can hold any number of accounts, of various different types. Suppose that the bank then imposes a restriction on its customers, stating that at least one of the accounts held must be a current account.

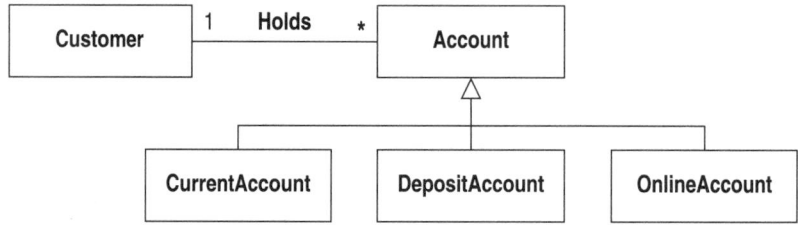

Figure 12.8 Polymorphic account holding

It would be natural to try to formalize this restriction by means of a constraint, but we cannot do this with the OCL notation presented so far in this chapter. Within the context of a customer object, navigation across the association in Figure 12.8 only provides us with a collection of account objects: we need in addition some way of finding out the run-time type of these objects.

OCL defines the operation `oclIsTypeOf`, which takes a type as an argument and is true only if the actual type of the object is equal to the specified type. Using this operation, the required constraint could be written in the following way.

```
context Customer inv:
    account->size > 0 implies
        account->select(oclIsTypeOf(CurrentAccount))->size > 1
```

Another use for run-time type information in constraints is to express in textual form constraints that must hold between parallel hierarchies in a model. For example, Figure 12.9 shows a situation where the bank has identified two different kinds of customer and is offering different types of account tailored for each.

It is quite common in such situations to want to restrict the links that can exist between instances of subclasses. For example, the bank might want to insist that only individuals can hold personal accounts and only companies can hold business accounts. This could be done by replacing the 'Holds' association with two lower-level associations, but, as discussed in Section 8.5, it is in general desirable to keep the higher-level association. An alternative approach, therefore, is to define a constraint that expresses the required property of instances of Figure 12.9.

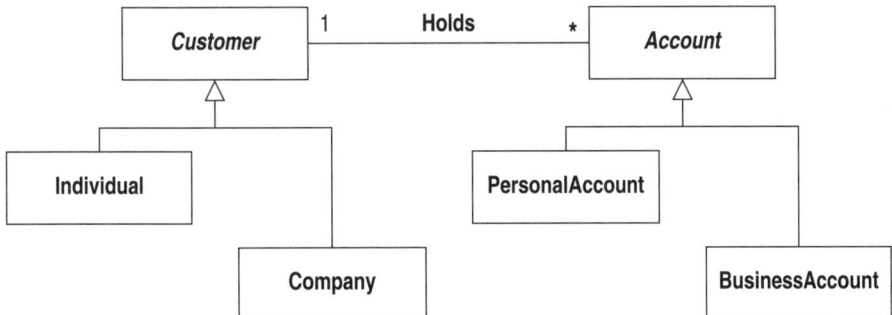

Figure 12.9 Parallel generalization hierarchies

The required constraint can be expressed by using the operation `oclType` which, when applied to an object, simply returns the type of that object. Using this operation, the following constraint asserts that all the accounts held by an individual must be personal accounts.

```
context Individual inv:
    account->forAll(a | a.oclType = PersonalAccount)
```

12.9 SUMMARY

- *Constraints* are assertions about model elements that specify properties which instances of a model must possess.

- UML defines a few standard constraints that can be represented graphically. UML defines OCL, the Object Constraint Language, for writing more general constraints.

- A constraint in OCL is a Boolean expression that asserts certain properties of a specified model element or relationships between model elements.

- Every constraint has a *context*, representing the model element that is being constrained or in terms of which the constraint is expressed. The context of a constraint can be either a class or an operation.

- *Navigation expressions* allow constraints to refer to objects that are linked, directly or indirectly, to the context object. This enables constraints to describe relationships between objects.

- Navigation expressions can denote, or return, individual objects or *collections* of objects. Collections can be *sets*, *bags* or *sequences* and OCL defines a wide range of operations on collections.

- Constraints are built up from *basic* constraints using Boolean operators and *iterative* constraints, resembling quantifiers.

> • Class specifications are often written using stereotyped constraints. An *invariant* describes properties of the class's attributes. *Preconditions* and *postconditions* specify the class's operations.

12.10 EXERCISES

12.1 Draw an object diagram showing some customer and account instances which violates the xor constraint given in Figure 12.2.

12.2 Draw an object diagram showing some person and committee instances which violates the subset constraint given in Figure 12.3.

12.3 Write an OCL constraint with the same meaning as the subset constraint shown in Figure 12.3. Give a general rule explaining how subset constraints could be replaced by OCL constraints.

12.4 Write an OCL constraint with the same meaning as the xor constraint in Figure 12.2. Give a general rule explaining how xor constraints could be replaced by OCL constraints.

12.5 Draw the class diagram implied by the object diagram in Figure 12.4. Can the requirement that the same customer holds an account and any debit cards belonging to it be expressed in any way without using an OCL constraint?

12.6 In the context suggested by Figure 12.4, suppose that the bank introduces a special credit card that is only available to customers who hold a savings account. Could this restriction be modelled using the subset constraint? Give reasons in support of your answer.

12.7 The diagram in Figure 12.6 states that employees of a company can have zero or one managers. Suppose that in fact the company operates a strict line management system whereby every employee apart from the managing director has exactly one manager. Change the diagram so that it models this new situation more accurately.

12.8 Write OCL navigation expressions based on Figure 12.6 for the objects described below. If necessary, add suitable role names to the diagram to avoid ambiguity.
  (*a*) The department that the employee with payroll number 123456 works in.
  (*b*) The department an employee's manager works for.
  (*c*) The employees at a specified grade in a given department.

12.9 Write OCL constraints expressing the following properties of the class diagram in Figure 12.6.
  (*a*) An employee's manager works for the same department as the employee.
  (*b*) Managers earn more than the people they manage.
  (*c*) Every department has a staff member earning at least £100,000.

12.10 What is wrong with the following attempt to write a constraint for the model of Figure 12.6 stating that nobody can be their own manager?

```
context Person inv:
    self <> self.manager
```

Write a correct OCL constraint for this requirement.

12.11 Write an OCL constraint for the class diagram in Figure 12.1, which states that every account a customer holds has a balance greater than £100.

12.12 Show how the multiplicity annotations on the associations in Figure 12.6 could be stated formally in OCL.

12.13 With reference to the class diagram of Figure 8.22, write a navigation expression denoting the companies that a given person works for. Use this navigation expression to write a constraint in OCL specifying that a person can only work for one company.

12.14 With reference to Figure 5.6, write an OCL constraint stating that the dates of the current bookings must all be equal to the current date stored in the booking system object.

12.15 With reference to the class diagram of Figure 8.43, write navigation expressions or constraints expressing the following.
   (*a*) The set of modules that a student is taking.
   (*b*) The mark a student gains for a particular module.
   (*c*) A student's average mark on all modules taken.
   (*d*) The set of modules a student has passed.
   (*e*) The set of students appearing on a given mark sheet.
   (*f*) The fact that a mark sheet records all the marks for exactly one module.

12.16 Add an association to Figure 12.6 so that the model can record details of which person is the head of each department. Write a constraint in OCL to express the requirement that the head of each department must be on the staff of the department.

12.17 With reference to Figure 12.7, write a suitable precondition and postcondition for the deposit operation on the savings account class.

12.18 With reference to Figure 12.9, write a general constraint in the context of the customer class expressing the restrictions on what accounts can be held by different types of customer.

13

IMPLEMENTATION STRATEGIES

It is clear from the examples considered earlier in this book that many of the features found in the design models used in UML can be implemented in a very straightforward manner in object-oriented programming languages. For example, the classes in a class diagram can be implemented as classes in Java, generalization by using inheritance and so on. Many case tools provide a code generation facility by implementing a set of rules such as these.

The fact that the transition from design models to code is so straightforward is a significant benefit of object-oriented design, but nevertheless there are certain features of the design models that do not map directly into programming language structures. This chapter considers the most prominent of these features and discusses various strategies for dealing with their implementation.

Associations are the most significant feature of class diagrams with no direct analogue in programming languages. The implementation of the restaurant booking system in Chapter 7 gave some simple examples of implementing associations using references and this approach is described in detail in Section 13.1 and the following sections. This chapter also describes ways in which more complex types of association, such as qualified associations and association classes, can be implemented.

The information contained in the dynamic models of an application is reflected not in the declarative structure of the implementation, but procedurally, in the methods of a class. Object interaction diagrams describe the order in which messages are sent in the execution of an operation, and this information is naturally used to guide the implementation of individual operations.

Statecharts, on the other hand, describe constraints that apply across all the operations of a class and which can therefore affect all its methods. It is a good idea to adopt a consistent strategy to ensure that these constraints are correctly reflected in the implementation of the methods of the class. Section 13.7 discusses various approaches to the implementation of statecharts.

13.1 IMPLEMENTING ASSOCIATIONS

Associations describe the properties of the links that exist between objects when a system is running. A link from one object to another informs each object of the identity, or the location, of the other object. Among other things, this enables the objects to send messages to each other, using the link as a kind of communication channel. Whatever implementation of links is chosen must support these properties of links. As explained in Section 7.6, references provide the appropriate functionality, and by far the commonest way to implement a simple association is by using references to linked objects.

The major difference between links and references is that links are symmetrical, whereas references only refer in one direction. If two objects are linked, a single link serves as a channel for sending messages in either direction. By using a reference, however, one object can send messages to another, but the other object has no knowledge of the object referring to it, and no way of sending messages back to that object. This implies that if a link has to support message passing in both directions, it will need to be implemented by a pair of references, one in each direction.

The use of two references incurs a considerable implementation overhead as it is crucial for the correctness of the implementation that inverse references are consistently maintained. In many cases, however, particular links only need to be traversed in one direction. Where this is the case, the association is often marked with a navigability constraint. This simplifies the implementation of the association considerably: if an association is only navigable in one direction, it can be implemented by a single reference, pointing in the direction of traversal.

Considerable simplification can therefore be obtained by only implementing links in one direction. On the other hand, if future modifications to the system require an association to be traversed in the other direction as well, significant changes to the program and reformatting of data may be required. Deciding whether to implement an association in just one direction involves a tradeoff between implementation simplicity and the likelihood of future modifications to the association, and this decision can only be taken on a case by case basis.

Section 13.2 discusses how to implement associations when the decision has been taken to maintain the association in only one direction. These are known as *unidirectional* implementations. Section 13.3 discusses *bidirectional* implementations, where it has been decided that the association must be maintained in both directions.

In general there are two distinct aspects to the implementation of associations. First, it is necessary to define the data declarations that will enable the details of actual links to be stored. Usually this will consist of defining data members in one class that can store references to objects of the associated class.

Second, it is necessary to consider the means by which these pointers will be manipulated by the rest of the application. In general, the details of the underlying implementation of the association should be hidden from client code. This implies that each class that participates in an association should define a suitable range of interface operations for maintaining the semantics of the associations defined in the class diagram.

13.2 UNIDIRECTIONAL IMPLEMENTATIONS

This section discusses cases where it has been decided that an association only needs to be supported in one direction. This design decision can be shown on a class diagram by writing a navigation arrow on the association to show the required direction of traversal. Different cases arise depending on the multiplicity of the association at the end where the arrowhead is written; the multiplicity at the tail of the arrow has no effect on the implementation of the association and is usually omitted. The following sections discuss the cases where the multiplicity of the directed association is 'optional', 'exactly one' and 'many'.

Optional associations

Figure 13.1 shows an association that is only to be implemented unidirectionally. Every account can have a debit card issued for use with the account, but, as this is an entirely new facility offered by the bank, it is envisaged that many account holders will not immediately take up the chance to have such a card.

Figure 13.1 An optional association

This association can be implemented using a simple reference variable, as shown below. This allows an account object to hold a reference to at most one debit card object. Cases where an account is not linked to a card are modelled by allowing the reference variable to hold a null reference. This implementation therefore provides exactly the multiplicity requirements specified by the association.

```
public class Account
{
  private DebitCard theCard ;

  public DebitCard getCard() {
    return theCard;
  }

  public void setCard(DebitCard card) {
    theCard = card;
  }

  public void removeCard() {
    theCard = null;
  }
}
```

The operations provided to maintain this link would in practice be derived from a more detailed examination of the relevant application. The code above does not assume that a card is supplied when an account is created. In addition, operations are provided to change the card linked to an account or to remove a link to a card altogether.

This implementation allows different cards to be linked to an account at different times during its lifetime. Associations with this property are sometimes called *mutable* associations. *Immutable* associations, on the other hand, are those which require that a link to one object cannot subsequently be replaced by a link to a separate object. In this case, an immutable association would correspond to the requirement that only one card was ever issued for a particular account.

If the association between accounts and debit cards was intended to be immutable, the alternative declaration of the account class given below might be more appropriate. This provides an operation to add a card to an account and only allows a card to be added if no card is already held. Once allocated, a card cannot be changed or even removed and the relevant operations have been removed from the interface.

```
public class Account
{
  private DebitCard theCard ;

  public DebitCard getCard() {
    return theCard ;
  }

  public void setCard(DebitCard card) {
    if (theCard != null) {
      // throw ImmutableAssociationError
    }
    theCard = card ;
  }
}
```

One-to-one associations

This example of an immutable association demonstrates that in general only some of the properties of associations can be implemented directly by providing suitable declarations of data members in the relevant classes. Other semantic features of an association can be enforced either by providing only a limited range of operations in the class's interface or by including code in the implementation of member functions that ensures that the necessary constraints are maintained.

Consider the association shown in Figure 13.2. This association describes a situation where bank accounts must have a guarantor who will underwrite any debts incurred by the account holder. It may frequently be necessary to find the details of the guarantor of an account, but in general it will not be necessary to find the account or accounts that an individual guarantor is responsible for. It has therefore been decided to implement the association only in the direction from account to guarantor.

Figure 13.2 A one-to-one association

The previous example showed that a variable holding a reference has a natural multiplicity of zero or one, because it can hold a null reference. If a multiplicity of exactly one is required, additional code must be written to check at run-time for the presence of a null reference. In the following implementation of the account class, the constructor throws an exception if a null reference to a guarantor object is provided, and no operation is defined in the interface to update the reference held.

```
public class Account
{
  private Guarantor theGuarantor ;

  public Account(Guarantor g) {
    if ( g == null ) {
      // throw NullLinkError
    }
    theGuarantor = g ;
  }

  public Guarantor getGuarantor() {
    return theGuarantor ;
  }
}
```

This code implements the association between account and guarantor objects as an immutable association. If the association was mutable, so that the guarantor of an account could be changed, a suitable function could be added to this class provided that, like the constructor, it checked that the new guarantor reference was non-null.

Associations with multiplicity 'many'

Figure 13.3 shows an association with multiplicity 'many' for which a unidirectional implementation is required. Each manager within the bank is responsible for looking after a number of accounts, but the model assumes that it is never necessary to find out directly who the manager of any particular account is. The new feature of this association is that a manager object could be linked not just to one, but potentially to many account objects.

In order to implement this association the manager object must maintain multiple pointers, one to each linked account, and hence some suitable data structure must be used to store all the pointers. In addition, it is likely that the interface of the manager class will provide operations to maintain the collection of pointers: for example, to add or remove details of particular accounts.

Figure 13.3 An association with multiplicity 'many'

The simplest and most reliable way to implement such an association is to make use of a suitable container class from a class library. For simple implementations in Java, the Vector class is a natural choice for this purpose. A skeleton implementation of the manager class using vectors is given below. The class declares a vector of accounts as a private data member, and the functions to add and remove accounts from this collection simply call the corresponding functions defined in the interface of the vector class.

```
public class Manager
{
  private Vector theAccounts ;

  public void addAccount(Account acc) {
    theAccounts.addElement(acc) ;
  }

  public void removeAccount(Account acc) {
    theAccounts.removeElement(acc) ;
  }
}
```

Part of the semantics of a class diagram such as Figure 13.3 is that there can be at most one link between a manager and any particular account. In this implementation, however, there is no reason why many pointers to the same account object could not be stored in the vector held by the manager. This is a further example of the inability of programming languages to capture in declarations every constraint expressible in UML's class diagrams. A correct implementation of the addAccount function should check that the account being added is not already linked to the manager object.

13.3 BIDIRECTIONAL IMPLEMENTATIONS

If a bidirectional implementation of an association is required, each link could be implemented by a pair of references, as discussed above. The declarations and code required to support such an implementation are essentially the same as those discussed above, the only difference being that suitable fields must be declared in both classes participating in the association.

The extra complexity involved in dealing with bidirectional implementations arises from the need to ensure that at run-time the two pointers implementing a link are kept consistent. This property is often referred to as *referential integrity*. Figure 13.4(*a*) shows the desired situation, where a pair of 'equal and opposite' pointers implement a single link. By contrast, Figure 13.4(*b*) shows the violation of referential integrity.

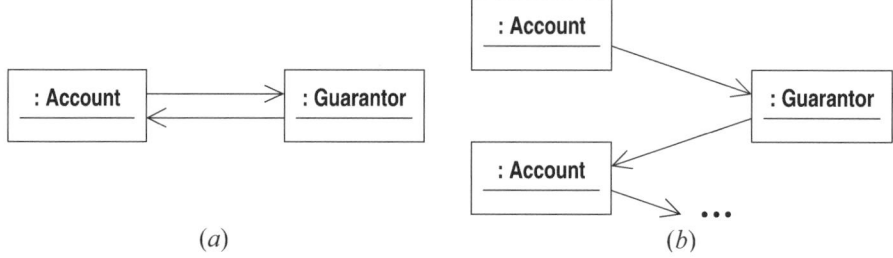

(a)   (b)

Figure 13.4 Referential integrity and its violation

For the association between accounts and guarantors, the required property can be stated informally as 'the guarantor of an account must guarantee that same account'. Figure 13.4(*b*) violates this: the top account object holds a reference to a guarantor object, which in turn holds a reference to a completely different account. These two references cannot be understood as being an implementation of a single link.

It should be clear from this example that referential integrity cannot be ensured by simply giving appropriate definitions of data members in the relevant classes. Such declarations only assert that a reference or references will be held, but give no information about the nature of the objects referred to, or about relationships holding between distinct references. As with certain aspects of unidirectional implementations, the relevant constraints can only be enforced in the code of the operations that maintain the links.

As with unidirectional implementations, not every association needs to support all possible forms of manipulation of links. What behaviour needs to be supported will depend on the details of individual applications and will be defined by the operational interfaces of the classes participating in the association. This section will consider a few representative cases and draw attention to the issues that an implementation needs to bear in mind.

One-to-one and optional associations

Figure 13.5 shows the association of Figure 13.1, but with multiplicities added at both ends. Assume that we are now required to provide a bidirectional implementation of this association. We will also assume that the association is immutable in the debit card to account direction, or in other words that, once a debit card is linked to an account, it must stay linked to that account until the end of its lifetime. An account, on the other hand, can have different cards associated with it at different times, to cater for situations where the account holder loses a card, for example.

Figure 13.5 A bidirectional association

This association can be thought of as a combination of a mutable and optional association in the left-to-right direction with an immutable association in the other. A simple approach to its implementation would simply combine the implementations of those associations given in Section 13.2, as shown below. For simplicity, the bodies of the methods in the classes are omitted.

```
public class Account
{
  private DebitCard theCard ;

  public DebitCard getCard() { ... }
  public void setCard(DebitCard card) { ... }
  public void removeCard() { ... }
}

public class DebitCard
{
  private Account theAccount ;

  public DebitCard(Account a) { ... }
  public Account getAccount() { ... }
}
```

This implementation certainly provides the data members necessary to store the bidirectional links, but the methods maintain the two directions of the link independently. For example, the pointer from the account to the card is set up in the account constructor and the pointer from card to account in the card constructor.

This division of labour makes it harder than necessary to maintain referential integrity for this association. For example, to create a link between a new debit card and an account two separate operations are required, first to create the card and second to link it to the account. The link from card to account is created when the card itself is created. Code to implement this might be as follows.

```
Account acc1 = new Account() ;
DebitCard card1 = new DebitCard(acc1) ;
acc1.setCard(card1) ;
```

To ensure that referential integrity is maintained, it is necessary to ensure that these two operations are always performed together. However, as two separate statements are needed, there is a real possibility that one may be omitted, or an erroneous parameter supplied, leading to an inconsistent data structure, as in the following example, in which the debit card is initialized with the wrong account.

```
Account acc1 = new Account(), acc2 = new Account() ;
DebitCard card1 = new DebitCard(acc2) ;
acc1.setCard(card1) ;
```

A better solution is explicitly to give the responsibility for maintaining the association to one of the classes involved. A link between two objects could then be created by means of a single function call and encapsulation could be used to ensure that only trusted functions have the ability to directly manipulate links.

The choice of which class to give the maintenance responsibility to often arises naturally out of other aspects of the overall design. In the current case, it is likely that there would be an operation on the account class to create a new debit card for the account and this would provide a strong argument for making the account class responsible for maintaining the association. If this was the case, the classes could be defined as follows.

```
public class Account
{
  private DebitCard theCard ;

  public DebitCard getCard() {
    return theCard;
  }

  public void addCard() {
    theCard = new DebitCard(this);
  }
}

public class DebitCard
{
  private Account theAccount ;

  DebitCard(Account a) { theAccount = a; }

  public Account getAccount() {
    return theAccount;
  }
}
```

Debit cards are now actually created by the addCard operation in the account class. The implementation of this operation dynamically creates a new debit card object, passing the address of the current account as an initializer. The constructor in the debit card class uses this initializer to set up the pointer back to the account object creating the card. A single call to the add card operation is now guaranteed to set up a bidirectional link correctly.

In an attempt to ensure that there is no other way of setting up links, the constructor of the debit card class is not declared to be public. The effect of this is to limit the classes that can create debit cards to those in the same package and to provide some measure of protection against the arbitrary creation of debit cards. The equivalent of the 'friend' mechanism in C++ would be needed to ensure that debit cards could only be created by functions in the account class.

This example is particularly simple because the association was declared to be immutable in one direction. In general, if both directions of an association are mutable, a wide range of situations can arise in which links can be altered, and a correct implementation must ensure that these are all correctly handled.

For example, suppose that a customer can hold many accounts but only one debit card, and has the facility to nominate which account is debited when the card is used. The association between accounts and debit cards will now be mutable in both directions and it will be reasonable for the card class to provide an operation to change the account that the card is associated with.

The manipulations involved in such an operation are quite involved, however. First, the existing link between the card and its account must be broken. Second, a new link must be established between the new account and the card. Finally, this should only happen if the new account is not already linked to a card.

The implementation sketched below follows the strategy given above of allocating the responsibility of manipulating references exclusively to the account class. As explained above, this makes consistency easier to guarantee, as there is only one place where changes are being made to links. This means that the card class must call functions in the account class to update references, as shown in the implementation of the changeAccount operation given below.

```
public class Account
{
   private DebitCard theCard ;

   public DebitCard getCard() { ... }
   public void addCard(DebitCard c) { ... }

   public void removeCard() {
      theCard = null ;
   }
}

public class DebitCard
{
   private Account theAccount ;

   public DebitCard(Account a) { ... }
   public Account getAccount() { ... }

   public void changeAccount(Account newacc) {
      if (newacc.getCard() != null) {
         // throw AccountAlreadyHasACard
      }
      theAccount.removeCard() ;
      newacc.addCard(this) ;
   }
}
```

Although in this function it may seem more 'efficient' to let the card class directly maintain its data elements, a significant amount of security and robustness can be achieved by delegating that responsibility to the account class, as shown.

One-to-many associations

The bidirectional implementation of one-to-many associations raises no significantly different problems from those discussed above. For example, Figure 13.6 shows an association specifying that customers can hold many accounts, each of which is held by a single customer.

Figure 13.6 Customers holding accounts

As before, the customer class could contain a data member to store a collection of pointers to accounts, and additionally each account should store a single pointer to a customer. It would seem most sensible to give the customer class the responsibility of maintaining the links of this association, though in practice this decision would only be made in the light of the total processing requirements of the system.

Many-to-many associations

The most general case of many-to-many associations does not raise any new issues of principle. For example, consider the relationship in Figure 13.7, which allows a number of signatories, people who are authorized to sign cheques, to be defined for each account. At the same time, a person can be a signatory for any number of accounts. This association may need to be traversed in both directions, and is mutable at both ends.

Figure 13.7 A general many-to-many association

There is no reason in principle why this association should not be implemented using the techniques discussed above. Because of the symmetry of many-to-many associations, however, it is often difficult sensibly to assign the responsibility of maintaining the links to one of the two classes involved and it can be quite complex to ensure that the operations in each class correctly maintain the referential integrity of the links.

An alternative approach that can sometimes be useful is to apply the technique of *reifying* the association, as discussed in Section 8.4. In the present case, this would involve replacing the many-to-many association by a new class and a pair of one-to-many associations, as shown in Figure 13.8.

Figure 13.8 Reifying a many-to-many association

Now the responsibility of maintaining the signatory relationship can be given to the new signatory class. Each instance of this class maintains references to the linked account and customer objects and should be made responsible for ensuring that the inverse references are maintained consistently.

Immutable bidirectional associations

Suppose that the association between accounts and guarantors is intended to be immutable and needs to be traversed in both directions. Figure 13.9 shows the relevant class diagram, which preserves the restriction that each guarantor can only guarantee one account.

Figure 13.9 An immutable one-to-one association

As before, each class can define a data member holding a reference to an object of the other class. The class declarations may be as follows.

```
public class Account
{
    private Guarantor theGuarantor ;

    public Account(Guarantor g)      { theGuarantor = g; }
    public Guarantor getGuarantor() { return theGuarantor; }
}

public class Guarantor
{
    private Account theAccount ;

    public Guarantor(Account a) { theAccount = a; }
    public Account getAccount() { return theAccount; }
}
```

These declarations seem to introduce a certain circularity. When an account is created, it must be supplied with an already existing guarantor object, and likewise when a guarantor is created it must be supplied with an already existing account. It might be thought that this could be achieved by creating the two objects simultaneously, as shown in the following code.

```
Account a   = new Account(new Guarantor(a)) ;
Guarantor g = a.getGuarantor() ;
```

However, although an analogous approach works in C++, this is not legal Java code, because the object a has not been initialized by the time it is used in the constructor of the guarantor class. In order to create the required link, one of the objects must be created using a default constructor and the link subsequently established with a suitable 'set' operation. It will then be necessary to check explicitly that the constraints on the association are maintained at all times.

13.4 IMPLEMENTING QUALIFIED ASSOCIATIONS

The previous sections have addressed some of the issues involved in the implementation of simple associations. Specialized forms of associations, such as the qualified associations considered in this section, have properties that suggest that alternative or enhanced implementation strategies are necessary. In these cases, is it worth considering how the designer's intentions are best preserved in the implementation of the association.

As explained in Section 8.11, a qualifier is a piece of data that can be used as a key to pick out one of a set of objects. For example, Figure 13.10 shows an association modelling the fact that a bank can maintain many different accounts. Each account is identifiable by a single piece of data, namely the account number, and this attribute is shown as a qualifier attached to the bank class. For simplicity, we assume that the association is to be given a unidirectional implementation.

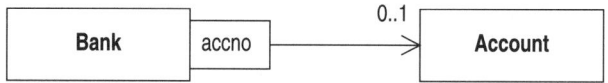

Figure 13.10 A qualified association

The most common use of such an association is to provide efficient access to objects based on the values of the qualifying attributes. This implies that it will often be necessary to provide some kind of data structure that supports such access in the object to which the qualifier is attached.

For example, we may need to retrieve information about accounts given only an account number. If the bank simply held a pointer to each of its accounts, this operation could be implemented by searching through all the pointers until the matching account was found. This could be very slow, however, and a better approach might be to maintain a lookup table mapping account numbers to accounts, as illustrated in Figure 13.11. As account numbers can be ordered, for example, this gives the possibility of using much more efficient search techniques.

This kind of structure is relatively easy to implement, the major issue being to decide how to implement the lookup table. In Java, an obvious and straightforward choice is to use a utility class such as `java.util.HashTable`.

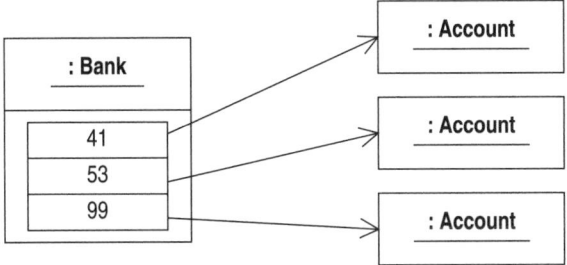

Figure 13.11 How qualifiers can be implemented

As a unidirectional implementation is being considered, the bank object must have the responsibility of maintaining the association. Operations to add and remove accounts, and to look up an account given its number, could be declared as follows.

```
public class Bank
{
  private Hashtable theAccounts ;

  public void addAccount(Account a) {
    theAccounts.put(new Integer(a.getNumber()), a);
  }
  public void removeAccount(int accno) {
    theAccounts.remove(new Integer(accno));
  }
  public Account lookupAccount(int accno) {
    return (Account) theAccounts.get(new Integer(accno));
  }
}
```

Qualifiers, then, can still be handled using the simple model that implements individual links by references. The implementation given above treats a qualified association in much the same way as an association with multiplicity 'many'. The most significant difference is in the data structure used to hold the multiple pointers at one end of the association. A bidirectional implementation of a qualified association, therefore, does not raise any significantly new problems and implementation of the association in Figure 13.10 as a bidirectional association is left as an exercise.

13.5 IMPLEMENTING ASSOCIATION CLASSES

Unlike the situation with qualifiers, it is not possible to handle association classes with a simple implementation of associations based on references. For example, consider the diagram in Figure 13.12, which shows that many students can be registered as taking modules and that a mark is associated with each such registration. The semantics of this notation were discussed in Section 8.9.

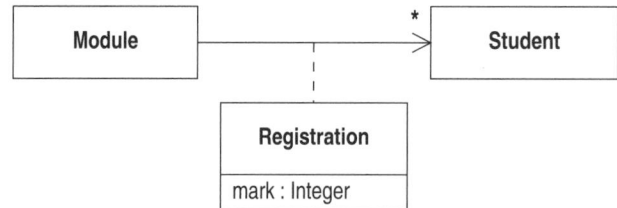

Figure 13.12 An association class

The association class shown in Figure 13.12 needs to be implemented as a class, to provide a place to store the attribute values representing marks. The links corresponding to the association cannot then be implemented as references between the module and student classes, however, as there would then be no way of associating the correct mark with a student and module pair.

A common strategy in this case is to transform the association class into a simple class linked to the two original classes with two new associations, as shown in Figure 13.13. In this diagram, the fact that many students can take a module is modelled by stating that the module can be linked to many objects of the registration class, each of which is further linked to a unique student, namely the student for whom the registration applies.

Figure 13.13 Transforming the association into a class

As a result of this transformation, the association class has been replaced by two straightforward associations, which can be implemented using references. The way in which these associations should be manipulated by client code repays some thought, however.

The original association shown in Figure 13.12 would naturally have been maintained by the module class, which might provide operations to add a link to a student and to record a mark stored for a student. Despite the fact that the association is now being implemented as a class, the interface presented to client code should remain unchanged. This implies that the module class must maintain both the registration class in Figure 13.13 and also the two new associations, and therefore that the operation to add a student to a module must create a new object and two new links. A possible outline implementation for this operation is shown below.

The implementation of the registration class is very simple. It must store a reference to the linked student object and the mark gained by that student. As this class is manipulated exclusively by the module class, we do not bother to provide an operational interface for it.

```
class Registration
{
  Registration(Student st) { student = st; mark = 0; }

  private Student student ;
  private int mark ;
}
```

The relevant parts of the definition of the module class are sketched out below. The very simple implementation given in this example does not perform any of the validation discussed above.

```
public class Module
{
  public void enrol(Student st)
    { registrations.addElement(new Registration(st)); }

  private Vector registrations ;
}
```

Implementing an association as a class is clearly a strategy that is required whenever a class diagram contains an association class. It is not limited to these cases, however, and, as discussed in Section 13.1, it is a strategy that can be applied to implement a general many-to-many association. This might be particularly appropriate if it was envisaged that there was a possibility of link attributes being added at some later date. A simple pointer-based implementation would not cope at all well with such a change, whereas if the association had been implemented as a class, it would then be almost trivial to add link attributes.

A further consideration in the implementation of this association is that the two class diagrams in Figure 13.12 and Figure 13.13 in fact have slightly different meanings. Figure 13.12 states that a student can only take a module once, as only one link is permitted between any given pair of module and student objects. With Figure 13.13 on the other hand, there is nothing to prevent a student being linked to the same module many times, through the mediation of different registration instances. An implementation of Figure 13.13 should bear this in mind and check that the appropriate constraints are satisfied.

13.6 IMPLEMENTING CONSTRAINTS

Section 12.7 explained how stereotyped constraints can be used to specify certain desirable properties of a class. Class invariants describe relationships that must exist between the attribute values of an instance of the class, and preconditions and postconditions specify what must be true before and after an operation is called. Often the robustness of an implementation can be increased by including code in the class that checks these conditions at the appropriate times.

In particular, all the preconditions that are specified for an operation should be explicitly checked in an implementation. Preconditions state properties of an operation's parameters that must be satisfied if the operation is to be able to run to completion successfully. However, it is the responsibility of the caller of the operation to ensure that the preconditions are satisfied when an operation is called. When the operation is called, it is simply provided with parameter values with no guarantee that they are sensible.

If an operation does not check its parameter values, there is a danger that erroneous or meaningless values will go undetected, resulting in unpredictable run-time errors. A better strategy is for an operation to check its preconditions and perhaps to raise an exception if a violation of the preconditions is detected. The following example provides a possible implementation of the withdraw operation of the savings account class specified in Section 12.7.

```
public class SavingsAccount
{
  public void withdraw(double amt) {
    if (amt >= balance) {
      // throw PreconditionUnsatisfied
    }
    balance -= amt ;
  }

  private double balance ;
}
```

A postcondition was also given for this operation, specifying that the result of the operation was to deduct the amount given from the balance of the account. It might seem logical to check at the end of the operation that the postcondition is satisfied, but in practice this would often involve duplicating much of the effort put into the implementation of the operation and it is rarely done.

If a class has a non-trivial invariant, it can sometimes be worthwhile writing an operation in the class which checks that the invariant is satisfied. This operation can then be called at suitable times to ensure that instances' attribute values are in a legal state. For example, this could be checked at the end of every operation that changed the state of an instance, such as the withdraw operation shown above.

In general, any constraint can be checked at run-time by writing code that will validate the current state of the model. However, the overheads of such checking can be significant and, except for the case of precondition checking, constraints are rarely implemented explicitly.

13.7 IMPLEMENTING STATECHARTS

If a statechart is defined for a class, the information it contains can be used to structure the implementation of the methods of the class in a fairly mechanical way. This ensures that the behaviour of the class is consistent with that specified in the statechart, and in many cases this can make the job of implementing the class correctly much easier. This section summarizes a simple approach to implementing some features of a statechart.

Figure 13.14 models two states of a bank account, recording whether it is in credit or overdrawn. The example assumes that the only relevant operations are those to deposit and withdraw money to and from the account, and guard conditions and actions document the effect of these operations in terms of the amount of money involved in the transaction, 'amt', and the current balance of the account, 'bal'. Notice that when the account is overdrawn, no withdrawals can be made.

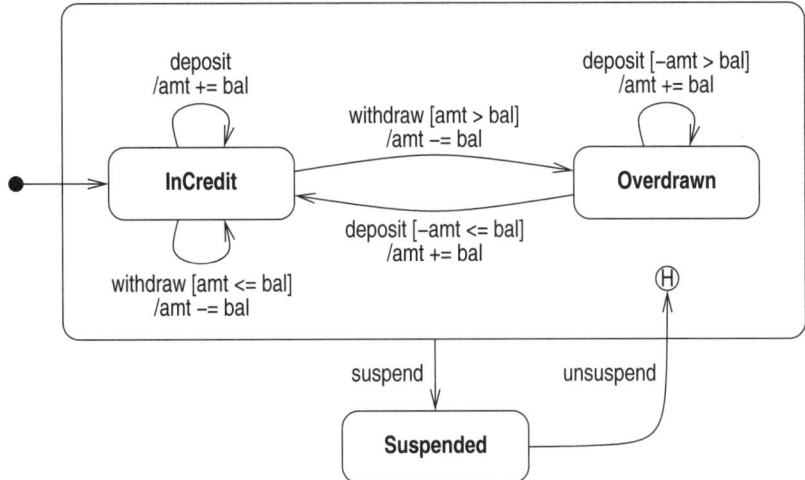

Figure 13.14 A statechart for bank accounts

The most important aspects of any implementation of the behaviour specified in a statechart are to record the current state of an object and to ensure that its response to a message is correctly determined by its current state.

Perhaps the easiest way to record the current state is to enumerate the different states as constants and to store the current state in a suitable data member. The following code shows how this could be done, and also shows how the constructor sets the initial state of the object to 'InCredit', as specified in Figure 13.14.

```
public class Account
{
  private final int InCredit = 0 ;
  private final int Overdrawn = 1 ;
  private final int Suspended = 2 ;

  private int state ;

  public Account() {
    state = InCredit ;
  }
}
```

Operations whose effect is state-dependent can be implemented as switch statements, with a separate case for each state. Each case represents all the transitions leading from the specified state that are labelled with the appropriate message. It should check any applicable guard conditions, perform any actions and if necessary change the state of the object by assigning a new value to the data member recording the state. If an operation is not applicable in a given state, that case can simply be left empty. For example, the following is a possible implementation of the 'withdraw' operation in the account class.

```
public void withdraw(double amt) {
  switch (state) {
  case InCredit:
    if (amt > bal) {
      state = Overdrawn ;
    }
    amt -= bal ;
    break ;
  case Overdrawn: case Suspended:
    break ;
  }
}
```

Composite states are essentially a device for simplifying the structure of a statechart and do not need to be represented as separate states. Their major role is to denote by a single transition a set of equivalent transitions from each of their substates. The 'suspend' transition in Figure 13.14 provides an example of this. This transition can be implemented simply by grouping together the cases that refer to the substates, as shown in the following outline implementation of the 'suspend' operation in the account class.

```
public void suspend() {
  switch (state) {
  case InCredit: case Overdrawn:
    state = Suspended ;
    break ;
  case Suspended:
    break ;
  }
}
```

History states are not additional states in a statechart, but rather a device for recording the most recent substate in a composite state. The history state in Figure 13.14 can therefore be represented by a variable storing a state, and this stored state can be used when an account is unsuspended, as shown below.

```
private int historyState ;
```

```
public void unsuspend() {
  switch (state) {
  case Suspended:
    state = historyState ;
    break ;
  // other cases
  }
}
```

Two bits of housekeeping need to be performed on the history state. The first time the composite state is entered, the history state is not active and the account enters the 'InCredit' state, as specified by the initial state in the composite state. In general, this behaviour can be simulated by initializing the history state variable to the specified initial state.

In addition, the history state variable needs to be set whenever a transition leaves the composite state. In the current example, this would be in the `suspend` method, just before the state is set to `Suspended`.

This general approach to the implementation of statecharts is simple and generally applicable, but it also has a few disadvantages. First, it does not provide much flexibility in the case where a new state is added to the statechart. In principle, the implementation of every member function of the class would have to be updated in such a case, even if they were quite unaffected by the change. Second, the strategy assumes that most functions have some effect in the majority of the states of the object. If this is not the case, the switch statements will be full of 'empty cases' and the implementation will contain a lot of redundant code.

13.8 REVERSE ENGINEERING

As previous sections have illustrated, the similarities in meaning between UML and object-oriented programming languages are such that many features of a design can be implemented in code by following a relatively small number of quite straightforward rules. By reversing the direction in which these rules are applied, it is possible produce UML documentation from the source code of a program. This process is known as *reverse engineering*.

Reverse engineering is useful in many situations where undocumented code has to be modified or maintained. This can happen when the original documentation has been lost, or is obsolete, as in many legacy systems, or where it was never produced in the first place. In these situations, abstract design documentation can be useful for becoming familiar with the code and ensuring that important functional properties of the code are preserved.

To illustrate the process of reverse engineering, we will consider some simple source code extracts representing a playlist of various music tracks and derive UML diagrams from them. First, the classes representing different kinds of tracks that the program will deal with are defined.

```
abstract class Track
{
  protected String title ;
  protected int duration ;

  Track(String t, int d) {
    title = t ;
    duration = d ;
  }

  abstract void play() ;
}
```

This class can be modelled as a UML class as shown in Figure 13.15. Fairly obviously, the data members of the class are modelled as attributes and the methods as operations. The constructor is underlined to indicate that it has class scope. The class itself and the 'play' operation are shown as abstract, reflecting the declaration in the code. Access levels in the code are made explicit using UML's visibility symbols: note that the class and its methods have package visibility in Java, not public visibility, and the diagram reflects this.

Track
title : String # duration : int
~ Track(t:String, d:int)
~ *play( )*

Figure 13.15 The track class

Different music file formats are represented by subclasses of Track, with implementations of the play method that are specialized for each format. Here, for example, is partial code for a class representing MP3 files.

```
class mp3 extends Track
{
  mp3(String t, int d) {
    super(t, d) ;
  }

  void play() {
    // Implementation omitted
  }
}
```

This class is defined by extending the track class, a relationship naturally modelled by using generalization in UML. Figure 13.16 shows this, together with a parallel 'wav' class, which is assumed to be defined for handling .wav files.

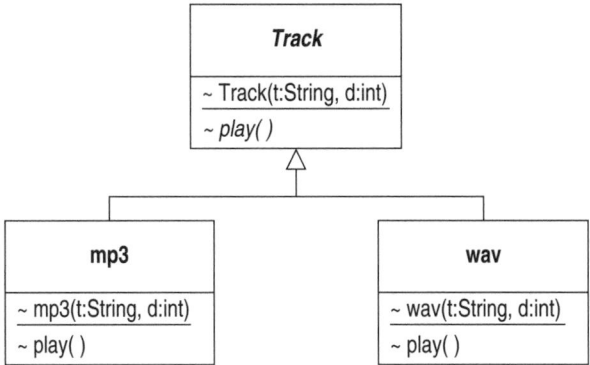

Figure 13.16 The track hierarchy

Finally, consider the following code for a simple playlist facility. A playlist simply stores a set of references to tracks and playing a playlist simply results in each of the stored tracks being played in turn.

```
public class Playlist
{
  private Vector tracks ;

  public Playlist() {
    tracks = new Vector() ;
  }

  public void add(Track t) {
    tracks.addElement(t) ;
  }

  public void play() {
    Enumeration enum = tracks.elements() ;
    while (enum.hasMoreElements()) {
      ((Track) enum.nextElement()).play() ;
    }
  }
}
```

Now, when generating code from a UML diagram, class attributes are normally implemented as fields in Java classes. Turning this rule around, it would seem natural to model the tracks vector in the playlist class as an attribute.

However, attributes are not the only source of fields in a class: associations are also often implemented by means of fields, which hold a reference to a linked object. The presence of a data field in a class, then, does not always indicate that there should be a corresponding attribute in the reverse engineered model. An attempt should be made to determine whether the field is implementing an attribute or an association.

The answer to this really depends on whether the field is meant to hold data values or objects. Sometimes this cannot be determined by the information available, however, and a reasonable guideline to follow is that a field holding a reference, or references, to objects of another class in the model should be reverse engineered to an association, not to an attribute.

Following this guideline, then, the `tracks` field will be reverse engineered not as an attribute but as an association, as shown in Figure 13.17. As the playlist class holds a vector of references to tracks, the association should be navigable towards the track class and have a 'zero or more' multiplicity, as shown in Figure 13.17.

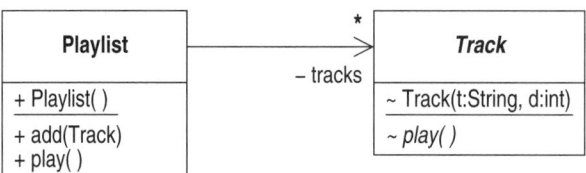

Figure 13.17 A model of playlists and tracks

This simple example has illustrated how structural features of a program can be captured using UML notation. Behavioural features are harder to identify, in general. For example, there are many different ways of implementing the behaviour specified in a statechart and, without knowing in advance exactly what is going on, it can be very hard to represent the behaviour of a class using a statechart.

Individual interactions can be documented quite straightforwardly on interaction diagrams, however. For example, consider the following method, which tests some of the functionality of the playlist classes.

```
public static void main(String[] args)
{
  Playlist list = new Playlist() ;

  list.add(new mp3("Who let the dogs out?", 193)) ;
  list.add(new wav("Meowth song", 253)) ;
  list.add(new mp3("Thunderball", 480)) ;

  list.play() ;
}
```

The collaboration diagram in Figure 13.18 shows the objects and links that are created at the beginning of this method and then the messages that are passed between these objects when the 'play' message is sent to the playlist.

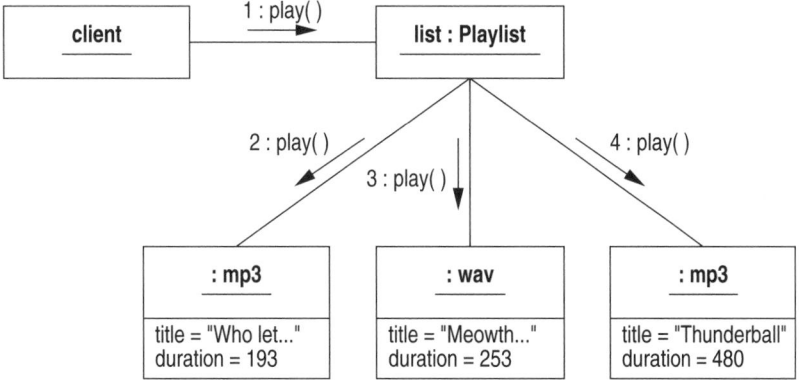

Figure 13.18 Playing a playlist

13.9 SUMMARY

- A simple strategy for implementing associations uses references to model links. Implementations can be either *unidirectional* or *bidirectional*, depending on how the association needs to be navigated.

- Not all the semantic properties of associations can be captured by data declarations. Further precision can be obtained by limiting the functions available to manipulate links and by ensuring that they check and maintain any relevant constraints.

- Bidirectional implementations of associations need to maintain the referential integrity of the references implementing a link. A strategy for robustness is to assign the responsibility for maintaining references to only one of the classes involved.

- Qualified associations can be implemented by providing some form of data structure mapping qualifiers onto the objects they identify.

- Association classes should be implemented as classes. This involves introducing additional associations connecting the association class to the original classes.

- Implementing an association as a class is a general strategy for the implementation of associations that can increase the ability of a system to withstand future modifications, at the expense of a more complex implementation now.

- Constraints in a model can be explicitly checked in code, but often it is only worth doing this for the preconditions of operations.

- The information provided in a statechart can be used to guide the implementation of a class. A simple strategy is to enumerate the possible states, store the current state and structure the implementation of the operations so that the effect of a message in each state is made clear, perhaps by using a switch statement.

> • Reverse engineering is the activity of producing design documentation for existing code. It is of importance when dealing with legacy code. One approach is to apply in reverse the rules used for generating code from a design.

13.10 EXERCISES

13.1 Change the account class in Section 13.2 so that the association between 'Account' and 'Guarantor' is implemented as a mutable association.

13.2 Implement the `addAccount` method in the manager class in Section 13.2 so that multiple references to the same account are not stored in the vector.

13.3 Provide an outline implementation of the association shown in Figure 13.6. Assume that the association is immutable in the account to customer direction, or in other words that an account cannot be switched from one customer to another.

13.4 Implement the signatory relationship between accounts and bank customers, first as a many-to-many relationship, as shown in Figure 13.7, and second using a reification, as shown in Figure 13.8.

13.5 In your answers to the previous exercise, is it possible for a single person to be recorded as a signatory for the same account more than once? If so, add run-time checks to ensure that this cannot happen. Is this constraint easier to enforce in one case rather than the other?

13.6 Provide a bidirectional implementation of the qualified association shown in Figure 13.10.

13.7 Provide a bidirectional implementation of the association class shown in Figure 13.12.

13.8 Complete the implementation of the savings account class that was discussed in Section 13.6. Provide a class constructor and an implementation of the deposit operation that checks a suitable precondition. Provide a function to check the class invariant and include calls to this function at suitable places in the class.

13.9 Provide an outline implementation of the association shown in Figure 12.2, together with code which checks that the xor constraint is maintained.

13.10 Provide an outline implementation of the association shown in Figure 12.3, together with code which checks that the subset constraint is maintained.

13.11 Produce a complete implementation of the account class, using the approach discussed in Section 13.7 to implement all the details specified in the statechart of Figure 13.14.

13.12 How could the strategy for the implementation of statecharts discussed in Section 13.7 be extended to deal with the following features of statecharts discussed in Chapter 10: entry and exit actions; activities; activity states; time events?

13.13 Using the approach discussed in Section 13.7, write a class simulating the behaviour of the ticket machine whose behaviour is summarized in Figure 10.20.

13.14 Many CASE tools, such as Rational Rose, support both code generation and reverse engineering. If you have access to such a tool, compare the rules that it uses for code generation with those described in this chapter.

13.15 Draw a UML class icon representing the following Java class.

```java
public class Counter
{
  private int value ;

  public Counter() {
    value = 0 ;
  }
  public int getValue() {
    return value;
  }
  public void increment(int i) {
    value += i;
  }
  public void reset() {
    value = 0;
  }
}
```

13.16 The program below defines a number of classes for handling invoices. An invoice is produced for a *client*, and contains a number of *lines*, each of which records a component of the total invoice, either the cost of some materials or a charge for labour.

(*a*) Draw a class diagram showing as much information as possible from the following class definitions.

```java
class Client
{
  private String name ;

  public Client(String n) { name = n; }
  public String getName() { return name; }
}

abstract class Line
{
```

```java
  protected String description ;

  public Line(String d) { description = d; }
  public String getDescription() { return description; }
  public abstract double getCost() ;
}

class Material extends Line
{
  private double cost ;

  public  Material(String d, double c) {
    super(d) ;
    cost = c ;
  }
  public double getCost() { return cost; }
}

class Labour extends Line
{
  private double rate ;
  private double time ;

  public Labour(String d, double r, double t) {
    super(d) ;
    rate = r ;
    time = t ;
  }
  public double getCost() { return time * rate; }
}

class Invoice
{
  private static int nInvoice = 0 ;

  private int invoiceNumber ;
  private Client client ;
  private Vector lines = new Vector() ;

  public Invoice(Client c) {
    invoiceNumber = ++nInvoice ;
    client = c ;
  }
  public void add(Line l) { lines.addElement(l); }
  public void print() {
    double total = 0 ;
    System.out.println(invoiceNumber + client.getName()) ;
    Enumeration enum = lines.elements() ;
    while (enum.hasMoreElements()) {
```

```
      Line l = (Line) enum.nextElement() ;
      System.out.println(l.getDescription() + l.getCost()) ;
      total += l.getCost() ;
    }
    System.out.println("Total: " + total) ;
  }
}
```

(*b*) The main program below creates a simple invoice and causes it to be printed out. Draw an object diagram showing the objects that are created when the method main runs and the messages that are passed between these objects when the invoice is printed.

```
public class Main
{
  public static void main(String[] args)
  {
    Client smith = new Client("John Smith") ;
    Invoice inv = new Invoice(smith) ;
    inv.add(new Material("new engine", 500.0)) ;
    inv.add(new Labour("labour", 35, 2)) ;
    inv.print() ;
  }
}
```

14

PRINCIPLES AND PATTERNS

In order to make effective use of a design notation such as UML, it is not enough simply to have a good grasp of the syntax and semantics of the various types of diagram. The availability of a formal notation does not ensure that good use will be made of it, and it is equally possible to express both good and bad designs in UML.

It is, of course, hard to characterize in purely formal terms the differences between good and bad designs, and it is probably impossible to do this with any degree of completeness. It is also very hard to make methodological recommendations which will ensure that designers produce only good designs. Nevertheless, a large amount of experience of object-oriented modelling and design has now been gained and, with this experience, some of the properties that can make a design successful or not are becoming better understood.

The knowledge accumulated by the community of object-oriented designers falls into two distinct categories. First, a number of widely accepted high-level principles have been identified. These principles describe particular properties that designs ought to have, or alternatively ought to avoid. The rationale for such principles is to point out characteristics of designs that experience has shown to have predictable consequences for the systems based on them.

These high-level principles are valuable, but provide little guidance to a designer trying to come up with a model for a particular application. To address these situations, it is necessary to document a different kind of design knowledge, more concerned with specific problems and strategies for overcoming them. Recent work on *design patterns* attempts to meet this need by identifying common modelling problems and providing verified solutions for them.

This chapter discusses a number of well-known and widely accepted principles of object-oriented design and then introduces the concept of design patterns. The use of patterns is illustrated by considering modifications to the programs presented in earlier chapters in this book.

14.1 THE OPEN–CLOSED PRINCIPLE

The open–closed principle was enunciated by Bertrand Meyer in 1988 in the influential book *Object-Oriented Software Construction*. This principle is concerned with the effects of change within a system, and in particular with maximizing the extent to which modules can be insulated from changes to other modules that they use.

Consider the situation where one module in a system makes use of the services provided by another. It is usual to call the first module the *client* and the second the *supplier*. Although the concepts involved apply more widely, this chapter will consider in detail only the relationship between classes. This can be modelled as a usage dependency in UML and the general situation is shown in Figure 14.1.

Figure 14.1 A usage dependency between client and supplier classes

A module is said to be *closed* if it is not subject to further change. This means that it can be freely used by client modules without the worry that future changes to the module will necessitate changes to the clients. Closing a module is desirable because it means that it can then be used as a stable component of the system, which is not subject to further change that may adversely affect the rest of the design.

A module is *open*, in Meyer's terminology, if it is still available for extension. Extending a module means adding to its capabilities, or enlarging its functionality. Having open modules is desirable, because this will make it possible to extend and modify the system. As system requirements are seldom stable, the ability to extend modules easily is an important aspect of keeping maintenance costs down.

The open–closed principle states that developers should try to produce modules that are simultaneously open and closed. As indicated above, there are significant benefits to be gained from both open and closed modules. The principle seems rather paradoxical, however, because it is hard to see how a single module can be both open and closed at the same time.

If the definition of 'open' was that it should be possible to change a module, then there would be a clear contradiction between a module being open and its being closed. However, the definition of 'open' only states that a module should be available for extension. In order to avoid contradiction, then, it is necessary to find a way in which modules can be extended without being changed.

A general solution to this problem is to distinguish between the *interface* and the *implementation* of a module. If these two aspects of a module could be separated in such a way that client modules only depend on the interfaces of their suppliers, then the implementations of modules could be modified without affecting clients in any way. Object-oriented programming languages provide a number of ways in which the interface of a class can be distinguished from its implementation, and in the remainder of this section these are briefly described and evaluated as suitable mechanisms for supporting the requirements of the open–closed principle.

Data abstraction

The use of data abstraction is intended to separate the interface of a data type or class from its implementation by making the implementation details inaccessible to client code. Data abstraction might therefore be thought to enable the construction of modules that are simultaneously open and closed. Data abstraction is provided in object-oriented programming languages by assigning to each feature of a class an *access level*, such as 'public' or 'private'. Figure 14.2 shows the generic client–supplier relationship with typical access levels defined for the features of the supplier class.

Figure 14.2 Client–supplier relationship using data abstraction

Access levels are also known as *visibilities* in UML and they indicate which features of a class can be 'seen' by clients. In Figure 14.2, the operation in the supplier class is declared to be public, and hence visible to the client, whereas the attribute is private and invisible.

From a client's point of view, the interface of a class is simply those features that are visible. It follows that invisible features can be changed, removed or added to without effect on clients, provided that the visible interface is preserved. In Java, for example, the supplier class in Figure 14.2 could be implemented as follows.

```
public class Supplier
{
  private int attribute ;

  public void operation() {
    // Implementation of operation
  }
}
```

The implementation of the public method in this class can be changed without having any effect on clients and, similarly, private fields can be added or removed as required to support the implementation of the methods of the class. What must be preserved to avoid having to make changes to clients is the visible interface consisting of the name and signature of the public methods of the class.

However, this approach to the implementation of the open–closed principle has a number of limitations. In the first place, the client module is technically not even closed, as modifications to the system require changes to the code in the client class. This might be treated as a violation of the letter rather than the spirit of the principle if its more substantial goals were achieved, but there are further, more substantial, problems with the data abstraction approach.

First, although it is the case in Java that private fields can be added to classes without any effect on clients, this is not the case in all programming environments. In C++, for example, a class definition is typically split between a header file, which is physically incorporated into the client module, and an implementation file. Any change to a header file, such as the addition of a new field, requires client modules to be recompiled, even if the change is invisible to them. It would be preferable if an implementation of the open–closed principle could be found that was language-independent.

Second, in the data abstraction approach the interface required by client modules is left implicit. Clients can make use of all features of the supplier that are visible to them, but need not do so. In practice, different clients of a module may make use of different subsets of the visible interface of a module. This makes it difficult to know exactly what changes to a module will affect a given client. Both documentation and maintainability would be improved by an approach that explicitly documented the interface required by a client module.

Abstract interface classes

An alternative approach to the implementation of the open–closed principle is to use an *abstract interface class*. A class diagram showing the general structure of the design using this technique is shown in Figure 14.3.

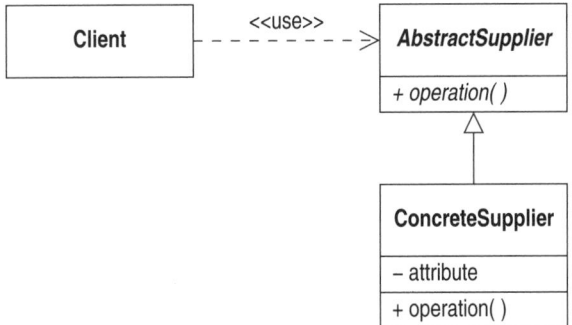

Figure 14.3 Client–supplier relationship using an abstract interface class

Here the abstract supplier class defines the interface for the supplier class. As it is an abstract class, it defines no attributes. The implementation of the supplier is deferred to a concrete subclass, which defines any necessary attributes and implements the functions declared in the abstract class. The client class declares its dependence on the interface class, which contains only those implementation details, if any, that it is known will not be subject to modification.

In Java, the abstract supplier class could be declared as an abstract class extended by the concrete supplier. The concrete subclass defines any necessary attributes for the chosen implementation and defines all the necessary member functions.

```
public abstract class AbstractSupplier
{
  public abstract void operation() ;
}

public class ConcreteSupplier extends AbstractSupplier
{
  private int attribute ;

  public void operation() {
    // Implementation of operation
  }
}
```

From the point of view of the open–closed principle, the important thing about this implementation is the effect on the dependency relationships between the three classes. As explained in Chapter 11, a generalization relationship induces a dependency between the subclass and the superclass. The usage dependencies between three classes in Figure 14.3 are therefore those shown in Figure 14.4.

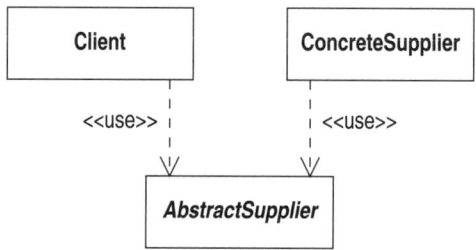

Figure 14.4 Dependencies with abstract interface class

Figure 14.4 makes it clear that the client class has no dependency on the concrete supplier class. A consequence of this is that any aspect of the concrete class can be changed without having any effect on the client module.

It should be remembered that we are talking about compile-time dependencies. Typically, at run-time the client would hold or manipulate a reference to an instance of a concrete supplier class, but through a field declared to hold a reference to an abstract supplier. Thanks to the polymorphic properties of references, such a field is not restricted to holding references to instances of the abstract supplier class.

The abstract supplier class is therefore an example of a module that is open, at least in the sense that it can be extended by the addition of further subclasses. These extra subclasses may provide alternative implementations of the interface, or may add features that were not previously present in the system. For example, the booking class in the booking system exhibits this feature of extensibility. Further subclasses could be added to it to enable the system to handle new kinds of bookings, but this would not affect any of the client modules, such as the restaurant or the booking system.

Is the abstract supplier class also closed? It is certainly more closed than the supplier class in Figure 14.2, in that typical changes to the implementation of supplier objects will be made to its concrete subclasses rather than to the abstract supplier itself. However, changes to the interface may be required as the system evolves and these will require changes to the abstract class. It may be asked if there is any way of closing a module against such changes and this issue will be considered in the Section 14.3.

The use of abstract interface classes, as exemplified in Figure 14.3, is a fundamental technique in object-oriented design and examples of its use will appear repeatedly in the patterns examined later in this chapter.

14.2 NO CONCRETE SUPERCLASSES

Section 14.1 has discussed the utility of abstract interface classes in providing software modules that satisfy the open–closed principle. A related principle states that all subclasses in generalization relationships should be concrete, or conversely that all non-leaf classes in a generalization hierarchy should be abstract. This principle can be summarized in the slogan 'no concrete superclasses'.

The rationale for this principle can best be appreciated by means of an example. Suppose that a bank is implementing classes to model different types of account, as in the examples considered in Section 8.5, and that in the initial version of the model only one class is defined, representing current accounts, which have the normal withdraw and deposit operations.

Subsequently the bank introduces savings accounts, which add the facility to pay interest on the balance in an account. As these new accounts share most of their functionality with current accounts, the decision is taken to define the savings account class as a specialization of the current account class, so that the shared functionality can be inherited. This situation is shown in Figure 14.5.

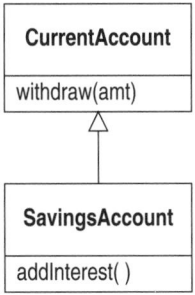

Figure 14.5 An example of a concrete superclass

This design is clearly a violation of the 'no concrete superclasses' principle, as the current account class in Figure 14.5 is both concrete and a superclass. Violation of this principle can lead to significant problems as a design evolves, as the following development of the example above will illustrate.

For example, suppose that the withdrawal operation that was originally defined did not permit accounts to become overdrawn. This restriction made the bank's current accounts unpopular with customers, however, so the decision is made to allow overdrafts on current accounts but not on savings accounts. It is not easy, however, to modify the design of Figure 14.5 to provide this functionality.

It would not be correct, for example, simply to modify the withdrawal operation defined in the current account class to permit overdrafts. As this operation is inherited by the savings account class, this would have the incorrect consequence of also permitting overdrafts on savings accounts. It would be possible to get round this by overriding the operation in the savings account class, to provide the original functionality, but this is rather an artificial solution. More seriously, it would have the consequence of replicating the code that actually performed the withdrawal in both classes. This may be trivial in this case, but, in general, code replication is a strong sign of a design error.

Another possibility would be to define the withdrawal operation in the current account class in such a way that it checked the run-time type of the account the withdrawal was being made from, and then chose an appropriate course of action. In outline, the implementation of the operation might be as follows.

```
public class CurrentAccount
{
  void withdraw(double amt) {
    if (this instanceof SavingsAccount) {
      // Check if becoming overdrawn
    }
    balance -= amt ;
  }
}
```

This style of programming has a number of serious drawbacks, however, including the fact that the superclass 'CurrentAccount' makes explicit reference to its subclasses. This means that when a new subclass is added, the code in the current account class will in general have to change, making it impossible for the current account class to be closed, in Meyer's sense. For this reason, among others, recourse to this style of programming is also taken as evidence of shortcomings in the design of a system.

Similar problems arise if a function has to be defined on current accounts only. For example, suppose the bank wants to add the capability for cheques to be cashed against a current account, but that this facility is not available for savings accounts. The only obvious implementation of this function is for it to check the run-time type of its argument, as shown below.

```
void cashCheque( CurrentAccount a ) {
  if (a instanceof SavingsAccount) {
    return ;
  }
  // Cash cheque
}
```

The problems in these cases arise from the fact that the current account class in Figure 14.5 is performing two roles. As a superclass, it is defining the interface that must be implemented by all account objects, but it is also providing a default implementation of that interface. In the cases we have examined, these roles conflict. In particular, this happens when specialized functionality must be associated in some way with instances of the concrete superclass.

A general solution to this sort of problem is to adopt the rule that all superclasses should be abstract. This means that the design shown in Figure 14.5 should be replaced by the one shown in Figure 14.6.

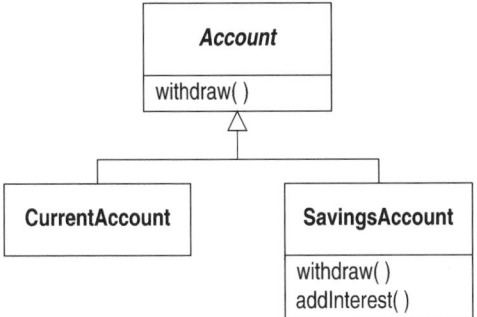

Figure 14.6 Applying the 'no concrete superclasses' rule

Now the withdraw operation in the 'Account' superclass can perform the basic withdrawal and the code that checks that a savings account is not becoming overdrawn can be placed in the function that overrides it. If necessary, the implementation of the operation in the superclass can be called from the subclass in order to make use of common functionality. Furthermore, as 'SavingsAccount' is no longer a subclass of 'CurrentAccount', instances of the subclass can no longer be passed to functions like 'cashCheque', above, and there is no need for that function to check the run-time type of its arguments.

14.3 DECOUPLE THE INTERFACE HIERARCHY

Suppose that an abstract interface class has been implemented along the lines shown in Figure 14.3. A modification request is then received, to add a function to the interface provided by the abstract supplier class, to satisfy the requirements of a new client class.

The design shown in Figure 14.3 seems to offer no alternative to adding this function directly to the abstract supplier class. There are serious problems with this approach, however. First, the aim is to close the abstract supplier and hence it should not be modified. Second, it is possible that such a change may lead to further changes to existing clients, at least to the extent of forcing them all to be recompiled. Third, the new function will have to be implemented in all existing concrete supplier classes, or a default implementation provided by the abstract supplier.

These problems can be avoided by defining abstract suppliers not as a base class in a hierarchy of supplier classes, but as an interface. If this is done, concrete supplier classes are no longer subclasses of abstract supplier, but instead provide realizations of the interface it defines. The new design, an alternative to that shown in Figure 14.3, is shown in Figure 14.7.

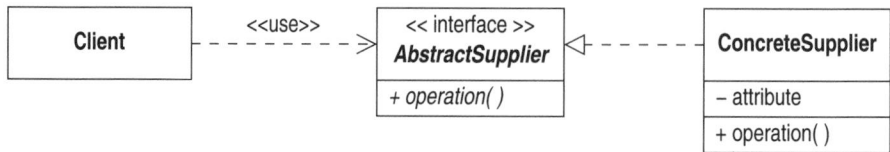

Figure 14.7 Using an interface

Now it is possible to handle the request to extend the abstract supplier interface to deal with the requirements of the new client without modifying the interface itself. Instead, a new interface can be defined, which is a specialization of the abstract supplier interface. The new client uses this new interface and the original client can continue to use the original, unchanged interface. The new interface can itself be realized by a new concrete supplier class. The abstract supplier is unchanged and so is a contender for being a genuinely closed module. The resulting situation is shown in Figure 14.8.

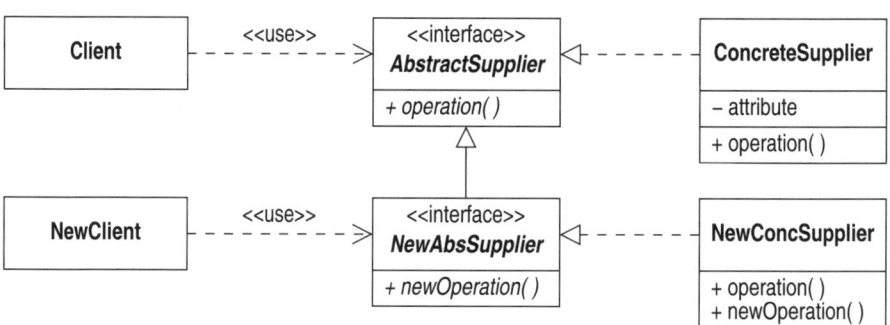

Figure 14.8 Extending an interface by specialization

Notice that Figure 14.8 does not show a generalization relationship between the concrete supplier and the new concrete supplier classes. One way to implement new concrete supplier would be to inherit the implementation of abstract supplier's functions from concrete supplier (at the risk of running foul of the no concrete superclasses rule), but alternative implementations are possible. For example, a reference to an instance of concrete supplier could be included in the new concrete supplier class and the appropriate function calls delegated, or everything could simply be re-implemented from scratch. Because client modules are now only indirectly related to concrete suppliers, different suppliers do not need to be related by generalization in order to provide polymorphic client interfaces: this is provided by the generalization between interfaces.

14.4 THE LISKOV SUBSTITUTION PRINCIPLE

If abstract interface classes are used, as described in Section 14.1, then any client module that programs to the interface defined by the abstract interface class will make extensive use of polymorphism. For example, in Figure 14.3 the client class only knows about abstract suppliers. This means that the clients will call supplier operations through a reference of type `AbstractSupplier`, as shown below.

```
AbstractSupplier supplier ;
...
supplier.operation() ;
```

When this code runs, the `supplier` variable does not contain a reference to an instance of `AbstractSupplier`: as this is an abstract class, it can have no instances. Instead, it will hold a reference to an instance of `ConcreteSupplier` or some other subclass of the abstract supplier class.

If this kind of polymorphism is not to cause problems in programs, the semantics of the language must ensure that something like the following is true: if a client is expecting to hold a reference to an object of class T, then it will work equally well when provided with a reference to an object of class S, where S is a specialization of T.

The *Liskov substitution principle*, named after the computer scientist Barbara Liskov, who gave a classic statement of it in 1988, provides a definition of what it means for one type to be a subtype of another, which in effect provides the required guarantee. In this context the principle can be stated as follows.

> Class S is correctly defined as a specialization of class T if the following is true: for each object *s* of class S there is an object *t* of class T such that the behaviour of any program P defined in terms of T is unchanged if *s* is substituted for *t*.

Less formally, this means that instances of a subclass can stand in for instances of a superclass without any effect on client classes or modules. One consequence of this is that associations on superclasses can be considered to be inherited by their subclasses, as it makes no difference to an object at the other end of a link if it is linked to a subclass object in place of a superclass object.

Although it is formulated in terms of types and subtypes, the Liskov substitution principle effectively defines the meaning of the notion of generalization as used in object-oriented design languages. In UML, the various forms of generalization that are defined, between classes, use cases and actors for example, share the property that instances of the specialized entity in such a relationship can always be substituted for instances of the more general entity.

Exactly what this means will depend on the type of entity being considered. In the case of actors, for example, it means that specialized actors can participate in all the interactions with use cases that are available to the more general actors of which they are specializations, as shown in Figure 4.5.

Generalization between classes can therefore only be correctly used in situations where occurrences of the superclass can be freely substituted by occurrences of the subclass, and where such substitution is undetectable by client modules. If there are any circumstances where a program would behave differently if a subclass object was used in place of a superclass object, then generalization is being used incorrectly.

Programming languages check for substitutability at a syntactic level and will check that subclasses are defined in such a way that certain classes of error will not occur at run-time, such as an object being sent a message that it does not understand. There is always the possibility that a programmer will implement an operation in a derived class in such a way as to undermine substitutability, however, perhaps by providing an implementation that causes subclass instances to behave in a completely different way from superclass instances.

Attempts have been made in the research literature to characterize a stronger notion of substitutability, which will ensure that subclasses provide behaviour that is in some way compatible with the behaviour defined in superclasses. This requirement has to be carefully phrased, however: it is not appropriate to demand that subclasses provide the same behaviour as superclasses, because in many cases the whole point of defining a subclass is to define specialized behaviour for certain classes of objects. One approach to this problem is to specify relationships between the constraints defined for the classes in a generalization relationship.

14.5 INTERACTIONS DETERMINE STRUCTURE

This example is based on an article by Robert Martin (1998). It illustrates a heuristic used in the development of the booking system, namely that interactions between objects can be used as a basis for identifying structural relationships between the classes to which the objects in the design belong.

Suppose that we are modelling a simple mobile phone, whose interface consists of a set of buttons for dialling numbers, a 'send' button for initiating a call and a 'clear' button for terminating a call. A component known as a 'dialler' interacts with the various buttons and keeps track both of the state of the current call and of the digits that have been dialled so far. A cellular radio deals with the connection to the cellular network and the telephone has in addition a microphone, a speaker and a display on which the number dialled is shown.

Figure 14.9 shows a naive design for the mobile phone based on this description. This diagram gives an intuitively clear model of the physical structure of the mobile phone. Each component is represented by a class and aggregation is used to indicate that the various components are parts of the whole assembly, represented by the mobile phone class.

The adequacy of this design can be tested by seeing whether it supports the interactions that implement the required behaviour of the phone. For example, consider the following scenario, which describes the basic course of events that might take place when a user is making a call with the phone.

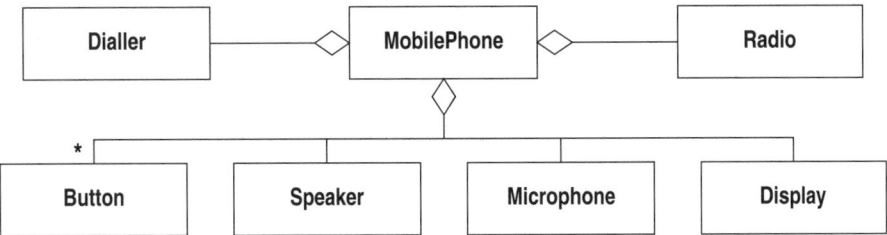

Figure 14.9 A 'physical' model of the mobile phone

1. The user presses buttons to enter the phone number being called.
2. Each digit pressed is added to the display.
3. The user presses the 'send' button.
4. The radio establishes a connection to the network and places the call.
5. The display indicates that the phone is now in use.
6. At the end of the call, the user presses the 'clear' button.
7. The display is cleared.

Figure 14.10 shows a realization of this scenario, up to the point at which the connection is made. When the user presses a button, a message is sent to the dialler giving the information about which digit has been pressed; this digit is then added to the display. When the user presses the send button, the dialler sends the complete number to the radio, which places the call and, once a connection is made, updates the display.

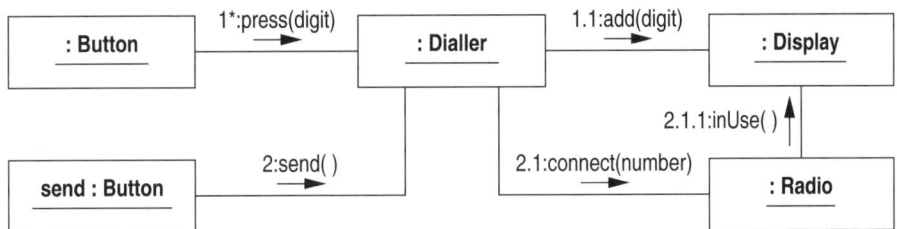

Figure 14.10 Making a call on the mobile phone

It is immediately obvious from these diagrams that the associations on the class diagram in Figure 14.9 do not support the messages that are sent in the course of the interaction shown in Figure 14.10. To obtain a consistent design, either the static model of the mobile phone should be altered or the realization of the scenario made consistent with the model in Figure 14.9.

In this example, it is probably preferable to adopt the structure implied by the interactions shown in Figure 14.10. A realization of the scenario above could be based on the structure shown in Figure 14.9, but by forcing all the interactions between objects to be routed through the central mobile phone object this approach would lead to a more complex interaction, which forced the phone object to keep track of every detail of what was going on.

A better approach is to adopt a static structure that is modelled on the structure required to support the system's interactions. The model of the mobile phone that is obtained by following this approach is shown in Figure 14.11.

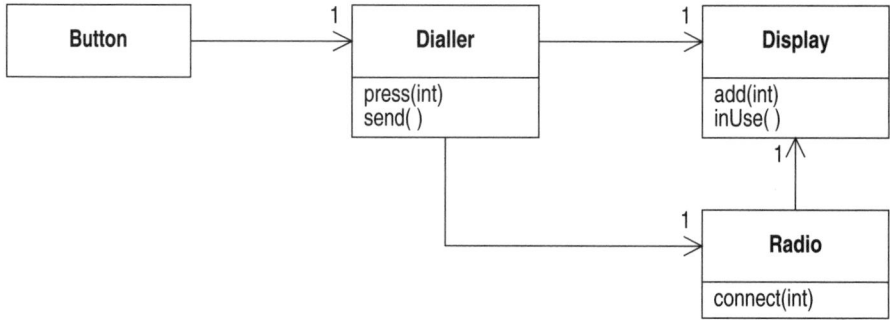

Figure 14.11 A better model of the mobile phone

Perhaps the most striking difference between this model and the one shown above in Figure 14.9 is that there is no longer any need for an object representing the mobile phone itself and hence the mobile phone class and the aggregation relationships linking it to the various components of the phone no longer appear in the model.

As a result, it could perhaps be claimed that the new model does not represent the real world as well as the original one. However, the notion that there is a 'real world' that can only be correctly modelled in one way is rather over-simplistic. The moral of this example is that the physical relationships between the objects we are modelling may not provide a suitable basis to support the interactions that provide the functionality required of the system. In such cases, it is usually advisable to adopt the static model that best supports the necessary interactions.

14.6 DESIGN PATTERNS

In any design activity, there are certain characteristic problems that occur repeatedly. Different designers will arrive at different solutions to these problems, but as design experience becomes more widely shared among practitioners, it is often the case that a substantial body of knowledge evolves, which describes these common problems and methods of solving them. Often the solutions are not altogether obvious and involve 'tricks of the trade' that are not widely known.

There are obvious advantages to making such knowledge explicit and publicly available. Most important among these, perhaps, is that inexperienced designers can then gain access to a library of techniques that are immediately applicable, thus making the process of developing expertise in the relevant design technique easier. In the case of object-oriented design, *design patterns* have been proposed as a way of codifying the ways in which expert designers tackle and solve particular commonly occurring problems in design.

The classic reference to the subject is the book *Design Patterns* published in 1995 by Erich Gamma, Richard Helm, Ralph Johnson and John Vlissides. This book is widely known by the nickname of the 'gang of four book' and will be referred to as such in the rest of this chapter.

The problems that designers face come at a number of levels. At a very low level, there are problems concerning the details of the interface or implementation of a single class. At the highest level, the problems concern the creation of an overall architecture for a system. Design patterns address an intermediate level of concern, where particular localized properties of a design have to be guaranteed.

Typical problems addressed by design patterns might include the following. How can a design ensure that only one instance of a class is ever created inside a system? How can recursive, tree-like structures be modelled? How can additional functionality be attached to an object dynamically?

The solution to the problem posed by a design pattern is typically expressed as a fragment of an object-oriented design, consisting of a number of interacting classes, which, taken together, provide a ready-made solution for the problem raised. A pattern can usually be applied in a great many situations, however, so the solution describes a template, or stereotypical, design that can be adapted and reused as required.

Definition of patterns

A pattern is often defined as 'a solution to a problem in a context'. The solution to a problem in object-oriented design can most succinctly be described by using a formal notation such as a class diagram or an interaction diagram, but this formal representation should not be identified with the pattern, for at least two reasons.

First, many patterns share a similar formal structure, while being designed for use in completely different situations. An integral part of distinguishing one pattern from another is to understand the problem that is being addressed, even if the proposed solutions in two or more cases may seem formally similar.

Second, most patterns can be manifested or implemented in a variety of different ways, using class structures or interactions that can differ in detail. Thus designs that are quite different in detail can in fact be applications of the same pattern.

The gang of four book defines the following essential elements of a pattern.

1. A *name*. Having a memorable name for a pattern helps designers to remember it. A collection of named patterns also provides a language that permits designers to discuss designs at the level of patterns.
2. The *problem*. This defines the situation in which the pattern is applicable.
3. The *solution*. This describes design elements that address the problem. Often the solution is expressed using suitable formal notation, but, as emphasized above, a pattern will usually encompass a number of variations round a common idea.
4. The *consequences*. These are the results and tradeoffs of applying the pattern. Knowledge of the consequences of using a pattern is essential if an informed decision is to be made about whether or not the pattern should be applied in a particular situation.

The concept of a design pattern is therefore rather informal. This informality can make it hard to give unequivocal answers to questions of when two patterns are the same, or whether a design does or does not make use of a given pattern. Many people within the patterns community defend this informality, arguing that a pattern captures a 'design insight' that resists formalization and loses its scope for applicability if it is defined too narrowly.

On the other hand, without a clear idea of what actually constitutes the definition of a pattern, it is difficult to tell whether two authors are describing the same pattern, variations on a pattern or two distinct patterns, for example, or to find a pattern that is applicable to a given situation. These problems are becoming more serious as the published pattern literature expands.

Patterns versus frameworks

Patterns and frameworks are two approaches to the problem of enabling certain elements of designs to be recorded and reused, and as such they are sometimes confused. They differ significantly, however, in terms of both what they provide and how they are intended to be used.

First, patterns and frameworks differ in terms of *size*. A framework defines an architecture for a complete application or a class of related applications. A pattern, on the other hand, describes a solution to a single design problem, which may be applicable in many applications or frameworks.

Second, patterns and frameworks have different *contents*. A pattern is a pure design idea, which can be adapted and implemented in various ways in different languages. A framework typically is a mixture of design and code, which can be extended in various ways by application programmers.

Third, as a consequence of the second point, patterns tend to be more *portable* than frameworks. Frameworks are already implemented, although without necessarily constituting a complete application, and are therefore usually restricted to a single implementation environment. Patterns are language-independent and can be applied in widely differing situations.

A third concept, which also carries connotations of reuse, is that of a 'component'. Components are usually thought of as enabling code reuse and permitting at most a limited degree of customization. The formula 'frameworks equal components plus patterns' has been used in the literature, but this rather underplays the role of a framework in defining a complete architecture for a system.

14.7 RECURSIVE STRUCTURES

In several examples earlier in the book, we have considered cases where an object has been linked to several objects of related classes, possibly including the object's own class, and has needed to treat them all in a similar manner. An example of this is provided by assemblies in the stock control program considered in Chapter 2.

In this example, an assembly could contain an unspecified number of other objects, some of which were simple parts and others which were themselves assemblies. These subassemblies could in turn contain further subassemblies in addition to parts, and this nesting of assemblies could continue to whatever level is required. In many ways, however, parts and assemblies were treated in an identical manner and the classes share aspects of a common interface.

This situation was modelled by introducing a new class to define the common features shared by files and directories. In Chapter 2 this class was called 'Component', and the relevant part of the class diagram describing the structure of components is shown in Figure 14.12.

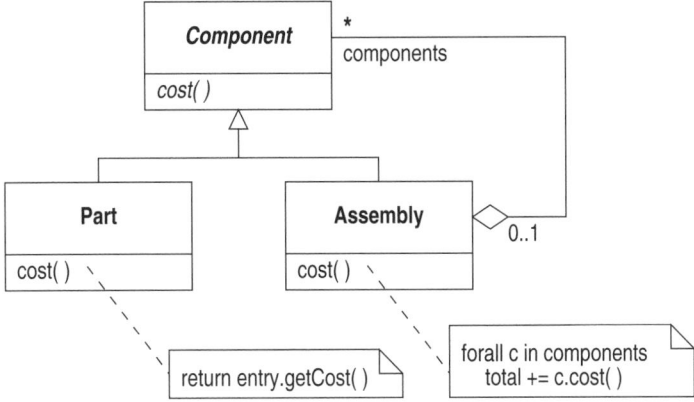

Figure 14.12 Parts and assemblies

'Component' is an abstract class that describes the common features of parts and assemblies. The operation to determine the cost of a component is abstract and is overridden in each of the subclasses. In the case of parts, the operation retrieves the cost of the part from the associated catalogue entry object (not shown in Figure 14.12). In the case of assemblies, the operation iterates through all the components contained in the assembly, calls the cost operation for each and returns the sum of the values returned. These properties are shown in the notes attached to the operations in Figure 14.12.

The link between an assembly and the components it contains is modelled by means of an association from the assembly class back to the superclass 'Component'. This states that an assembly can have zero or more components, each of which can be either a part or an assembly. The association in Figure 14.12 differs from that given in Chapter 2 in that an assembly is defined to be an aggregate of its components. As explained in Section 8.7, this guarantees that the assembly has a strict tree structure and that an assembly can never contain itself, either directly or indirectly.

There are two important semantic properties of parts and assemblies that make the generalization in Figure 14.12 appropriate. First, they share a common interface, which is defined in the common superclass. Second, the overall structure of an assembly is a recursively defined tree structure, in which the contents of an assembly can be either parts or other assemblies.

The Composite pattern

The structure exemplified by Figure 14.12 is very common and its essential properties are captured in the pattern named 'Composite' given in the gang of four book. The intention of the Composite pattern is to 'compose objects into tree structures to represent part–whole hierarchies. Composite lets clients treat individual objects and compositions of objects uniformly'.

The solution presented by a pattern is typically documented in a class diagram, which shows how a number of classes can interact together to provide the required functionality. In the case of Composite, the description of the pattern is very similar to its application shown in Figure 14.12, but with more general names given to the participating classes. A slightly simplified version of the structure of the Composite pattern as defined in the gang of four book is shown in Figure 14.13.

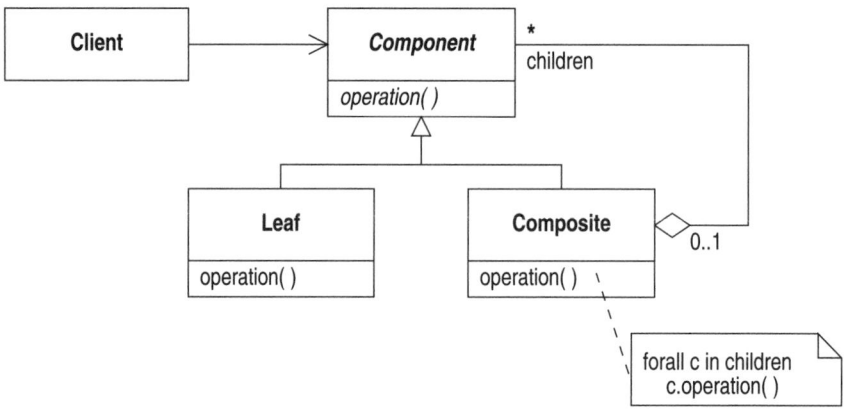

Figure 14.13 The structure of the Composite pattern

This diagram shows that a component of a recursive structure can either be a leaf, which has no subcomponents of its own, or a composite, which can have any number of child components. In the stock control example, the part class corresponds to the 'Leaf' class and the assembly class to the class called 'Composite'.

The component class defines a uniform interface through which clients can access and manipulate composite structures. In Figure 14.13 this is represented by an abstract operation. This interface must be defined explicitly in each of the subclasses, and normally the implementation of the operation in the composite class will call the operation on each of its children. This is indicated by the note attached to the operation in the composite class.

The class diagram in Figure 14.13, then, defines a generic structure that enables tree-like structures to be built up by programs. A designer who wished to apply this pattern would take this diagram and identify classes in the application corresponding to the leaf and composite classes and create a common superclass for them. The definition of the operation then provides a reusable implementation of an operation to visit every node in the tree.

Patterns in UML

A design pattern is intended to be a general-purpose design solution that can be reused in many different situations. The classes in Figure 14.13 are not application classes, but are more like placeholders, which will be identified with different classes in different applications of the pattern.

To reflect this, patterns are represented in UML as *parameterized collaborations*. The pattern is treated as a single unit, a collaboration, and names of classes in the pattern are defined as parameters, which can be replaced by real class names when the pattern is applied. Figure 14.14 shows the Composite pattern represented in this form.

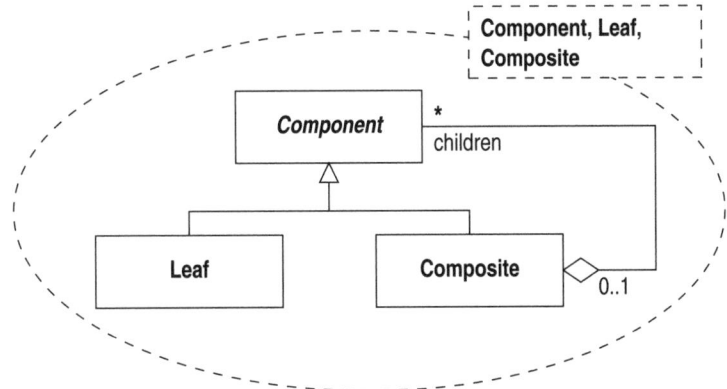

Figure 14.14 The Composite pattern as a parameterized collaboration

One of the advantages of representing patterns in this form is that the application of a pattern can be documented on a class diagram. Figure 14.15 shows a simplified class diagram for the stock control program together with an abstract representation of the Composite pattern. Links from the pattern to classes are labelled with the names of the classes in the pattern, and this documents which classes in the design correspond to particular roles in an instantiation of the pattern.

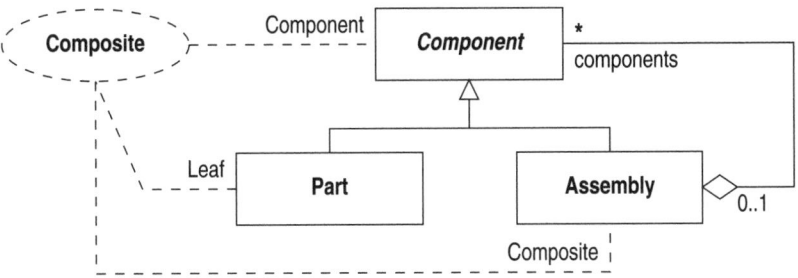

Figure 14.15 Documenting the application of a pattern

14.8 THE STATE AND STRATEGY PATTERNS

An alternative implementation of statecharts to that described in Section 13.7 can be based on an application of a design pattern called 'State' from the gang of four book. The intent of the State pattern is to 'allow an object to alter its behaviour when its internal state changes. The object will appear to change its class.'.

The class diagram summarizing the structure of the State pattern is given in Figure 14.16. The 'Context' class represents the entities that display state-dependent behaviour. The different states of context objects are represented by classes in the state hierarchy; every context object is linked to exactly one of these at a time, representing its current state.

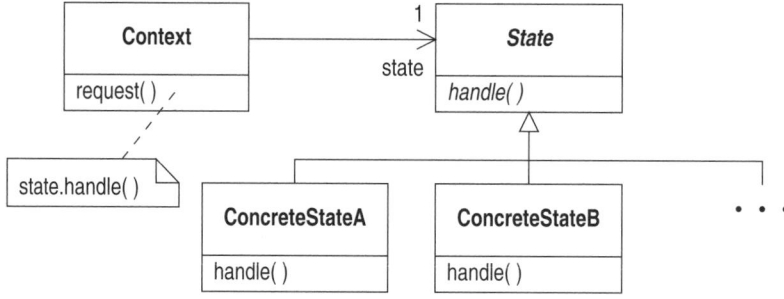

Figure 14.16 The State pattern

When a context object receives a request, it does not attempt to deal with it itself, but instead delegates it to an operation in the state class that will handle it. By providing different implementations of this operation in the subclasses of the state class, the context object appears to be providing dynamically varying behaviour.

A related pattern called 'Strategy', shown in Figure 14.17, allows alternative implementations of an algorithm to be provided in such a way that different instances of a class can support different implementations of the same operation, or even change implementation at run-time. Here, the interface of the context object defines an operation, but the class does not implement it. Rather, the implementation is provided by a linked object of class 'Strategy', to which calls to the operation are delegated. Despite these differences, however, the structure of the Strategy pattern is almost indistinguishable from that of the State pattern, apart from the naming of the classes and operations involved.

Nevertheless, the State and Strategy patterns are thought to be distinct patterns because they are supposed to be addressing different problems. This example illustrates that there is more to a pattern than the diagram giving its structure, but on the other hand it may raise doubts about how patterns are to be distinguished from one another. Perhaps the different states of an object can be thought of as alternative strategies for implementing the object's operations, for example. To complicate the situation still further, the next section considers a family of patterns that are essentially implementations of the same idea, but which are nevertheless structurally distinct.

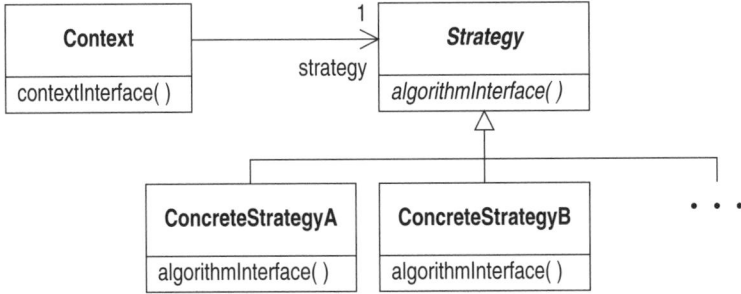

Figure 14.17 The Strategy pattern

14.9 MVC, DOCUMENT/VIEW AND OBSERVER

A basic idea behind the model–view–controller architecture, which was described in Chapter 5, is the separation of the data being used from the user interface through which it is viewed and manipulated. This idea was originally proposed in the context of the Smalltalk programming languages. This section will briefly describe the structure of MVC and the way that its key ideas have been used in Microsoft's document/view architecture and in the Observer pattern.

Models, views and controllers

Figure 14.18 shows the generic structure of an application using the model–view–controller architecture. There is a single *model* object, which stores and maintains the data of interest. Linked to the model are a number of *view* objects, each of which is responsible for displaying the data in a particular way. For example, if the model contained some statistical data, different views might display this in either bar chart or pie chart format. Also linked to the model are a number of *controllers*, responsible for detecting user input and forwarding it to other objects.

The three components of this architecture communicate by message passing and Figure 14.18 shows the details of a typical interaction whereby some action on the part of the user causes the model and its associated views to be updated.

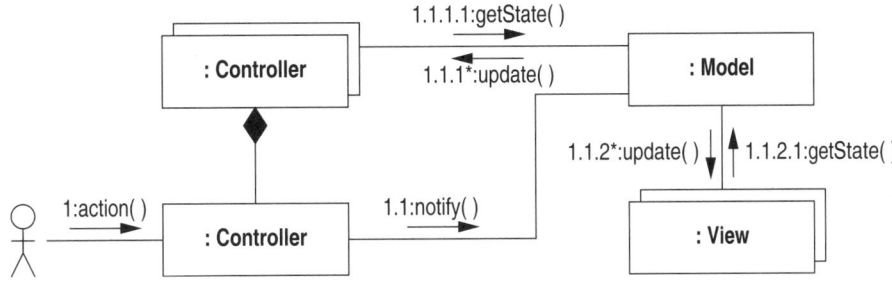

Figure 14.18 A standard interaction cycle in MVC

User input is detected by a specific controller, shown in Figure 14.18 to be one of the set of controllers. In general, user input can change the state of the model, so the controller then sends a notification message to the model informing it of the change. This message, along with others in the interaction, would typically pass some data as arguments that, for clarity, are not shown in Figure 14.18.

When it receives a change notification, the model sends an update message to all the controllers and views linked to it, collectively known as its dependents. On receiving an update message, a dependent will query the model for the latest information about its state and then redisplay whatever portions of the user interface are affected. Notice that, in general, controllers as well as views can be affected by changes to the model: a simple example might be a menu option that needs to be enabled or disabled.

The benefits of this architecture lie in the clear separation it makes between the code that processes an application's data and that which deals with its user interface. This makes it easy, for example, to develop new types of view without affecting the model. This approach was particularly valuable in the Smalltalk environment, which was one of the first to make large-scale use of graphical user interfaces.

Document/view architecture

The *document/view architecture* was proposed by Microsoft as a standard way of structuring applications supporting a graphical user interface. Document/view can be viewed as a simplification of the MVC architecture, in which documents correspond to models, but views combine the functionality of both the controllers and views of MVC. The structural relationship between the document and view classes, together with some of the operations that cause them to interact, is shown in Figure 14.19.

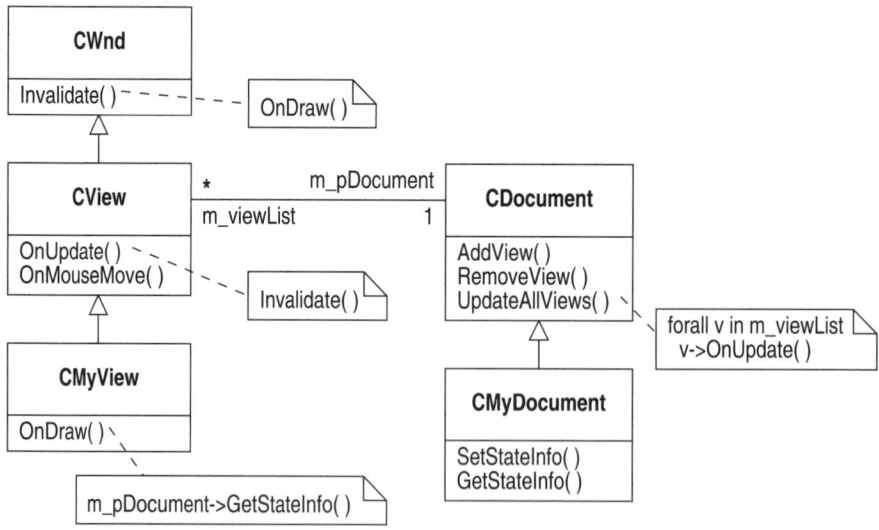

Figure 14.19 The document/view architecture (simplified)

Figure 14.20 shows the details of a typical interaction that would take place in the document/view architecture following a user action such as a mouse move. Notice that this collaboration is drawn using instances rather than roles, to emphasize the fact that the objects participating are instances of the two user-defined classes 'CMyDocument' and 'CMyView' and not simply objects playing the roles of document and view.

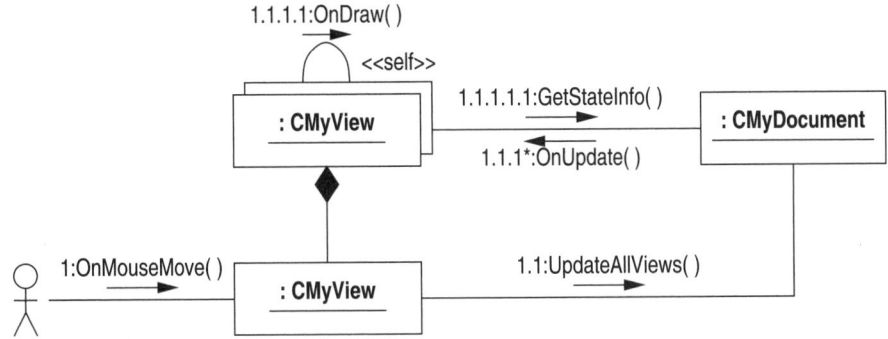

Figure 14.20 A typical document/view interaction

The overall structure of the document/view interaction is similar to the one shown in Figure 14.18 for the MVC architecture. The view that detects the user's action sends the notification message 'UpdateAllViews' to its document. The document then sends an update message to all the views linked to it, including the one that sent the notification. This update message gets translated into a call to the view's 'OnDraw' method and, in the course of executing this, a view will typically retrieve information about the current state of its linked document before displaying it.

The Observer pattern

Another variation on this theme of separating model and view is provided by the Observer pattern defined in the gang of four book. This pattern is intended to 'define a one-to-many dependency between objects so that when one object changes state, all its dependents are notified and updated accordingly'. A class diagram showing the classes involved in the pattern is shown in Figure 14.21. This diagram shows the by now familiar relationship between a model, called a subject in this pattern, and a number of views, now known as observers.

The Observer pattern is meant to be applicable in a wider range of circumstances than simply updating a graphical display in response to a user's actions. Observer objects, therefore, do not necessarily have any responsibility for detecting user input, and so the interactions involved in the use of Observer are often simpler than in the MVC and document/view. Nevertheless, as Figure 14.22 shows, the basic structure of the interaction is the same as those considered earlier. An unspecified client sends a notification message to the subject, which then sends update messages to all its observers; these in turn may then query the state of the subject.

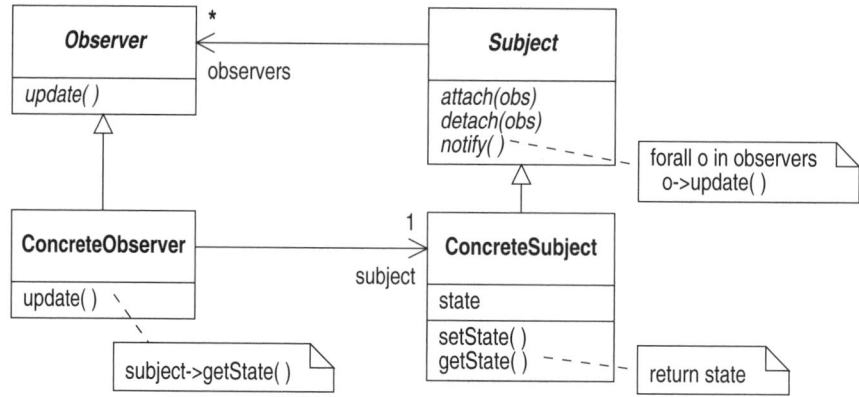

Figure 14.21 The Observer pattern

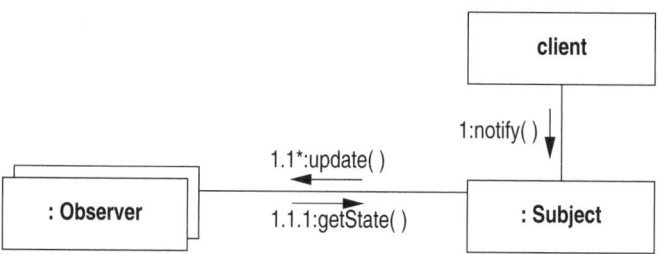

Figure 14.22 Interactions in the Observer pattern

14.10 APPLYING VISITOR TO THE STOCK CONTROL PROGRAM

Suppose there is a requirement to add a function to the stock control program to print out a list of all the parts and subassemblies in an assembly. Such a report is often called a 'parts explosion'. A simple approach might be to add an 'explode' function to the hierarchy, analogous to the existing 'cost' function. The implementation of this function in the part class would print out the details of a simple part, and in the assembly class it would iterate through all the components of the assembly calling 'explode' on each. There are potential problems with this approach, however, including the following.

1. Every class in the hierarchy must be altered to add 'explode'. If the hierarchy was large, this might be an unfeasible, or very expensive, operation.
2. The code that controls the iteration through the components of an assembly is repeated in both the 'cost' and 'explode' functions. It would be preferable to avoid this redundancy by having the iteration implemented in a single place.
3. The 'Part' class is part of the model in this application and yet this proposal makes it directly responsible for producing output. The basic principle of the patterns discussed in the previous section, however, is that user-interface code should be separated from the model, to allow easy modification and extension.

These issues are addressed by the Visitor pattern, whose intent is to 'represent an operation to be performed on the elements of an object structure. Visitor lets you define a new operation without changing the classes of the elements on which it operates.' Visitor therefore provides a method for implementing classes that are simultaneously open and closed, in the sense discussed in Section 14.1.

Visitor works by separating the classes that represent data, the part hierarchy in this example, from operations that can be applied to that data. Operations are represented by classes in a new hierarchy of 'visitors'. The connection between the two is made by defining a single operation in the part hierarchy that 'accepts a visitor'. Figure 14.23 shows how a single operation, to find the cost of a component, can be implemented using this technique.

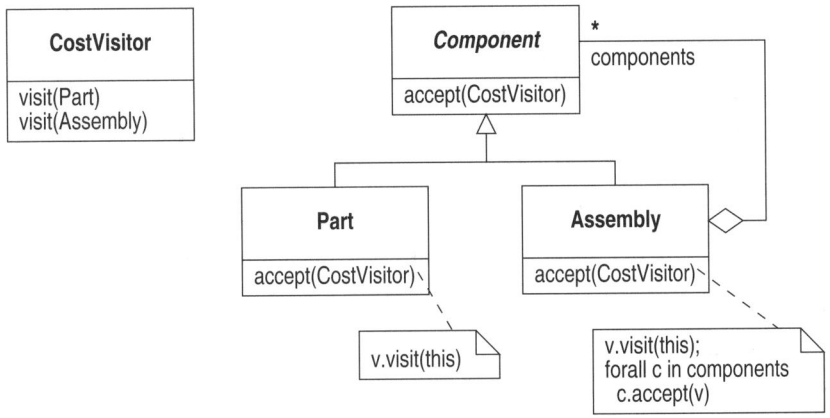

Figure 14.23 Finding the costs of components using Visitor

With this design, a programmer can no longer simply call an operation in the component class to find out the cost of a component. Instead, a cost visitor object must be created, and passed to the component, as follows.

```
CostVisitor visitor = new CostVisitor() ;
int cost = component.accept(visitor) ;
```

What happens when a component accepts a visitor depends on the run-time type of the component. If the component is a part, the job of working out the cost of the part is delegated to a function in the visitor object; to make the required information available, a reference to the part is passed to this function. If the component is an assembly, however, an iteration through all the subcomponents of the assembly is performed and each subcomponent in turn is asked to accept the visitor. In this way, the visitor object is passed from component to component until every part in the assembly has been visited.

The actual business of working out the cost of the assembly is carried out in the cost visitor object. The definition of this class given below shows how the total cost is preserved as the iteration is being carried out.

```
public class CostVisitor
{
  private int total ;

  public void visit(Part p) {
    total += p.cost() ;
  }

  public void visit(Assembly a) {
    // null implementation
  }
}
```

As this shows, the cost visitor class contains all the code that is specific to working out the cost of a component. The generic code that traverses the part hierarchy, however, appears in the accept function in the assembly class. In order to work out the cost of an assembly, there is nothing to do apart from ensuring that all its components are visited, so the cost visitor class contains no specific code for working out the cost of an assembly. In other cases, however, this function may not be empty and it has been left in this example to indicate its general role.

Figure 14.24 shows the interactions that take place when the code above is used to work out the cost of a simple assembly consisting of two parts. Notice that every component in the assembly is asked in turn to accept the visitor and in response sends a 'visit' message to the cost visitor, with the component itself as a parameter. Finally, the client object retrieves the total cost of the assembly (this operation is trivial and not shown in the code above).

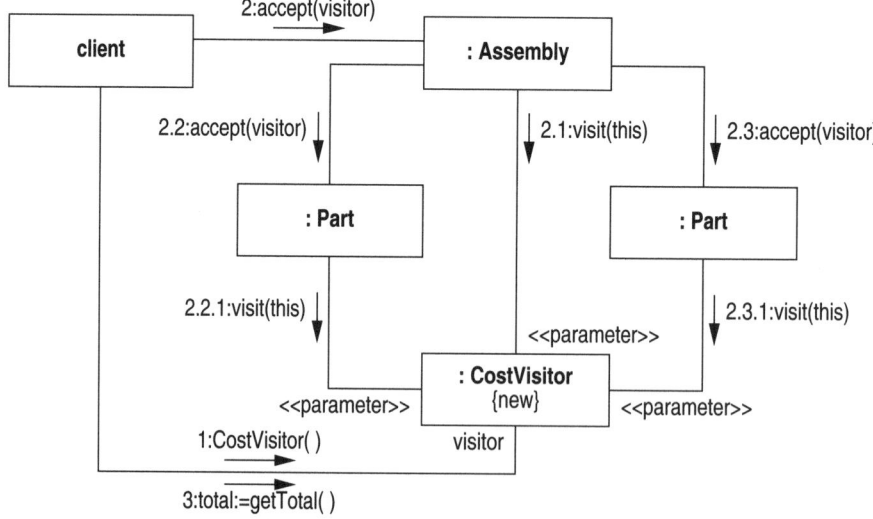

Figure 14.24 Working out the cost of an assembly with visitors

At the cost of making the overall design more complex, then, this use of visitors makes it possible to define a new operation on the part hierarchy without changing any of the classes in that hierarchy. All that is required is to define a suitable visitor class and to pass visitors to components using the 'accept' operation.

In order to complete the design, it is necessary to define an abstract visitor class, so that references to particular types of visitor do not have to be made in the part hierarchy. Classes defining visitors for different types of operation, such as calculating the cost or printing a parts explosion, can then be defined as subclass of the abstract class, as shown in Figure 14.25.

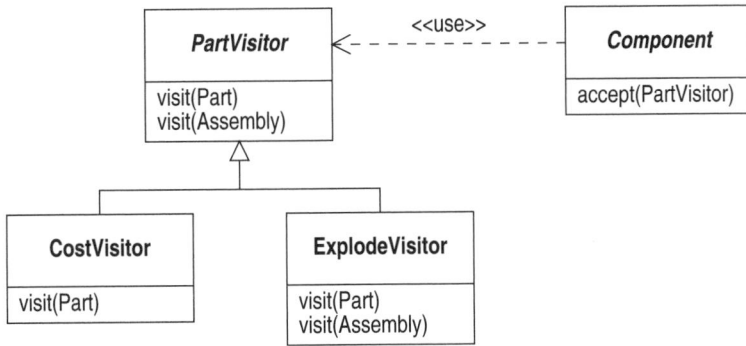

Figure 14.25 The visitor hierarchy

In general, a visitor class must provide an operation corresponding to each class in the hierarchy that is being visited. In Figure 14.25, therefore, the part visitor class provides two overloaded operations to visit parts and assemblies.

Specific visitor classes should override these functions to provide appropriate functionality for each type of component. As it may not be necessary to override every function, null implementations of these are provided in the part visitor class. For example, cost visitors do not need to perform any specific processing when visiting assemblies, so the null function in implementation of this class above could be removed and simply inherited from the superclass.

The use of the Visitor pattern in this case neatly addresses the problems identified above with the proposal to define new functions with new operations in the part hierarchy. First, the classes in the original hierarchy are now untouched when the explode operation is added: all new code is contained in the class 'ExplodeVisitor'. Second, the code that controls the iteration through assemblies is kept separate from the code that implements particular operations and is automatically reused for all operations. Finally, user-interface code can be localized in the 'ExplodeVisitor' class, thus preserving a kind of model–view distinction.

The Visitor pattern has limitations of its own, however. For example, references to the classes in the part hierarchy are hard-coded in the visitor classes, which means that if a new part subclass is created, all the visitor classes will have to be modified. The Visitor pattern is most suitable, therefore, when operations are to be added to a relatively stable class hierarchy.

14.11 SUMMARY

- The open–closed principle calls for modules that are simultaneously extensible and yet immune from change. The use of abstract interface classes is a way of defining classes that have this property.

- Decoupling interface and implementation hierarchies protects classes even further, by allowing the interfaces of existing classes to be changed without affecting existing code.

- In order to prevent any ambiguity between polymorphic and non-polymorphic operations, a rule can be adopted that all superclasses in a design should be abstract.

- The Liskov substitution principle provides the definition of interchangeability between instances, which is the foundation of the semantics of generalization in UML.

- Static relationships in a design should be based on the interactions they are to support, not on the perceived physical structure of application domain objects.

- Design patterns provide examples of tested solutions to commonly occurring problems in design.

- The separation of a system's data from its presentation to the user is a principle widely applied in object-oriented design, appearing in the MVC and document/view architectures and also in the Observer pattern.

- The Visitor pattern provides a way to add operations to an existing hierarchy without changing the definitions of the classes in the hierarchy.

14.12 EXERCISES

14.1 Add a new type of booking to the booking system, such as provisional bookings that must be confirmed 24 hours before they are due, and check that the 'Booking' class is in fact open and closed in the sense of Section 14.1.

14.2 Implement the structure shown in Figure 14.8 and confirm that the abstract supplier interface is in fact a closed module. An implementation in a language that does not provide interfaces should replace them by abstract classes, and use multiple inheritance where necessary.

14.3 Extend the interaction shown in Figure 14.10 so that it includes the messages sent when the user presses the clear button to terminate a call. Make any necessary changes to the class diagram in Figure 14.11 to keep it consistent with the updated collaboration diagram.

14.4 Write a simulation of the mobile phone based on the design given in Figures 14.10 and 14.11 and the amendments made to these in the previous exercise.

14.5 Draw up a table identifying in detail correspondences between the document/view architecture and Observer, as presented in the class diagrams above. For example, the operation called 'Attach' in Observer corresponds to the one called 'AddView' in document/view. Also, list any significant discrepancies between the two. Discuss the extent to which document/view can be considered to be an instantiation of the Observer pattern.

14.6 One of the implementation considerations for the Observer pattern given in the gang of four book concerns the question of which object should trigger the update operation. Observers will only stay consistent with their subjects if the notification operation is called at appropriate times. This operation should be called whenever the subject's state has changed, but it could be called either by the subject itself or by the client object that has caused the change. Explain how these two approaches would be applied in MVC and outline the advantages and disadvantages of each.

14.7 The Java AWT contains a faithful implementation of the Observer pattern in the interface `java.util.Observer` and class `java.util.Observable`. Consult documentation for the Java AWT and document this instantiation of the pattern formally, in class and interaction diagrams, commenting explicitly on the correspondences and differences between Observer and its Java implementation.

14.8 One weakness of the stock control program is that each individual part is represented by an object. This could lead to a very large number of identical objects being created, with a consequent waste of storage. Consult the definition of the Flyweight pattern in the gang of four book and apply it to the stock control program to remove this problem.

14.9 In the mobile phone example, instances of the button class need to know what type of button they are so that they can send the appropriate message to the dialler when they are pressed. This means that any application that requires to use a button for a new purpose will have to modify the button class to support the new functionality. However, the button class is potentially a useful reusable component if it can be turned into a closed module. Investigate how this could be done by applying the Adaptor pattern given in the gang of four book.

14.10 Reimplement the account class discussed in Section 13.7 using the State pattern to capture the information in the statechart of Figure 13.14. What are the advantages and shortcomings, if any, of the State pattern over the simple implementation presented in Section 13.7?

APPENDIX A

UML NOTATION SUMMARY

This appendix summarizes the notation that has been used in the course of this book. As far as possible, the notation is consistent with the specification of version 1.4 of UML.

A.1 GENERAL CONCEPTS

Model elements

A model element is an application of a single modelling concept, such as 'class' or 'message'. A model is a set of interrelated model elements containing all the information held about the system being designed.

Diagrams

A diagram is a graphical presentation of a subset of the model elements in a model, chosen to illustrate a certain aspect of the system's structure or behaviour.

Notes

Notes are graphical symbols containing text or other information. They can be attached to model elements using dashed lines, as shown in Figure A.1.

Comments

A comment is a string giving an informal description of one or more model elements. Comments appear on diagrams in notes attached to the relevant model elements, as shown in Figure A.1.

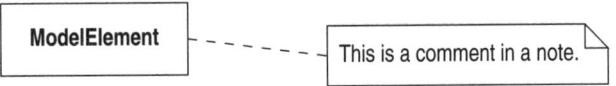

Figure A.1 Notation for comments

Constraints

A constraint is a Boolean expression describing desired properties of one or more model elements. A state of the system described by the model is only valid if all constraints evaluate to true.

UML does not define a language for writing general constraints; they can be written informally, or using a formal language such as OCL. Constraints are shown on diagrams inside braces ({ ... }), either written near the model element they describe or in a note attached to the relevant elements.

Stereotypes

A stereotype is an annotation attached to a model element, which gives some additional information about what the element means or how it is used. A stereotype consists of a *keyword* written in guillemets (<< ... >>).

Tagged values

Tagged values provide a way of recording on a diagram information about a model element for which no graphical notation exists. They are shown on diagrams inside braces ({ ... }), as a comma-separated list of *property specifications* of the form *name = value*. In the case of a Boolean property, *name* can be written as an abbreviation for *name = true*.

Standard elements

UML predefines a number of stereotypes, tagged values and constraints, known collectively as *standard elements*, and others are widely used in both the specification of UML and elsewhere.

Classifiers and Instances

UML makes a fundamental distinction between *classifiers* and *instances*. Instances are entities that have state, represented by a set of attribute values, and to which operations can be applied. Classifiers describe sets of instances that share a common structure and behaviour. The relationship between a class and the objects it describes is the most familiar example of the distinction between classifiers and instances. UML consistently uses the same notation for classifiers and the related instances, distinguishing between the two by underlining the names of instances.

Confusingly, the same terminology is also used to describe a link as an instance of an association. Links are not instances in the same way that objects are, however, as they have no state and no operations can be applied to them.

Diagrams as graphs

Many UML diagrams are presented as *graphs* in which the nodes represent various model elements, and the arcs the relationships between them. Four different types of relationship are frequently depicted on diagrams, represented by different types of arrow. These are summarized in Figure A.2, in the context of a class diagram, though they can occur on other diagrams as well.

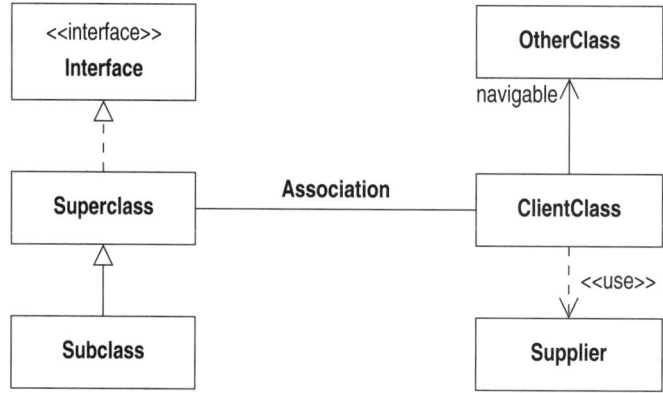

Figure A.2 Types of relationship in UML

Associations connect classes and other classifiers, such as actors and use cases. Associations have instances, called *links*, which connect instances of these classifiers. Associations are represented by solid lines between classifiers. Association ends have a property of *navigability*, which is denoted by an open arrowhead.

Generalization is a relationship between classifiers, which implies that instances of the specialized classifier can be substituted for those of the more general one. Generalization is represented by a solid arrow with a hollow arrowhead. Generalization relationships can connect classes, interfaces, actors, use cases and associations.

Realization, or implementation, describes the relationship between a class and an interface that it supports. It also describes the relationship between a use case and an interaction that realizes it, though this is rarely shown on diagrams. Realization is shown by a dashed arrow with a hollow arrowhead.

Dependencies show any other, less specific, relationship between model elements. Dependencies are shown with a dashed arrow with an open arrowhead and are often labelled with a stereotype to give more information about the type of relationship being shown.

Multiplicity

Multiplicities are used in a variety of places to specify how many occurrences of a model element are permitted in a given context. A multiplicity specification consists of a comma-separated list of *number ranges*, of the form *lower-bound .. upper-bound*. The lower bound can be any non-negative integer; the upper bound can be any integer greater than 0 or the symbol '*', which denotes that the range is unbounded. If the lower and upper bounds are the same, the range specifies a single number and can be written as such. Some common multiplicity specifications are shown in Table A.1.

Table A.1 Common multiplicity specifications

Symbol	Meaning
1	exactly one
0..1	zero or one ("optional")
* (or 0..*)	zero or more ("many")
1..*	one or more

Visibility

Features declared inside classifiers such as classes and packages have a visibility property, which specifies to what extent the feature can be used by other elements. Four visibility levels are defined, as listed in Table A.2. Tools are allowed to define alternative symbols to represent visibility.

Table A.2 Visibility symbols

Symbol	Keyword	Meaning
+	public	can be used by any classifier
#	protected	can be used by descendent classifiers
−	private	can only be used by the classifier itself
~	package	can be used by classifiers defined within the same package

A.2 MODEL STRUCTURE

Packages

Packages are collections of model elements, possibly including nested packages, used to structure large models. They are represented by a folder icon, as shown in Figure A.3.

The model elements in a package can be drawn inside the package. The package name is written in the tab or the body of the folder, depending on the presence of nested elements. An alternative notation for nested packages is also shown in Figure A.3.

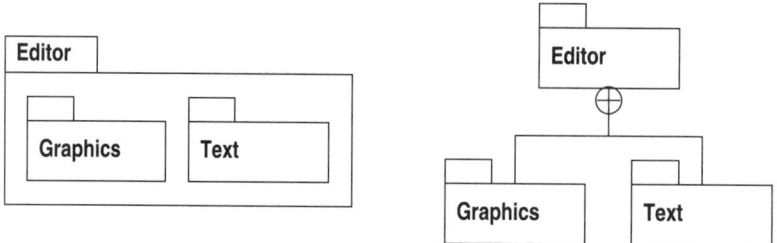

Figure A.3 Two forms of notation for nested packages

A.3 USE CASE DIAGRAMS

Use case diagrams show the actors who interact with a system and the use cases that define the ways in which such interaction can take place. Actors are linked to the use cases they participate in by an association. Figure A.4 summarizes the notation used on use case diagrams.

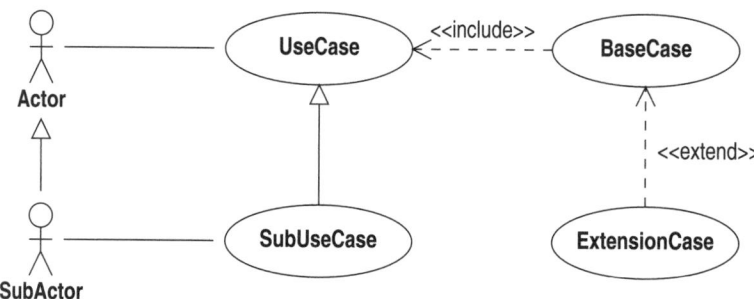

Figure A.4 Use case diagrams

Both use cases and actors can be related by generalization. Two stereotyped dependencies can exist between use cases. The 'include' stereotype is used in the case where one use case 'calls' another at some point in its execution. The 'extend' stereotype is used when a use case allows some optional processing at a given point (the 'extension point'); the optional processing is represented as a separate use case, which extends the base case.

A.4 OBJECT DIAGRAMS

Object diagrams show individual objects and the links between them. Objects are instances of classes, and object and class names can be shown, underlined, in object icons. Attributes and their values can be shown in a separate compartment under the name compartment. The notation for objects is illustrated in Figure A.5.

Objects are connected by links, which are instances of associations. Links can be labelled with the name of the association of which they are instances.

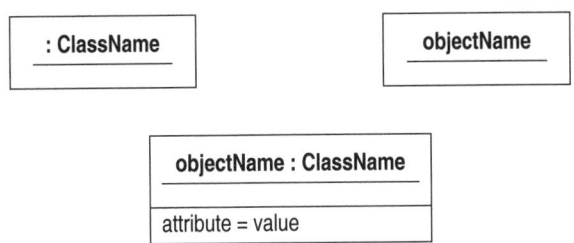

Figure A.5 Notation for objects

Link ends can be labelled with the role names from the association, and with an arrowhead, denoting navigability. Notation for links is illustrated in Figure A.6.

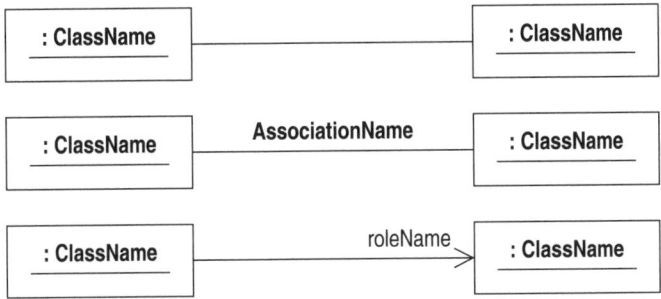

Figure A.6 Notation for links

The standard elements that can be used on object diagrams are listed in Table A.3.

A.5 COLLABORATIONS

Collaborations describe collections of linked objects that can participate in interactions. Collaborations at *specification level* consist of classifier roles linked by association roles. Classifier roles have a name and may have a specified base class. Association roles can have a base association or may represent one of a number of transient forms of link, such as parameters or local variables. A classifier role can have a multiplicity, specifying the number of objects that can play that role in an interaction. The notation for specification level collaborations is shown in Figure A.7.

Collaborations at *instance level* show actual instances in a collaboration. Object diagrams are used to show instance level collaborations. The name compartment of an instance in a collaboration can additionally contain the name of the role that the instance is playing in the collaboration, as shown in Figure A.8.

Multiobjects can be used on instance level collaborations to represent a set of objects playing a particular role, with individual instances in the set being linked to the multiobject using composition.

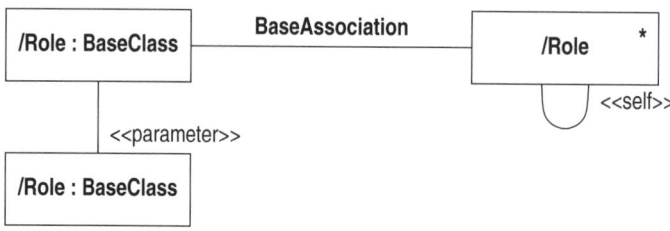

Figure A.7 Specification level collaborations

Figure A.8 Instances in collaborations and a multiobject

A collaboration as a whole is denoted by a dashed oval, containing the name of the collaboration. The structure of roles defining the collaboration can be drawn inside the oval. A *collaboration usage diagram* shows how the roles in a parameterized collaboration can be mapped to classifiers, as shown in Figure A.9.

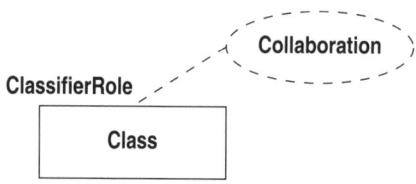

Figure A.9 Notation for collaboration usage diagrams

Table A.3 lists the standard elements that can be used on collaborations.

A.6 MESSAGES

Interactions consist of a collaboration together with a specification of the messages that make up the interaction. The notation for messages is shown in Figure A.10. Messages with a solid arrowhead are *synchronous* messages and correspond to normal procedure calls with nested control, where a message sender waits for the call to return before continuing. The return of control to the sender of a message is shown by a return message with a dashed arrow.

A message has a label, with the following general form:

sequence-expression return-value := *message-name argument-list*

A *sequence-expression* consists of a sequence number optionally followed by a recurrence. A sequence number is a dot-separated list of integers.

Table A.3 Standard elements for collaborations and object diagrams

	Applies to	**Standard elements**
Stereotypes	link and association role ends	`<<association>>`
		`<<global>>`
		`<<local>>`
		`<<parameter>>`
		`<<self>>`
Constraints	objects, links and roles	`{destroyed}`
		`{new}`
		`{transient}`

A recurrence of the form *[iteration-clause]* represents an iterated message, repeated as specified by the iteration clause. A recurrence of the form *[condition-clause]* represents a branch. UML does not specify the syntax to be used for iteration and condition clauses, and programming languages notation can be used.

1.2*: value := operation(arg) return value

Figure A.10 Notation for messages

Table A.4 lists the standard elements that can be used on messages.

Table A.4 Standard elements for messages

	Applies to	**Standard elements**
Stereotypes	messages	`<<create>>`
		`<<destroy>>`

A.7 COLLABORATION DIAGRAMS

Collaboration diagrams consist of messages added to a collaboration. The messages are written adjacent to the association roles or links in the collaboration, and must respect any navigability constraints. The basic notation for collaboration diagrams is shown in Figure A.11.

Messages on collaboration diagrams are usually numbered, either sequentially or using a hierarchical number scheme to indicate nested control. Return messages are not usually shown: instead, return values are written in the message labels.

A.8 SEQUENCE DIAGRAMS

Sequence diagrams show an interaction between roles or prototypical objects in a collaboration. The basic notation for sequence diagrams is shown in Figure A.12.

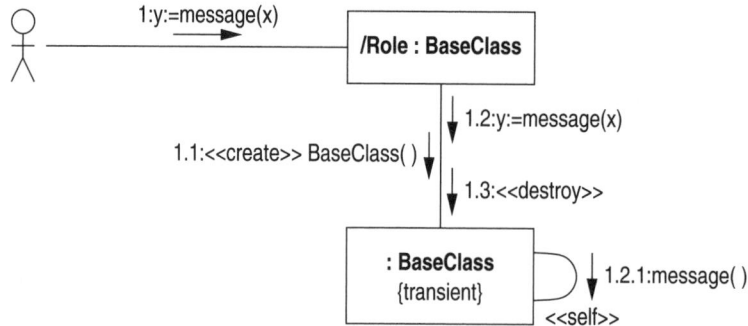

Figure A.11 Notation for collaboration diagrams

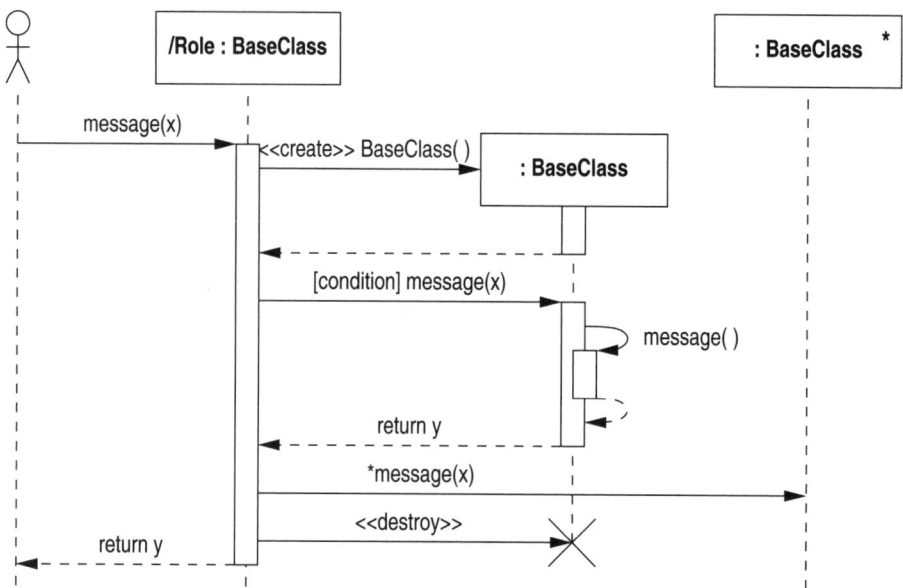

Figure A.12 Notation for sequence diagrams

Each role has a *lifeline* extending below it. Messages are represented by labelled arrows going from one lifeline to another. Messages give rise to *activations*. At the end of an activation, a return message indicates that the flow of control returns to the calling object. Parameters and return values can be shown on messages. Messages sent to an object by itself give rise to nested activations.

Object creation is shown by a constructor message terminating at the newly created role. This is the position at the point in time at which it is created. Object destruction is shown by a stereotyped 'destroy' message. The destroyed object's lifeline terminates at the point of destruction.

A.9 CLASS DIAGRAMS

Classes categorize the objects that can exist in a system and define their shared properties. Class diagrams show the classes in a system and a variety of relationships between those classes. The basic notation for classes is illustrated in Figure A.13.

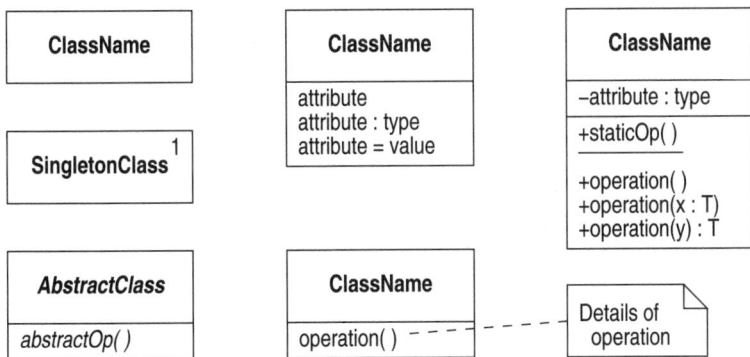

Figure A.13 Basic notation for classes

Class icons consist of three compartments. The top compartment contains the class name and optionally a multiplicity and any standard elements that apply to the class. The lower compartments are optional and show the *features* of the class.

The second compartment contains the attributes of the class. An attribute has a name and optionally a visibility, a type, a multiplicity and an initial value.

The third compartment contains the operations of the class. An operation has a name and optionally a visibility, parameters and a return type.

Table A.5 lists the standard elements that can be used on classes.

Table A.5 Standard elements for classes

	Applies to	**Standard elements**
Stereotypes	classes	`<<enumeration>>`
		`<<interface>>`
Tagged values	classes	`persistence = persistent`
		`persistence = transitory`

Generalization

Classes can be related by generalization. Generalization relates one superclass to one or more subclasses. A discriminator can be used to describe the aspect of the classes that is being generalized upon.

Attributes and operations of the superclass are inherited by the subclasses, where they can be redefined if necessary, or new features added. Notation for generalization is shown in Figure A.14.

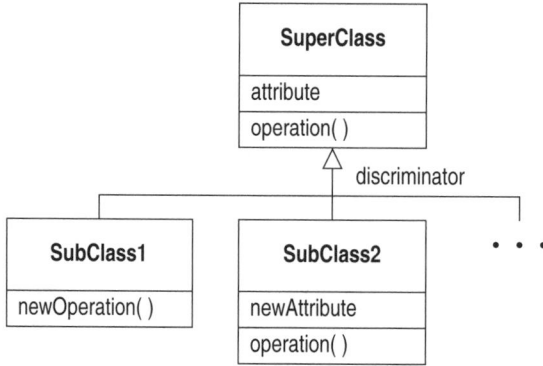

Figure A.14 Notation for generalization

Associations

Classes can be connected by means of *associations*. An association between two classes implies the possibility of links between instances of the classes. Associations can optionally be labelled with an association name, together with a small arrowhead indicating the direction in which the name should be understood.

Association ends can optionally be labelled with *role names*, multiplicities and navigability annotations. Notation for associations is shown in Figure A.15.

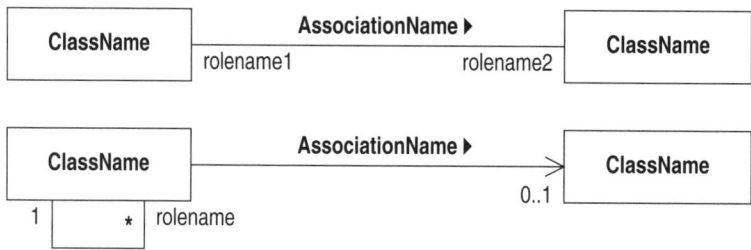

Figure A.15 Notation for associations

Aggregation models a transitive and antisymmetric 'whole–part' relationship between classes. It can be decorated with multiplicity symbols to show various different properties of the aggregation relationship.

Composition defines a stronger form of the whole–part relationship than simple aggregation, where a part can only belong to one composite and has a lifetime bounded by that of the composite. Notation for aggregation and composition is shown in Figure A.16.

A composite object can contain classes and associations. If an association lies wholly within the composite, the objects it connects must be parts of the same composite. Objects from different composites can only be connected by an association that crosses the boundary of the composite. The notation for composite objects is shown in Figure A.17.

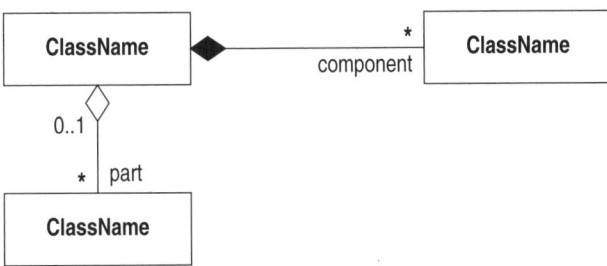

Figure A.16 Notation for aggregation and composition

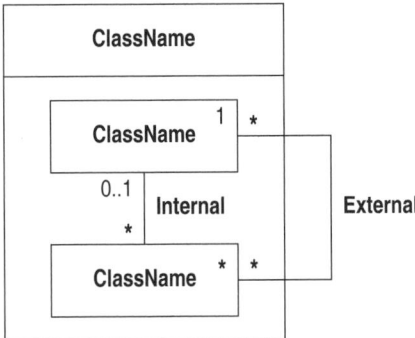

Figure A.17 Notation for composite objects

Association classes have all the properties of both classes and associations. They provide a means whereby data can be associated with the links between objects, and associations can themselves participate in further associations.

Qualifiers are a special form of association class attribute, which specify that one or more attributes function as a key to enable access to instances of one class from another. Notation for association classes and qualifiers is shown in Figure A.18.

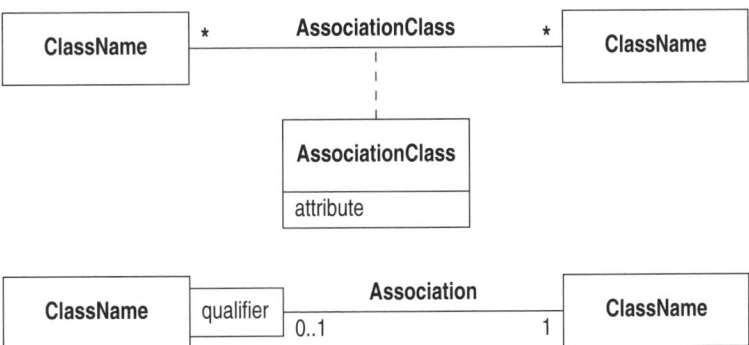

Figure A.18 Notation for association classes and qualifiers

A.10 STATECHART DIAGRAMS

A *statechart* can be drawn for any class whose instances respond to messages in different ways depending on their current state. The basic notation for statecharts, shown in Figure A.19, allows the *states* of an object to be shown, along with the *events* the object can detect and the *transitions* between states consequent on detecting an event.

Events can be followed by *conditions*; the relevant transition will then only be followed if the condition is true when the event is detected. Events can also be followed by *actions*, which are performed whenever the transition is followed.

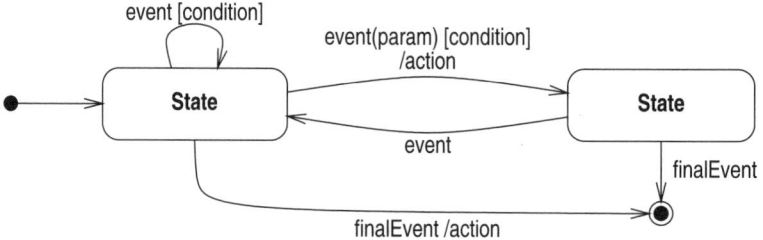

Figure A.19 Notation for states, events and transitions

The internal properties of a state can be specified to show attributes of the object that are relevant to that state, and also the operations that an object performs while entering or exiting a state. *Internal transitions* specify the response to an event that does not involve leaving the current state.

A state can have an *activity* specified. When the activity finishes, a *completion transition* from the state will be followed, if one exists. *Time events* can be attached to transitions that must fire after an object has spent a certain length of time in a state.

The notation for these properties is shown in Figure A.20.

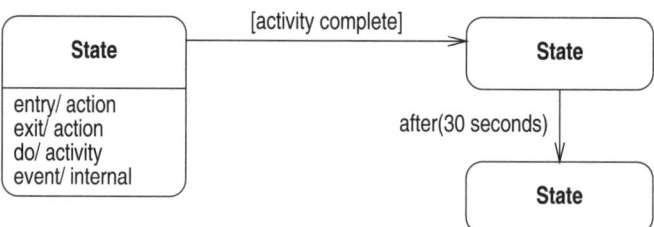

Figure A.20 Notation for the internal details of a state

In order to simplify complex statecharts, a number of states can be grouped together into a *composite state*. A composite state can contain initial and final states and also a *history state*.

A transition from a composite state is equivalent to a set of transitions, one from each of its substates. A transition to the final state of a composite triggers a completion transition defined on the composite, if any.

A transition to a composite state is equivalent to a transition to a nested initial state if the composite has not been entered previously, and to a nested history state if it has. The transitions from nested initial and history states fire automatically in these cases.

Notation for composite states is shown in Figure A.21.

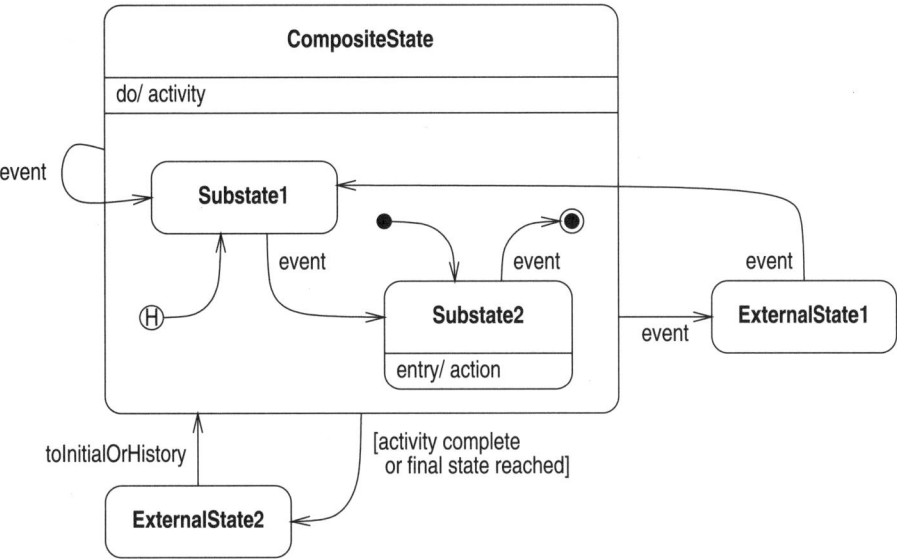

Figure A.21 Notation for composite states

A.11 COMPONENT DIAGRAMS

Component diagrams show *components* and *dependencies* between them. Figure A.22 shows the notation for components and the interfaces they realize, and how to express a usage dependency between two components.

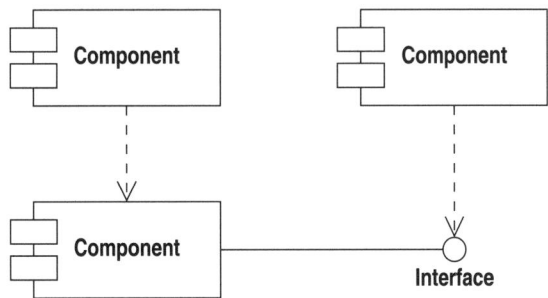

Figure A.22 Notation for components and dependencies

A.12 TEMPLATES

A number of types of model elements, including classes and collaborations, can be parameterized and represented as templates. Templates can then be instantiated by *binding* a suitable model element to the template parameter. Figure A.23 shows the notation for template classes and two ways of showing template instantiation.

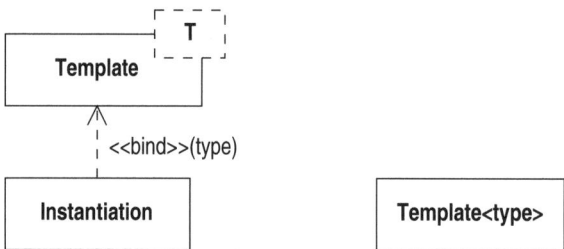

Figure A.23 Templates and template instantiation

APPENDIX B

SUMMARY OF THE OBJECT CONSTRAINT LANGUAGE (OCL)

B.1 CONSTRAINTS

A constraint consists of a *context declaration* followed by a list of stereotyped expressions. To write a constraint applying to instances of a class, the context declaration specifies the class being constrained and the *invariant* stereotype is used. Optionally, the context declaration can provide a name for the instance being constrained.

```
context c : Classifier
    inv: Boolean expression
```

To write a constraint applying to an operation, the context declaration gives the operation's signature, and the *precondition* and *postcondition* stereotypes are used.

```
context class::operation(x:T1) : T2
    pre: Boolean expression
    post: Boolean expression
```

B.2 EXPRESSIONS

Expressions evaluate to an element of an OCL type. Expressions are built up from *primary expressions* by applying *properties* of appropriate types. The properties of the various OCL types are listed in Sections B.3 and B.5. Primary expressions are commonly the name of the context object, or one of its properties if the name is left implicit. The expression `self` can be used to refer to the current context object. Properties are applied in *postfixed expressions*, in one of the following forms.

object . property
collection- >property

A number of prefix and infix operators are defined for various types. Expressions formed using these operators can be parenthesized and used as a primary expression for forming further property applications.

```
(x + y).abs()
```

B.3 BASIC TYPES

OCL defines four basic types, namely `Boolean`, `Integer`, `Real` and `String`. `OclAny` is an abstract supertype that defines properties shared by all the basic types. The metatypes `OclType` and `OclExpression` represent the OCL types and expressions respectively.

The properties of the basic types defined by OCL are listed below. The signatures of the properties are given in the following styles.

T :: *property* (*parameters*) : *returnType*
T :: "*prefixOp*" () : *returnType*
T :: "*infixOp*" (*t* : *T*) : *returnType*

If *t* and *u* are expressions of type *T*, properties can be applied by means of expressions of the following forms.

t.property (*arguments*)
prefixOp t
t infixOp u

Properties of OCL types

The following operations allow certain information about a type to be retrieved from the model. The `allInstances` property returns all the instances of the specified type that exist when the expression is evaluated, not the set of all possible instances.

```
OclType::name() : String
OclType::attributes() : Set(String)
OclType::associationEnds() : Set(String)
OclType::operations() : Set(String)
OclType::supertypes() : Set(OclType)
OclType::allSuperTypes() : Set(OclType)
OclType::allInstances() : Set(T)
```

Properties of all types

Equality of objects can be tested with = and <>. `oclIsTypeOf` tests the type of the object, whereas `oclIsKindOf` tests whether an object belongs to a descendent of a type. `oclAsType` is a type conversion operation.

```
oclAny::"="(object : OclAny) : Boolean
oclAny::"<>"(object : OclAny) : Boolean
oclAny::oclIsKindOf(type : OclType) : Boolean
oclAny::oclIsTypeOf(type : OclType) : Boolean
oclAny::oclAasType(type : oclType) : T
```

Properties of numeric types

The standard numerical operations are defined for the types `Integer` and `Real`. In the signatures below the type variable *Number* should be replaced consistently by `Integer` or `Real` to arrive at a fully defined operation. `Integer` is a subtype of `Real`, so `Integer` values can be supplied for `Real` parameters.

> *Number*::"+"(n : *Number*) : *Number*
> *Number*::"-"() : *Number*
> *Number*::"-"(n : *Number*) : *Number*
> *Number*::"*"(n : *Number*) : *Number*
> *Number*::"/"(n : *Number*) : Real
> Integer::"div"(r : Integer) : Integer
> Integer::"mod"(r : Integer) : Integer
> *Number*::"abs"() : *Number*
> *Number*::"max"(n : *Number*) : *Number*
> *Number*::"min"(n : *Number*) : *Number*
> Real::floor() : Integer
> Real::round() : Integer
> Real::"<"(r : Real) : Boolean
> Real::">"(r : Real) : Boolean
> Real::"<="(r : Real) : Boolean
> Real::">="(r : Real) : Boolean

Properties of Booleans

```
Boolean::"or"(b : Boolean) : Boolean
Boolean::"xor"(b : Boolean) : Boolean
Boolean::"and"(b : Boolean) : Boolean
Boolean::"not"() : Boolean
Boolean::"implies"(b : Boolean) : Boolean
```

Properties of strings

```
String::size() : Integer
String::concat(s : String) : String
String::toUpper() : String
String::toLower() : String
String::substring(lower : Integer, upper : Integer) : String
```

B.4 MODEL TYPES

In addition to these basic types, each classifier defined in the UML model gives rise to a *model type*.

B.5 COLLECTIONS

OCL defines three kinds of collections, namely sets, bags and sequences. A set is a collection of distinct elements, whilst bags and sequences can contain duplicate elements, and in addition the elements in a sequence are ordered. Collections in OCL cannot be nested: a set of sets, for example, would be 'flattened' into a set containing the elements from all the given sets.

These various types of collection are represented in OCL by four types. `Collection` is an abstract supertype representing the common properties of all collections, and `Set`, `Bag` and `Sequence` represent the specific kinds of collection. The type of a collection is defined by the kind of collection and the type of the elements contained. For example, the type of a set of integers would be written `Set(Integer)`. In the operation signatures below, a type variable T is used to indicate the contained types. Collection types are not subtypes of `OclAny`.

Specific collections can be denoted by literals of the following forms.

```
Set(Integer) { 6, 2, 8, 4 }
Bag(String) { "hello", "hello", "hello" }
Sequence(Integer) { 1, 2, 1, 2, 3 }
```

The properties of collections defined by OCL are listed below. The signatures of the properties are given in the following styles.

CollectionType (*T*) ::*property* (*parameters*) : *returnType*
CollectionType (*T*) :: "*infixOp*" (*d* : *CollectionType* (*T*)) : *returnType*

If *c* and *d* are expressions of type *CollectionType* (*T*), properties can be applied by means of expressions of the following forms.

c->*property* (*arguments*)
c infixOp *d*

Properties of collections can also be applied to objects of type *T* using the above notation, but the object is converted into a collection containing the single element before the property is applied.

Collection predicates

A number of predicates are defined for all collections. These allow the size and membership of a collection to be tested.

```
Collection(T)::size() : Integer
Collection(T)::count(object : T) : Integer
Collection(T)::isEmpty() : Boolean
Collection(T)::notEmpty() : Boolean
Collection(T)::includes(object : T) : Boolean
Collection(T)::excludes(object : T) : Boolean
Collection(T)::includesAll(c : Collection(T)) : Boolean
Collection(T)::excludesAll(c : Collection(T)) : Boolean
Bag(T)::"="(Bag(T)) : Boolean
Set(T)::"="(Set(T)) : Boolean
Sequence(T)::"="(Sequence(T)) : Boolean
```

The following operations apply Boolean conditions to the elements of a collection, to test whether the condition is true for all, some or exactly one of the elements of the collection. isUnique is true if and only if exp evaluates to a different value for every element of the collection.

```
collection(T)::any(exp : OclExpression) : T
collection(T)::exists(exp : OclExpression) : Boolean
collection(T)::forAll(exp : OclExpression) : Boolean
collection(T)::isUnique(exp : OclExpression) : Boolean
collection(T)::one(exp : OclExpression) : Boolean
```

If the elements in a collection support the operation +, the sum of all elements in the collection can be found using the operation sum. The basic types Integer and Real support +, and certain model types may also do so.

```
Collection(T)::sum() : T
```

Type conversions

Collections can be changed from one type to another. Converting a bag or a sequence to a set causes duplicate elements to be lost. The ordering of a sequence returned by asSequence is undefined.

```
Collection(T)::sortedBy(exp : OclExpression) : Sequence(T)
Set(T)::asBag() : Bag(T)
Set(T)::asSequence() : Sequence(T)
Bag(T)::asSet() : Set(T)
Bag(T)::asSequence() : Sequence(T)
Sequence(T)::asBag() : Bag(T)
Sequence(T)::asSet() : Set(T)
```

Collection operations

The collection operations provide ways of creating one collection out of another. `select` and `reject` generate subcollections of the original collection, formed by keeping or removing specified elements. `collect` applies an expression to each element of the collection and forms a new collection out of the results of these applications.

```
Collection(T)::iterate(exp : OclExpression)
                  : exp.evaluationType
Set(T)::select(exp : OclExpression) : Set(T)
Set(T)::reject(exp : OclExpression) : Set(T)
Set(T)::collect(exp : OclExpression) : Set(exp.evaluationType)
Bag(T)::select(exp : OclExpression) : Bag(T)
Bag(T)::reject(exp : OclExpression) : Bag(T)
Bag(T)::collect(exp : OclExpression) : Bag(exp.evaluationType)
Sequence(T)::select(exp : OclExpression) : Sequence(T)
Sequence(T)::reject(exp : OclExpression) : Sequence(T)
Sequence(T)::collect(exp : OclExpression)
                : Sequence(exp.evaluationType)
```

Set-theoretic operations

```
Set(T)::"-"(s : Set(T)) : Set(T)
Set(T)::intersection(s : Set(T)) : Set(T)
Bag(T)::intersection(s : Bag(T)) : Bag(T)
Bag(T)::intersection(s : Set(T)) : Set(T)
Set(T)::intersection(s : Bag(T)) : Set(T)
Set(T)::symmetricDifference(s : Set(T)) : Set(T)
Bag(T)::union(s : Bag(T)) : Bag(T)
Bag(T)::union(s : Set(T)) : Bag(T)
Set(T)::union(s : Set(T)) : Set(T)
Set(T)::union(s : Bag(T)) : Bag(T)
Sequence(T)::union(s : Sequence(T)) : Sequence(T)
```

Individual elements can be added to or removed from a set, and the number of elements in a set counted.

```
count(object : T) : Integer
Bag(T)::excluding(object : T) : Bag(T)
```

```
Set(T)::excluding(object : T) : Set(T)
Sequence(T)::excluding(object : T) : Sequence(T)
Bag(T)::including(object : T) : Bag(T)
Set(T)::including(object : T) : Set(T)
Sequence(T)::including(object : T) : Sequence(T)
```

Operations on sequences

```
Sequence(T)::append(object : T) : Sequence(T)
Sequence(T)::prepend(object : T) : Sequence(T)
Sequence(T)::at(i : Integer) : T
Sequence(T)::first() : T
Sequence(T)::last() : T
Sequence(T)::subsequence(lower : Integer, upper : Integer)
           : Sequence(T)
```

APPENDIX C

A TEMPLATE FOR USE CASE DESCRIPTIONS

UML does not define a standard template for writing use case descriptions, but it is useful to adopt a consistent format for a project. This appendix presents a representative list of headings under which a use case can be defined, though it should be emphasized that it is usually more important to concentrate on writing complete and understandable courses of events than on filling in every section of a specified template.

Name

The name of a use case should be expressed as a short verb phrase, stating what task the user will accomplish with the use case.

Summary, or short description

It is often useful to provide a one paragraph summary of what the use case accomplishes.

Actors

Lists the actors that are involved in the use case and the *primary* actor, who is responsible for initiating its execution.

Triggers

Triggers are the events that start the use case. Triggers do not have to be input events to the system: for example, in the booking system example, a trigger for the 'Make Reservation' use case could be 'a potential customer phones the restaurant to make a booking'. In other cases, however, the trigger may be the same as the first system event in the use case.

Preconditions

Preconditions summarize what must be true before the use case can start. Often preconditions state which other use cases must have run before the one being specified: a typical precondition might be 'the user has successfully logged on'.

Postconditions, or guarantees

Postconditions summarize what will be true when the use case has finished. In many cases, this will depend on the exact series of interactions that takes place in a particular use case instance. It can be useful to distinguish between 'minimal guarantees', which describe what will or will not happen in all cases, and 'success guarantees', which describe what will happen if the normal course of event completes successfully.

Courses of events, or scenarios

The basic, or normal, course of events should normally be presented as an unbroken sequence of interactions. The interactions within a course of events are normally numbered, for easy reference later on.

Alternative and exceptional courses of events

Alternative and exceptional courses of events can be written out in full. Often, however, it is adequate simply to specify the points at which the alternative flow diverges from the basic course of events. This can be done by giving the number of the step where behaviour can vary and specifying what condition causes the divergence.

Extension points

This section should list the points in the courses of events at which extensions can take place, and give the condition or event that determines whether or not this will happen. The extensions themselves should be written as separate use cases; otherwise, an alternative course of events can be specified.

Inclusions

This section simply summarizes the use cases that are included into the use case being defined. The points at which inclusion takes place should be specified in the courses of events. This section is redundant if a use case diagram showing the same information is readily available.

REFERENCES AND BIBLIOGRAPHY

The specification of UML is maintained by the Object Management Group (2001), and the language is described in detail by its principal developers in the *User Guide*, by Booch, Rumbaugh and Jacobson (1999) and the *Reference Manual*, by Rumbaugh, Jacobson and Booch (1999). The specification has moved on since these books were written, however, and they are not necessarily accurate references to the current state of the language.

The original books written by the developers of UML are good sources of background information about object-oriented modelling and the development of modelling languages. The classic descriptions of these are contained in the books by James Rumbaugh and others (1991), Grady Booch (1994) and Ivar Jacobson and others (1992). A book by Robert Martin (1995) describes the Booch method from a programming perspective similar to the one adopted in this book.

Many books describe UML with more of an emphasis on the analysis and design of information systems. A good representative of these is the textbook by Bennet *et al.* (2002). Larman (2002) has more of an emphasis on programming and would be a suitable follow-up book to this one. These and other books that have been consulted in the writing of this book are listed below.

The primary reference for the Unified Process is the book by Jacobson *et al.* (1999). A readable short introduction to Rational's instantiation of it is provided by Kruchten (2000). Extreme programming is described in a very readable manner by Beck (2000). Raymond (1999) is the classic statement of the open source philosophy and Moody (2001) describes in detail the development of Linux. More general accounts of software development and the role of design in the process can be found in Sommerville (2000).

The following references provide more detailed coverage of some of the topics introduced in this book. Use cases are discussed in detail in Cockburn (2001). OCL is described in detail by Warmer and Kleppe (1999). The book by Blaha and Premerlani (1998) contains a comprehensive account of object-oriented design for database applications. The classic source for material on design patterns is the 'gang of four' book by Erich Gamma and others (1995). For C++ users, a very thorough treatment of the issues of physical design is provided by Lakos (1996).

Beck, K. (2000) *Extreme Programming Explained*, Addison-Wesley, Boston.

Bennett, S., McRobb, S. and Farmer, R. (2002) *Object-Oriented Systems Analysis and Design using UML*, 2nd edn, McGraw-Hill, London.

Bennett, S., Skelton, J. and Lunn, K. (2001) *Schaum's Outline of UML*, McGraw-Hill, New York.

Blaha, M. and Premerlani, W. (1998) *Object-Oriented Modeling and Design for Database Applications*, Prentice Hall, Upper Saddle River, NJ.

Boehm, B. W. (1988) A spiral model of software development and enhancement, *Computer*, vol. 5, pp. 61–72.

Booch, G. (1994) *Object-Oriented Analysis and Design with Applications*, 2nd edn, Benjamin Cummings, Redwood City, CA.

Booch, G., Rumbaugh, J. and Jacobson, I. (1999) *The Unified Modeling Language User Guide*, Addison-Wesley, Reading, MA.

Cockburn, A. (2001) *Writing Effective Use Cases*, Addison-Wesley, Boston, MA.

Fowler, M. and Scott, K. (1999) *UML Distilled: Applying the Standard Object Modeling Language*, 2nd edn, Addison-Wesley, Reading, MA.

Gamma, E., Helm, R., Johnson, R. and Vlissides, J. (1995) *Design Patterns*, Addison-Wesley, Reading, MA.

Jacobson, I., Booch, G. and Rumbaugh, J. (1999) *The Unified Software Development Process*, Addison-Wesley, Reading, MA.

Jacobson, I., Christerson, M., Johnsson, P. and Övergaard, G. (1992), *Object-Oriented Software Engineering*, Addison-Wesley, Reading, MA.

Kruchten, P. (2000) *The Rational Unified Process*, 2nd edn, Addison-Wesley, Reading, MA.

Lakos, J. (1996) *Large-Scale C++ Software Design*, Addison-Wesley, Reading, MA.

Larman, C. (2002) *Applying UML and Patterns*, Prentice Hall PTR, Upper Saddle River, NJ.

Liskov, B. (1988) Data abstractions and hierarchy, *SIGPLAN Notices*, vol. 23. no. 5, pp. 17–34.

Martin, R. C. (1998) UML Tutorial: Collaboration Diagrams, *C++ Report*, vol. 10. no. 1, pp. 6–9.

Martin, R. (1995) *Designing Object-Oriented C++ Applications Using the Booch Method*, Prentice Hall, Englewood Cliffs, NJ.

Meyer, B. (1988) *Object-Oriented Software Construction*, Prentice Hall, London.

Moody, G. (2001) *Rebel Code*, Penguin Books, Harmondsworth.

Object Management Group (2001) *OMG Unified Modeling Language Specification, Version 1.4*. http://www.omg.org.

Raymond, E. S. (1999) *The Cathedral and the Bazaar*, O'Reilly, Sebastopol, CA.

Royce, W. W. (1970) Managing the development of large software systems, *Proceedings, IEEE WESCON*, August 1970, pp. 1–9. Reprinted in *Proceedings of the 9th International Conference on Software Engineering*, 1987, pp. 328–338.

Rumbaugh, J., Blaha, M., Premerlani, W., Eddy, F. and Lorensen, W. (1991) *Object-Oriented Modeling and Design*, Prentice Hall, Englewood Cliffs, NJ.

Rumbaugh, J., Jacobson, I. and Booch, G. (1999) *The Unified Modeling Language Reference Manual*, Addison-Wesley, Reading, MA.

Sommerville, I. (2000) *Software Engineering*, 6th edn, Addison-Wesley, Reading, MA.

Stevens, P. and Pooley, R. (2000) *Using UML*, updated edn, Addison-Wesley, Harlow.

Warmer, J. and Kleppe A. (1999) *The Object Constraint Language*, Addison-Wesley, Reading, MA.

Wirfs-Brock, R., Wilkerson, B. and Wiener, L. (1991) *Designing Object-Oriented Software*, Prentice Hall, Englewood Cliffs, NJ.

INDEX